Financial Accounting
for Decision Makers

Visit the *Financial Accounting for Decision Makers, fourth edition*
Companion Website at **www.pearsoned.co.uk/atrillmclaney** to find
valuable **student** learning material including:

- Learning objectives for each chapter
- Multiple choice questions to help test your learning
- Additional exercises and revision questions
- Solutions to end of chapter review questions
- Links to relevant sites on the web
- An online glossary to explain key terms
- Flashcards to test your knowledge of key terms and definitions

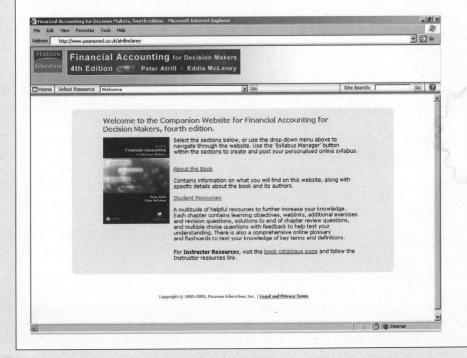

4th Edition

Financial Accounting
for Decision Makers

Peter Atrill

and

Eddie McLaney

FT Prentice Hall
FINANCIAL TIMES

An imprint of **Pearson Education**
Harlow, England • London • New York • Boston • San Francisco • Toronto
Sydney • Tokyo • Singapore • Hong Kong • Seoul • Taipei • New Delhi
Cape Town • Madrid • Mexico City • Amsterdam • Munich • Paris • Milan

Pearson Education Limited

Edinburgh Gate
Harlow
Essex CM20 2JE
England

and Associated Companies throughout the world

Visit us on the World Wide Web at:
www.pearsoned.co.uk

Second edition published 1999 by Prentice Hall Europe
Third edition published 2002 by Pearson Education Limited
Fourth edition published 2005

© Prentice Hall Europe 1996, 1999
© Pearson Education Limited 2002, 2005

ISBN 0 273 68847 2

British Library Cataloguing-in-Publication Data
A catalogue record for this book is available from the British Library

Library of Congress Cataloging-in-Publication Data
Atrill, Peter.
  Financial accounting for decision makers / Peter Atrill and Eddie McLaney. – 4th ed.
    p. cm.
  Rev. ed of: Financial accounting for non-specialists / Peter Atrill and Eddie McLane.
3rd ed. 2002.
  Includes bibliographical references and index.
  ISBN 0-273-68847-2 (alk. paper)
  1. Accounting. 2. Decision making. I. McLaney, E. J. II. Atrill, Peter.
Financial accounting for non-specialists. III. Title.

  HF5635.A884 2004
  657—dc22

                                                          2004057757

10 9 8 7 6 5 4 3 2 1
09 08 07 06 05

Typeset in 9.5/12.5pt Stone Serif by 35
Printed and bound by Mateu Cromo Artes Graficas, Spain

The publisher's policy is to use paper manufactured from sustainable forests.

Contents

3 Measuring and reporting financial performance 58

7 Analysing and interpreting financial statements   197

8 Reporting the financial results of groups of companies

Companion Website and Instructor resources

Visit **www.pearsoned.co.uk/atrillmclaney** to find valuable online resources

For students
- Learning objectives for each chapter
- Multiple choice questions to help test your learning
- Additional exercises and review questions
- Solutions to end of chapter review questions
- Links to relevant sites on the web
- An online glossary to explain key terms
- Flashcards to test your knowledge of key terms and definitions

For instructors
- Complete, downloadable Instructor's Manual
- PowerPoint slides that can be downloaded and used as OHTs
- Case study material with solutions
- Progress tests, consisting of various questions and exercise material with solutions
- Tutorial/seminar questions and solutions
- Solutions to end of chapter review questions

Also: The Companion Website provides the following features:

- Search tool to help locate specific items of content
- E-mail results and profile tools to send results of quizzes to instructors
- Online help and support to assist with website usage and troubleshooting

For more information please contact your local Pearson Education sales representative or visit **www.pearsoned.co.uk/atrillmclaney**

Guided tour of the book

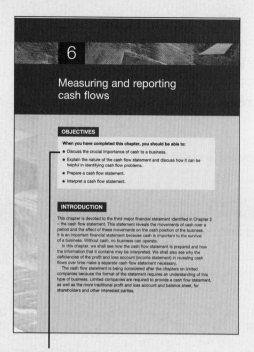

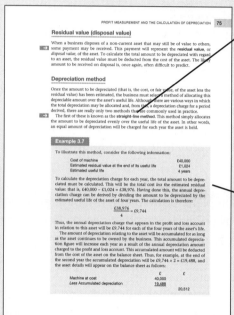

Key terms   The key concepts and techniques in each chapter are highlighted in colour where they are first introduced, with an adjacent icon in the margin to help you refer back to the most important points.

Examples   At frequent intervals throughout most chapters, there are numerical examples that give you step-by-step workings to follow through to the solution.

Learning objectives   Bullet points at the start of each chapter show what you can expect to learn from that chapter, and highlight the core coverage.

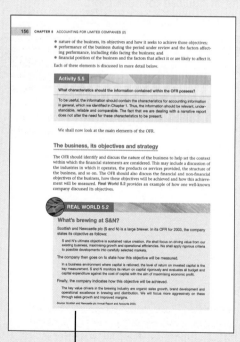

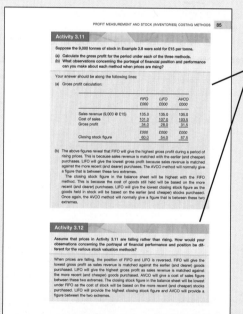

Activities   These short questions, integrated throughout each chapter, allow you to check your understanding as you progress through the text. They comprise either a narrative question requiring you to review or critically consider topics, or a numerical problem requiring you to deduce a solution. A suggested answer is given immediately after each activity.

'Real World' illustrations   Integrated throughout the text, these illustrative examples highlight the practical application of accounting concepts and techniques by real businesses, including extracts from company reports and financial statements, survey data and other interesting insights from business.

Self-assessment questions   Towards the end of most chapters you will encounter one of these questions, allowing you to attempt a comprehensive question before tackling the end-of-chapter assessment material. To check your understanding and progress, solutions are provided in Appendix C.

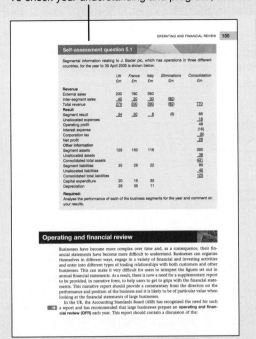

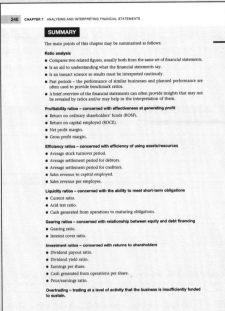

Bullet point chapter summary   Each chapter ends with a 'bullet-point' summary. This highlights the material covered in the chapter and can be used as a quick reminder of the main issues.

Key terms summary   At the end of each chapter, there is a listing (with page reference) of all the key terms, allowing you to refer back easily to the most important points.

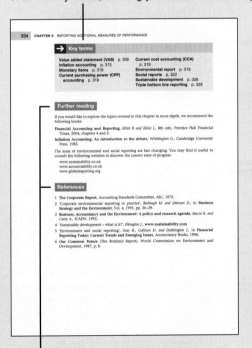

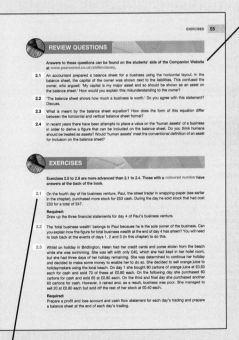

Review questions These short questions encourage you to review and/or critically discuss your understanding of the main topics covered in each chapter, either individually or in a group. Solutions to these questions can be found on the Companion Website at **www.pearsoned.co.uk/ atrillmclaney**.

Further reading   This section comprises a listing of relevant chapters in other textbooks that you might refer to in order to pursue a topic in more depth or gain an alternative perspective.

References   Provides full details of sources of information referred to in the chapter.

Exercises   There are eight of these comprehensive questions at the end of most chapters. The more advanced questions are separately identified. Solutions to five of the questions (those with coloured numbers) are provided in Appendix D, enabling you to assess your progress. Solutions to the remaining questions are available for lecturers only. An additional exercise for each chapter can be found on the Companion Website at **www.pearsoned.co.uk/atrillmclaney**.

Guided tour of the Companion Website

Extra material has been prepared to help you study using *Financial Accounting for Decision Makers*. This material can be found on the book's Companion Website at **www.pearsoned.co.uk/atrillmclaney**. You will find links to websites of interest, as well as a range of material including:

Interactive quizzes

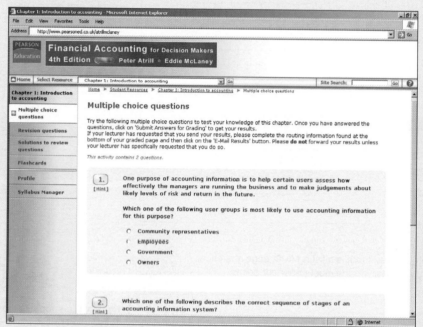

For each chapter there is a set of interactive multiple choice questions, plus a set of fill-in-the blanks questions and an extra exercise. Test your learning and get automatic grading on your answers.

Revision questions

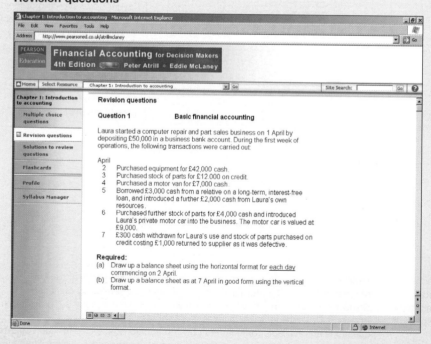

Sets of questions covering the whole book are designed to help you check your overall learning whilst you are revising.

Solutions to review questions

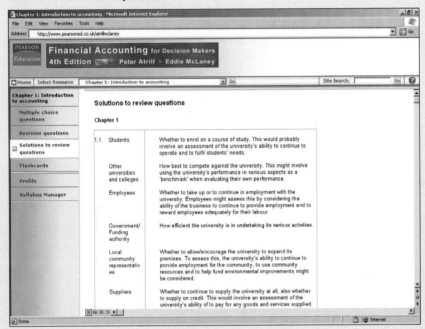

Answers to the end-of-chapter review questions that appear in the book are to be found on the website, so you can check your progress.

Glossary and flashcards

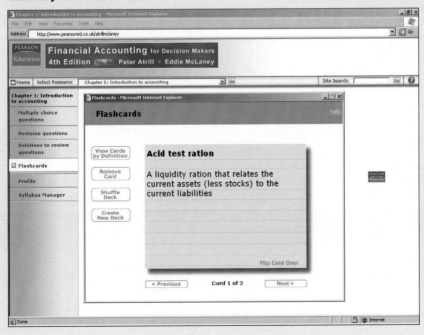

Full version of the book's glossary to help you check definitions while you are online. Flashcards help you to learn and test yourself on definitions of key terms. A term is displayed on each card: 'flip over' for the definition. 'Shuffle' the cards to randomly test your knowledge.

Preface

This text provides a comprehensive introduction to financial accounting. It is aimed both at students who are not majoring in accounting as well as those who are. Those studying introductory-level financial accounting as part of their course in business, economics, hospitality management, tourism, engineering or some other area should find that the book provides complete coverage of the material at the level required. Students who are majoring in accounting should find the book useful as an introduction to the main principles, which can serve as a foundation for further study. The text does not focus on the technical aspects, but rather examines the basic principles and underlying concepts. The ways in which financial statements and information can be used to improve the quality of decision making are the main focus of the book. To reinforce this practical emphasis, there are, throughout the text, numerous illustrative extracts with commentary from company reports, survey data and other sources.

In this fourth edition, we have taken the opportunity to make improvements that have been suggested by students and lecturers who used the previous edition. We have brought up to date and expanded the number of examples from real life. We have also introduced 'bullet-point' chapter summaries. These should help to remind you of the key issues in each chapter. From 2005, most of the larger UK companies will have to adopt a new set of international rules relating to the preparation of their main financial statements. These new rules form the basis of the section of the book that deals specifically with financial accounting for limited companies.

The text is written in an 'open-learning' style. This means that there are numerous integrated activities, worked examples and questions throughout the text to help you to understand the subject fully. You are encouraged to interact with the material and to check your progress continually. Irrespective of whether you are using the book as part of a taught course or for personal study, we have found that this approach is more 'user-friendly' and makes it easier for you to learn.

We recognise that most of you will not have studied financial accounting before, and we have therefore tried to write in a concise and accessible style, minimising the use of technical jargon. We have also tried to introduce topics gradually, explaining everything as we go. Where technical terminology is unavoidable we try to provide clear explanations. In addition, you will find all the key terms highlighted in the text. These are then listed at the end of each chapter with a page reference. All of these key terms are also listed alphabetically, with a concise definition, in the glossary given in Appendix B towards the end of the book. This should provide a convenient point of reference from which to revise.

A further important consideration in helping you to understand and absorb the topics covered is the design of the text itself. The page layout and colour scheme have been carefully considered to allow for the easy navigation and digestion of material. The layout features a large page format, an open design, and clear signposting of the various features and assessment material.

More detail about the nature and use of these features is given in the 'How to use this book' section on page xv; and the main points are also summarised, using example pages from the text, in the Guided tour on pages xviii–xix hereafter.

We hope that you will find the book readable and helpful.

Peter Atrill
Eddie McLaney

How to use this book

We have organised the chapters to reflect what we consider to be a logical sequence and, for this reason, we suggest that you work through the text in the order in which it is presented. We have tried to ensure that earlier chapters do not refer to concepts or terms that are not explained until a later chapter. If you work through the chapters in the 'wrong' order, you will probably encounter concepts and terms that were explained previously.

Irrespective of whether you are using the book as part of a lecture/tutorial-based course or as the basis for a more independent mode of study, we advocate following broadly the same approach.

Integrated assessment material

Interspersed throughout each chapter are numerous **Activities**. You are strongly advised to attempt all of these questions. They are designed to simulate the sort of quick-fire questions that your lecturer might throw at you during a lecture or tutorial. Activities serve two purposes:

- To give you the opportunity to check that you understand what has been covered so far.
- To encourage you to think about the topic just covered, either to see a link between that topic and others with which you are already familiar, or to link the topic just covered to the next.

The answer to each Activity is provided immediately after the question. This answer should be covered up until you have deduced your solution, which can then be compared with the one given.

Towards the middle/end of each chapter there is a **Self-assessment question**. This is more comprehensive and demanding than most of the Activities, and is designed to give you an opportunity to check and apply your understanding of the core coverage of the chapter. The solution to each of these questions is provided in Appendix C at the end of the book. As with the Activities, it is important that you attempt each question thoroughly before referring to the solution. If you have difficulty with a Self-assessment question, you should go over the relevant chapter again.

End-of-chapter assessment material

At the end of each chapter there are four **Review questions**. These are short questions requiring a narrative answer or discussion within a tutorial group. They are intended to help you assess how well you can recall and critically evaluate the core terms and concepts covered in each chapter. Answers to these questions are provided in the student access Companion Website. At the end of each chapter, except for Chapter 1, there are eight **Exercises**. These are mostly computational and are designed to re-inforce your knowledge and understanding. Exercises are graded as 'basic' and 'more advanced' according to their level of difficulty. The basic-level questions are fairly straightforward; the more advanced ones can be quite demanding but are capable of being successfully completed if you have worked conscientiously through the chapter and have attempted the basic exercises. Solutions to five of the exercises in each chapter are provided in Appendix D at the end of the book. A coloured exercise number identifies these five questions. Here, too, a thorough attempt should be made to answer each exercise before referring to the solution. Solutions to the other three exercises and to the review questions in each chapter are provided in a separate Instructors' Manual.

To familiarise yourself with the main features and how they will benefit your study of this text, an illustrated Guided tour is provided on pages xviii–xix.

Content and structure

The text comprises nine main chapters. The market research for this text revealed a divergence of opinions, given the target market, on whether or not to include material on double-entry bookkeeping techniques. So as to not interrupt the flow and approach of the main chapters, Appendix A on recording financial transactions (including Activities and three Exercise questions) has been placed after Chapter 9.

Supplements and website

A comprehensive range of supplementary materials is available to lecturers adopting this text at **www.pearsoned.co.uk/atrillmclaney**.

Acknowledgements

We are grateful to the following for permission to reproduce copyright material:

Real World 7.6 from *Marks and Spencer Plc Annual Report, 2003* (Marks and Spencer Plc 2003); Figure 7.7 from Financial ratios as predictors of failure in *Empirical Research in Accounting: Selected Studies*, Institute of Professional Accounting, University of Chicago, Blackwell Publishers (Beaver, W. H. 1966); Figure 9.4 from *Tate and Lyle Plc Annual Report 2003* (Tate and Lyle Plc 2003); Chapter 9, p. 329: Global Reporting Initiative Sustainability Reporting Guidelines from *Global Reporting Initiative Sustainability Reporting Guidelines 2002* (GRI Secretariat 2002); Real World 9.4 from 'Reported cases of bribery', *The Shell Report 2002*, p. 48 (Royal Dutch/Shell Group of Companies).

Real World 1.3 Profit without honour from *The Financial Times Limited*, 29/30 June 2002, © John Kay. Times Newspapers Limited for an extract (Real World 1.2) adapted from the article 'Margin of success for clothing retailers' published in *The Times* 20th November 2002 © The Times 2002; Thorntons plc for an extract (Real World 3.3) from the 2003 Thorntons plc Annual Report and Accounts; Kingfisher plc for an extract (Real World 4.4) from the 2003 Annual Review of Kingfisher plc; Tesco Stores Ltd for an extract (Real World 4.5) from the 2003 Tesco Annual Report and Financial Statements; Rolls-Royce International Ltd for an extract (Real World 4.9) from the 2002 Annual Financial Statements of Rolls-Royce; Today's CPA, a publication of the Texas Society of Certified Public Accountants for an extract (Real World 5.11) from the article 'The rise and fall of Enron' by C. W. Thomas published in *Journal of Accountancy* Vol. 194 Issue 3, April 2002; Unilever plc for an extract (Exercise 5.8) from a segmental report for 2002 of Unilever plc; Cadbury Schweppes plc for an extract (Real World 8.2) from the 2002 Report and Accounts of Cadbury Schweppes; and Business in the Community for an extract (p. 327) adapted from the report 'Winning with Integrity – A Guide to Social Responsibility' published by *Business in the Community* November 2000.

We are grateful to the Financial Times Limited for permission to reprint the following material:

Real World 4.1 Monotub industries in a spin as founder gets Titan for £1, FT.com, © *Financial Times*, 23 January 2003; Real World 6.1 Eurotunnel takes £1.3bn impairment charge, FT.com, © *Financial Times*, 9 February 2004; Real World 7.4 Market statistics for some well known businesses, © *Financial* Times, 3 January 2004.

In some instances we have been unable to trace the owners of copyright material and we would appreciate any information that would enable us to do so.

1

Introduction to accounting

OBJECTIVES

When you have completed this chapter, you should be able to:

● Explain the nature and role of accounting.

● Identify the main users of financial information and discuss their needs.

● Distinguish between financial and management accounting.

● Identify and discuss the main forms of business enterprise.

INTRODUCTION

In this opening chapter we begin by considering the role and nature of accounting. We shall identify the main users of accounting information and discuss the ways in which accounting can improve the quality of the decisions that they make. We shall then go on to consider the particular role of financial accounting and the differences that exist between financial and management accounting. As this book is concerned with accounting and financial decision making for private sector businesses, we shall also examines the main forms of business enterprise and considers what the key objectives of a business are likely to be.

What is accounting?

 Accounting is concerned with collecting, analysing and communicating financial information. The purpose is to help people that use this information to make more informed decisions. If the financial information that is communicated is not capable of improving the quality of decisions made, there would be no point in producing it. Sometimes the impression is given that the purpose of accounting is simply to prepare financial reports on a regular basis. While it is true that accountants undertake this kind of work, it does not represent an end in itself. The ultimate purpose of the accountant's work is to give people better financial information on which to base their decisions. This decision-making perspective of accounting fits in with the theme of this book and shapes the way in which we deal with each topic.

Accounting and user needs

For accounting information to be useful, the accountant must be clear about *for whom* the information is being prepared and *for what purpose* the information will be used. There are likely to be various groups of people (known as 'user groups') with an interest in a particular organisation, in the sense of needing to make decisions about that organisation. For the typical private sector business, the most important of these groups are shown in Figure 1.1.

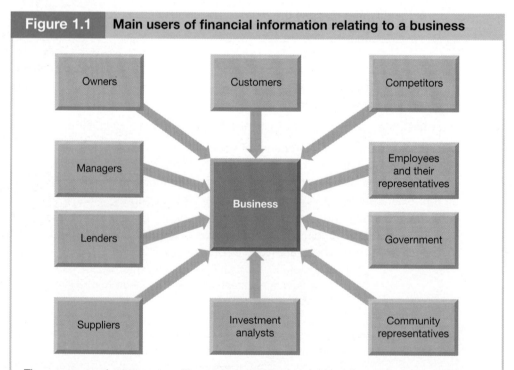

Figure 1.1	Main users of financial information relating to a business

There are several user groups with an interest in the accounting information relating to a business. The majority of these are outside the business but, nevertheless, they have a stake in the business. This is not meant to be an exhaustive list of potential users; however, the groups identified are normally the most important.

Activity 1.1

Ptarmigan Insurance plc (PI) is a large motor insurance business. Taking the user groups identified above, suggest what sort of decisions each one is likely to make about PI.

Your answer may be as follows:

User group	Decision
Customers	Whether to take up further insurance policies with PI. This would probably involve an assessment of PI's ability to continue in business and to supply customers' needs.
Competitors	How best to compete against PI or, perhaps, whether to leave the market on the grounds that it is not possible to compete profitably with PI. This might involve using PI's performance in various aspects as a 'benchmark' when evaluating their own performance. They might also try to assess PI's competitive strength and to identify significant changes that may signal PI's future actions (for example, expanding its ability to provide its service as a prelude to market expansion).
Employees	Whether to take up or to continue in employment with PI. Employees might assess this by considering the ability of the business to continue to provide employment and to reward employees adequately for their labour.
Government	Whether PI should pay tax and, if so, how much, whether it complies with agreed pricing policies, whether financial support is needed and so on. In making these decisions an assessment of PI's profits, sales and financial strength would be made.
Community representatives	Whether to allow PI to expand its premises or whether to provide economic support for PI. To assess these, PI's ability to continue to provide employment for the community, to use community resources and to help fund environmental improvements might be considered.
Investment analysts	Whether or not to advise clients to buy shares in PI. This would involve an assessment of the likely risks and returns associated with PI.
Suppliers	Whether to continue to supply PI and, if so, whether to supply on credit. This would involve an assessment of PI's ability to pay for any goods and services supplied.
Lenders	Whether to lend money to PI and/or whether to require repayment of any existing loans. To assess this, PI's ability to meet its obligations to pay interest and to repay the principal would be considered.
Managers	Whether the performance of the business requires improvement. Here, performance to date would be compared with earlier plans or some other 'benchmark' to decide whether action needs to be taken. Whether there should be a change in PI's future direction. In making such decisions, management will need to look at PI's ability to perform and at the opportunities available to it.
Owners (shareholders)	Whether to buy additional shares in PI or to sell some or all of those currently held. This would involve an assessment of the likely risks and returns associated with PI. Owners would also be involved with decisions on the employment of senior managers. Here, past performance of the business would be assessed.

You may have thought of other reasons why each group would find accounting information useful.

The conflicting interests of users

Conflicts of interest may arise between the various user groups over the ways in which the wealth of the business is generated and/or distributed. For example, a conflict of interest may arise between the managers and the owners of the business. Although managers are appointed to act on behalf of the owners, there is always a risk that they will put their own interests first. They may use the wealth of the business to, for example, furnish large offices or buy expensive cars. Accounting information has an important role to play in reporting the extent to which various groups have benefited from the business. Thus, owners may rely on accounting information to check whether the pay and benefits of managers are in line with agreed policy. A further example of potential conflict is between lenders and owners. There is a risk that the funds loaned to a business will not be used for purposes that have been agreed. Lenders may, therefore, rely on accounting information to check that the funds have been applied in an appropriate manner and that the terms of the loan agreement are being adhered to.

Activity 1.2

Can you think of other examples where accounting information may be used to monitor potential conflicts of interest between the various user groups identified?

Two possible examples that spring to mind are:

● Employees (or their representatives) wishing to check that they are receiving a 'fair share' of the wealth created by the business and that agreed profit-sharing schemes are being adhered to.
● Government wishing to check that the profits made from a contract that it has given to a business are not excessive.

You may have thought of other examples.

Not-for-profit organisations

Though the focus of this book is accounting as it relates to private sector businesses, there are many organisations that do not exist mainly for the pursuit of profit yet produce accounting information for decision-making purposes. Examples include: charities, clubs and associations, universities, local government authorities, churches and trade unions. User groups need accounting information about these types of organisation to help them to make decisions. These groups are often the same as, or similar to, those identified for private sector businesses. They may have a stake in the future viability of the organisation and may use accounting information to check that the wealth of the organisation is being properly controlled and used in a way that is consistent with the organisation's objectives.

How useful is accounting information?

No one would seriously claim that accounting information fully meets all of the needs of each of the various user groups. Accounting is still a developing subject and we still have much to learn about user needs and the ways in which these needs should be met. Nevertheless, the information contained in accounting reports should help users make decisions relating to the business. The information should reduce uncertainty over the financial position and performance of the business. It should help to answer questions concerning the availability of cash to pay owners a return for their investment or to repay loans and so on. Typically, there is no close substitute for the information that is provided by financial statements. This is to say that if users are not to get the information from the financial statements, they will not get it at all. Other sources of information concerning the financial health of a business are normally regarded as less useful than the financial statements.

Activity 1.3

What other sources of information might users employ to gain an impression of the financial position and performance of a business? What kind of information might be gleaned from these sources?

Other sources of information available include:

- Meetings with managers of the business
- Public announcements made by the business
- Newspaper and magazine articles
- Radio and TV reports
- Information-gathering agencies (for example, Dun and Bradstreet)
- Industry reports
- Economy-wide reports.

These sources can provide information on various aspects of the business, such as new products or services being offered, management changes, new contracts offered or awarded, the competitive environment within which the business operates, the impact of new technology, changes in legislation, changes in interest rates and future levels of inflation. However, the various sources of information identified are not really substitutes for accounting reports. Rather, they should be used in conjunction with the reports in order to obtain a clearer picture of the financial health of a business.

The evidence on the usefulness of accounting

There are arguments and convincing evidence that accounting information is at least *perceived* as being useful to users. There have been numerous research surveys that asked users to rank the importance of accounting information, in relation to other sources of information, for decision-making purposes. Generally speaking, these studies have found that users rank accounting information very highly. There is also considerable evidence that businesses choose to produce accounting information that exceeds the minimum requirements imposed by accounting regulations. (For example, businesses often produce a considerable amount of accounting information for managers, which is not required by any regulations.) Presumably, the cost of producing this additional accounting information is justified on the grounds that users believe it to be useful to them. Such arguments and evidence, however, leave unanswered the question as to whether the information produced is actually being used for decision-making purposes, that is: does it affect people's behaviour?

It is normally very difficult to assess the impact of accounting on decision-making. One situation arises, however, where the impact of accounting information can be observed and measured. This is where the **shares** (portions of ownership of a business) are traded on a stock exchange. The evidence reveals that, when a business makes an announcement concerning its accounting profits, the prices at which shares are traded and the volume of shares traded often change significantly. This suggests that investors are changing their views about the future prospects of the business as a result of this new information available to them and that this, in turn, leads them to make a decision either to buy or to sell shares in the business.

Thus, we can see that there is evidence that accounting reports are perceived as being useful and are used for decision-making purposes. It is impossible, however, to measure just how useful accounting reports are to users and whether the cost of producing those reports represents value for money. Accounting information will usually represent only one input to a particular decision and the precise weight attached to the accounting information by the decision maker and the benefits which flow as a result cannot be accurately assessed. We shall see below, however, that it is at least possible to identify the kinds of qualities which accounting information must possess in order to be useful. Where these qualities are lacking, the usefulness of the information will be diminished.

Accounting as a service function

One way of viewing accounting is as a form of service. Accountants provide economic information to their 'clients', who are the various users identified in Figure 1.1. The quality of the service provided would be determined by the extent to which the information needs of the various user groups have been met. It can be argued that, to be useful, accounting information should possess certain key qualities, or characteristics. These are:

- **Relevance.** Accounting information must have the ability to influence decisions. Unless this characteristic is present, there is really no point in producing the information. The information may be relevant to the prediction of future events (for example, in predicting how much profit is likely to be earned next year) or relevant in helping confirm past events (for example, in establishing how much profit was earned last year). The role of accounting in confirming past events is important because users often wish to check on the accuracy of earlier predictions that they have made. The accuracy (or inaccuracy) of earlier predictions may enable users to judge the likely accuracy of current predictions.
- **Reliability.** Accounting should be free from significant errors or bias. It should be capable of being relied upon by users to represent what it is supposed to represent. Though both relevance and reliability are very important, the problem that we often face in accounting is that information that is highly relevant may not be very reliable, and that which is reliable may not be very relevant.

Activity 1.4

To illustrate this last point, let us assume that a manager has to sell a custom-built machine owned by the business and has recently received a bid for it. What information would be relevant to the manager when deciding whether to accept the bid? How reliable would that information be?

The manager would probably like to know the current market value of the machine before deciding whether or not to accept the bid. The current market value would be highly relevant to the final decision, but it might not be very reliable because the machine is unique and there is likely to be little information concerning market values.

Where a choice has to be made between providing information that has either more relevance or more reliability, the maximisation of relevance tends to be the guiding rule.

- **Comparability.** This quality will enable users to identify changes in the business over time (for example, the trend in sales over the past five years). It will also help users to evaluate the performance of the business in relation to other similar businesses. Comparability is achieved by treating items that are basically the same in the same manner for accounting purposes. Comparability tends also to be enhanced by making clear the policies that have been adopted in measuring and presenting the information.

- **Understandability.** Accounting reports should be expressed as clearly as possible and should be understood by those at whom the information is aimed.

Activity 1.5

Do you think that accounting reports should be understandable to those who have not studied accounting?

It would be useful if everyone could understand accounting reports, but realistically, this is not likely it to be the case. Complex financial events and transactions cannot always be reported easily. It is probably best that we regard accounting reports in the same way as we regard a report written in a foreign language. To understand either of these, we need to have had some preparation. Generally speaking, accounting reports assume that the user not only has a reasonable knowledge of business and accounting, but is also prepared to invest some time in studying the reports.

The threshold of materiality

The qualities, or characteristics, that have just been described will help us to decide if a particular piece of financial information is potentially useful. However, in order to make a final decision, we also have to consider whether the information is material, or significant. This means that we should ask whether its omission or misrepresentation in the financial reports would really alter the decisions that users make. Thus, in addition to possessing the characteristics mentioned above, financial information must

→ also achieve a threshold of **materiality**. If the information is not regarded as material, it should not be included within the reports as it will merely clutter them up and, perhaps, interfere with the users' ability to interpret the financial results. The type of information and amounts involved will normally determine whether it is material.

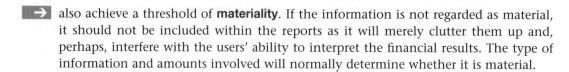

Costs and benefits of accounting information

Having read the previous sections you may feel that, when considering a piece of financial information, provided the four main qualities identified are present and it is material it should be included in the financial reports. Unfortunately, there is one more hurdle to jump. A piece of financial information may still be excluded from the financial reports even when it is considered to be useful. Consider Activity 1.6 below.

Activity 1.6

Suppose an item of information is capable of being provided. It is relevant to a particular decision, it is also reliable, comparable and can be understood by the decision maker concerned and is material.

Can you think of a reason why, in practice, you might choose not to produce the information?

The reason that you may decide not to produce, or discover, the information is that you judge the cost of doing so to be greater than the potential benefit of having the information. This cost–benefit issue will place limits on the extent to which accounting information is provided.

In theory, financial information should only be produced if the costs of providing a particular item of information are less than the benefits, or value, to be derived from its use. Figure 1.2 shows the relationship between the costs and value of providing additional financial information. The figure shows how the value of information received by the decision maker eventually begins to decline. This is, perhaps, because additional information becomes less relevant, or because of the problems that a decision maker may have in processing the sheer quantity of information provided. The costs of providing the information, however, will increase with each additional piece of information. The broken line indicates the point at which the gap between the value of information and the cost of providing that information is at its greatest. This represents the optimal amount of information that can be provided. This theoretical model, however, poses a number of problems in practice, as discussed below.

To illustrate the practical problems of establishing the value of information, suppose that we wish to buy a particular DVD system that we have seen for sale in a local shop at £250. We believe that other local shops may have the same system on offer for a lower price. The way of finding out the prices at other shops is either to telephone them or to visit them. Telephone calls cost money and involve some of our time. Visiting the shops may not involve the outlay of money, but more of our time will be involved. Is it worth the cost of finding out the price of the system at various shops? The answer, as we have seen, is that if the cost of discovering the price is less than the potential benefit, it is worth having that information.

| Figure 1.2 | Relationship between costs and the value of providing additional financial information |

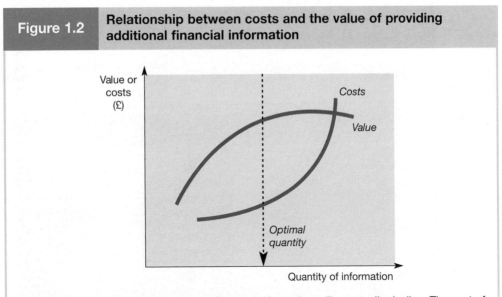

The benefits of each additional item of financial information will eventually decline. The cost of providing information, however, will rise with each additional piece of information. The optimal level of information provision is where the gap between the value of the information and the costs of providing it is at its greatest.

To identify the various selling prices of the DVD system, there are several points to be considered, including:

● How many shops shall we telephone or visit?
● What is the cost of each telephone call?
● How long will it take to make all the telephone calls or visits?
● How much do we value our time?

The economic benefit of having the information on the price of the system is probably even harder to assess and the following points need to be considered:

● What is the cheapest price that we might be quoted for the DVD system?
● How likely is it that we shall be quoted prices cheaper than £250?

The answers to these questions may be far from clear. When assessing the value of accounting information we are confronted with similar problems.

The provision of accounting information can be very costly; however, the costs are often difficult to quantify. The direct, out-of-pocket, costs such as salaries of accounting staff are not really a problem, but these are only part of the total costs involved. There are also less direct costs, such as the cost of the manager's time spent on analysing and interpreting the information contained in reports. In addition, costs will also be incurred if users employ the accounting information to the disadvantage of the business. For example, if suppliers discovered from the accounting reports that the business was in a poor financial state, they might decide to impose strict conditions or refuse to supply further goods.

The economic benefit of having accounting information is even harder to assess. It is possible to apply some 'science' to the problem of weighing the costs and benefits, but a lot of subjective judgement is likely to be involved. Whilst no one would seriously advocate that a typical business should not produce accounting information, at the

Figure 1.3	The characteristics that influence the usefulness of accounting information

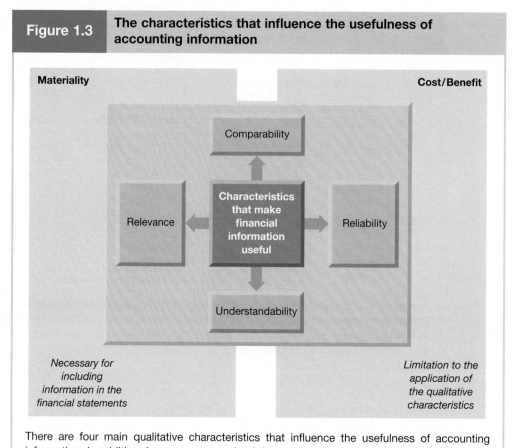

There are four main qualitative characteristics that influence the usefulness of accounting information. In addition, however, accounting information should be material and the benefits of providing the information should outweigh the costs.

same time, no one would advocate that every item of information that could be seen as possessing one or more of the key characteristics should be produced, irrespective of the cost of producing it.

When weighing the costs of providing additional financial information against the benefits, there is also the problem that those who bear the burden of the costs may not be the ones who benefit from the additional information. The costs of providing accounting information are usually borne by the owners of the business, but other user groups may be the beneficiaries.

The characteristics that influence the usefulness of accounting information and which have been discussed in this section and the preceding section are set out in Figure 1.3.

Accounting as an information system

We have already seen that accounting can be seen as the provision of a service to 'clients'. Another way of viewing accounting is as a part of the business's total information system. Users, both inside and outside the business, have to make decisions concerning the allocation of scarce economic resources. To try to ensure that these

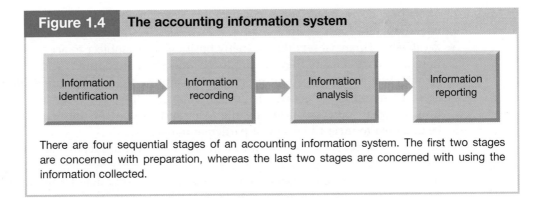

Figure 1.4   The accounting information system

Information identification → Information recording → Information analysis → Information reporting

There are four sequential stages of an accounting information system. The first two stages are concerned with preparation, whereas the last two stages are concerned with using the information collected.

resources are allocated in an efficient manner, users require economic information on which to base decisions. It is the role of the accounting system to provide that information and this will involve information gathering and communication.

The **accounting information system** has certain features that are common to all information systems within a business. These are:

● identifying and capturing relevant information (in this case economic information);
● recording in a systematic manner the information collected;
● analysing and interpreting the information collected;
● reporting the information in a manner that suits the needs of users.

The relationship between these features is set out in Figure 1.4.

Given the decision-making emphasis of this book, we shall be concerned primarily with the final two elements of the process – the analysis and reporting of financial information. We shall consider the way in which information is used by, and is useful to, managers rather than the way in which it is identified and recorded. In this context, information technology is playing an increasingly important role. It has created opportunities for analysis and reporting that were not possible before.

Management and financial accounting

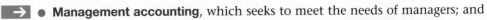

Accounting is usually seen as having two distinct strands. These are:

● **Management accounting**, which seeks to meet the needs of managers; and
● **Financial accounting**, which seeks to meet the accounting needs of all of the other users that were identified in Figure 1.1, earlier in the chapter.

The differences between the two types of accounting reflect the different user groups that they address. Briefly, the major differences are as follows:

● *Nature of the reports produced.* Financial accounting reports tend to be general-purpose. That is, they contain financial information that will be useful for a broad range of users and decisions rather than being specifically designed for the needs of a particular group or set of decisions. Management accounting reports, on the other hand, are often specific-purpose reports. They are designed either with a particular decision in mind or for a particular manager.
● *Level of detail.* Financial accounting reports provide users with a broad overview of the performance and position of the business for a period. As a result, information is aggregated and detail is often lost. Management accounting reports, however,

often provide managers with considerable detail to help them with a particular operational decision.

● *Regulations.* Financial reports, for many businesses, are subject to accounting regulations that try to ensure they are produced with standard content and in a standard format. Law and the accounting profession impose these regulations. Since management accounting reports are for internal use only, there are no regulations from external sources concerning the form and content of the reports. They can be designed to meet the needs of particular managers.

● *Reporting interval.* For most businesses, financial accounting reports are produced on an annual basis, though large businesses may produce half-yearly reports and a few produce quarterly ones. Management accounting reports may be produced as frequently as required by managers. In many businesses, managers are provided with certain reports on a weekly or monthly basis, which allows them to check progress frequently. In addition, special-purpose reports will be prepared when required (for example, to evaluate a proposal to purchase a piece of machinery).

● *Time horizon.* Financial accounting reports reflect the performance and position of the business for the past period. In essence, they are backward looking. Management accounting reports, on the other hand, often provide information concerning future performance as well as past performance. It is an oversimplification, however, to suggest that financial accounting reports never incorporate expectations concerning the future. Occasionally, businesses will release projected information to other users in an attempt to raise capital or to fight off unwanted takeover bids.

● *Range and quality of information.* Financial accounting reports concentrate on information that can be quantified in monetary terms. Management accounting also produces such reports, but is also more likely to produce reports that contain information of a non-financial nature such as measures of physical quantities of stocks and output. Financial accounting places greater emphasis on the use of objective, verifiable evidence when preparing reports. Management accounting reports may use information that is less objective and verifiable, but they provide managers with the information they need.

We can see from this that management accounting is less constrained than financial accounting. It may draw on a variety of sources and use information that has varying degrees of reliability. The only real test to be applied when assessing the value of the information produced for managers is whether or not it improves the quality of the decisions made.

Activity 1.7

Are the information needs of managers and those of other users so very different?
Is there any overlap between the information needs of managers and the needs of other users?

The distinction between management and financial accounting suggests that there are differences between the information needs of managers and those of other users. Whilst differences undoubtedly exist, there is also a good deal of overlap between these needs. For example, managers will, at times, be interested in receiving an historic overview of business operations of the sort provided to other users. Equally, the other users would be interested in receiving information relating to the future, such as the planned level of profits, and non-financial information such as the state of the sales order book and the extent of product innovations.

The distinction between the two areas reflects, to some extent, the differences in access to financial information. Managers have much more control over the form and content of information they receive. Other users have to rely on what managers are prepared to provide or what the financial reporting regulations state must be provided. Though the scope of financial accounting reports has increased over time, fears concerning loss of competitive advantage and user ignorance concerning the reliability of forecast data have led businesses to resist providing other users with the detailed and wide-ranging information that is available to managers.

Scope of this book

This book is concerned with financial accounting rather than management accounting. In Chapter 2 we begin by introducing the three principal financial statements:

- Balance sheet
- Profit and loss account (also called the income statement)
- Cash flow statement.

These statements are briefly reviewed before we go on to consider the balance sheet in more detail. We shall see that the balance sheet provides information concerning the wealth held by a business at a particular point in time and the claims against this wealth. Included in our consideration of the balance sheet will be an introduction to **accounting conventions**. Conventions are the generally accepted rules that accountants tend to follow when preparing financial statements. Chapter 3 introduces the second of the major financial statements, the profit and loss account. This statement provides information concerning the wealth created by a business during a period. In this chapter we shall be looking at such issues as how profit is measured, the point in time at which we recognise that a profit has been made, and the accounting conventions that apply to this particular statement.

In the UK and throughout much of the industrialised world, the limited company is the major form of business unit. Chapter 4 considers the accounting aspects of limited companies. Although there is nothing of essence that makes the accounting aspects of limited companies different from other types of private sector business, there are some points of detail that we need to consider. Chapter 5 continues our examination of limited companies and, in particular, considers the framework of rules that must be adhered to when presenting accounting reports to owners and external users.

Chapter 6 deals with the last of the three principal financial statements, the cash flow statement. This financial statement is important in identifying the financing and investing activities of the business over a period. It sets out how cash was generated and how cash was used during a period.

Reading the three statements will provide information about the performance and position of a business. It is possible, however, to gain even more helpful insights to the business by analysing the statements using financial ratios and other techniques. Combining two figures in the financial statements in a ratio and comparing this with a similar ratio for, say, another business, can often tell us much more than just reading the figures themselves. Chapter 7 is concerned with techniques for analysing financial statements.

Many of the larger businesses in the UK are a group of companies rather than just a single company. A group of companies will exist where one company controls one or more other companies. In Chapter 8 we shall see why groups exist and consider the accounting issues raised by the combination of companies into groups.

Finally, we shall consider the way in which the reporting of financial information has expanded in recent years. The increasing complexity of business and the increasing demands of users for additional information have led to a number of supplementary financial reports being produced. Chapter 9 considers some of the more important of these.

Has accounting become too interesting?

In recent years, accounting has become front-page news both in the US and Europe and has become a major talking point among those connected with the world of business. Unfortunately, the attention that accounting has attracted has been for all the wrong reasons. We have seen that investors rely on financial reports to help them keep an eye on both their investment and the managers. However, what if the managers provide misleading financial reports to investors? Recent revelations suggest that the managers of some large companies have been doing just this.

Two of the most notorious cases have been those of Enron, an energy-trading business based in Texas, which was accused of entering into complicated financial arrangements in order to obscure losses and to inflate profits, and WorldCom, a major long-distance telephone operator in the US, which was accused of reclassifying $3.9 billion of expenses so as to inflate the profit figure that the business reported to its owners (shareholders) and to others. In the wake of these scandals, there was much closer scrutiny by investment analysts and investors of the financial reports that businesses produce. This has led to further businesses, in both the US and Europe, being accused of using dubious accounting practices to bolster profits.

Various reasons have been put forward to explain this spate of scandals. Some may have been caused by the pressures on managers to meet unrealistic expectations of investors for continually rising profits, others by the greed of unscrupulous executives whose pay is linked to financial performance. However, they may all reflect a particular economic environment.

Real World 1.1 gives some comments suggesting that when all appears to be going well with a business, people can be quite gullible and over-trusting.

REAL WORLD 1.1

The thoughts of Warren Buffett

Warren Buffett is one of the world's shrewdest and most successful investors. He believes that the accounting scandals mentioned above were perpetrated during the 'new economy boom' of the late 1990s when confidence was high and exaggerated predictions were being made concerning the future. He states that during that period:

> You had an erosion of accounting standards. You had an erosion, to some extent, of executive behaviour. But during a period when everybody 'believes', people who are inclined to take advantage of other people can get away with a lot.

He believes that the worst is now over and that the 'dirty laundry' created during this heady period is being washed away and that the washing machine is now in the 'rinse cycle'. However, he points out that:

> It's only in the rinse cycle that you find out how dirty the laundry has been.

Source: The Times, Business section, 26 September 2002, p. 25.

Whatever the causes, the result of these accounting scandals has been to undermine the credibility of financial statements and to introduce much stricter regulations concerning the quality of financial information. We shall return to this issue in later chapters when we consider the financial statements.

The changing nature of accounting

Over the past two decades, the environment in which businesses operate has become increasingly turbulent and competitive. Various reasons have been identified to explain these changes, including:

- the increasing sophistication of customers;
- the development of a global economy where national frontiers become less important;
- rapid changes in technology;
- the deregulation of domestic markets (for example, electricity, water and gas);
- increasing pressure from owners (shareholders) for competitive economic returns; and
- the increasing volatility of financial markets.

This new, more complex, environment has brought new challenges for both financial accounting and management accounting. To meet the changing needs of users there has been a radical review of what kind of information is reported and how it is reported.

In recent years, there have been various attempts to set out the principles upon which financial accounting is based. This is designed to help users to understand more clearly the nature and purpose of financial accounting reports and to provide a more solid foundation for the development of accounting rules. These principles try to address fundamental questions such as 'Who are the users of financial accounting information?', 'What kinds of financial accounting reports should be prepared and what should they contain?' and 'How should items be measured?'

In response to criticisms that the financial reports of some businesses are too opaque, accounting rule-makers have tried to improve the framework of rules to ensure that the accounting policies of businesses are more comparable, more transparent and portray economic reality more faithfully. The recent spate of accounting scandals, however, suggests that there is still work to be done.

The internationalisation of business and businesses, has created a need for accounting rules to have an international reach. It can no longer be assumed that users of accounting information relating to a particular business are based in the country in which the business operates or are familiar with the accounting rules of that country. Thus, there has been increasing harmonisation of accounting rules across national frontiers. A more detailed review of these developments is included in Chapter 6.

Management accounting has also changed by becoming more outward looking. In the past, information provided to managers has been largely restricted to that collected within the business. However, the attitude and behaviour of customers and rival businesses have now become the object of much information gathering. Increasingly, successful businesses are those that are able to secure and maintain competitive advantage over their rivals.

To obtain this advantage, businesses have become more 'customer driven' (that is, concerned with satisfying customer needs). This has led to management accounting information that provides details of customers and the market, such as customer evaluation of services provided and market share. In addition, information about the costs and profits of rival businesses, which can be used as 'benchmarks' by which to gauge competitiveness, is gathered and reported.

To compete successfully, businesses must also find ways of managing costs. The cost base of modern businesses is under continual review and this, in turn, has led to the development of more sophisticated methods of measuring and controlling costs.

Forms of business unit

Businesses may be classified according to their form of ownership. The particular classification has important implications when accounting for businesses – as we shall see in later chapters – and so it is useful to be clear about the main forms of ownership that can arise.

There are basically three arrangements:

- Sole proprietorship
- Partnership
- Limited company.

Each of these is considered below.

Sole proprietorship

Sole proprietorship, as the name suggests, is where an individual is the sole owner of a business. This type of business is often quite small in terms of size (as measured, for example, by sales generated or number of staff employed), however, the number of such businesses is very large indeed. Examples of sole-proprietor businesses can be found in most industrial sectors but particularly within the service sector. Hence, services such as electrical repairs, picture framing, photography, driving instruction, retail shops and hotels have a large proportion of sole-proprietor businesses. The sole-proprietor business is easy to set up. No formal procedures are required and operations can often commence immediately (unless special permission is required because of the nature of the trade or service, such as running licensed premises). The owner can decide the way in which the business is to be conducted and has the flexibility to restructure or dissolve the business whenever it suits. The law does not recognise the sole-proprietor business as being separate from the owner, so the business will cease on the death of the owner.

Although the owner must produce accounting information to satisfy the taxation authorities, there is no legal requirement to produce accounting information relating to the business for other user groups. However, some user groups may demand accounting information about the business and may be in a position to have their demands met (for example, a bank requiring accounting information on a regular basis as a condition of a loan). The sole proprietor will have unlimited liability which means that no distinction will be made between the proprietor's personal wealth and that of the business if there are business debts that must be paid.

Partnership

A **partnership** exists where at least two individuals carry on a business together with the intention of making a profit. Partnerships have much in common with sole-proprietor businesses. They are often quite small in size (although some, such as partnerships of accountants and solicitors, can be large). Partnerships are also easy to set up as no formal procedures are required (and it is not even necessary to have a written agreement between the partners). The partners can agree whatever arrangements suit them concerning the financial and management aspects of the business, and the partnership can be restructured or dissolved by agreement between the partners.

Partnerships are not recognised in law as separate entities and so contracts with third parties must be entered into in the name of individual partners. The partners of a business usually have unlimited liability.

Activity 1.8

What are the main advantages and disadvantages that should be considered when deciding between a sole proprietorship and a partnership?

The main advantages of a partnership over a sole-proprietor business are:

- Sharing the burden of ownership.
- The opportunity to specialise rather than cover the whole range of services (for example, a solicitors' practice, where each partner tends to specialise in a different aspect of the law).
- The ability to raise capital where this is beyond the capacity of a single individual.

The main disadvantages of a partnership compared with a sole proprietorship are:

- The risks of sharing ownership of a business with unsuitable individuals.
- The limits placed on individual decision making that a partnership will impose.

Limited company

Limited companies can range in size from quite small to very large. The number of individuals who subscribe capital and become the owners may be unlimited, which provides the opportunity to create a very large-scale business. The liability of owners, however, is limited (hence 'limited' company), which means that those individuals subscribing capital to the company are liable only for debts incurred by the company up to the amount that they have agreed to invest. This cap on the liability of the owners is designed to limit risk and to produce greater confidence to invest. Without such limits on owner liability, it is difficult to see how a modern capitalist economy could operate. In many cases, the owners of a limited company are not involved in the day-to-day running of the business and will invest in a business only if there is a clear limit set on the level of investment risk.

The benefit of limited liability, however, imposes certain obligations on such a company. To start up a limited company, documents of incorporation must be prepared that set out, amongst other things, the objectives of the business. Furthermore, a framework of regulations exists that places obligations on the way in which such a company conducts its affairs. Part of this regulatory framework requires annual financial reports to be made available to owners and lenders and an annual general meeting of the owners to be held to approve the reports. In addition, a copy of the annual financial reports must be lodged with the Registrar of Companies for public inspection.

In this way, the financial affairs of a limited company enter the public domain. With the exception of small companies, there is also a requirement for the annual financial reports to be subject to an audit. This involves an independent firm of accountants examining the annual reports and underlying records to see whether the reports provide a true and fair view of the financial health of the company and whether they comply with the relevant accounting rules established by law and by the accounting profession.

The features of limited companies will be considered in more detail in Chapters 4 and 5.

Activity 1.9

What are the main advantages and disadvantages that should be considered when deciding between a partnership business and a limited liability company?

The main advantages of a partnership over a limited company are:

- The ease of setting up the business.
- The degree of flexibility concerning the way in which the business is conducted.
- The degree of flexibility concerning restructuring and dissolution of the business.
- Freedom from administrative burdens imposed by law (for example, the annual general meeting and the need for an independent audit).

The main disadvantage of a partnership compared with a limited company is:

- The fact that it is not possible to limit the liability of partners.

This book concentrates on the accounting aspects of limited liability companies because this type of business is by far the most important in economic terms. However, the accounts of limited companies are a little more complex than those of partnerships and sole proprietorships and so it is not really a good idea to introduce the basic principles of accounting using examples based on this form of business unit. The early chapters will tend, therefore, to introduce accounting concepts through examples based on sole-proprietor businesses, this being the simplest form of business unit. Once we have dealt with the basic accounting principles, which are the same for all three types of business, we can then go on to see how they are applied to limited companies. It must be emphasised that there are no differences in the way that all three of these forms of business keep their day-to-day accounting records. In preparing their periodic financial statements, there are certain differences that need to be considered. These differences are not ones of principle, however, but of detail.

Business objectives

A business seeks to enhance the wealth of its owners, and throughout this book we shall assume that this is its main objective. This may come as a surprise, as there are other objectives that a business may pursue that are related to the needs of others associated with the business. For example, a business may seek to provide good working conditions for its employees, or it may seek to conserve the environment for the local community. While a business may pursue these objectives, it is normally set up with a view to increasing the wealth of its owners, and in practice the behaviour of businesses over time appears to be consistent with this objective.

Real World 1.2 provides an example of how many clothes retailers pursue the search for profit.

REAL WORLD 1.2

From rags to riches

Progress in the search for profit is reported by the accounting information system. Realisation that the reported profits are inadequate this can be an important driver for change within a business. This change can, in turn, have a profound effect on the working lives of those both inside and outside the business.

Many clothes retailers have been concerned with profit levels in recent years. This has led them to make radical changes to the ways in which they operate. Low inflation and increased competition in the high street have forced the retailers to keep costs under strict control in order to meet their profit objectives. This has been done in various ways, including:

- moving production to cheaper countries and closing inflexible manufacturing offshoots;
- using fewer manufacturers and working more closely with manufacturers in the design of clothes. This has enabled the retailers to add details, such as embroidery or unusual design features, and to command a higher price for relatively little cost;
- improving communication to suppliers of materials and to manufacturers so that design and sourcing decisions can be made faster and more accurately. This has meant that the time to make garments has been reduced from as much as nine months to just a few weeks;
- predicting more accurately what customers want in order to avoid being left with stocks of unwanted items.

The effect of implementing these changes has been to reduce costs, and thereby improve profits, and to have more flexibility in the cost structure so that the clothes retailers are more able to weather a downturn.

Source: Adapted from 'Margin of success for clothing retailers', *The Times*, 20 November 2002, p. 30.

Does this mean that the needs of other groups associated with the business (employees, customers, suppliers, the community and so on) are not really important? The answer to this question is almost certainly no if the business wishes to survive and prosper over the longer term. Satisfying the needs of other groups will normally be consistent with the need to increase the wealth of the owners over the longer term. A dissatisfied workforce, for example, may result in low productivity, strikes and so forth, which will in turn have an adverse effect on the wealth of the owners. Similarly, a business that upsets the local community by polluting the environment may attract bad publicity, resulting in a loss of customers and heavy fines.

We should be clear that businesses need to do more than just maximise this year's profit if they are to generate as much wealth as possible for their owners. In the short term, corners can be cut and risks taken that will improve profit. Wealth is a longer-term concept, since it relates not only to this year's profit, but to that of future years as well. **Real World 1.3** gives some examples of how emphasis on short-term profits can damage wealth.

REAL WORLD 1.3

Short-term gains, long-term problems   **FT**

In recent years, many businesses have been criticised for failing to consider the long-term implications of their policies on the wealth of the owners. John Kay argues that some businesses have achieved growth in short-term increases in wealth by sacrificing their longer-term prosperity. He points out that:

> . . . The business of Marks and Spencer, the retailer, was unparalleled in reputation but mature. To achieve earnings growth consistent with a glamour rating the company squeezed suppliers, gave less value for money, spent less on stores. In 1998, it achieved the highest [profit] margin in sales in the history of the business. It had also compromised its position to the point where sales and profits plummeted.
>
> Banks and insurance companies have taken staff out of branches and retrained those that remain as sales people. The pharmaceuticals industry has taken advantage of mergers to consolidate its research and development facilities. Energy companies have cut back on exploration.
>
> We know that these actions increased corporate earnings. We do not know what effect they have on the long-run strength of the business – and this is the key point – do the companies themselves know? Some rationalisations will genuinely lead to more productive businesses. Other companies will suffer the fate of Marks and Spencer.

Source: 'Profit without honour', John Kay, *Financial Times Weekend*, 29/30 June 2002.

SUMMARY

The main points of this chapter may be summarised as follows:

What is accounting?

● Accounting provides financial information for a range of users to help them make better judgements and decisions concerning a business.

Accounting and user needs

● For accounting to be useful, there must be a clear understanding of *for whom* and *for what purpose* the information will be used.

● There may be conflicts of interest between different users over the ways in which the wealth of a business is generated or distributed.

● There is evidence that users find accounting information useful and use it to make decisions.

● Accounting can be viewed as a form of service as it involves providing financial information required by the various users.

● To provide a useful service, accounting must possess certain qualities, or characteristics. These are relevance, reliability, comparability and understandability. In addition, accounting information must be material.

● Providing a service to users can be costly and financial information should be produced only if the cost of providing the information is less than the benefits gained.

Accounting information

● Accounting is part of the total information system within a business. It shares the features that are common to all information systems within a business, which are the identification, recording, analysis and reporting of information.

Management and financial accounting

● Accounting has two main strands – management accounting and financial accounting.

● Management accounting seeks to meet the needs of the business's managers and financial accounting seeks to meet the needs of the other user groups.

● These two strands differ in terms of the types of reports produced, the level of reporting detail, the time horizon, the degree of standardisation, and the range and quality of information provided.

Is accounting too interesting?

● In recent years, there has been a wave of accounting scandals in the US and Europe.

● This appears to reflect a particular economic environment, although other factors may also play a part.

Accounting change

● Changes in the economic environment have led to changes in the nature and scope of accounting.

● Financial accounting has improved its framework of rules and there has been greater international harmonisation of accounting rules.

● Management accounting has become more outward looking and new methods for managing costs have emerged.

Forms of business

There are three main forms of business unit:

● Sole proprietorship – easy to set up and flexible to operate but the owner has unlimited liability.

● Partnership – easy to set up and spreads the burdens of ownership but partners usually have unlimited liability and there are ownership risks if the partners are unsuitable.

● Limited company – limited liability for owners but obligations imposed on the way a company conducts its affairs.

Business objectives

● The main business objective is to enhance the wealth of the owners.

→ **Key terms**

Further reading

If you would like to explore the topics covered in this chapter in more depth, we recommend the following books:

Accounting Theory, *Riahi-Belkaoui A.*, 4th edn, Thomson Learning Business Press, 2000, chapters 1 and 2.

Management and Cost Accounting, *Horngren C., Bhimani A., Foster G. and Datar S*, 2nd edn, Prentice Hall, 2002, chapter 1.

Financial Accounting and Reporting, *Elliot B. and Elliot J.*, 8th edn, Financial Times Prentice Hall, 2004, chapter 1.

Corporate Financial Accounting and Reporting, *Sutton T.*, 2nd edn, Financial Times Prentice Hall, 2004, chapter 1.

REVIEW QUESTIONS

Answers to these questions can be found on the students' side of the Companion Website at www.pearsoned.co.uk/atrillmclaney.

1.1 Identify the main users of accounting information for a university. Do these users differ very much from the users of accounting information for private sector businesses? Is there a difference in the ways in which accounting information for a university would be used, compared with that of a private sector business?

1.2 What, in economic principle, should be the determinate of what accounting information is produced? Should economics be the only issue here? (Consider who are the users of accounting information.)

1.3 Financial accounting statements tend to reflect past events. In view of this, how can they be of any assistance to a user in making a decision when decisions, by their very nature, can only be made about future actions?

1.4 'Accounting reports should be understandable. As some users of accounting information have a poor knowledge of accounting, we should produce simplified financial reports to help them.' To what extent do you agree with this view?

2

Measuring and reporting financial position

OBJECTIVES

When you have completed this chapter, you should be able to:

- Explain the nature and purpose of the three major financial statements.

- Prepare a simple balance sheet and interpret the information that it contains.

- Discuss the accounting conventions underpinning the balance sheet.

- Discuss the limitations of the balance sheet in portraying the financial position of a business.

INTRODUCTION

We saw in the previous chapter that accounting has two distinct strands – financial accounting and management accounting. This chapter, and Chapters 3 to 7, will examine the three major financial statements that form the core of financial accounting. We begin our examination by providing an overview of these statements and we shall see how each contributes towards an assessment of the overall financial position and performance of a business.

Following this overview, we begin a more detailed examination by turning our attention towards one of these financial statements – the balance sheet. We shall see how it is prepared, and examine the principles underpinning this statement. We shall also consider its value for decision-making purposes.

The major financial statements – an overview

The objective of the major financial accounting statements is to provide a picture of the overall financial position and performance of the business. To achieve this objective, the business's accounting system will normally produce three particular statements on a regular, recurring basis. These three are concerned with answering the following questions:

- What cash movements (that is, cash in and cash out) took place over a particular period?
- How much wealth (that is, profit) was generated, or lost, by the business over that period?
- What is the accumulated wealth of the business at the end of that period?

These questions are addressed by the following three financial accounting statements, with each one addressing a particular question. The financial statements are:

- the **cash flow statement**
- the **profit and loss account** (also known as the **income statement**)
- the **balance sheet**.

Taken together, they provide an overall picture of the financial health of the business.

Perhaps the best way to introduce these financial statements is to look at an example of a very simple business. From this we shall be able to see the sort of information that each of the statements can usefully provide. It is, however, worth pointing out that, whilst a simple business is our starting point, the principles that we consider are also applied to more complex businesses. This means that we shall frequently encounter these principles again in later chapters.

Example 2.1

Paul was unemployed and unable to find a job. He therefore decided to embark on a business venture. Christmas was approaching, and so he decided to buy gift wrapping paper from a local supplier and to sell it on the corner of his local high street. He felt that the price of wrapping paper in the high street shops was excessive, and that this provided him with a useful business opportunity.

He began the venture with £40 in cash. On the first day of trading, he purchased wrapping paper for £40 and sold three-quarters of his stock for £45 cash.

- **What cash movements took place during the first day of trading?**
  On the first day of trading, a *cash flow statement* showing the cash movements for the day can be prepared as follows:

Cash flow statement for day 1

	£
Opening balance (cash introduced)	40
Add Cash from sales of wrapping paper	45
	85
Less Cash paid to purchase wrapping paper	40
Closing balance of cash	45

Example 2.1 continued

● **How much wealth (that is, profit) was generated by the business during the first day of trading?**

A *profit and loss account* can be prepared to show the wealth (profit) generated on the first day. The wealth generated will represent the difference between the value of the sales made and the cost of the goods (that is, wrapping paper) sold:

Profit and loss account for day 1

	£
Sales revenue	45
Less Cost of goods sold ($^3/_4$ of £40)	30
Profit	15

Note that it is only the *cost* of the wrapping paper sold that is matched against the sales revenue in order to find the profit, and not the whole of the cost of wrapping paper acquired. Any unsold stock (in this case $^1/_4$ of £40 = £10) will be charged against the future sales revenue that it generates.

● **What is the accumulated wealth at the end of the first day?**

To establish the accumulated wealth at the end of the first day, we can draw up a *balance sheet*. This will list the resources held at the end of that day:

Balance sheet at the end of day 1

	£
Cash (closing balance)	45
Stock of goods for resale ($^1/_4$ of £40)	10
Total business wealth	55

We can see from the above financial statements that each statement provides part of a picture that sets out the financial performance and position of the business. We begin by showing the cash movements. Cash is a vital resource that is necessary for any business to function effectively. Cash is required to meet debts that may become due and to acquire other resources (such as stock). Cash has been described as the 'lifeblood' of a business, and movements in cash are usually given close scrutiny by users of financial statements.

However, it is clear that reporting cash movements alone would not be enough to portray the financial health of the business. The changes in cash over time do not give an insight to the profit generated. The profit and loss account provides us with information concerning this aspect of performance. For day 1, for example, we saw that the cash balance increased by £5, but the profit generated, as shown in the profit and loss account, was £15. The cash balance did not increase by the amount of the profit made because part of the wealth generated (£10) was held in the form of stocks.

To gain an insight to the total wealth of the business, a balance sheet can be drawn up at the end of the day. Cash is only one form in which wealth can be held. In the case of this business, wealth is also held in the form of a stock of goods for resale (also known as inventories). Hence, when drawing up the balance sheet, both forms of wealth held will be listed. In the case of a large business, there may be many other forms in which wealth will be held, such as land and buildings, equipment, motor vehicles and so on.

Let us now continue with our example.

Example 2.1 continued

On the second day of trading, Paul purchased more wrapping paper for £20 cash. He managed to sell all of the new stock and all of the earlier stock, for a total of £48.

The cash flow statement on day 2 will be as follows:

Cash flow statement for day 2

	£
Opening balance (from the end of day 1)	45
Add Cash from sales of wrapping paper	48
	93
Less Cash paid to purchase wrapping paper	20
Closing balance	73

The profit and loss account for day 2 will be as follows:

Profit and loss account for day 2

	£
Sales revenue	48
Less Cost of goods sold (£20 + £10)	30
Profit	18

The balance sheet at the end of day 2 will be:

Balance sheet at the end of day 2

	£
Cash (closing balance)	73
Stock of goods for resale	–
Total business wealth	73

We can see that the total business wealth increased to £73 by the end of day 2. This represents an increase of £18 (that is, £73 – £55) over the previous day – which, of course, is the amount of profit made during day 2 as shown on the profit and loss account.

Activity 2.1

On the third day of his business venture, Paul purchased more stock for £46 cash. However, it was raining hard for much of the day and sales were slow. After Paul had sold half of his total stock for £32, he decided to stop trading until the following day.

Have a go at drawing up the three financial statements for day 3 of Paul's business venture.

→

Cash flow statement for day 3

	£
Opening balance (from the end of day 2)	73
Add Cash from sales of wrapping paper	32
	105
Less Cash paid to purchase wrapping paper	46
Closing balance	59

Profit and loss account for day 3

	£
Sales revenue	32
Less Cost of goods sold ($^1/_2$ of £46)	23
Profit	9

Balance sheet at the end of day 3

	£
Cash (closing balance)	59
Stock of goods for resale ($^1/_2$ of £46)	23
Total business wealth	82

Note that the total business wealth had increased by £9 (that is, the amount of the day's profit) even though the cash balance had declined. This is because the business is holding more of its wealth in the form of stock rather than cash, compared with the end of day 2.

We can see that the profit and loss account and cash flow statement are both concerned with measuring flows (of wealth and cash respectively) during a particular period (for example, a particular day, a particular month or a particular year). The balance sheet, however, is concerned with the financial position at a particular moment in time.

Figure 2.1 illustrates this point. The profit and loss account, cash flow statement and balance sheet, when taken together, are often referred to as the **final accounts** of the business.

For external users, these statements are normally backward looking because they are based on information concerning past events and transactions. This can be useful in providing feedback on past performance, and in identifying trends that provide clues to future performance. However, the statements can also be prepared using projected data to help assess likely future profits, cash flows and so on. The financial statements are normally prepared on a projected basis for internal decision-making purposes only. Managers are usually reluctant to publish these projected statements for external users, as they may reveal valuable information to competitors.

Now that we have an overview of the financial statements, we shall consider each statement in more detail. We shall go straight on to look at the balance sheet. Chapter 3 looks at the profit and loss account, Chapter 6 goes into more detail on the cash flow statement. (Chapters 4 and 5 consider the balance sheet and profit and loss accounts of limited companies.)

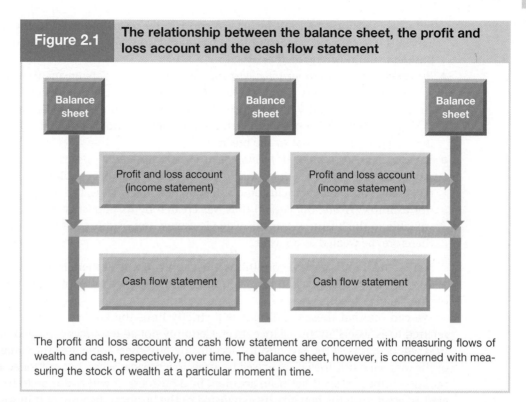

Figure 2.1   **The relationship between the balance sheet, the profit and loss account and the cash flow statement**

The profit and loss account and cash flow statement are concerned with measuring flows of wealth and cash, respectively, over time. The balance sheet, however, is concerned with measuring the stock of wealth at a particular moment in time.

The balance sheet

The purpose of the balance sheet is simply to set out the financial position of a business at a particular moment in time. (The balance sheet is sometimes referred to as the *position statement*, because it seeks to provide the user with a picture of financial position.) We saw above that the balance sheet will reveal the forms in which the wealth of the business is held and how much wealth is held in each form. We can, however, be more specific about the nature of the balance sheet by saying that it sets out the **assets** of the business on the one hand, and the **claims** against the business on the other. Before looking at the balance sheet in more detail, we need to be clear about what these terms mean.

Assets

An asset is essentially a resource held by the business. For a particular item to be treated as an asset for accounting purposes:

● *a probable future benefit must exist*. This simply means that the item must be expected to have some future monetary value. This value can arise through its use within the business or through its hire or sale. Thus, an obsolete piece of equipment that could be sold for scrap would still be considered an asset, whereas an obsolete piece of equipment that could not be sold for scrap would not be regarded as one.

● *the business must have an exclusive right to control the benefit*. Unless the business has exclusive rights over the resource it cannot be regarded as an asset. Thus, for a business offering holidays on barges, the canal system may be a very valuable resource, but as the business will not be able to control the access of others to the canals, it cannot be regarded as an asset of the business. (However, the barges owned by the business would be regarded as assets.)

● *the benefit must arise from some past transaction or event.* This means that the transaction (or other event) giving rise to the business's right to the benefit must have already occurred, and will not arise at some future date. Thus an agreement by a business to purchase a piece of machinery at some future date would not mean the item is currently an asset of the business.

● *the asset must be capable of measurement in monetary terms.* Unless the item can be measured in monetary terms, with a reasonable degree of reliability, it will not be regarded as an asset for inclusion on the balance sheet. Thus, the title of a magazine (for example '*Hello!*' or '*Vogue*') that was created by its publisher may be extremely valuable to the business, but this value is usually impossible to quantify. It will not, therefore, be treated as an asset.

Note that all four of these conditions must apply. If one of them is missing, the item will not be treated as an asset, for accounting purposes, and will not, therefore, appear on the balance sheet.

We can see that these conditions will strictly limit the kind of items that may be referred to as 'assets' in the balance sheet. Certainly not all resources exploited by a business will be assets of the business for accounting purposes. Some, like the canal system or the magazine title '*Hello!*', may well be assets in a broader sense, but not for accounting purposes. Once an asset has been acquired by a business, it will continue to be considered an asset until the benefits are exhausted or the business disposes of it in some way.

Activity 2.2

Indicate which of the following items could appear as an asset on the balance sheet of a business. Explain your reasoning in each case.

1 £1,000 owing to the business by a customer who is unable to pay.
2 The purchase of a patent from an inventor that gives the business the right to produce a new product. Production of the new product is expected to increase profits over the period during which the patent is held.
3 The business hiring a new marketing director who is confidently expected to increase profits by over 30 per cent over the next three years.
4 The purchase of a machine that will save the business £10,000 each year. It is currently being used by the business but it has been acquired on credit and is not yet paid for.

Your answer to the above problems should be along the following lines:

1 Under normal circumstances a business would expect a customer to pay the amount owed. Such an amount is therefore typically shown as an asset under the heading 'debtors' or 'receivables'. However, in this particular case the debtor is unable to pay. Hence the item is incapable of providing future benefits, and the £1,000 owing would not be regarded as an asset. Debts that are not paid are referred to as 'bad debts'.
2 The purchase of the patent would meet all of the conditions set out above and would therefore be regarded as an asset.
3 The hiring of a new marketing director would not be considered as the acquisition of an asset. One argument against its classification as an asset is that the business does not have exclusive rights of control over the director. (Nevertheless, it may have an exclusive right to the services that the director provided.) Perhaps a stronger argument is

that the value of the director cannot be measured in monetary terms with any degree of reliability.

4 The machine would be considered an asset even though it is not yet paid for. Once the business has agreed to purchase the machine, and has accepted it, the machine is legally owned by the business even though payment is still outstanding. (The amount outstanding would be shown as a claim, as we shall see below.)

The sorts of items that often appear as assets in the balance sheet of a business include:

- freehold premises
- machinery and equipment
- fixtures and fittings
- patents and trademarks
- debtors (receivables)
- investments.

Activity 2.3

Can you think of three additional items that might appear as assets in the balance sheet of a business?

You may be able to think of a number of other items. Some that you may have identified are:

- motor vehicles
- stock of goods (inventories)
- computer equipment
- cash at bank.

Note that an asset does not have to be a physical item – it may also be a non-physical right to certain benefits. Assets that have a physical substance and can be touched are referred to as **tangible assets**. Assets that have no physical substance but which, nevertheless, provide expected future benefits (such as patents) are referred to as **intangible assets**.

Claims

A claim is an obligation on the part of the business to provide cash, or some other form of benefit, to an outside party. A claim will normally arise as a result of the outside party providing funds in the form of assets for use by the business. There are essentially two types of claim against a business:

- **Capital**. This represents the claim of the owner(s) against the business. This claim is sometimes referred to as the *owner's equity*. Some find it hard to understand how the owner can have a claim against the business, particularly when we consider the example of a sole-proprietor-type business where the owner *is*, in effect, the business. However, for accounting purposes, a clear distinction is made between the business (whatever its size) and the owner(s). The business is viewed as being quite separate from the owner and this is equally true for a sole proprietor like Paul, the wrapping-paper seller in Example 2.1, or a large company like Marks and Spencer plc. It is seen as a separate entity with its own separate existence, and when financial statements are prepared, they are prepared for the business rather than for the owner(s). This means that the balance sheet should reflect the financial position of the business as a separate entity. Viewed from this perspective, any funds contributed by the owner will be seen as coming from outside the business and will appear as a claim against the business in its balance sheet.

As we have just seen, the business and the owner are separate for accounting purposes, irrespective of the type of business concerned. It is also true that the operation of the capital section of the balance sheet is broadly the same irrespective of the type of business concerned. As we shall see in Chapter 4, with limited companies the capital figure must be analysed according to how each part of the capital first arose. For example, companies must make a distinction between that part of the capital that arose from retained profits and that part that arose from the owners putting in cash to start up the business.

● **Liabilities**. Liabilities represent the claims of individuals and organisations, apart from the owner, that have arisen from past transactions or events such as supplying goods or lending money to the business.

Once a claim has been incurred by a business, it will remain as an obligation until it is settled.

Now that the meaning of the terms *assets* and *claims* has been established, we can go on and discuss the relationship between the two. This relationship is quite simple and straightforward. If a business wishes to acquire assets, it will have to raise the necessary funds from somewhere. It may raise the funds from the owner(s) or from outside parties or from both. To illustrate the relationship, let us take the example of a business as set out in Example 2.2.

Example 2.2

Jerry and Co. deposits £20,000 in a bank account on 1 March in order to commence business. Let us assume that the cash is supplied by the owner (£6,000) and by a lender (£14,000) and paid into the business bank account. The raising of the funds in this way will give rise to a claim on the business by both the owner (capital) and the lender (liability). If a balance sheet of Jerry and Co. is prepared following the above transactions, the assets and claims of the business will appear as follows:

Jerry and Co.
Balance sheet as at 1 March

Assets	£	Claims	£
Cash at bank	20,000	Capital	6,000
		Liability – loan	14,000
	20,000		20,000

We can see from the balance sheet that has been prepared that the total claims are the same as the total assets. Thus:

$$\text{Assets} = \text{Capital} + \text{Liabilities}$$

This equation – which is often referred to as the *balance sheet equation* – will always hold true. Whatever changes that may occur to the assets of the business or the claims against the business, there will be compensating changes elsewhere that will ensure that the balance sheet always 'balances'. By way of illustration, consider the following transactions for Jerry and Co:

2 March   Purchased a motor van for £5,000, paying by cheque.
3 March   Purchased stock in trade (that is, goods to be sold) on one month's credit for £3,000.
4 March   Repaid £2,000 of the loan from the lender.
6 March   Owner introduced another £4,000 into the business bank account.

A balance sheet may be drawn up after each day in which transactions have taken place. In this way, the effect can be seen of each transaction on the assets and claims of the business. The balance sheet as at 2 March will be as follows:

Jerry and Co.
Balance sheet as at 2 March

Assets	£	Claims	£
Cash at bank (20,000 – 5,000)	15,000	Capital	6,000
Motor van	5,000	Liabilities – loan	14,000
	20,000		20,000

As can be seen, the effect of purchasing a motor van is to decrease the balance at the bank by £5,000 and to introduce a new asset – a motor van – to the balance sheet. The total assets remain unchanged. It is only the 'mix' of assets that will change. The claims against the business will remain the same because there has been no change in the way in which the business has been funded.

The balance sheet as at 3 March, following the purchase of stock, will be as follows:

Jerry and Co.
Balance sheet as at 3 March

Assets	£	Claims	£
Cash at bank	15,000	Capital	6,000
Motor van	5,000	Liabilities – loan	14,000
Stock (inventories)	3,000	Liabilities – trade creditor	3,000
	23,000		23,000

The effect of purchasing stock has been to introduce another new asset (stock) to the balance sheet. In addition, the fact that the goods have not yet been paid for means that the claims against the business will be increased by the £3,000 owed to the supplier, who is referred to as a *trade creditor* (or trade payable) on the balance sheet.

Activity 2.4

Try drawing up a balance sheet for Jerry and Co. as at 4 March.

The balance sheet as at 4 March, following the repayment of part of the loan, will be as follows:

Jerry and Co.
Balance sheet as at 4 March

Assets	£	Claims	£
Cash at bank (15,000 – 2,000)	13,000	Capital	6,000
Motor van	5,000	Liabilities – loan (14,000 – 2,000)	12,000
Stock (inventories)	3,000	Liabilities – trade creditor (payable)	3,000
	21,000		21,000

The repayment of £2,000 of the loan will result in a decrease in the balance at the bank of £2,000 and a decrease in the loan claim against the business by the same amount.

Activity 2.5

Try drawing up a balance sheet as at 6 March for Jerry and Co.

The balance sheet as at 6 March, following the introduction of more funds, will be as follows:

Jerry and Co.
Balance sheet as at 6 March

Assets	£	Claims	£
Cash at bank (13,000 + 4,000)	17,000	Capital (6,000 + 4,000)	10,000
Motor van	5,000	Liabilities – loan	12,000
Stock (inventories)	3,000	Liabilities – trade creditor (payable)	3,000
	25,000		25,000

The introduction of more funds by the owner will result in an increase in the capital of £4,000 and an increase in the cash at bank by the same amount.

Example 2.2 illustrates the point that the balance sheet equation (assets equals capital plus liabilities) will always hold true, because it reflects the fact that, if a business wishes to acquire assets, it must raise funds equal to the cost of those assets. The funds raised must be provided by the owners (capital), or by others (liabilities) or by both the owners and others. Hence the total cost of assets acquired should always equal the total capital plus liabilities.

It is worth pointing out that a business would not draw up a balance sheet after each day of transactions as shown in the example above. Such an approach is likely to be impractical, given even a relatively small number of transactions each day. A balance sheet for the business is usually prepared at the end of a defined reporting period. Determining the length of the reporting interval will involve weighing up the costs of producing the information against the perceived benefits of the information for decision-making purposes. In practice, the reporting interval will vary between businesses, and could be monthly, quarterly, half-yearly or annually. For external reporting purposes, an annual reporting cycle is the norm (although certain businesses, typically larger ones, report more frequently than this). However, for internal reporting purposes to managers, many businesses produce monthly financial statements.

The effect of trading operations on the balance sheet

In the example we considered earlier, we dealt with the effect on the balance sheet of a number of different types of transactions that a business might undertake. These transactions covered the purchase of assets for cash and on credit, the repayment of a loan, and the injection of capital. However, one form of transaction, trading, has not yet been considered. To deal with the effect of trading transactions on the balance sheet, let us return to our earlier example.

Example 2.2 continued

The balance sheet that we drew up for Jerry and Co. as at 6 March was as follows:

Jerry and Co.
Balance sheet as at 6 March

	£		£
Assets		Claims	
Cash at bank	17,000	Capital	10,000
Motor van	5,000	Liabilities – loan	12,000
Stock (inventories)	3,000	Liabilities – trade creditor (payable)	3,000
	25,000		25,000

Let us assume that, on 7 March, the business managed to sell all of the stock for £5,000 and received a cheque immediately from the customer for this amount. The balance sheet on 7 March, after this transaction has taken place, will be as follows:

Jerry and Co.
Balance sheet as at 7 March

	£		£
Assets		Claims	
Cash at bank (17,000 + 5,000)	22,000	Capital [10,000 + (5,000 – 3,000)]	12,000
Motor van	5,000	Liabilities – loan	12,000
Stock (inventories) (3,000 – 3,000)	–	Liabilities – trade creditor (payable)	3,000
	27,000		27,000

We can see that the stock (£3,000) has now disappeared from the balance sheet, but the cash at bank has increased by the selling price of the stock (£5,000). The net effect has therefore been to increase assets by £2,000 (that is, £5,000 – £3,000). This increase represents the net increase in wealth (the profit) that has arisen from trading. Also note that the capital of the business has increased by £2,000, in line with the increase in assets. This increase in capital reflects the fact that increases in wealth, as a result of trading or other operations, will be to the benefit of the owners and will increase their stake in the business.

Activity 2.6

What would have been the effect on the balance sheet if the stock had been sold on 7 March for £1,000 rather than £5,000?

The balance sheet on 7 March would be as follows:

Jerry and Co.
Balance sheet as at 7 March

Assets	£	Claims	£
Cash at bank (17,000 + 1,000)	18,000	Capital [10,000 + (1,000 – 3,000)]	8,000
Motor van	5,000	Liabilities – loan	12,000
Stock (inventories) (3,000 – 3,000)	–	Liabilities – trade creditor (payable)	3,000
	23,000		23,000

As we can see, the stock (£3,000) will disappear from the balance sheet, but the cash at bank will rise by only £1,000. This will mean a net reduction in assets of £2,000. This reduction represents a loss arising from trading and will be reflected in a reduction in the capital of the owner.

We can see that any decrease in wealth (loss) arising from trading or other transactions will lead to a reduction in the owner's stake in the business. If the business wished to maintain the level of assets as at 6 March, it would be necessary to obtain further funds from the owner or from lenders, or both.

What we have just seen means that the balance sheet equation can be extended as follows:

Assets = Capital + Profit (or − Loss) + Liabilities

As we have seen, the profit or loss for the period impacts on the balance sheet as an addition or reduction to capital. Any funds introduced or withdrawn by the owner for living expenses or other reasons also affect capital, but are shown separately. By doing this, we provide more comprehensive information for users of the financial statements. If we assume that the above business sold the stock for £5,000, as in the earlier example, and further assume that the owner withdrew £1,500 for his or her own use, the capital of the owner would appear as follows on the balance sheet:

	£
Capital (owner's equity)	
Opening balance	10,000
Add Profit	2,000
	12,000
Less Drawings	1,500
Closing balance	10,500

If the drawings were in cash, the balance of cash would decrease by £1,500 in the balance sheet.

Note that, like all balance sheet items, the amount of capital is cumulative. This means that any profit made that is not taken out as drawings by the owner(s) remains in the business. These retained profits have the effect of expanding the business.

The classification of assets

If the items on the balance sheet are listed haphazardly, with assets listed on one side and claims on the other, it can be confusing. To help users to understand more clearly the information that is presented, assets and claims are usually grouped into categories. Assets may be categorised as being either current or non-current.

Current assets

Current assets are basically assets that are held for the short term. To be more precise, they are assets that meet any one of four criteria. These are:

- they are held for sale or consumption in the normal course of a business's operating cycle;
- they are for the short term (that is, to be sold within the next year);
- they are held primarily for trading; and
- they are cash, or near cash such as easily marketable, short-term investments.

The most common current assets are stock (or inventories), customers who owe money for goods or services supplied on credit (known as trade debtors or receivables) and cash.

Perhaps it is worth making the point here that most sales made by most businesses are made on credit. This is to say that the goods pass to, or the service is rendered to, the customer, at one point but the customer pays later. Retail sales are the only significant exception to this general point.

For businesses that sell goods, rather than render a service, the current assets of stock, trade debtors and cash are interrelated. They circulate within a business as shown in Figure 2.2. We can see that cash can be used to purchase stock, which is then sold on credit. When the credit customers (trade debtors) pay, the business receives an injection of cash, and so on.

| Figure 2.2 | The circulating nature of current assets |

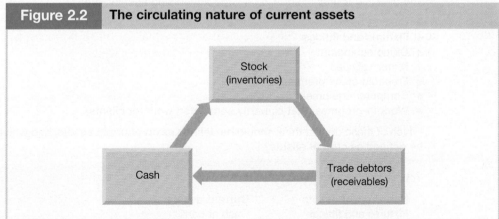

Stock may be sold on credit to customers. When the customers pay, the trade debts will be converted into cash, which can then be used to purchase more stock, and so the cycle begins again.

Non-current assets

→ **Non-current assets** (also called **fixed assets**) are assets that do not meet the above criteria. They are held for the long-term operations of the business. Essentially, they are the 'tools' of the business and are held with the objective of generating wealth.

This distinction between assets that are continuously circulating within the business and assets used for long-term operations may be helpful when trying to assess the appropriateness of the mix of assets held. A business will need a certain amount of both types of asset to operate effectively.

Activity 2.7

Can you think of two examples of assets that may be classified as non-current assets?

Examples of assets that may be defined as being non-current are:

- freehold premises
- plant and machinery
- motor vehicles
- patents.

This is not an exhaustive list. You may have thought of others.

It is important to appreciate that how a particular asset is classified (that is, between current and non-current) varies according to the nature of the business. This is because the *purpose* for which a particular type of asset is held may differ from business to business. For example, a motor vehicle manufacturer will normally hold a stock of the motor vehicles produced for resale, and would therefore classify them as part of the current assets. On the other hand, a business that uses motor vehicles for delivering its goods to customers (that is, as part of its long-term operations) would classify them as non-current assets.

Activity 2.8

The assets of Kunalun and Co., a large advertising agency, are:

- Cash at bank
- Fixtures and fittings
- Office equipment
- Motor vehicles
- Freehold office premises
- Computer equipment
- Work-in-progress (that is, partly completed work for clients).

Which of these do you think should be defined as non-current assets, and which should be defined as current assets?

Your answer should be as follows:

Non-current assets	Current assets
Fixtures and fittings	Cash at bank
Office equipment	Work-in-progress
Motor vehicles	
Freehold office premises	
Computer equipment	

The classification of claims

As we have already seen, claims are normally classified into capital (owner's claim) and liabilities (claims of outsiders). Liabilities are further classified into two groups:

- **Current liabilities** are basically amounts due for settlement in the short term. To be more precise, they are liabilities that meet any one of four criteria:
  - they expect to be settled within the normal course of the business's operating cycle;
  - they are due to be settled within 12 months of the balance sheet date;
  - they are held primarily for trading purposes; and
  - the business does not have the right to defer settlement beyond 12 months after the balance sheet date.
- **Non-current liabilities** represent those amounts due to outside parties that are not current liabilities.

Activity 2.9

Can you think of an example of each of a current liability and a non-current liability?

An example of a current liability would be amounts owing to suppliers for goods supplied on credit (known as trade creditors or trade payables) or a bank overdraft (a form of bank borrowing that is repayable on demand). An example of a non-current liability would be a long-term loan.

This classification of liabilities can help gain an insight to the ability of the business to meet its maturing obligations (that is, claims that must shortly be met). The current liabilities, which show the amounts that must be paid within the normal operating cycle, can be compared with the current assets, which show the assets to be sold within the same period. It should also help to highlight how the long-term finance of the business is raised. If a business relies on long-term loans to finance the business, the financial risks associated with the business will increase. This is because these loans will bring a commitment to make interest payments and capital repayments and the business may be forced to stop trading if this commitment is not fulfilled. Thus when raising long-term finance, a business must strike the right balance between non-current liabilities and owners' capital. We shall consider this issue in more detail in Chapter 7.

Balance sheet formats

Now that we have looked at the classification of assets and liabilities, it is possible to consider the format of the balance sheet. Although there is an almost infinite number of ways in which the same balance sheet information could be presented, we shall consider two basic formats. The first of these follows the style we adopted with Jerry and Co. earlier. A more comprehensive example of this style is shown in Example 2.3, below.

Example 2.3

Brie Manufacturing
Balance sheet as at 31 December 2005

	£	£		£
Non-current assets			**Capital**	
Freehold premises		45,000	Opening balance	50,000
Plant and machinery		30,000	*Add* Profit	14,000
Motor vans		19,000		64,000
		94,000	*Less* Drawings	4,000
				60,000
			Non-current liabilities	
			Loan	50,000
Current assets			**Current liabilities**	
Stock (inventories)	23,000		Trade creditors (payables)	37,000
Trade debtors				
(receivables)	18,000			
Cash at bank	12,000			
		53,000		
		147,000		147,000

Within each category of asset (non-current and current), shown in Example 2.3, the items are listed in reverse order of liquidity (nearness to cash). Thus, the assets that are furthest from cash are listed first and the assets that are closest to cash are listed last. In the case of non-current assets, freehold premises are listed first as these assets are usually the most difficult to turn into cash, and motor vans are listed last as there is usually a ready market for them. In the case of current assets, we have already seen that stock is converted to debtors and then debtors are converted to cash. Hence, under the heading of current assets, stock is listed first, followed by debtors and finally cash itself.

This ordering of assets is a normal practice, which is followed irrespective of the format used. Note also that the current assets are listed individually in the first column, and a subtotal of current assets (£53,000) is carried over to the second column to be added to the subtotal of non-current assets (£94,000). This convention is designed to make the balance sheet easier to read.

An obvious change to the format illustrated in Example 2.3 is to show claims on the left and assets on the right. Some people prefer this approach because the claims can be seen as the source of finance for the business, and the assets show how that finance has been deployed. It could be seen as more logical to show sources first and uses second.

The format shown in Example 2.3 is sometimes referred to as the *horizontal layout*. However, in recent years, a more common form of layout for the balance sheet is the *vertical* (or *narrative*) form of layout. This format is really based on a rearrangement of the balance sheet equation. With the horizontal format above, the balance sheet equation is set out as in Figure 2.3. The vertical format merely rearranges this equation as shown in Figure 2.4.

The vertical layout not only rearranges the equation but, as the name suggests, presents the information vertically rather than horizontally. The balance sheet starts with non-current assets and works downwards towards capital at the end. The balance sheet of Brie Manufacturing which was arranged in horizontal format in Example 2.3 can be rearranged in vertical format as shown in Example 2.4.

Figure 2.3   The horizontal balance sheet

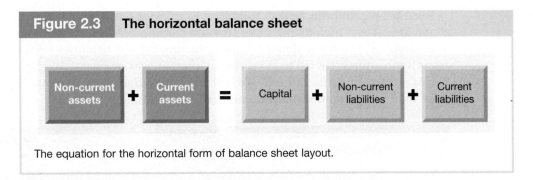

The equation for the horizontal form of balance sheet layout.

Figure 2.4   The vertical balance sheet

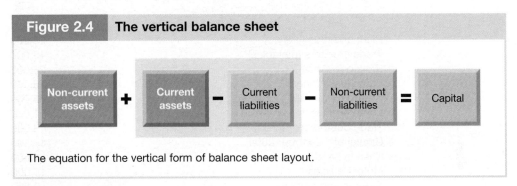

The equation for the vertical form of balance sheet layout.

Example 2.4

Brie Manufacturing
Balance sheet as at 31 December 2005

	£	£
Non-current assets		
Freehold premises		45,000
Plant and machinery		30,000
Motor vans		19,000
		94,000
Current assets		
Stock (inventories)	23,000	
Trade debtors (receivables)	18,000	
Cash at bank	12,000	
	53,000	
Less **Current liabilities**		
Trade creditors (payables)	37,000	
		16,000
Total assets *less* current liabilities		110,000
Less **Non-current liabilities**		
Loan		50,000
Net assets		60,000
Capital		
Opening balance		50,000
Add Profit		14,000
		64,000
Less Drawings		4,000
		60,000

Some people find the vertical format of Example 2.4 easier to read than the horizontal format as it usefully highlights the relationship between current assets and current liabilities. The figure derived from deducting current liabilities from the current assets is sometimes referred to as *net current assets* or *working capital*. We can see that for Brie Manufacturing this figure is £16,000, indicating that the short-term liquid assets more than cover the short-term claims against the business.

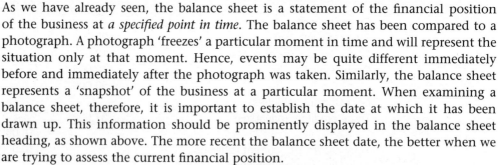

Self-assessment question 2.1

The following information relates to Simonson Engineering as at 30 September 2005:

	£
Plant and machinery	25,000
Trade creditors (payables)	18,000
Bank overdraft	26,000
Stock (inventories)	45,000
Freehold premises	72,000
Long-term loans	51,000
Trade debtors (receivables)	48,000
Capital at 1 October 2004	117,500
Cash in hand	1,500
Motor vehicles	15,000
Fixtures and fittings	9,000
Profit for the year to 30 September 2005	18,000
Drawings for the year to 30 September 2005	15,000

Required:
Prepare a balance sheet in the vertical format.

The balance sheet as a position at a point in time

As we have already seen, the balance sheet is a statement of the financial position of the business at *a specified point in time*. The balance sheet has been compared to a photograph. A photograph 'freezes' a particular moment in time and will represent the situation only at that moment. Hence, events may be quite different immediately before and immediately after the photograph was taken. Similarly, the balance sheet represents a 'snapshot' of the business at a particular moment. When examining a balance sheet, therefore, it is important to establish the date at which it has been drawn up. This information should be prominently displayed in the balance sheet heading, as shown above. The more recent the balance sheet date, the better when we are trying to assess the current financial position.

A business will normally prepare a balance sheet as at the close of business on the last day of its accounting year. In the UK, businesses are free to choose their accounting year. When making a decision on which year-end date to choose, commercial convenience can often be a deciding factor. Thus, a business operating in the retail trade may choose to have a year-end date early in the calendar year (for example, 31 January) because trade tends to be slack during that period and more staff time is available to help with the tasks involved in the preparation of the annual financial statements (such as checking the amount of stock held). Since trade is slack, it is also a time when the amount of stock held by the retail business is likely to be low as compared with other times of the year. Thus the balance sheet, though showing a fair view of what it purports to show, may not show a picture of what is more typically the position of the business over the rest of the year.

Accounting conventions and the balance sheet

Accounting is based on a number of rules or conventions that have evolved over time. They have evolved as attempts to deal with practical problems experienced by preparers and users, rather than to reflect some theoretical ideal. In preparing the balance sheets earlier, we have followed various **accounting conventions**, although they have not been explicitly mentioned. We shall now identify and discuss the major conventions that we have applied.

Business entity convention

For accounting purposes, the business and its owner(s) are treated as being quite separate and distinct. This is why owners are treated as being claimants against their own business in respect of their investment in the business. The **business entity convention** must be distinguished from the legal position that may exist between businesses and their owners. For sole proprietorships and partnerships, the law does not make any distinction between the business and its owner(s). For limited companies, on the other hand, there is a clear legal distinction between the business and its owners. (As we shall see in Chapter 4, the limited company is regarded as having a separate legal existence.) For accounting purposes these legal distinctions are irrelevant, and the business entity convention applies to all businesses.

Money measurement convention

Accounting normally deals with only those items that are capable of being expressed in monetary terms. Money has the advantage that it is a useful common denominator with which to express the wide variety of resources held by a business. However, not all such resources are capable of being measured in monetary terms and so will be excluded from a balance sheet. The **money measurement convention**, therefore, limits the scope of accounting reports.

Activity 2.10

Can you think of resources held by a business that cannot be quantified in monetary terms?

In answering this activity you may have thought of the following:

- the quality of the workforce
- the reputation of the business's products
- the location of the business
- the relationship with customers
- the ability of the managers.

Over the years, attempts have been made to measure, and then include on the balance sheet, resources of a business that have been previously excluded. For example, we have seen attempts to measure the 'human assets' of the business. It is often claimed that employees are the most valuable 'assets' of a business. By measuring these assets and putting the amount on the balance sheet, it is sometimes argued that we have a more complete picture of the financial position. However, these attempts are resisted because they involve softening the recognition criteria for an asset that we discussed earlier in the chapter. In particular, the ability to measure the value of the staff in monetary terms is an issue here.

Real World 2.1 shows how one business has succeeded in putting people on the balance sheet.

REAL WORLD 2.1

Rio's on the team sheet and the balance sheet

It may be surprising to learn that although human 'assets' are not shown on the balance sheet of a business as a general rule, there are exceptions to this rule. The most common exception arises with professional football clubs. Although football clubs cannot own players, they can own the rights to the players' services. Where these rights are acquired by compensating other clubs for releasing the players from their contracts, the amounts paid provide a reliable basis for measurement. This means that the rights to services can be regarded as an asset of the club for accounting purposes (assuming, of course, the player will also bring benefits to the club).

Manchester United Football Club has acquired several key players in this way and reports the cost of acquiring those rights to the players' services in its balance sheet. The balance sheet for 2003 shows the cost of registering its current squad of players as £89m. The item of players' registrations is shown as an intangible asset in the balance sheet as it is the rights to services not the players that are the assets. The figure of £89m includes the cost of bought-in players such as Rio Ferdinand but not 'home-grown' players such as Paul Scholes and the Neville brothers. The 'home-grown' players are not included because the club did not pay a transfer fee for them, so no clear-cut value can be placed on their services.

Source: Manchester United Annual Report 2003.

Historic cost convention

Assets are shown on the balance sheet at a value that is based on their **historic cost** (that is, acquisition cost). This method of measuring asset value has been adopted by accountants in preference to methods based on some form of current value. Many people find the **historic cost convention** difficult to support, as outdated historic costs are unlikely to help in the assessment of current financial position. It is often argued that recording assets at their current value would provide a more realistic view of financial position and would be relevant for a wide range of decisions. However, a system of measurement based on current values can present a number of problems.

Activity 2.11

Can you think of reasons why current value accounting may pose problems for both preparers and users of financial statements?

··

The term 'current value' can be defined in a number of ways. For example, it can be defined broadly as either the current replacement cost or the current realisable value (selling price) of an asset. These two types of valuation may result in quite different figures being produced to represent the current value of an item. (Think, for example, of second-hand car values: there is often quite a difference between buying and selling prices.) In addition, the broad terms 'replacement cost' and 'realisable value' can be defined in different ways. We must therefore be clear about what kind of current value accounting we wish to use. There are also practical problems associated with attempts to implement any system of current value accounting. For example, current values, however defined, are often difficult to establish with any real degree of objectivity. This may mean that the figures produced are heavily dependent on the opinion of managers. Unless the current value figures are capable of some form of independent verification, there is a danger that the financial statements will lose their credibility among users.

By reporting assets at their historic cost, it is argued that more reliable information is produced. Reporting in this way reduces the need for subjective opinion, as the amount paid for a particular asset is usually a matter of demonstrable fact. However, information based on past costs may not always be relevant to the needs of users.

Later in the chapter, we shall consider the valuation of assets in the balance sheet in more detail. We shall see that the historic cost convention is not always rigidly adhered to, and that departures from this convention often occur.

Going concern convention

→ The **going concern convention** holds that the financial statements should be prepared on the assumption that the business will continue operations for the foreseeable future, unless this is known not to be true. In other words, it is assumed that there is no intention, or need, to sell off the assets of the business. Such a sale may arise where the business is in financial difficulties and it needs to pay the creditors. This convention is important because the market (sale) value of non-current assets is often low in relation to the values at which they appear in the balance sheet, and an expectation of having to sell off the assets would mean that anticipated losses on sale should be fully recorded. However, where there is no expectation of a need to sell off the assets, the value of non-current assets can continue to be shown at their recorded values (that is, based on historic cost). This convention therefore provides some support for the historic cost convention under normal circumstances.

Dual aspect convention

Each transaction has two aspects, both of which will affect the balance sheet. Thus the purchase of a motor car for cash results in an increase in one asset (motor car) and a decrease in another (cash). The repayment of a loan results in the decrease in a liability (loan) and the decrease in an asset (cash/bank).

Activity 2.12

What are the two aspects of each of the following transactions?

- Purchase £1,000 stock on credit.
- Owner withdraws £2,000 in cash.
- Repayment of a loan of £3,000.

Your answer should be as follows:

- Stock increases by £1,000, creditors increase by £1,000.
- Capital reduces by £2,000, cash reduces by £2,000.
- Loan reduces by £3,000, cash reduces by £3,000.

→ Recording the **dual aspect** of each transaction ensures that the balance sheet will continue to balance.

Prudence convention

→ The **prudence convention** holds that financial statements should err on the side of caution. The convention represents an attempt to deal with the uncertainty surrounding many events reported in the financial statements, and evolved to counteract the excessive optimism of some managers and owners, which resulted in an overstatement of financial position. This convention requires the recording of all losses in full, and applies to both actual losses and expected losses. For example, if certain goods purchased for resale proved to be unpopular with customers and, as a result, the goods are to be sold below their original cost, the prudence convention requires that the expected loss from the future sales should be recognised immediately rather than when the goods are eventually sold. Profits, on the other hand, are not recognised until they are realised (that is, when the goods are actually sold). When the prudence convention conflicts with another convention, it is prudence that will normally prevail.

Activity 2.13

Can you think of a situation where certain users might find a prudent view of the financial position of a business will work to their disadvantage?

Applying the prudence convention can result in an understatement of financial position as unrealised profits are not recognised but expected losses are recognised in full. This may result in owners selling their stake in the business at a price that is lower than they would have received if a more balanced approach to valuation were employed.

The degree of bias towards understatement may be difficult to judge. It is likely to vary according to the views of the individual carrying out the valuation.

Stable monetary unit convention

The **stable monetary unit convention** holds that money, which is the unit of measurement in accounting, will not change in value over time. However, in the UK and throughout much of the world, inflation has been a persistent problem. This has meant that the value of money has declined in relation to other assets. In past years, high rates of inflation have resulted in balance sheets, which are drawn up on an historic cost basis, reflecting figures for assets that were much lower than if current values were employed. This sparked a big debate within the accounting profession and business community and there were calls to abandon historic costs in favour of current values in accounting. In more recent years, however, there have been lower rates of inflation and the debate has lost its intensity.

Objectivity convention

The **objectivity convention** seeks to reduce personal bias in financial statements. As far as possible, financial statements should be based on objective, verifiable evidence rather than on matters of opinion.

Activity 2.14

Which of the above conventions does the objectivity convention support and which does it conflict with?

The objectivity convention provides further support (along with the going concern convention) for the use of historic cost as a basis of valuation. It can conflict, however, with the prudence convention, which requires the use of judgement in determining values.

Accounting for goodwill and product brands

Some intangible non-current assets are similar to tangible non-current assets in so far as they have a clear and separate identity and the cost of the asset can be reliably determined. Patents, trademarks, copyrights and licences would normally fall into this category. Some intangible non-current assets, however, are quite different in nature. They lack a clear and separate identity and are really a hotch-potch of attributes that form part of the essence of the business. Goodwill and product brands fall into this category.

The term 'goodwill' is often used to cover various attributes of the business such as the quality of the products, the skill of the workforce and the relationship with customers. Product brands are similar to goodwill in that they are made up of various attributes, such as the brand image, the quality of the product, the trademark and so on. Although goodwill and product brands may be valuable to a business, this does not mean that they meet the recognition criteria for accounting assets that were discussed earlier in the chapter. Where they have been generated internally by the business it is often difficult to measure their cost or even to verify their existence. They are, therefore, excluded from the balance sheet.

When these items are acquired through an arm's-length transaction, however, the problems of verification and measurement are resolved. (An 'arm's-length' transaction is one that is undertaken between two unconnected parties.) If goodwill is acquired when taking over another business, or if a business acquires a particular product brand from another business, these items will be clearly identified and a price agreed for them. Under these circumstances, they should be reported as assets by the business that acquired them. **Real World 2.2** provides an example of a purchase of goodwill.

REAL WORLD 2.2

Where there's goodwill

CRH is a Dublin-based building materials business that has expanded its operations in recent years. In October 2003 it was reported that it had purchased Cementbouw, Handel and Industrie, a Dutch building materials business. CRH paid €646m for Cementbouw's distribution and building products operations. This was made up of €354m for the net assets (that is, assets less liabilities taken over), leaving a payment of €292m for goodwill. The payment for goodwill, which represents around 45 per cent of the total purchase price, will be recorded as an asset on the balance sheet of CRH.

Source: Based on information in 'CRH purchase of Cementbouw gets approval', *Financial Times*, 1 October 2003.

The basis of valuation of assets on the balance sheet

It was mentioned earlier that, when preparing the balance sheet, the historic cost convention is normally applied for the reporting of assets. However, this point requires further elaboration as, in practice, it is not simply a matter of recording each asset on the balance sheet at its original cost. We shall see that things are a little more complex than this. Before discussing the valuation rules in some detail, however, we should point out that these rules are based on international accounting standards. These are a set of rules that are generally accepted world-wide. The nature and role of accounting standards will be discussed in detail in Chapter 5.

Tangible non-current assets (property, plant and equipment)

Tangible non-current assets tend to be referred to as 'property, plant and equipment' and we shall use this terminology from now on. Property, plant and equipment should be measured initially at their historic cost. However, they will normally be used up over time as a result of wear and tear, obsolescence and so on. The amount used up, which is referred to as *depreciation,* must be measured for each accounting period that the assets are held. Although we shall leave a detailed examination of depreciation until Chapter 3, we need to know that when an asset has been depreciated, this fact should be reflected in the balance sheet. The total depreciation that has accumulated over the period since the asset was acquired must be deducted from its cost. This net figure (that is, the cost of the asset less the total depreciation to date) is referred to as the *net book value, written-down value* or *carrying amount*. The procedure described is not really a contravention of the historic cost convention. It is simply recognition of the fact that a proportion of the cost of the non-current asset has been consumed in the process of generating benefits for the business.

Although using depreciated cost is the 'benchmark treatment' for these assets, an alternative is allowed. Property, plant and equipment can be measured using **fair values** provided that these values can be measured reliably. The 'fair values', in this case, are usually the current market values (that is, the exchange values in an arm's-length transaction). By using fair value a more up-to-date figure than the depreciated cost figure is provided to users, which may be more relevant to their needs. It may also place the business in a better light, as assets such as freehold property may increase significantly in value over time. Of course, increasing the balance sheet value of an asset does not make that asset more valuable. However, perceptions of the business may be altered by such a move.

Activity 2.15

Refer to the vertical format balance sheet of Brie Manufacturing shown earlier (p. 41). What would be the effect of revaluing the freehold land to a figure of £110,000 on the balance sheet?

The effect on the balance sheet would be to increase the freehold land to £110,000 and the gain on revaluation (that is, £110,000 − £45,000 = £65,000) would be added to the capital of the owner, as it is the owner who will benefit from the gain. The revised balance sheet would therefore be as follows:

Brie Manufacturing
Balance sheet as at 31 December 2004

	£	£
Non-current assets		
Freehold premises		110,000
Plant and machinery		30,000
Motor vans		19,000
		159,000
Current assets		
Stock (inventories)	23,000	
Trade debtors (receivables)	18,000	
Cash at bank	12,000	
	53,000	
Less Current liabilities		
Trade creditors (payables)	37,000	
		16,000
Total assets less current liabilities		175,000
Less Non-current liabilities		
Loan		50,000
Net assets		125,000
Capital		
Opening balance		50,000
Add Revaluation gain		65,000
Profit		14,000
		129,000
Less Drawings		4,000
		125,000

One consequence of revaluing the freehold premises is that the depreciation charge will be increased. This is because the depreciation charge is based on the increased value of the asset.

Real World 2.3 shows that one well-known business revalued its land and buildings and, by doing so, greatly improved the looks of its balance sheet.

REAL WORLD 2.3

Retailer marks up land and buildings

The balance sheet of Marks and Spencer plc, a major high street retailer, as at 29 March 2003 reveals land and buildings at a net book value, or carrying amount, of £2,148.4m. These land and buildings are shown at an open market value and were valued by a firm of independent surveyors. If the land and buildings of the business had not been valued in this way, the net book value at 29 March 2003 would have been £1,451.3m. The effect of using market values was, therefore, to increase the net book value of these assets by £697.1m. This represents approximately 20 per cent of the net book value of all the tangible non-current assets of the business.

Source: Marks and Spencer plc Annual Report 2003, www.marksandspencer.com.

Once assets are revalued, the frequency of revaluation then becomes an important issue as assets recorded at out-of-date values can mislead users. Using out-of-date revaluations on the balance sheet is the worst of both worlds. It lacks the objectivity and verifiability of historic cost; it also lacks the realism of current values. Revaluations should therefore be frequent enough to ensure that the net book value, or carrying amount, of the revalued asset does not differ materially from its fair value at the balance sheet date.

When an item of property, or plant, or equipment is revalued on the basis of fair values, all assets within that particular group must be revalued. Thus, it is not acceptable to revalue some property but not others. Although this provides some degree of consistency within a particular group of assets, it does not, of course, prevent the balance sheet from containing a mixture of valuations.

Intangible non-current assets

For these assets, the balance sheet treatment used for tangible non-current assets broadly applies. The 'benchmark treatment' is that they are measured initially at historic cost and any depreciation (or *amortisation* as it is usually termed in this context) incurred following acquisition will be deducted to obtain a net book value. Once again, the alternative of revaluing intangible assets using fair values is available. However, this can only be used where fair values can be properly determined by reference to an active market. In practice, this is likely to be a rare occurrence.

The impairment of non-current assets

There is always a risk that both types of non-current asset may suffer a significant fall in value. This may be due to factors such as changes in market conditions, technological obsolescence and so on. In some cases, this fall in value may lead to the net book value, or carrying amount, of the asset being higher than the amount that could be recovered from the asset through its continued use or through its sale. When this situation arises, the asset figure on the balance sheet should be reduced to its recoverable amount. Unless this is done, the asset will be overstated on the balance sheet.

Activity 2.16

With which of the accounting conventions described earlier is this accounting treatment consistent?

The answer is the prudence convention, which states that actual or anticipated losses should be recognised in full.

We have seen that, under normal circumstances, a business may have a choice of using either depreciated cost or a value-based measure when reporting its non-current assets. However, under the circumstances just described, the business has no choice; the use of depreciated cost is not an option. **Real World 2.4** provides an example of where the application of this 'impairment rule' as it is called, resulted in huge write-downs for a business.

REAL WORLD 2.4

Talking telephone numbers

mmO_2 plc is a major mobile phone operator. During the year to 31 March 2003, the business was badly affected by a downturn in market conditions, which led to a review of the carrying amounts of its non-current assets. Following this review, the business decided to reduce the value of its intangible non-current assets by a total of £8,300m on the year-end balance sheet. This amount included write-downs for licences and goodwill in its operations in the UK and Germany of £2,300m and £4,700m respectively, and a write-down of goodwill in its operations in Ireland of £1,300m.

Source: mmO_2 Annual Report 2003.

Stocks (inventories)

It is not only non-current assets that run the risk of a significant fall in value. The stocks, or inventories, of a business could also suffer this fate, which could be caused by factors such as obsolescence, deterioration, damage and so on. Where a fall in value means that the amount likely to be recovered from the sale of the stocks will be lower than their cost, this loss must be reflected in the balance sheet. Thus, if the net realisable value (that is, selling price less any selling costs) falls below the cost of stocks held, the former should be used as the basis of valuation. Once again, this reflects the influence of the prudence convention on the balance sheet.

Real World 2.5 shows how stocks may be reported in the financial statements of large businesses.

REAL WORLD 2.5

Reporting the valuation basis of stocks

The published financial statements of large businesses normally show the basis on which the stocks of the business are valued. For example, Unilever plc, a large business selling food and home- and personal-care products, stated in its 2002 financial statements:

> Stocks are stated at the lower of cost and estimated net realisable value.

In some cases, the way in which the cost of stocks has been derived (usually when the goods are manufactured by the business rather than bought in) will be stated and, in a few cases, the basis for deriving net realisable value is stated. For example, the published financial statements of Thorntons plc, the chocolate maker, include the following statement:

> Cost includes materials, direct labour and an attributable part of the overheads according to the stage of production reached. Net realisable value is the estimated value which would be realised after deducting all costs of completion, marketing and selling.

Source: Unilever plc Annual Report 2002; Thorntons plc Annual Report 2003.

Interpreting the balance sheet

We have seen that the conventional balance sheet has a number of limitations. This has led some users of financial information to conclude that the balance sheet has little to offer in the way of useful information. However, this is not really the case. The balance sheet can provide useful insights to the financing and investing activities of a business. We shall consider this in detail in Chapter 7 when we deal with the analysis and interpretation of the financial statements.

SUMMARY

The main points of this chapter may be summarised as follows:

The major financial statements

- There are three major financial statements – the cash flow statement, the profit and loss account (income statement) and the balance sheet.
- The cash flow statement shows the cash movements over a particular period.
- The profit and loss account shows the wealth (profit) generated over a particular period.
- The balance sheet shows the accumulated wealth at a particular point in time.

The balance sheet

- Sets out the assets of the business, on the one hand, and the claims against those assets, on the other.
- Assets are resources of the business that have certain characteristics, such as the ability to provide future benefits.
- Claims are obligations on the part of the business to provide cash, or some other benefit, to outside parties.
- Claims are of two types – capital and liabilities.
- Capital represents the owner's claim and liabilities represent the claims of others, apart from the owner.

Classification of assets and liabilities

- Assets are normally categorised as being current or non-current (fixed).
- Current assets are held for sale or consumption in the normal course of business or are held for the short term.
- Non-current assets are held for use within the business for long-term operations.
- Liabilities are normally categorised as being current or non-current liabilities.
- Current liabilities represent amounts due in the normal course of the business's operating cycle or due for repayment within 12 months.
- Non-current liabilities represent amounts due that are not current liabilities.

Balance sheet formats

- The horizontal format sets out the assets on one side of the balance sheet and the capital and liabilities on the other side.
- The vertical format begins with the assets at the top of the balance sheet and deducts the liabilities. The resulting figure represents the net assets of the business. The capital of the business is shown at the bottom of the balance sheet.

Accounting conventions

- Accounting conventions have evolved to deal with practical problems experienced by preparers.
- The main conventions relating to the balance sheet include business entity, money measurement, historic cost, going concern, dual aspect, prudence, stable monetary unit and objectivity.

Asset valuation

- Property, plant and equipment are shown at historic cost less any amounts written off for depreciation. However, fair values may be used rather than depreciated cost.
- Where the amount that can be recovered from the tangible non-current assets is below the net book value, this lower amount should be reflected in the balance sheet.
- Intangible non-current assets broadly follow the same valuation rules as just described.
- Current assets are shown at the lower of cost or net realisable value.

→ Key terms

Further reading

If you would like to explore the topics covered in this chapter in more depth, we recommend the following books:

Financial Reporting, *Alexander D. and Britton A.*, 6th edn, International Thomson Business Press, 2001, chapter 3.

Corporate Financial Accounting and Reporting, *Sutton T.*, 2nd edn, Financial Times Prentice Hall, 2004, chapters 2 and 8.

International Financial Reporting Standards (IFRSs) 2003, *International Accounting Standards Board*, IASCF, 2003, IAS 16, IAS 36 and IAS 38.

Accounting Theory and Practice, *Glautier M. and Underdown B.*, 7th edn, Financial Times Prentice Hall, 2001, chapter 12.

REVIEW QUESTIONS

Answers to these questions can be found on the students' side of the Companion Website at www.pearsoned.co.uk/atrillmclaney.

2.1 An accountant prepared a balance sheet for a business using the horizontal layout. In the balance sheet, the capital of the owner was shown next to the liabilities. This confused the owner, who argued: 'My capital is my major asset and so should be shown as an asset on the balance sheet.' How would you explain this misunderstanding to the owner?

2.2 'The balance sheet shows how much a business is worth.' Do you agree with this statement? Discuss.

2.3 What is meant by the balance sheet equation? How does the form of this equation differ between the horizontal and vertical balance sheet format?

2.4 In recent years there have been attempts to place a value on the 'human assets' of a business in order to derive a figure that can be included on the balance sheet. Do you think humans should be treated as assets? Would 'human assets' meet the conventional definition of an asset for inclusion on the balance sheet?

EXERCISES

Exercises 2.5 to 2.8 are more advanced than 2.1 to 2.4. Those with a coloured number have answers at the back of the book.

2.1 On the fourth day of his business venture, Paul, the street trader in wrapping-paper (see earlier in the chapter), purchased more stock for £53 cash. During the day he sold stock that had cost £33 for a total of £47.

Required:
Draw up the three financial statements for day 4 of Paul's business venture.

2.2 The 'total business wealth' belongs to Paul because he is the sole owner of the business. Can you explain how the figure for total business wealth at the end of day 4 has arisen? You will need to look back at the events of days 1, 2 and 3 (in this chapter) to do this.

2.3 Whilst on holiday in Bridlington, Helen had her credit cards and purse stolen from the beach while she was swimming. She was left with only £40, which she had kept in her hotel room, but she had three days of her holiday remaining. She was determined to continue her holiday and decided to make some money to enable her to do so. She decided to sell orange juice to holidaymakers using the local beach. On day 1 she bought 80 cartons of orange juice at £0.50 each for cash and sold 70 of these at £0.80 each. On the following day she purchased 60 cartons for cash and sold 65 at £0.80 each. On the third and final day she purchased another 60 cartons for cash. However, it rained and, as a result, business was poor. She managed to sell 20 at £0.80 each but sold off the rest of her stock at £0.40 each.

Required:
Prepare a profit and loss account and cash flow statement for each day's trading and prepare a balance sheet at the end of each day's trading.

2.4 On 1 March, Joe Conday started a new business. During March he carried out the following transactions:

1 March Deposited £20,000 in a bank account
2 March Purchased fixtures and fittings for £6,000 cash, and stock £8,000 on credit
3 March Borrowed £5,000 from a relative and deposited it in the bank
4 March Purchased a motor car for £7,000 cash and withdrew £200 for own use
5 March A further motor car costing £9,000 was purchased. The motor car purchased on 4 March was given in part exchange at a value of £6,500. The balance of purchase price for the new car was paid in cash
6 March Conday won £2,000 in a lottery and paid the amount into the business bank account. He also repaid £1,000 of the loan

Required:
Draw up a balance sheet for the business at the end of each day.

2.5 The following is a list of the assets and claims of Crafty Engineering Ltd at 30 June last year:

	£000
Trade creditors (payables)	86
Motor vehicles	38
Loan from Industrial Finance Co. (long-term)	260
Machinery and tools	207
Bank overdraft	116
Stock (inventories)	153
Freehold premises	320
Trade debtors (receivables)	185

Required:
(a) Prepare the balance sheet of the business as at 30 June last year from the above information using the vertical format. *Hint*: There is a missing item that needs to be deduced and inserted.
(b) Discuss the significant features revealed by this financial statement.

2.6 The balance sheet of a business at the start of the week is as follows:

Assets	£	Claims	£
Freehold premises	145,000	Capital	203,000
Furniture and fittings	63,000	Bank overdraft	43,000
Stock in trade	28,000	Trade creditors (payables)	23,000
Trade debtors (receivables)	33,000		
	269,000		269,000

During the week the following transactions take place:

(a) Stock sold for £11,000 cash; this stock had cost £8,000.
(b) Sold stock for £23,000 on credit; this stock had cost £17,000.
(c) Received cash from trade debtors totalling £18,000.
(d) The owners of the business introduced £100,000 of their own money, which was placed in the business bank account.
(e) The owners brought a motor van, valued at £10,000, into the business.
(f) Bought stock in trade on credit for £14,000.
(g) Paid trade creditors £13,000.

Required:
Show the balance sheet after all of these transactions have been reflected.

2.7 The following is a list of assets and claims of a manufacturing business at a particular point in time:

	£
Bank overdraft	22,000
Freehold land and buildings	245,000
Stock (inventories) of raw materials	18,000
Trade creditors (payables)	23,000
Plant and machinery	127,000
Loan from Industrial Finance Co. (long-term)	100,000
Stock (inventories) of finished goods	28,000
Delivery vans	54,000
Trade debtors (receivables)	34,000

Required:

Write out a balance sheet in the standard vertical form incorporating these figures. *Hint*: There is a missing item that needs to be deduced and inserted.

2.8 You have been talking to someone who had read the first chapter of an accounting text some years ago. During your conversation the person made the following statements:

(a) The profit and loss account (income statement) shows how much cash has come into and left the business during the accounting period and the resulting balance at the end of the period.

(b) In order to be included in the balance sheet as an asset, an item needs to be worth something in the market, that is all.

(c) The balance sheet equation is:

$$\text{Assets} + \text{Capital} = \text{Liabilities}$$

(d) Non-current assets are things that cannot be moved.

(e) Working capital is the name given to the sum of the current assets.

Required:

Comment critically on each of the above statements, going into as much detail as you can.

Measuring and reporting financial performance

INTRODUCTION

In this chapter we continue our examination of the major financial statements by looking at the profit and loss account (income statement). This statement was briefly considered in Chapter 2 and is now examined in some detail. We shall see how this statement is prepared and how it links with the balance sheet. We shall also consider some of the key measurement problems to be faced when preparing this statement.

The profit and loss account (income statement)

In Chapter 2, we examined the nature and purpose of the balance sheet. We saw that this statement was concerned with setting out the financial position of a business at a particular moment in time. However, it is not usually enough for users to have information relating only to the amount of wealth held by a business at one moment in time. Businesses exist for the primary purpose of generating wealth, or profit, and it is the profit generated *during a period* that is the main concern of many users of financial statements. Although the amount of profit generated is of particular interest to the owners of a business, other groups such as managers, employees and suppliers will also have an interest in the profit-making ability of the business. The purpose of the profit and loss account – or income statement, as it is sometimes called – is to measure and report how much **profit** (wealth) the business has generated over a period. As with the balance sheet that we examined in Chapter 2, the profit and loss account is prepared following the same principles, irrespective of whether the business is a sole proprietorship or a limited company.

The measurement of profit requires that the total revenue of the business, generated during a particular period, be identified. **Revenue** is simply a measure of the inflow of economic benefits arising from the ordinary activities of a business. These benefits, which accrue to the owners, will result in either an increase in assets (such as cash or amounts owed to the business by debtors) or a decrease in liabilities. Different forms of business enterprise will generate different forms of revenue. Some examples of the different forms that revenue can take are as follows:

- sales of goods (for example, of a manufacturer);
- fees for services (for example, of a solicitor);
- subscriptions (for example, of a club);
- interest received (for example, of an investment fund).

The total expenses relating to each accounting period must also be identified. **Expense** is really the opposite of revenue. It represents the outflow of economic benefits arising from the ordinary activities of a business. This loss of benefits will result in either a decrease in assets or an increase in liabilities. Expenses are incurred in the process of generating revenue, or attempting to generate them. The nature of the business will again determine the type of expenses that will be incurred. Examples of some of the more common types of expenses are:

- the cost of buying goods that are subsequently sold – known as *cost of sales* or *cost of goods sold*;
- salaries and wages;
- rent and rates;
- motor vehicle running expenses;
- insurances;
- printing and stationery;
- heat and light;
- telephone and postage, and so on.

The profit and loss account for a particular period simply shows the total revenue generated during that period and deducts from this the total expenses incurred in generating that revenue. The difference between the total revenue and total expenses will represent either profit (if sales revenue exceeds expenses) or loss (if expenses exceed revenue). Thus, we have:

> **Profit (loss) for the period = Total revenue for the period**
> ***less* Total expenses incurred**
> **in generating the revenue**

Relationship between the profit and loss account and the balance sheet

The profit and loss account and the balance sheet should not be viewed in any way as substitutes for one another. Rather they should be seen as performing different functions. The balance sheet is, as stated earlier, a statement of the financial position of a business at a single moment in time – a 'snapshot' of the stock of wealth held by the business. The profit and loss account, on the other hand, is concerned with the *flow* of wealth over a period of time. The two statements are closely related. The profit and loss account can be viewed as linking the balance sheet at the beginning of the period with the balance sheet at the end. Thus, at the start of a new business, a balance sheet will be produced to reveal the opening financial position. After an appropriate period, a profit and loss account will be prepared to show the wealth generated over the period. A balance sheet will also be prepared to reveal the new financial position at the end of the period covered by the profit and loss account. This balance sheet will incorporate the changes in wealth that have occurred since the previous balance sheet was drawn up.

We saw in the previous chapter (p. 36) that the effect on the balance sheet of making a profit (loss) means that the equation can be extended as follows:

> **Assets = Capital + Profit (or – Loss) + Liabilities**

The amount of profit or loss for the period affects the balance sheet as an adjustment to capital.

The above equation can be extended to:

> **Assets = Capital + (Sales revenue – Expenses) + Liabilities**

In theory, it would be possible to calculate profit and loss for the period by making all adjustments for revenue and expenses through the capital section of the balance sheet. However, this would be rather cumbersome. A better solution is to have an 'appendix' to capital, in the form of a profit and loss account. By deducting expenses from revenue for the period, the profit and loss account derives the profit (loss) for adjustment in the capital item in the balance sheet. This figure represents the net effect of trading for the period. Providing this 'appendix' means that a detailed and more informative view of performance is presented to users.

The format of the profit and loss account

→ The format of the **profit and loss account** will vary according to the type of business to which it relates. To illustrate a profit and loss account, let us consider the case of a retail business (that is, a business that purchases goods in their completed state and resells them). This type of business usually has straightforward operations and, as a result, the profit and loss account is relatively easy to understand.

Example 3.1 sets out a typical format for the profit and loss account of a retail business.

Example 3.1

Hi-Price Stores
Profit and loss account for the year ended 31 October 2005

	£	£
Sales revenue		232,000
Less Cost of sales		154,000
Gross profit		78,000
Add Interest received from investments		2,000
		80,000
Less Salaries and wages	24,500	
Rent and rates	14,200	
Heat and light	7,500	
Telephone and postage	1,200	
Insurance	1,000	
Motor vehicle running expenses	3,400	
Loan interest	1,100	
Depreciation – fixtures and fittings	1,000	
Depreciation – motor van	600	
		54,500
Net profit		25,500

→ The first part of the statement is concerned with calculating the **gross profit** for the period. The trading revenue, which arises from selling the goods, is the first item that appears. Deducted from this item is the cost of sales, which is the cost of the goods sold during the period. The difference between the trading revenue and cost of sales is referred to as gross profit. This represents the profit from simply buying and selling goods without taking into account any other expenses or revenues associated with the business.

Having calculated the gross profit, any additional sources of revenue of the business are then added to this figure. In the above example, interest from investments represents an additional source of revenue. From this subtotal of gross profit and additional revenues, the other expenses (overheads) that have to be incurred in operating the business (salaries and wages, rent and rates and so on) are deducted. The final figure
→ derived is the **net profit** for the period. This net profit figure represents the wealth generated during the period that is attributable to the owner(s) of the business and which will be added to their capital in the balance sheet. As can be seen, net profit is

a residual – that is, the amount left over after deducting all expenses incurred in generating the sales for the period.

The profit and loss account – some further aspects

Having set out the main principles involved in preparing a profit and loss account, we need to consider some further points.

Cost of sales

The **cost of sales** figure for a period can be identified in different ways. In some businesses, the cost of sales is identified at the time a sale has been made. Sales are closely matched with the cost of those sales and so identifying the cost of sales figure for inclusion in the profit and loss account is not a problem. Many large retailers (for example, supermarkets) have point-of-sale (checkout) devices that not only record each sale but also simultaneously pick up the cost of the particular sale. Other businesses that sell a relatively small number of high-value items (for example, an engineering business that produces custom-made equipment) also tend to match sales revenue with the cost of the goods sold at the time of the sale. However, some businesses (for example, small retailers) do not usually find it practical to match each sale to a particular cost of sales figure as the accounting period progresses. They find it easier to identify the cost of sales figure at the end of the accounting period.

To understand how this is done, it is important to recognise that the cost of sales figure represents the cost of goods that were *sold* during the period rather than the cost of goods that were *purchased* during the period. Part of the goods purchased during a particular period may remain in stock and not be sold until a later period. To derive the cost of sales for a period, it is necessary to know the amount of opening and closing stocks (inventories) for the period and the cost of goods purchased during the period. Example 3.2 below illustrates how the cost of sales is derived.

Example 3.2

Hi-Price Stores, which we considered in Example 3.1 above, began the accounting year with unsold stock of £40,000 and during that year purchased stock at a cost of £189,000. At the end of the year, unsold stock of £75,000 was still held by the business.

The opening stock at the beginning of the year *plus* the goods purchased during the year will represent the total goods available for resale. Thus:

	£
Opening stock	40,000
Plus Goods purchased	189,000
Goods available for resale	229,000

The closing stock will represent that portion of the total goods available for resale that remains unsold at the end of the period. Thus, the cost of goods actually sold during the period must be the total goods available for resale *less* the stocks remaining at the end of the period. That is:

	£
Goods available for resale	229,000
Less Closing stock	75,000
Cost of goods sold (or cost of sales)	154,000

These calculations are sometimes shown on the face of the profit and loss account as in Example 3.3.

Example 3.3

	£	£
Sales revenue		232,000
Less Cost of sales		
Opening stock	40,000	
Plus Goods purchased	189,000	
	229,000	
Less Closing stock	75,000	154,000
Gross profit		78,000

The above is simply an expanded version of the first section of the profit and loss account for Hi-Price Stores, as set out in Example 3.1. We have simply included the additional information concerning stock balances and purchases for the year provided in Example 3.2.

Classification of expenses

The classifications for the revenue and expense items, as with the classifications of various assets and claims in the balance sheet, are often a matter of judgement by those who design the accounting system. In the profit and loss account in Example 3.1, the insurance expense could have been included with telephone and postage under a single heading – say, general expenses. Such decisions are normally based on how useful a particular classification will be to users. This will usually mean, however, that expense items of material size will be shown separately. For businesses that trade as limited companies, there are rules that dictate the classification of various items appearing in the accounts for external reporting purposes. These rules will be discussed in Chapter 5.

In the case of the balance sheet, we saw that the information could be presented in either a horizontal format or a vertical format. This is also true of the profit and loss account. Where a horizontal format is used, expenses are listed on the left-hand side and revenues on the right, the difference being either net profit or net loss. The vertical format has been used above as it is easier to understand and is now almost always used.

Activity 3.1

The following information relates to the activities of H & S Retailers for the year ended 30 April 2005:

	£
Motor vehicle running expenses	1,200
Rent received from subletting	2,000
Closing stock	3,000
Rent and rates payable	5,000
Motor vans	6,300
Annual depreciation – motor vans	1,500
Heat and light	900
Telephone and postage	450
Sales revenue	97,400
Goods purchased	68,350
Insurance	750
Loan interest payable	620
Balance at bank	4,780
Salaries and wages	10,400
Opening stock	4,000

Prepare a profit and loss account (in vertical format) for the year ended 30 April 2005. (*Hint*: Not all items shown above should appear on this statement.)

Your answer to this activity should be as follows:

H & S Retailers
Profit and loss account for the year ended 30 April 2005

	£	£
Sales revenue		97,400
Less Cost of sales		
Opening stock	4,000	
Plus Purchases	68,350	
	72,350	
Less Closing stock	3,000	69,350
Gross profit		28,050
Rent received		2,000
		30,050
Less Salaries and wages	10,400	
Rent and rates	5,000	
Heat and light	900	
Telephone and postage	450	
Insurance	750	
Motor vehicle running expenses	1,200	
Loan interest	620	
Depreciation – motor van	1,500	
		20,820
Net profit		9,230

The reporting period

We have seen already that for reporting to those outside the business, a financial reporting cycle of one year is the norm, though some large businesses will produce a half-yearly, or interim, financial statement to provide more frequent feedback on progress. For those who manage a business, however, it is important to have much more frequent feedback on performance. Thus it is quite common for profit and loss accounts to be prepared on a quarterly, monthly, weekly or even daily basis in order to show how things are progressing.

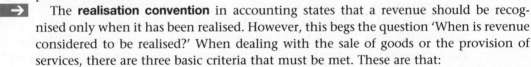

Profit measurement and the recognition of revenue

A key issue in the measurement of profit concerns the point at which revenue is recognised. Where there is a sale of goods or provision of services, the revenue arising from a particular sale could be recognised at one of the different points in the process.

For example, a firm of solicitors undertakes to handle a house purchase for a client for which it will charge a fixed fee. In theory, the firm could recognise the revenue at any one of several different points in the process. The obvious possibilities seem to be:

- at the time of agreeing to do the work;
- at the time of completing the work; or
- at the time the client pays.

The particular point chosen is not simply a matter of academic interest: it can have a profound impact on the total revenues, and therefore total profits, reported for a particular period. If the solicitors' case (above) straddled the end of an accounting period, the choice made among the three possible times for recognising the revenue could determine whether the revenue is included as a revenue of an earlier accounting period or a later one.

 The **realisation convention** in accounting states that a revenue should be recognised only when it has been realised. However, this begs the question 'When is revenue considered to be realised?' When dealing with the sale of goods or the provision of services, there are three basic criteria that must be met. These are that:

- the amount of revenue can be measured reliably;
- it is probable that the economic benefits will be received; and
- the costs associated with the transaction can be measured reliably.

However, there is an additional criterion to be applied where the revenue comes from the sale of goods.

The sale of goods

Where there is a sale of goods, there is the additional criterion that ownership and control of the items should pass to the buyer before revenue is recognised. Activity 3.2 below provides an opportunity to apply the various criteria discussed to a practical problem.

Activity 3.2

A manufacturing business sells goods on credit (that is, the customer pays for the goods some time after they are received). Below are four points in the production/selling cycle at which revenue might be recognised by the business:

- when the goods are produced;
- when an order is received from a customer;
- when the goods are delivered to, and accepted by, the customer; and
- when the cash is received from the customer.

A significant amount of time may elapse between these different points. At what point do you think the business should recognise revenue?

The criteria will usually be fulfilled at point 3: when the goods are passed to, and accepted by, the customer. By this point the buyer and seller will have agreed both the selling price and the settlement terms and both parties will have legally enforceable rights. As a result, the revenue can be reliably measured, it is probable that the amounts due will be paid, and ownership and control will have passed to the buyer. (At this point, the costs of the transaction can also normally be established.)

We can see that the effect of applying these criteria is that a sale on credit is usually recognised *before* the cash is received. Thus, the total sales revenue figure shown in the profit and loss account may include sales transactions for which the cash has yet to be received. The total sales revenue figure in the profit and loss account for a period will often, therefore, be different from the total cash received from sales during that period.

Where goods are sold for cash rather than on credit, the revenue will normally be recognised at the point of sale. It is at this point that all the criteria will usually be met. For cash sales, there will be no difference in timing between reporting sales revenue and cash received.

Some products (and services, as we shall see shortly), have long production cycles. One example is a new building. A customer may enter a contract with a builder to build a new house, with all of the conditions regarding the work specified in the contract. The contract may also break the building work into a number of stages. Stage 1 might be clearing and levelling the land and putting in the foundations. Stage 2 might be building the walls. Stage 3 might be putting on the roof and so on. Each stage would have a separate price, the total for all the stages equalling the contract total for building the house. As each stage is completed, the builder recognises the price for it as a revenue and bills the customer. Were the builder to wait until the house is completed before recognising the revenue, all of the profit would be recognised in the accounting year in which the house was completed. If the building work were started in one accounting year and completed in the following one, none of the revenue and profit would be recognised in the earlier year, when perhaps nearly all of the work was done. This could provide misleading information in the profit and loss account. Other business activities, such as shipbuilding, where the time taken from the start of the work to completion is lengthy, adopt a similar approach to revenue recognition.

Providing services

Where a business provides a service, revenue may be recognised *before* the service is fully complete, provided a particular stage of completion can be reliably measured. In some cases, a service may be carried out over a long period of time, such as a management consultancy service to help restructure a large business. The consultants may work for some years on the restructuring project but will not wait until it is complete before recognising any part of the revenue. Such a large project is usually undertaken in stages and a proportion of the total revenue may be recognised when an agreed stage of the service is complete: for example, when an identifiable division of the business has been restructured. The proportion of revenue recognised will normally reflect the proportion of work done or costs incurred. This is exactly the same approach as used by builders in long contracts.

Another example of recognising revenue before the service is complete is when a business provides an unspecified number of services over an agreed period of time. For example, an Internet business may provide open access to the Internet for those who pay a subscription fee. In this case, it is usually assumed that the economic benefits flow evenly over time and so revenue would normally be recognised evenly over the subscription period.

For many services, however, it is not possible to recognise revenue in stages and so recognition will take place when the service is fully completed: for example, the solicitor handling a house sale that we discussed above. **Real World 3.1** provides some examples of how different kinds of businesses recognise revenue in practice.

REAL WORLD 3.1

Recognising revenue in practice

Large businesses often disclose the way in which revenue appearing in the profit and loss account is recognised. Here are a few examples:

mmO$_2$, the mobile phone operator, recognises:

● revenues from handsets at the point of sale;
● revenues from pre-pay call cards when the customer has used up the card to pay for calls;
● revenues from connection fees and subscriptions evenly over the period to which they relate.

Source: mmO$_2$ Annual Report 2003.

Brandon Hire plc operates tool and equipment hire services and recognises revenues from hiring over the period of the contract.

Source: Brandon Hire plc Annual Report and Accounts 2003.

Hyder Consulting plc is an engineering design, planning and management consultancy business which generates revenue principally from long-term contracts. Revenue from contracts is recognised on the basis of the sales value of the work performed in relation to the total sales value of the contract and its stage of completion.

Source: Hyder Consulting plc Annual Report 2003.

In all of the forms of service mentioned in Real World 3.1, there will normally be a timing difference between the recognition of revenue and the receipt of cash. Revenue for providing services is often recognised *before* the cash is received, just like the sale of goods on credit. However, there are occasions when it is the other way around; usually because the business demands payment before providing the service.

Activity 3.3

Can you think of any examples of where cash may be demanded in advance of a service being provided? *Hint*: Try to think of services that you may use.

Examples of where cash is received in advance of the service being provided may include:

- rent received from letting premises;
- telephone line rental charges;
- TV licence (BBC) or subscription (for example, Sky) fees; and
- subscriptions received for the use of health clubs or golf clubs.

You may have thought of others.

We have seen above that we should recognise revenue only when it has been earned and we are pretty confident that we shall receive the cash. In recent years, however, some businesses have been criticised for being a little too quick to recognise revenue. Early recognition can, of course, help to boost profits, at least in the short term. **Real World 3.2** looks at a business that was criticised for early recognition of revenue.

REAL WORLD 3.2

Looking on the sunny side   FT

MyTravel Group plc is a major tour operator that attracted considerable criticism for its revenue recognition policy. The policy of the business was to recognise revenue for holidays taken at the time the holiday was booked. However, this was seen as being premature by some commentators and was changed to a more conservative basis in response to criticisms. Now the business recognises revenue for holidays taken on the date of departure. This revised policy seems to be in line with other travel operators: Holidaybreak plc, for example, adopts this approach to revenue recognition.

The effect of introducing more conservative accounting policies was to reduce profits of MyTravel plc by £20.3m in 2002 and by £19.0m in 2001.

Sources: 'Crackdown on companies overstating turnover', *Financial Times*, 27 February 2003; Holiday Break plc Annual Report and Financial Statements 2003; MyTravel Group plc Annual Report and Accounts 2002.

Profit measurement and the recognition of expenses

Having decided on the point at which revenue is recognised, we must now turn to the issue of the recognition of expenses. The **matching convention** in accounting is designed to provide guidance concerning the recognition of expenses. This convention states that expenses should be matched to the revenue that they helped to generate. In other words, expenses must be taken into account in the same profit and loss account in which the associated sale is included in the total sales revenue figure. Applying this convention may mean that a particular expense reported in the profit and loss account for a period may not be the same figure as the cash paid for that item during the period. The expense reported may be either more or less than the cash paid during the period. Let us consider two examples that illustrate this point.

When the expense for the period is more than the cash paid during the period

Example 3.4

Domestic Ltd retails household electrical appliances. It pays its sales staff a commission of 2 per cent of sales revenue generated, and total sales revenue for the year amounted to £300,000. This will mean that the commission to be paid in respect of the sales for the period will be £6,000. However, by the end of the period, the sales commission paid to staff was £5,000. If the business reported only the amount paid, it would mean that the profit and loss account would not reflect the full expense for the year. This would contravene the *matching convention* because not all of the expenses associated with the revenue of the period would have been matched in the profit and loss account. This will be remedied as follows:

- Sales commission expense in the profit and loss account will include the amount paid *plus* the amount outstanding (that is, £6,000 = £5,000 + £1,000).
- The amount outstanding (£1,000) represents an outstanding liability at the balance sheet date and will be included under the heading **accrued expenses**, or 'accruals', in the balance sheet. As this item will have to be paid within 12 months of the balance sheet date, it will be treated as a current liability.
- The cash will already have been reduced to reflect the commission paid (£5,000) during the period.

These points are illustrated in Figure 3.1.

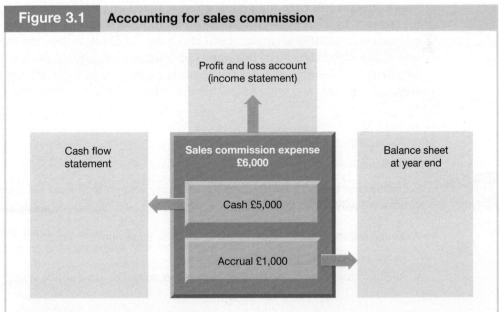

Figure 3.1   Accounting for sales commission

This illustrates the main points of Example 3.4. We can see that the sales commission expense of £6,000 (which appears in the profit and loss account) is made up of a cash element £5,000 and an accrued element £1,000. The cash element appears in the cash flow statement and the accrued element will appear as a year-end liability in the balance sheet.

In principle, all expenses should be matched to the period in which the sales revenue to which they relate is reported. However, it is sometimes difficult to match closely certain expenses to sales revenue in the same precise way that we have matched sales commission to sales revenue. It is unlikely, for example, that electricity charges incurred can be linked directly to particular sales in this way. As a result, the electricity charges incurred by, say, a retailer would be matched to the *period* to which they relate. Example 3.5 illustrates this.

Example 3.5

Domestic Ltd has reached the end of its accounting year and has only been charged electricity for the first three quarters of the year (amounting to £1,900). This is simply because the electricity company has yet to send out bills for the quarter that ends on the same date as Domestic Ltd's year end. In this situation, an estimate should be made of the electricity expense outstanding (that is, the bill for the last three months of the year is estimated). This figure (let us say the estimate is £500) is dealt with as follows:

● Electricity expense in the profit and loss account will include the amount paid, plus the amount of the estimate (that is, £1,900 + £500 = £2,400) in order to cover the whole year.
● The amount of the estimate (£500) represents an outstanding liability at the balance sheet date, and will be included under the heading 'accruals' or 'accrued expenses' in the balance sheet. As this item will have to be paid within 12 months of the balance sheet date, it will be treated as a current liability.
● The cash will already have been reduced to reflect the electricity paid (£1,900) during the period.

This treatment will have the desired effect of increasing the electricity expense to the 'correct' figure for the year in the profit and loss account, assuming that the estimate is reasonably accurate. It will also have the effect of showing that, at the end of the accounting year, Domestic Ltd owed the amount of the last quarter's electricity bill. Dealing with the outstanding amount in this way reflects the dual aspect of the item, and will ensure that the balance sheet equation is maintained.

Activity 3.4

Let us say the estimate for outstanding electricity was correct. How will the payment of the electricity bill be dealt with?

When the electricity bill is eventually paid, it will be dealt with as follows:

● Reduce cash by the amount of the bill.
● Reduce the amount of the accrued expense as shown on the balance sheet.

If there is a slight error in the estimate, a small adjustment (either negative or positive depending on the direction of the error) can be made to the following year's expense. Dealing with the estimation error in this way is not strictly correct, but the amount is likely to be insignificant.

Activity 3.5

Can you think of other expenses, apart from electricity charges, that cannot be linked directly to sales revenue and for which matching will therefore be done on a time basis?

You may have thought of the following examples:

- rent and rates
- insurance
- interest payments
- licences.

This is not an exhaustive list. You may have thought of others.

When the amount paid during the year is more than the full expense for the period

It is not unusual for a business to be in a situation where it has paid more during the year than the full expense for that year. Example 3.6 illustrates how we deal with this.

Example 3.6

Images Ltd, an advertising agency, normally pays rent for its premises quarterly in advance (on 1 January, 1 April, 1 July and 1 October). On the last day of the last accounting year (31 December), it paid the next quarter's rent (£4,000) to the following 31 March, which was a day earlier than required. This would mean that a total of five quarters' rent was paid during the year. If Images Ltd treats all of the cash paid as an expense in the profit and loss account, this would be more than the full expense for the year. This would contravene the matching convention because a higher figure than the expenses associated with the revenue of the year would appear in the profit and loss account.

The problem is overcome by dealing with the rental payment as follows:

- Show the rent for four quarters as the appropriate expense in the profit and loss account (that is, 4 × £4,000 = £16,000).
- The cash (that is, 5 × £4,000 = £20,000) would already have been paid during the year.
- Show the quarter's rent paid in advance (£4,000) as a **prepaid expense** on the asset side of the balance sheet. (The prepaid expense will appear as a current asset in the balance sheet, under the heading 'prepaid expenses' or 'prepayments'.)

In the next accounting period, this prepayment will cease to be an asset and will become an expense in the profit and loss account of that period. This is because the rent prepaid relates to that period and will be 'used up' during that period.

These points are illustrated in Figure 3.2.

In practice, the treatment of accruals and prepayments will be subject to the **materiality convention** of accounting. This convention states that, where the amounts involved are immaterial, we should consider only what is expedient. This may mean

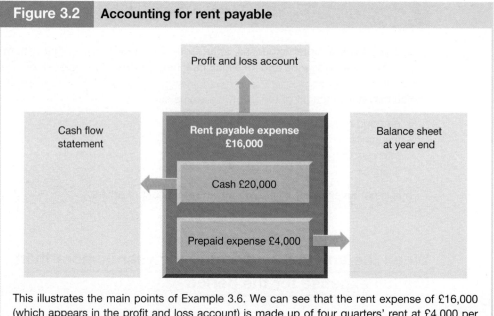

Figure 3.2 **Accounting for rent payable**

This illustrates the main points of Example 3.6. We can see that the rent expense of £16,000 (which appears in the profit and loss account) is made up of four quarters' rent at £4,000 per quarter. This is the amount that relates to the period and is 'used up' during the period. The cash paid of £20,000 (which appears in the cash flow statement) is made up of the cash paid during the period, which is five quarters at £4,000 per quarter. Finally, the prepayment of £4,000 (which appears on the balance sheet) represents the payment made on 31 December and relates to the next financial year.

that an item will be treated as an expense in the period in which it is paid, rather than being strictly matched to the revenue to which it relates. For example, a business may find that, at the end of an accounting period, there is a bill of £5 owing for stationery used during the year. For a business of any size, the time and effort involved in recording this as an accrual would have little effect on the measurement of profit or financial position. It would, therefore, be ignored when preparing the profit and loss account for the period. The bill would, presumably, be paid in the following period and therefore be treated as an expense of that period.

Profit, cash and accruals accounting

As we have just seen, revenue does not usually represent cash received and expenses are not the same as cash paid. As a result, the net profit figure (that is, total revenue minus total expenses) will not normally represent the net cash generated during a period. It is therefore important to distinguish between profit and liquidity. Profit is a measure of achievement, or productive effort, rather than a measure of cash generated. Although making a profit will increase wealth, as we have already seen in Chapter 2, cash is only one form in which that wealth may be held. These points are summarised as the **accruals convention** of accounting. This asserts that profit is the excess of revenue over expenses for a period, not the excess of cash receipts over cash payments.

Leading on from this, the approach to accounting encompassed in the accruals convention is frequently referred to as **accruals accounting**. Thus the balance sheet and the profit and loss account are both prepared on the basis of accruals accounting. On the other hand, the cash flow statement is not. It deals with cash receipts and payments.

Profit measurement and the calculation of depreciation

The expense of **depreciation**, which appeared in the profit and loss account in Activity 3.1, requires further explanation. Non-current assets (with the exception of freehold land) do not usually have a perpetual existence. They are eventually used up in the process of generating revenue for the business. In essence, depreciation is an attempt to measure that portion of the cost (or fair value) of a non-current asset that has been used up in generating the revenue recognised during a particular period. The depreciation charge is considered to be an expense of the period to which it relates. Depreciation tends to be relevant both to property, plant and equipment (tangible non-current assets) and to intangible non-current assets.

To calculate a depreciation charge for a period, four factors have to be considered:

● the cost (or fair value) of the asset;
● the useful life of the asset;
● the residual value of the asset; and
● the depreciation method.

The cost (or fair value) of the asset

The cost of an asset will include all costs incurred by the business to bring the asset to its required location and to make it ready for use. Thus, in addition to the costs of acquiring the asset, any delivery costs, installation costs (for example, setting up a new machine) and legal costs incurred in the transfer of legal title (for example, in the case of freehold property) will be included as part of the total cost of the asset. Similarly, any costs incurred in improving or altering an asset in order to make it suitable for its intended use within the business will also be included as part of the total cost.

Activity 3.6

Andrew Wu (Engineering) Ltd purchased a new motor car for its marketing director. The invoice received from the motor car supplier revealed the following:

	£	£
New BMW 325i		26,350
Delivery charge	80	
Alloy wheels	660	
Sun roof	200	
Petrol	30	
Number plates	130	
Road fund licence	160	1,260
		27,610
Part exchange – Reliant Robin		1,000
Amount outstanding		26,610

What is the total cost of the new car that will be treated as part of the business's property, plant and equipment?

Activity 3.6 continued

The cost of the new car will be as follows:

	£	£
New BMW 325i		26,350
Delivery charge	80	
Alloy wheels	660	
Sun roof	200	
Number plates	130	1,070
		27,420

These costs include delivery costs and number plates, as they are a necessary and integral part of the asset. Improvements (alloy wheels and sun roof) are also regarded as part of the total cost of the motor car. The petrol costs and road fund licence, however, represent a cost of operating the asset rather than a part of the total cost of acquiring the asset and making it ready for use: hence these amounts will be charged as an expense in the period incurred (although part of the cost of the licence may be regarded as a prepaid expense in the period incurred).

The part-exchange figure shown is part payment of the total amount outstanding, and is not relevant to a consideration of the total cost.

The fair value of an asset was defined in Chapter 2 as the exchange value that could be obtained in an arm's-length transaction. For land and buildings, this is normally the market value, as determined by professionally qualified valuers. For other types of property, plant and equipment, such as motor vehicles, market values may also be used. However, where the asset is very specialised and this value is difficult to determine, replacement cost may be used instead. The problems of using current values were discussed in Chapter 2.

The useful life of the asset

An asset has both a *physical life* and an *economic life*. The physical life of an asset will be exhausted through the effects of wear and tear and/or the passage of time. It is possible, however, for the physical life to be extended considerably through careful maintenance, improvements and so on. The economic life of an asset is decided by the effects of technological progress and by changes in demand. After a while, the benefits of using the asset may be less than the costs involved. This may be because the asset is unable to compete with newer assets, or because it is no longer relevant to the needs of the business. The economic life of an asset may be much shorter than its physical life. For example, a computer may have a physical life of eight years and an economic life of three years.

It is the economic life of an asset that will determine the expected useful life for the purpose of calculating depreciation. Forecasting the economic life of an asset, however, may be extremely difficult in practice: both the rate at which technology progresses and shifts in consumer tastes can be swift and unpredictable.

Residual value (disposal value)

When a business disposes of a non-current asset that may still be of value to others, some payment may be received. This payment will represent the **residual value**, or *disposal value*, of the asset. To calculate the total amount to be depreciated with regard to an asset, the residual value must be deducted from the cost of the asset. The likely amount to be received on disposal is, once again, often difficult to predict.

Depreciation method

Once the amount to be depreciated (that is, the cost, or fair value, of the asset less the residual value) has been estimated, the business must select a method of allocating this depreciable amount over the asset's useful life. Although there are various ways in which the total depreciation may be allocated and, from this, a depreciation charge for a period derived, there are really only two methods that are commonly used in practice.

The first of these is known as the **straight-line method**. This method simply allocates the amount to be depreciated evenly over the useful life of the asset. In other words, an equal amount of depreciation will be charged for each year the asset is held.

Example 3.7

To illustrate this method, consider the following information:

Cost of machine	£40,000
Estimated residual value at the end of its useful life	£1,024
Estimated useful life	4 years

To calculate the depreciation charge for each year, the total amount to be depreciated must be calculated. This will be the total cost *less* the estimated residual value: that is, £40,000 – £1,024 = £38,976. Having done this, the annual depreciation charge can be derived by dividing the amount to be depreciated by the estimated useful life of the asset of four years. The calculation is therefore:

$$\frac{£38,976}{4} = £9,744$$

Thus, the annual depreciation charge that appears in the profit and loss account in relation to this asset will be £9,744 for each of the four years of the asset's life.

The amount of depreciation relating to the asset will be accumulated for as long as the asset continues to be owned by the business. This accumulated depreciation figure will increase each year as a result of the annual depreciation amount charged to the profit and loss account. This accumulated amount will be deducted from the cost of the asset on the balance sheet. Thus, for example, at the end of the second year the accumulated depreciation will be £9,744 × 2 = £19,488, and the asset details will appear on the balance sheet as follows:

	£	£
Machine at cost	40,000	
Less Accumulated depreciation	19,488	
		20,512

→ The balance of £20,512 shown above is referred to as the **written-down value**, *net book value* or *carrying amount* of the asset. It represents that portion of the cost (or fair value) of the asset that has still to be written off (that is treated as an expense). It must be emphasised that this figure does *not* represent the current market value, which may be quite different.

The straight-line method derives its name from the fact that the written-down value of the asset at the end of each year, when plotted against time, will result in a straight line, as shown in Figure 3.3.

Figure 3.3	Graph of written-down value against time using the straight-line method

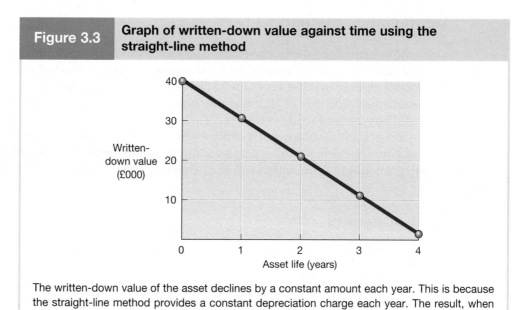

The written-down value of the asset declines by a constant amount each year. This is because the straight-line method provides a constant depreciation charge each year. The result, when plotted on a graph, is a straight line.

The second approach to calculating depreciation for a period is referred to as the → **reducing-balance method**. This method applies a fixed percentage rate of depreciation to the written-down value of an asset each year. The effect of this will be high annual depreciation charges in the early years and lower charges in the later years. To illustrate this method, let us take the same information used in Example 3.7. It can be shown that using a fixed percentage of 60 per cent of the written-down value to determine the annual depreciation charge will have the effect of reducing the written-down value to £1,024 after four years.

The calculations will be as follows:

	£
Cost of machine	40,000
Year 1 Depreciation charge (60%* of cost)	(24,000)
Written-down value (WDV)	16,000
Year 2 Depreciation charge (60% of WDV)	(9,600)
Written-down value	6,400
Year 3 Depreciation charge (60% of WDV)	(3,840)
Written-down value	2,560
Year 4 Depreciation charge (60% of WDV)	(1,536)
Residual value	1,024

* Deriving the fixed percentage to be applied requires the use of the following formula:

$$P = (1 - \sqrt[n]{R/C}) \times 100\%$$

where: P = the depreciation percentage;
     n = the useful life of the asset (in years);
     R = the residual value of the asset;
     C = the cost, or fair value, of the asset.

The fixed percentage rate will, however, be given in all examples used in this text.

We can see that the pattern of depreciation is quite different for the two methods. If we plot the written-down value of the asset, which has been derived using the reducing-balance method, against time, the result will be as shown in Figure 3.4.

Figure 3.4	Graph of written-down value against time using the reducing-balance method

Under the reducing-balance method, the written-down value of an asset falls by a larger amount in the earlier years than in the later years. This is because the depreciation charge is based on a fixed-rate percentage of the written-down value.

Activity 3.7

Assume that the machine used in the example above was owned by a business that made a profit *before* depreciation of £20,000 for each of the four years in which the asset was held.

Calculate the net profit for the business for each year under each depreciation method, and comment on your findings.

Your answer should be as follows:

Straight-line method

	(a) Profit before depreciation £	(b) Depreciation £	(a–b) Net profit £
Year 1	20,000	9,744	10,256
Year 2	20,000	9,744	10,256
Year 3	20,000	9,744	10,256
Year 4	20,000	9,744	10,256

Activity 3.7 continued

Reducing-balance method

	(a) Profit before depreciation £	(b) Depreciation £	(a–b) Net profit/ (loss) £
Year 1	20,000	24,000	(4,000)
Year 2	20,000	9,600	10,400
Year 3	20,000	3,840	16,160
Year 4	20,000	1,536	18,464

The straight-line method of depreciation results in a constant net profit figure over the four-year period because both the profit before depreciation and the depreciation charge are constant over the period. The reducing-balance method, however, results in a changing profit figure over time, despite the fact that, in this example, the pre-depreciation profit is the same each year. In the first year a net loss is reported, and thereafter a rising net profit is reported.

Although the *pattern* of net profit for each year over the four-year period will be quite different, depending on the depreciation method used, the *total* net profit for the period (£41,024) will remain the same. This is because both methods of depreciating will allocate the same amount of total depreciation (£38,976) over the four-year period. It is only the amount allocated *between years* that will differ.

In practice, the use of different depreciation methods may not have such a dramatic effect on profits as suggested in the activity above. Where a business replaces some of its assets each year, the total depreciation charge calculated under the reducing-balance method will reflect a range of charges (from high through to low), as assets will be at different points in the replacement cycle. This could mean that the total depreciation charge may not be significantly different from the total depreciation charge that would be derived under the straight-line method.

Selecting a depreciation method

How does a business choose which depreciation method to use for a particular asset? The most appropriate method should be the one that best matches the depreciation expense to the economic benefits that are consumed. The business may therefore decide to undertake an examination of the pattern of benefits consumed. Where the asset's benefits are likely to be consumed evenly over time (buildings, for example), the straight-line method may be considered appropriate. Where assets lose their efficiency and the benefits consumed decline over time as a result (for example, certain types of machinery), the reducing-balance method may be considered more appropriate. Where the pattern of economic benefits consumed is uncertain, the straight-line method is normally chosen.

There is an international accounting standard to deal with the problem of depreciation. As we shall see in Chapter 5, the purpose of accounting standards is to narrow areas of accounting difference and to ensure that information provided to users is transparent and comparable. The standard for handling depreciation endorses the view that the depreciation method chosen should reflect the pattern in which the asset's economic benefits are consumed. The standard also requires that businesses disclose a fair amount of detail concerning depreciation charges in their financial statements. Thus, information such as the methods of depreciation used, the accumulated amount of depreciation at the beginning and end of the financial period and either the depreciation rates applied or the useful lives of the assets must be disclosed.

Real World 3.3 sets out the depreciation policies of Thorntons plc.

REAL WORLD 3.3

Depreciation policies in practice

Thorntons plc, the manufacturer and retailer of confectionery, uses the straight-line method to depreciate its non-current assets. The financial statements for the year ended 30 June 2003 show the period over which different classes of tangible assets are depreciated as follows:

In equal annual instalments

Factory freehold premises	50 years
Short leasehold land and buildings	Period of the lease
Retail fixtures and fittings	5 years
Retail equipment	4 to 5 years
Retail shop improvements	10 years
Other equipment and vehicles	3 to 7 years
Manufacturing plant and machinery	12 to 15 years

We can see that there are wide variations in the expected useful lives of the various non-current assets held.

Source: Thorntons plc Annual Report and Accounts 2003.

The approach taken for the depreciation (or amortisation as it is usually called in this context) of intangible non-current assets is broadly the same as that of property, plant and equipment (tangible non-current assets). However, there is often much greater uncertainty surrounding the future economic benefits from intangible non-current assets. International accounting standards deal with this greater uncertainty by applying stricter rules. For example, there is a presumption that the depreciation (or amortisation) period for intangible assets is no more than twenty years. This presumption can only be rebutted if there is persuasive evidence to the contrary. International accounting standards also insist that a review of the depreciation period and depreciation method used must be carried out at least annually. For property, plant and equipment (tangible non-current assets), the review periods can be less frequent.

Depreciation and the replacement of non-current assets

There seems to be a misunderstanding in the minds of some people that the purpose of depreciation is to provide the funds for the replacement of an asset when it reaches the end of its useful life. However, this is *not* the purpose of depreciation as conventionally defined. It was mentioned earlier that depreciation represents an attempt to

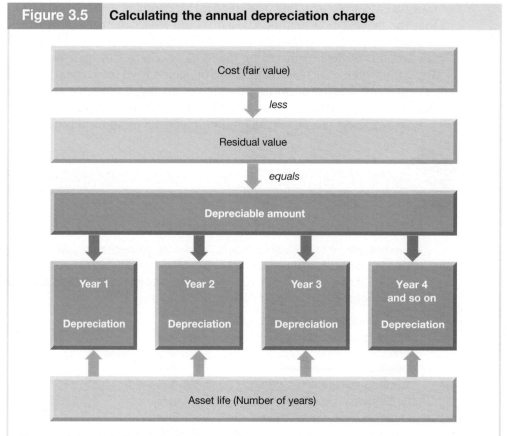

Figure 3.5   Calculating the annual depreciation charge

The cost (fair value) of an asset less the residual value will represent the amount to be depreciated. This amount is depreciated over the useful life (four years in this particular case) of the asset using an appropriate depreciation method.

allocate the cost, or fair value, (less any residual value) of an asset over its expected useful life. The resulting depreciation charge in each period represents an expense, which is then used in the calculation of net profit for the period. Calculating the depreciation charge for a period is therefore necessary for the proper measurement of financial performance, and must be done whether or not the business intends to replace the asset in the future. This principle is illustrated in Figure 3.5.

If there is an intention to replace the asset, the depreciation charge in the profit and loss account will not ensure that liquid funds are set aside by the business specifically for this purpose. Although the effect of a depreciation charge is to reduce net profit, and therefore to reduce the amount available for withdrawal by the owners, the amounts retained within the business as a result may be invested in ways that are unrelated to the replacement of the specific asset.

Activity 3.8

Suppose that a business sets aside liquid funds, equivalent to the depreciation charge each year, with the intention of using these to replace the asset at the end of its useful life.

Will this ensure that there will be sufficient funds available for this purpose?

No. Even if funds are set aside each year that are equal to the depreciation charge for the year, the total amount accumulated at the end of the asset's useful life may be insufficient for replacement purposes. This may be because inflation or technological advances have resulted in an increase in the replacement cost.

Depreciation and judgement

When reading the above sections on depreciation, it may have struck you that accounting is not as precise and objective as is sometimes suggested. There are areas where subjective judgement is required, and depreciation provides a good illustration of this.

Activity 3.9

What kinds of judgements must be made to calculate a depreciation charge for a period?

In answering this activity, you may have thought of the following:

● the expected residual or disposal value of the asset
● the expected useful life of the asset
● the choice of depreciation method.

Making different judgements on these matters would result in a different pattern of depreciation charges over the life of the asset, and therefore in a different pattern of reported profits. However, underestimations or overestimations that are made in relation to the above will be adjusted for in the final year of an asset's life, and so the total depreciation charge (and total profit) over the asset's life will not be affected by estimation errors.

Real World 3.4 shows the effect of changing the useful life of assets on the annual profit of one large business.

REAL WORLD 3.4

Changing the useful life of assets

In 2002, Euro-Disney, the theme park and hotel operator, extended the estimated life of some of its non-current assets relating to infrastructure and buildings. The management argued that the revisions were designed to reflect more faithfully the useful lives of these assets in relation to their intended use and in relation to industry practice. The effect of doing this was to decrease the depreciation charge (and, therefore, increase profit) in 2002 by €5.7m. As the profit for the year, before exceptional items, was €4.9m, this change turned a loss for the period into a profit.

Source: Euro-Disney plc 2002 Financial Report.

Activity 3.10

Sally Dalton (Packaging) Ltd purchased a machine for £40,000. At the end of its useful life of four years, the amount received on sale was £4,000. When the asset was purchased the business received two estimates of the likely residual value of the asset, which were: (a) £8,000, and (b) zero.

Show the pattern of annual depreciation charges over the four years and the total depreciation charges for the asset under each of the two estimates. The straight-line method should be used to calculate the annual depreciation charges.

The depreciation charge, assuming estimate (a), will be £8,000 a year ((£40,000 – £8,000)/4). The depreciation charge, assuming estimate (b), will be £10,000 a year (£40,000/4). As the actual residual value is £4,000, estimate (a) will lead to underdepreciation of £4,000 (£8,000 – £4,000) over the life of the asset, and estimate (b) will lead to overdepreciation of £4,000 (£0 – £4,000). These under- and overestimations will be dealt with in year 4.

The pattern of depreciation and total depreciation charges will therefore be:

| | | Estimate | |
| | | (a) | (b) |
Year		£	£
1	Annual depreciation	8,000	10,000
2	Annual depreciation	8,000	10,000
3	Annual depreciation	8,000	10,000
4	Annual depreciation	8,000	10,000
		32,000	40,000
4	Under/(over)depreciation	4,000	(4,000)
	Total depreciation	36,000	36,000

The final adjustment for underdepreciation of an asset is often referred to as 'loss on sale of non-current asset', as the amount actually received is less than the residual value. Similarly, the adjustment for overdepreciation is often referred to as 'profit on sale of non-current asset'.

Profit measurement and stock (inventories) costing methods

The way in which we measure the cost of stock (or inventories) is important because the cost of the stock sold during a period will affect the calculation of net profit, and the remaining stock held at the end of the period will affect the portrayal of the financial position. In the last chapter, we saw that historic cost is the basis for valuing assets, and so it is tempting to think that determining the cost of stocks held is not a difficult issue. However, in a period of *changing prices*, the costing of stock can be a problem.

A business must determine the cost of the stock sold during the period and the cost of the stock remaining at the end of the period. To do this, both of these costs are calculated as if the stock had been physically handled in a particular assumed manner. The assumption made has nothing to do with how the stock is *actually* handled; it is concerned only with which assumption is likely to lead to the most useful accounting information.

Two common assumptions used are:

- **first in, first out (FIFO)**: that is, the earliest stocks held are the first to be sold;
- **last in, first out (LIFO)**: that is, the latest stocks held are the first to be sold.

Another approach to deriving the cost of stocks is to assume that stocks entering the business lose their separate identity, and any issues of stock reflect the average cost of the stocks that are held. This is the **weighted average cost (AVCO)** method, where the weights used in deriving the average cost figures are the quantities of each batch of stock purchased. Example 3.8 below provides a simple illustration of the way in which each method is applied.

Example 3.8

A business that supplies coal to factories has the following transactions during a period:

		Tonnes	Cost/tonne
1 May	Opening stock	1,000	£10
2 May	Purchased	5,000	£11
3 May	Purchased	8,000	£12
		14,000	
6 May	Sold	(9,000)	
	Closing stock	5,000	

First in, first out (FIFO)

Using the first in, first out approach, the first 9,000 tonnes of coal are assumed to be those that are sold. This is the opening stock (1,000 tonnes), the stock bought on 2 May (5,000 tonnes) and 3,000 tonnes of the 3 May purchase. The remainder of the 3 May purchase (5,000 tonnes) will comprise the closing stock. Thus we have:

	Cost of sales			Closing stock		
	Tonnes	Cost/tonne £	Total £000	Tonnes	Cost/tonne £	Total £000
1 May	1,000	10	10.0			
2 May	5,000	11	55.0			
3 May	3,000	12	36.0	5,000	12	60.0
Cost of sales			101.0	Closing stock		60.0

Last in, first out (LIFO)

Using the last in, first out approach, the later purchases will be the first to be sold. This is the 3 May purchase (8,000 tonnes) and 1,000 tonnes of the 2 May purchase. The earlier purchases (the rest of the 2 May purchase and the opening stock) will comprise the closing stock. Thus we have:

	Cost of sales			Closing stock		
	Tonnes	Cost/tonne £	Total £000	Tonnes	Cost/tonne £	Total £000
3 May	8,000	12	96.0			
2 May	1,000	11	11.0	4,000	11	44.0
1 May				1,000	10	10.0
Cost of sales			107.0	Closing stock		54.0

Weighted average cost (AVCO)

Using this approach, a weighted average cost will be determined that will be used to derive both the cost of goods sold and the cost of the remaining stocks held. This simply means that the total cost of the opening stock, the 2 May and 3 May purchases are added together and divided by the total number of tonnes, to obtain the weighted average cost per tonne. Both the cost of sales and closing stock values are based on that average cost per tonne. Thus we have:

	Purchases		
	Tonnes	Cost/tonne £	Total £000
1 May	1,000	10	10.0
2 May	5,000	11	55.0
3 May	8,000	12	96.0
	14,000		161.0

Average cost = £161,000/14,000 = £11.5 per tonne.

Cost of sales			Closing stock		
Tonnes	Cost/tonne £	Total £000	Tonnes	Cost/tonne £	Total £000
9,000	11.5	103.5	5,000	11.5	57.5

Activity 3.11

Suppose the 9,000 tonnes of stock in Example 3.8 were sold for £15 per tonne.

(a) Calculate the gross profit for the period under each of the three methods.
(b) What observations concerning the portrayal of financial position and performance can you make about each method when prices are rising?

Your answer should be along the following lines:

(a) Gross profit calculation:

	FIFO £000	LIFO £000	AVCO £000
Sales revenue (9,000 @ £15)	135.0	135.0	135.0
Cost of sales	101.0	107.0	103.5
Gross profit	34.0	28.0	31.5
	£000	£000	£000
Closing stock figure	60.0	54.0	57.5

(b) The above figures reveal that FIFO will give the highest gross profit during a period of rising prices. This is because sales revenue is matched with the earlier (and cheaper) purchases. LIFO will give the lowest gross profit because sales revenue is matched against the more recent (and dearer) purchases. The AVCO method will normally give a figure that is between these two extremes.

The closing stock figure in the balance sheet will be highest with the FIFO method. This is because the cost of goods still held will be based on the more recent (and dearer) purchases. LIFO will give the lowest closing stock figure as the goods held in stock will be based on the earlier (and cheaper) stocks purchased. Once again, the AVCO method will normally give a figure that is between these two extremes.

Activity 3.12

Assume that prices in Activity 3.11 are falling rather than rising. How would your observations concerning the portrayal of financial performance and position be different for the various stock valuation methods?

When prices are falling, the position of FIFO and LIFO is reversed. FIFO will give the lowest gross profit as sales revenue is matched against the earlier (and dearer) goods purchased. LIFO will give the highest gross profit as sales revenue is matched against the more recent (and cheaper) goods purchased. AVCO will give a cost of sales figure between these two extremes. The closing stock figure in the balance sheet will be lowest under FIFO as the cost of stock will be based on the more recent (and cheaper) stocks purchased. LIFO will provide the highest closing stock figure and AVCO will provide a figure between the two extremes.

It is important to recognise that the different stock valuation methods will only have an effect on the reported profit *from one year to the next*. The figure derived for closing stock will be carried forward and matched with sales revenue in a later period. Thus, if the cheaper purchases of stocks are matched to sales revenue in the current period, it will mean that the dearer purchases will be matched to sales revenue in a later period. Over the life of the business, therefore, the total profit will be the same whichever valuation method has been used.

Stock valuation – some further issues

We saw in Chapter 2 that the closing stock figure will appear as part of the current assets of the business and that the convention of prudence requires current assets to be valued at the lower of cost and net realisable value. (The net realisable value of stocks is the estimated selling price less any further costs that may be necessary to complete the goods and any costs involved in selling and distributing the goods.) This rule may mean that the valuation method applied to stock will switch each year depending on which of cost and net realisable value is the lower. In practice, however, the cost of the stock held is usually below the current net realisable value – particularly during a period of rising prices. It is, therefore, the cost figure that will normally appear in the balance sheet.

Activity 3.13

Can you think of any circumstances where the net realisable value will be lower than the cost of stocks held, even during a period of generally rising prices?

The net realisable value may be lower where:

- Goods have deteriorated or become obsolete.
- There has been a fall in the market price of the goods.
- The goods are being used as a 'loss leader'.
- Bad purchasing decisions have been made.

There is an international accounting standard to deal with the issue of stock valuation. The 'benchmark treatment' is that the cost of stocks held should be determined using either FIFO or AVCO. The LIFO approach is not an acceptable method to use. The standard also supports the 'lower of cost or net realisable value' rule.

Real World 3.5 sets out the policies of two businesses with respect to their stockholdings.

REAL WORLD 3.5

Stock valuation in practice

Some businesses indicate the basis for establishing the cost of stocks held. For example, Tate and Lyle plc, the sugar and other starch-based food processor, reveals that stock is transferred to the profit and loss account on a 'first in, first out' basis whereas Euro-Disney uses weighted average cost.

Sources: Tate and Lyle plc Annual Report 2003; Euro-Disney 2002 Financial Report.

→ Stock valuation and depreciation provide two examples where the **consistency convention** must be applied. This convention holds that when a particular method of accounting is selected to deal with a transaction, this method should be applied consistently over time. Thus, it would not be acceptable to switch from, say, FIFO to AVCO between periods (unless there are exceptional circumstances that make this appropriate). The purpose of this convention is to try to ensure that users are able to make valid comparisons between periods.

Activity 3.14

Stock valuation provides a further example of where subjective judgement is required to derive the figures for inclusion in the financial statements. For a retail business, what are the main areas where judgement is required?

The main areas are:

- The choice of cost method (FIFO, LIFO, AVCO).
- Deriving the net realisable value figure for stocks held.

Profit measurement and the problem of bad and doubtful debts

Many businesses sell goods on credit. When credit sales are made, the revenue is usually recognised as soon as the goods are passed to, and accepted by, the customer. Recording the dual aspect of a credit sale will involve:

- increasing sales revenue;
- increasing debtors by the amount of the credit sale.

However, with this type of sale there is always the risk that the customer will not pay the amount due, however reliable the customer might have appeared to be at the time of the sale. When it becomes reasonably certain that the customer will never pay, the debt is considered to be 'bad' and this must be taken into account when preparing the financial statements.

Activity 3.15

When preparing the financial statements, what would be the effect on the profit and on the balance sheet, of not taking into account the fact that a debt is bad?

The effect would be to overstate the assets (debtors) on the balance sheet and to overstate profit in the profit and loss account, as the sale (which has been recognised) will not result in any future benefit arising.

→ To provide a more realistic picture of financial performance and position, the **bad debt** must be 'written off'. This will involve:

● reducing the debtors;
● increasing expenses (by creating an expense known as 'bad debts written off') by the amount of the bad debt.

The matching convention requires that the bad debt is written off in the same period as the sale, that gave rise to the debt, is recognised.

Note that, when a debt is bad, the accounting response is not simply to cancel the original sale. If this were done, the profit and loss account would not be so informative. Reporting the bad debts as an expense can be extremely useful in the evaluation of management performance.

At the end of the accounting period, it may not be possible to identify with reasonable certainty all the bad debts that have been incurred during the period. It may be that some debts appear doubtful, but only at some later point in time will the true position become clear. The uncertainty that exists does not mean that, when preparing the financial statements, we should ignore the possibility that some of the debtors outstanding will eventually prove to be bad. It would not be prudent to do so, nor would it comply with the need to match expenses to the period in which the associated sale is recognised. As a result, the business will normally try to identify all those debts that, at the end of the period, can be classified as doubtful (that is, there is a possibility that they may eventually prove to be bad). This can be done by examining individual accounts of debtors or by taking a proportion of the total debtors outstanding based on past experience.

Once a figure has been derived, a **provision for doubtful debts** can be created. This provision will be:

● shown as an expense in the profit and loss account; and
● deducted from the total debtors figure in the balance sheet.

By doing this, full account is taken, in the appropriate accounting period, of those debts where there is a risk of non-payment. This accounting treatment of doubtful debts will be in addition to the treatment of bad debts described above.

Example 3.9 illustrates the reporting of bad and doubtful debts.

Example 3.9

Desai Enterprises has debtors of £350,000 at the end of the accounting year to 30 June 2005. Investigation of these debtors revealed that £10,000 was likely to prove irrecoverable and that a further £30,000 was doubtful.

Extracts from the profit and loss account would have been as follows:

Profit and loss account (extracts) for the year ended 30 June 2005

	£
Bad debts written off	10,000
Provision for doubtful debts	30,000

Balance sheet (extracts) as at 30 June 2005

	£
Debtors	340,000*
Less Provision for doubtful debts	30,000
	310,000

* that is, £350,000 – £10,000 irrecoverable debts

The provision for doubtful debts is, of course, an estimate, and it is quite likely that the actual amount of debts that prove to be bad will be different from the estimate. Let us say that, during the next accounting period, it was discovered that £26,000 of the doubtful debts in fact proved to be irrecoverable. These debts must now be written off as follows:

- reduce debtors by £26,000; and
- reduce provision for doubtful debts by £26,000.

However, a provision for doubtful debts of £4,000 will remain. This amount represents an overestimate made when creating the provision in the profit and loss account for the year to 30 June 2005. As the provision is no longer needed, it should be eliminated. Remember that the provision was made by creating an expense in the profit and loss account for the year to 30 June 2005. As the expense was too high, the amount of the overestimate should be 'written back' in the next accounting period. In other words, it will be treated as revenue for the year to 30 June 2006. This will mean:

- reducing the provision for doubtful debts by £4,000; and
- increasing revenue by £4,000.

Ideally, of course, the amount should be written back to the 2005 profit and loss account; however, it is too late to do this. At the end of 2006, not only will 2005's overprovision be written back but a new provision should be created to allow for the debts, arising from 2006's sales that seem doubtful.

Activity 3.16

Clayton Conglomerates had debts of £870,000 outstanding at the end of the accounting year to 31 March 2005. The chief accountant believed that £40,000 of those debts were irrecoverable and that a further £60,000 were doubtful. In the subsequent year, it was found that an overpessimistic estimate of doubtful debts had been made and that only a further £45,000 of debts had actually proved to be bad.

Show the relevant extracts in the profit and loss account for both 2005 and 2006 to report the bad debts written off and the provision for doubtful debts. Also show the relevant balance sheet extract as at 31 March 2005.

Your answer should be as follows:

Profit and loss account (extracts) for the year ended 31 March 2005

	£
Bad debts written off	40,000
Provision for doubtful debts	60,000

Profit and loss account (extracts) for the year ended 31 March 2006

	£
Provision for doubtful debts written back (revenue)	15,000

Note: This figure will usually be netted off against any provision created for doubtful debts in respect of 2006.

Activity 3.16 continued

Balance sheet (extracts) as at 31 March 2005

	£
Debtors	830,000
Less Provision for doubtful debts	60,000
	770,000

Activity 3.17

Bad and doubtful debts represent further areas where judgement is required in deriving expenses figures for a particular period. What will be the effect of different judgements concerning the amount of bad and doubtful debts on the profit for a particular period and on the total profit reported over the life of the business?

Judgement is often required in deriving a figure for bad debts incurred during a period. There may be situations where views will differ concerning whether or not a debt is irrecoverable. The decision concerning whether or not to write off a bad debt will have an effect on the expenses for the period and, hence, the reported profit. However, over the life of the business the total reported profit would not be affected, as incorrect judgements in one period will be adjusted for in a later period.

Suppose, for example, that a debt of £100 was written off in a period and that, in a later period, the amount owing was actually received. The increase in expenses of £100 in the period in which the bad debt was written off would be compensated for by an increase in revenue of £100 when the amount outstanding was finally received (bad debt recoverable). If, on the other hand, the amount owing of £100 was never written off in the first place, the profit for the two periods would not be affected by the bad debt adjustment and would, therefore, be different – but the total profit for the two periods would be the same.

A similar situation would apply where there are differences in judgements concerning doubtful debts.

Real World 3.6 shows the effect of bad debt provisions on the profits of one well-known business.

REAL WORLD 3.6

Making a dent in profits

The size of bad debt provisions can be high in relation to reported profits. In February 2003, Barclays Bank plc announced annual profits for the preceding year of £3.2bn. The profits were lower than expected because of the need to increase bad debt provisions by nearly a third to £1.48bn. The reasons for the increase included lending problems in Argentina and business collapses in the telecoms and energy sectors.

Source: 'Barclays hit by bad debt provisions', FT.com, 13 February 2003.

Let us now try to bring together some of the points that we have raised in this chapter through a self-assessment question.

Self-assessment question 3.1

TT and Co. is a new business that started trading on 1 January 2004. The following is a summary of transactions that occurred during the first year of trading:

1   The owners introduced £50,000 of capital, which was paid into a bank account opened in the name of the business.
2   Premises were rented from 1 January 2004 at an annual rental of £20,000. During the year, rent of £25,000 was paid to the owner of the premises.
3   Rates (a tax on business premises) were paid during the year as follows:

For the period 1 January 2004 to 31 March 2004   £500
For the period 1 April 2004 to 31 March 2005   £1,200

4   A delivery van was bought on 1 January 2004 for £12,000. This is expected to be used in the business for four years and then to be sold for £2,000.
5   Wages totalling £33,500 were paid during the year. At the end of the year, the business owed £630 of wages for the last week of the year.
6   Electricity bills for the first three quarters of the year were paid totalling £1,650. After 31 December 2004, but before the final statements had been finalised for the year, the bill for the last quarter arrived showing a charge of £620.
7   Stock-in-trade totalling £143,000 was bought on credit.
8   Stock-in-trade totalling £12,000 was bought for cash.
9   Sales revenue on credit totalled £152,000 (cost of sales £74,000).
10   Cash sales revenue totalled £35,000 (cost of sales £16,000).
11   Receipts from trade debtors totalled £132,000.
12   Payments to trade creditors totalled £121,000.
13   Van running expenses paid totalled £9,400.

At the end of the year it was clear that a trade debtor who owed £400 would not be able to pay any part of the debt. The business uses the straight-line method for depreciating non-current assets.

Required:
Prepare a balance sheet as at 31 December 2004 and a profit and loss account for the year to that date. (Use the outline financial statements produced below to help you.)

TT and Co.
Balance sheet as at 31 December 2004

	£	£	£
Non-current assets			
Motor van			
Current assets			
Stock-in-trade			
Trade debtors			
Prepaid expenses			
Cash			
Less **Current liabilities**			
Trade creditors			
Accrued expenses			
Capital			
Original			
Add Profit			

→

Self-assessment question 3.1 continued

Profit and loss account for the year ended 31 December 2004

	£	£
Sales revenue		
Less Cost of sales		___
Gross profit		
Less Rent		
Rates		
Wages		
Electricity		
Bad debts		
Van expenses		
Van depreciation	___	___
Net profit for the year		___

Interpreting the profit and loss account

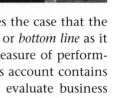

When a profit and loss account is presented to users it is sometimes the case that the only item that will concern them will be the final net profit figure, or *bottom line* as it is sometimes called. Although the net profit figure is a primary measure of perform-ance, and its importance is difficult to overstate, the profit and loss account contains other information that should also be of interest. To be able to evaluate business performance effectively, it is important to find out how the final net profit figure was derived. Thus the level of sales revenue, the nature and amount of expenses incurred, and the profit in relation to sales revenue are important factors in understanding the performance of the business over a period. The analysis and interpretation of financial statements is considered in detail in Chapter 7.

SUMMARY

The main points of this chapter may be summarised as follows:

The profit and loss account (income statement)

- Measures and reports how much profit (loss) has been generated over a period.
- Profit (loss) for the period is the difference between the total revenue and total expenses for the period.
- Links the balance sheets at the beginning and end of a financial period.
- The profit and loss account of a retail business will first calculate gross profit, then add any additional revenue and then deduct any overheads for the period. The final figure derived is the net profit (loss) for the period.
- Gross profit represents the difference between the sales revenue for the period and the cost of sales.

Expenses and revenue

- Cost of sales may be identified by either matching the cost of each sale to the particular sale or by adjusting the goods purchased during the period to take account of opening and closing stocks.
- The classification of expenses is often a matter of judgement, although there are statutory rules for businesses that trade as limited companies.
- The realisation convention states that revenue is recognised when it has been realised.
- Realisation occurs when the amount of revenue can be measured reliably, it is probable that the economic benefits will be received and the costs of the transactions can be measured reliably.
- Where there is a sale of goods, there is an additional criterion that ownership and control must pass to the buyer before revenue can be recognised.
- Revenue can be recognised after partial completion providing a particular stage of completion can be measured reliably.
- The matching convention states that expenses should be matched to the revenue that they help generate.
- A particular expense reported in the profit and loss account may not be the same as the cash paid. This will result in some adjustment for accruals or prepayments.
- The materiality convention states that where the amounts are immaterial, we should consider only what is expedient.
- 'Accruals accounting' is preparing the profit and loss account and balance sheet following the accruals convention, which says that profit = revenue – expenses (not cash receipts – cash payments).

Depreciation of non-current assets

- Depreciation requires a consideration of the cost (or fair value), useful life and residual value of an asset. It also requires a consideration of the method of depreciation.
- The straight-line method of depreciation allocates the amount to be depreciated evenly over the useful life of the asset.
- The reducing-balance method applies a fixed percentage rate of depreciation to the written-down value of an asset each year.
- The depreciation method chosen should reflect the pattern of benefits associated with the asset.
- Depreciation is an attempt to allocate the cost (or fair value), less the residual value, of an asset over its useful life. It does not provide funds for replacement of the asset.

Stock (inventory) costing methods

- The way in which we derive the cost of stocks is important in the calculation of profit and the presentation of financial position.
- The first in, first out (FIFO) method assumes that the earliest stocks held are the first to be sold.
- The last in, first out (LIFO) method assumes that the latest stocks are the first to be sold.
- The weighted average cost (AVCO) method applies an average cost to all stocks sold.
- When prices are rising, FIFO gives the lowest cost of sales and highest closing stock figure and LIFO gives the highest cost of sales figure and the lowest closing stock

figure. AVCO gives a figure for cost of sales and closing stock that lies between FIFO and LIFO.

- When prices are falling, the positions of FIFO and LIFO are reversed.
- Stocks are shown at the lower of cost and net realisable value.
- When a particular method of accounting, such as a stock costing method, is selected, it should be applied consistently over time.

Bad debts

- Where it is reasonably certain that a credit customer will not pay, the debt is regarded as 'bad' and written off.
- Where it is doubtful that a credit customer will pay, a provision for doubtful debts should be created.

→ Key terms

Profit p. 59	**Accruals accounting** p. 72
Revenue p. 59	**Depreciation** p. 73
Expense p. 59	**Residual value** p. 75
Profit and loss account p. 61	**Straight-line method** p. 75
Gross profit p. 61	**Written-down value** p. 76
Net profit p. 61	**Reducing-balance method** p. 76
Cost of sales p. 62	**First in, first out (FIFO)** p. 83
Realisation convention p. 65	**Last in, first out (LIFO)** p. 83
Matching convention p. 68	**Weighted average cost (AVCO)**
Accrued expenses p. 69	p. 83
Prepaid expense p. 71	**Consistency convention** p. 87
Materiality convention p. 71	**Bad debt** p. 87
Accruals convention p. 72	**Provision for doubtful debts** p. 88

Further reading

If you would like to explore the topics covered in this chapter in more depth, we recommend the following books:

Financial Reporting, *Alexander D. and Britton A.*, 6th edn, International Thomson Business Press, 2001, chapter 4.

Financial Accounting and Reporting, *Elliott B. and Elliott J.*, 8th edn, Financial Times Prentice Hall, 2004, chapters 14 and 17.

Corporate Financial Accounting and Reporting, *Sutton T.*, 2nd edn, Financial Times Prentice Hall, 2004, chapters 2, 8, 9 and 10.

International Financial Reporting Standards (IFRSs) 2003, *International Accounting Standards Board*, IASCF, 2003, IAS 16 and IAS 38.

REVIEW QUESTIONS

Answers to these questions can be found on the students' side of the Companion Website at www.pearsoned.co.uk/atrillmclaney.

3.1 'Although the profit and loss account is a record of past achievement, the calculations required for certain expenses involve estimates of the future.' What is meant by this statement? Can you think of examples where estimates of the future are used?

3.2 'Depreciation is a process of allocation and not valuation.' What do you think is meant by this statement?

3.3 What is the convention of consistency? Does this convention help users in making a more valid comparison *between* businesses?

3.4 'An asset is similar to an expense.' Do you agree?

EXERCISES

Exercises 3.6 to 3.8 are more advanced than 3.1 to 3.5. Those with a coloured number have answers at the back of the book.

3.1 You have heard the following statements made. Comment critically on them.

(a) 'Capital only increases or decreases as a result of the owners putting more cash into the business or taking some out.'
(b) 'An accrued expense is one that relates to next year.'
(c) 'Unless we depreciate this asset we shall be unable to provide for its replacement.'
(d) 'There is no point in depreciating the factory building. It is appreciating in value each year.'

3.2 Singh Enterprises has an accounting year to 31 December. On 1 January 2002 the business purchased a machine for £10,000. The machine had an expected useful life of four years and an estimated residual value of £2,000. On 1 January 2003 the business purchased another machine for £15,000. This machine had an expected useful life of five years and an estimated residual value of £2,500. On 31 December 2004 the business sold the first machine purchased for £3,000.

Required:
Show the relevant profit and loss account extracts and balance sheet extracts for the years 2002, 2003 and 2004.

3.3 The owner of a business is confused, and comes to you for help. The financial statements for his business, prepared by an accountant, for the last accounting period revealed an increase in profit of £50,000. However, during the accounting period the bank balance declined by £30,000. What reasons might explain this apparent discrepancy?

3.4 Spratley Ltd is a builders' merchant. On 1 September the business had 20 tonnes of sand in stock at a cost of £18 per tonne and at a total cost of £360. During the first week in September, the business purchased the following amounts of sand:

September	Tonnes	Cost per tonne £
2	48	20
4	15	24
6	10	25

On 7 September the business sold 60 tonnes of sand to a local builder.

Required:
Calculate the cost of goods sold and the closing stock figures from the above information using the following stock costing methods:

(a) first in, first out
(b) last in, first out
(c) weighted average cost.

3.5 Fill in the values (a) to (f) in the following table on the assumption that there were no opening balances involved:

	Relating to period		At end of period	
	Paid/ received £	Expense/ revenue for period £	Prepaid £	Accruals/ deferred revenues £
Rent payable	10,000	a	1,000	
Rates and insurance	5,000	b		1,000
General expenses	c	6,000	1,000	
Loan interest payable	3,000	2,500	d	
Salaries	e	9,000		3,000
Rent receivable	f	1,500		1,500

3.6 The following is the balance sheet of TT and Co. at the end of its first year of trading (from Self-assessment question 3.1):

TT and Co.
Balance sheet as at 31 December 2004

	£	£	£
Non-current assets			
Motor van: Cost			12,000
Less Depreciation			2,500
			9,500
Current assets			
Stock-in-trade	65,000		
Trade debtors	19,600		
Prepaid expenses*	5,300		
Cash	750		
		90,650	
Less **Current liabilities**			
Trade creditors	22,000		
Accrued expenses†	1,250		
		23,250	
			67,400
			£76,900
Capital			
Original			50,000
Add Profit			26,900
			£76,900

* The prepaid expenses consisted of rates (£300) and rent (£5,000).
† The accrued expenses consisted of wages (£630) and electricity (£620).

During 2005, the following transactions took place:

1   The owners withdrew capital in the form of cash of £20,000.
2   Premises continued to be rented at an annual rental of £20,000. During the year, rent of £15,000 was paid to the owner of the premises.
3   Rates on the premises were paid during the year as follows: for the period 1 April 2005 to 31 March 2006 £1,300.
4   A second delivery van was bought on 1 January 2005 for £13,000. This is expected to be used in the business for four years and then to be sold for £3,000.
5   Wages totalling £36,700 were paid during the year. At the end of the year, the business owed £860 of wages for the last week of the year.
6   Electricity bills for the first three quarters of the year and £620 for the last quarter of the previous year were paid totalling £1,820. After 31 December 2005, but before the accounts had been finalised for the year, the bill for the last quarter arrived showing a charge of £690.
7   Stock-in-trade totalling £67,000 was bought on credit.
8   Stock-in-trade totalling £8,000 was bought for cash.
9   Sales revenue on credit totalled £179,000 (cost £89,000).
10 Cash sales revenue totalled £54,000 (cost £25,000).
11 Receipts from trade debtors totalled £178,000.
12 Payments to trade creditors totalled £71,000.
13 Van running expenses paid totalled £16,200.

The business uses the straight-line method for depreciating non-current assets.

Required:
Prepare a balance sheet as at 31 December 2005 and a profit and loss account for the year to that date.

3.7 The following is the balance sheet of WW Limited as at 31 December 2004:

Balance sheet as at 31 December 2004

	£	£	£
Non-current assets			
Machinery			25,300
Current assets			
Stock-in-trade	12,200		
Trade debtors	21,300		
Prepaid expenses (rates)	400		
Cash	8,300		
		42,200	
Less **Current liabilities**			
Trade creditors	16,900		
Accrued expenses (wages)	1,700		
		18,600	
			23,600
			48,900
Capital			
Original			25,000
Retained profit			23,900
			48,900

During 2005 the following transactions took place:

1　The owners withdrew capital in the form of cash of £23,000.
2　Premises were rented at an annual rental of £20,000. During the year, rent of £25,000 was paid to the owner of the premises.
3　Rates on the premises were paid during the year for the period 1 April 2005 to 31 March 2006 and amounted to £2,000.
4　Some machinery, which was bought on 1 January 2004 for £13,000, has proved to be unsatisfactory. It was part-exchanged for some new machinery on 1 January 2005, and WW Limited paid a cash amount of £6,000. The new machinery would have cost £15,000 had the business bought it without the trade-in.
5　Wages totalling £23,800 were paid during the year. At the end of the year, the business owed £860 of wages.
6　Electricity bills for the four quarters of the year were paid totalling £2,700.
7　Stock-in-trade totalling £143,000 was bought on credit.
8　Stock-in-trade totalling £12,000 was bought for cash.
9　Sales revenue on credit totalled £211,000 (cost £127,000).
10　Cash sales revenue totalled £42,000 (cost £25,000).
11　Receipts from trade debtors totalled £198,000.
12　Payments to trade creditors totalled £156,000.
13　Van running expenses paid totalled £17,500.

The business uses the reducing-balance method of depreciation for non-current assets at the rate of 30 per cent each year.

Required:
Prepare a balance sheet as at 31 December 2005 and a profit and loss account for the year to that date.

3.8 The following is the profit and loss account for Nikov and Co. for the year ended 31 December 2005, along with information relating to the preceding year.

Profit and loss account for the year ended 31 December

	2004		2005	
	£000	£000	£000	£000
Sales revenue		382.5		420.2
Less Cost of sales		114.8		126.1
Gross profit		267.7		294.1
Less				
Salaries and wages	86.4		92.6	
Selling and distribution costs	75.4		98.9	
Rent and rates	22.0		22.0	
Bad debts written off	4.0		19.7	
Telephone and postage	4.4		4.8	
Insurance	2.8		2.9	
Motor vehicle expenses	8.6		10.3	
Loan interest	5.4		4.6	
Depreciation – Motor van	3.3		3.1	
– Fixtures and fittings	4.5		4.3	
		216.8		263.2
Net profit (loss)		50.9		30.9

Required:
Analyse the performance of the business for the year to 31 December 2005 in so far as the information allows.

4

Accounting for limited companies (1)

OBJECTIVES

When you have completed this chapter, you should be able to:

- Discuss the nature of the limited company.

- Explain the role of directors of limited companies.

- Outline and explain the particular features and restrictions of the owners' claim, in the context of limited companies.

- Prepare a profit and loss account and a balance sheet for a limited company.

INTRODUCTION

In the UK, most businesses, except the very smallest, trade in the form of limited companies. There are currently about 1.5 million limited companies in the UK. It is estimated that, in the UK, 80 per cent of business activity and 60 per cent of all employment occurs in limited companies. This is probably fairly representative of many of the world's countries, particularly the more industrialised ones.

In this chapter we shall examine the nature of limited companies to see how they differ in practical terms from sole proprietorships and partnerships. This involves considering the ways in which the owners provide finance. It also requires an examination of the ways in which the financial statements, which we discussed in the last two chapters differ between companies and sole proprietorships.

In Chapter 5 we shall continue our examination of the financial statements of limited companies, by looking at the framework of regulations that surround their preparation.

Generating wealth through limited companies

The nature of limited companies

Let us begin our examination of limited companies by discussing their legal nature. A **limited company** has been described as an artificial person that has been created by law. This means that a company has many of the rights and obligations that 'real' people have. For example, it can sue or be sued by others and can enter into contracts in its own name. This contrasts sharply with other types of business, such as that of a sole proprietor, where it is the owner(s) rather than the business that must sue, enter into contracts and so on, because the business has no separate legal identity.

With the rare exceptions of those that are created by Act of Parliament or by Royal Charter, all UK companies are created by registration. To create a company the person or persons (usually known as *promoters*) wishing to create it, fill in a few simple forms and pay a modest registration fee. After having ensured that the necessary formalities have been met, the Registrar of Companies, a government official, enters the name of the new company on the Registry of Companies. Thus, in the UK, companies can be formed very easily and cheaply (for about £100).

Companies may be owned by just one person, but most have more than one owner and some have many owners. The owners are usually known as *members* or *shareholders*. The ownership of a company is normally divided into a number, frequently a large number, of **shares**, each of equal size. Each owner, or shareholder, owns one or more shares in the company. Large companies typically have a very large number of shareholders. For example at 31 March 2003, BT Group plc, the telecommunications business, had over 1.6 million different shareholders.

As a limited company has its own legal identity, it is regarded as being quite separate from those who own and manage it. This fact leads to two important features of the limited company: perpetual life and limited liability. These are now explained.

Perpetual life

A company is normally granted a perpetual existence and so will continue even where an owner of shares in the company dies. The shares of the deceased person will simply pass to the beneficiary of his or her estate. The granting of perpetual existence means that the life of a company is quite separate from the lives of those individuals who own or manage it. It is not, therefore, affected by changes in ownership that arise when individuals buy and sell shares in the company.

Though a company may be granted a perpetual existence when it is first formed, it is possible for either the shareholders or the courts to bring this existence to an end. When this is done, the assets of the company are sold off to meet outstanding liabilities. Any surplus arising from the sale will then be used to pay the shareholders. Shareholders may agree to end the life of a company where it has achieved the purpose for which it was formed or where they feel that the company has no real future. The courts may bring the life of a company to an end where creditors have applied to the courts for this to be done because they have not been paid amounts owing.

Where shareholders agree to end the life of a company, it is referred to as a 'voluntary liquidation'. **Real World 4.1** describes the demise of one company by this method.

Monotub Industries in a spin as founder gets Titan for £1   **FT**

Monotub Industries, maker of the Titan washing machine, yesterday passed into corporate history with very little ceremony and with only a whimper of protest from minority shareholders.

At an extraordinary meeting held in a basement room of the group's West End headquarters, shareholders voted to put the company into voluntary liquidation and sell its assets and intellectual property to founder Martin Myerscough for £1. (The shares in the company were at one time worth 650p each.)

The only significant opposition came from Giuliano Gnagnatti who, along with other shareholders, has seen his investment shrink faster than a wool twin-set on a boil wash.

The not-so-proud owner of 100,000 Monotub shares, Mr Gnagnatti, the managing director of an online retailer, . . . described the sale of Monotub as a 'free gift' to Mr Myerscough. This assessment was denied by Ian Green, the chairman of Monotub, who said the closest the beleaguered company had come to a sale was an offer for £60,000 that gave no guarantees against liabilities, which are thought to amount to £750,000.

The quiet passing of the washing machine, eventually dubbed the Titanic, was in strong contrast to its performance in many kitchens.

Originally touted as the 'great white goods hope' of the washing machine industry with its larger capacity and removable drum, the Titan ran into problems when it kept stopping during the spin cycle, causing it to emit a loud bang and leap into the air.

Summing up the demise of the Titan, Mr Green said: 'Clearly the machine had some revolutionary aspects, but you can't get away from the fact that the machine was faulty and should not have been launched with those defects.'

The usually vocal Mr Myerscough, who has promised to pump £250,000 into the company and give Monotub shareholders £4 for every machine sold, refused to comment on his plans for the Titan or reveal who his backers were. But . . . he did say that he intended to 'take the Titan forward'.

Source: 'Monotub Industries in a spin as founder gets Titan for £1', Lisa Urquhart, *Financial Times*, 23 January 2003, FT.com.

Limited liability

Since the company is a legal person in its own right, it must take responsibility for its own debts and losses. This means that once the shareholders have paid what they have agreed to pay for the shares, their obligation to the company, and to the company's creditors, is satisfied. In this way, shareholders limit their losses to that which they have paid, or agreed to pay, for their shares. This is of great practical importance to potential shareholders, since they know that what they can lose, as part-owners of the business, is limited.

Contrast this with the position of sole proprietors or partners (that is the owners or part-owners of unincorporated businesses). Here there is not the opportunity that shareholders have to 'ring fence' assets that they choose not to put into the business. If a sole proprietary business finds itself in a position where liabilities exceed the business assets, the law gives unsatisfied creditors the right to demand payment out of what the sole proprietor may have regarded as 'non-business' assets. Thus the sole proprietor could lose everything – house, car, the lot. This is because the law sees Jill, the sole proprietor, as being the same as Jill the private individual. The shareholder, by contrast, can lose only the amount committed to that company. Legally, the business operating as a limited company, in which Jack owns shares, is not the same as Jack himself. This is true even were Jack to own all of the shares in the company.

Real World 4.2 gives an example of a well-known case where the shareholders of a particular company were able to avoid any liability to those that had lost money as a result of dealing with the company.

REAL WORLD 4.2

Carlton and Granada 1 – Nationwide Football League 0

A recent example of shareholders taking advantage of limited liability status is that of two television companies, Carlton and Granada, which each owned 50 per cent of ITV Digital (formerly ON Digital). ITV Digital collapsed because it was unable to meet its liabilities. Before its collapse, the company had signed a contract to pay the Nationwide Football League more than £89 million on both 1 August 2002 and 1 August 2003 for the rights to broadcast football matches over three seasons. However, the company was unable to meet this commitment and the shareholders could not be held legally liable for the amounts owing.

Carlton and Granada merged into one business in 2003, but at the time of ITV Digital were two independent companies.

Activity 4.1

We have just said that the fact that shareholders can limit their losses to that which they have paid, or have agreed to pay, for their shares is of great practical importance to potential shareholders.

Can you think of any practical benefit to a private sector economy, in general, of this ability of shareholders to limit losses?

Business is a risky venture – in some cases, very risky. People with money to invest will tend to be more content to do so where they know the limit of their liability. This means that more businesses will tend to be formed and that existing ones will find it easier to raise additional finance from existing and/or additional part-owners. This is good for the private sector economy, since businesses will tend to form and expand more readily. Thus, the wants of society are more likely to be met where limited liability exists.

→ Though **limited liability** has this advantage to the providers of capital (the shareholders), it is not necessarily to the advantage of all others who have a stake in the business, like the Nationwide Football League clubs (see Real World 4.2). Limited liability is attractive to shareholders because they can, in effect, walk away from the unpaid debts of the company if their contribution as shareholders has not been sufficient to meet those debts. This is likely to make any individual, or another business, that is considering advancing credit, wary of dealing with the limited company. This can be a real problem for smaller, less established companies. For example, suppliers may insist on cash payment before delivery of goods or the rendering of a service. Alternatively, a supplier may require a personal guarantee from a major shareholder that the debt will be paid before allowing a company trade credit. In the latter case, the supplier will circumvent the company's limited liability status by establishing the personal liability of an individual. However, larger, more established companies, tend to have built up the confidence of suppliers.

Legal safeguards

The fact that a company is limited must be indicated in the name of the company. This is mainly to warn individuals and other businesses contemplating dealing with a limited company that the liability of the owners (shareholders) is limited. As we shall see later in this chapter, there are other safeguards for those dealing with a limited company, in that the extent to which shareholders may withdraw their investment from the company is restricted.

Another important safeguard for those dealing with a limited company is that all limited companies must produce annual financial statements (profit and loss account (income statement), balance sheet and cash flow statement), and in effect make these available to the public. The rules surrounding the financial statements of limited companies will be discussed in Chapter 5.

Just before we leave the topic of the legal separateness of owners and the company, it is worth emphasising that this has no connection with the business entity convention of accounting, which we discussed in Chapter 2. This accounting convention applies equally well to all business types, including sole proprietorships where there is certainly no legal distinction between the owner and the business.

Public and private companies

When a company is registered with the Registrar of Companies, it must be registered either as a public or as a private company. The main practical difference between these is that a **public company** can offer its shares for sale to the general public, but a **private company** is restricted from doing so. A public limited company must signal its status to all interested parties by having the words 'public limited company', or its abbreviation 'plc' in its name. For a private limited company, the word 'limited' or 'Ltd' must appear as part of its name.

Private limited companies tend to be smaller businesses where the ownership is divided among relatively few shareholders who are usually fairly close to one another – for example, a family company. Numerically, there are vastly more private limited companies in the UK than there are public ones. Of the total of 1.5 million UK limited companies, about 99 per cent are private limited companies and just 1 per cent are public limited companies.

Since the public ones tend to be individually larger, they probably represent a much more important group economically. Many private limited companies are no more than the vehicle through which businesses, which are little more than sole proprietorships, operate.

Taxation

Another consequence of the legal separation of the limited company from its owners is that companies must be accountable to the Inland Revenue for tax on their profits and gains. This introduces the effects of tax into the accounting statements of limited companies. The charge for tax is shown in the profit and loss account (income statement). The tax charge for a particular year is based on that year's profit. Since only 50 per cent of a company's tax liability is due for payment during the year concerned, the other 50 per cent will appear on the end-of-year balance sheet as a current liability. This will be illustrated a little later in the chapter. The tax position of companies contrasts with that of sole proprietorships and partnerships, where tax is levied not on the business but on the owner(s). Thus tax does not impact on the financial statements of unincorporated businesses, but is an individual matter between the owner(s) and the Inland Revenue.

Companies are charged **corporation tax** on their profits and gains. The percentage rates of tax tend to vary from year to year, but have recently been in the low thirties for larger companies and in the low twenties for smaller companies. These rates of tax are levied on the company's taxable profit, which is not necessarily the same as the profit shown on the profit and loss account (income statement). This is because tax law does not, in every respect, follow the normal accounting rules. Generally, however, the taxable profit and the company's accounting profit are pretty close to one another.

Transferring share ownership – the role of the Stock Exchange

The point has already been made that shares in a company may be transferred from one owner to another. The desire of some shareholders to sell their shares, coupled with the desire of others to buy those shares, has led to the existence of a formal market in which shares can be bought and sold. The London Stock Exchange, and similar organisations around the world, provides a marketplace in which shares in public companies may be bought and sold. Share prices are determined by the laws of supply and demand, which are, in turn, determined by investors' perceptions of the future economic prospects of the companies concerned. Only the shares of certain companies (*listed* companies) may be traded on the London Stock Exchange. About 2,700 UK companies are listed. This represents only one in about 550 of all UK companies (public and private) and about one in six public limited companies. On the other hand, many of these 2,700 listed companies are massive. Nearly all of the 'household name' UK businesses (for example Tesco, Boots, BT, Cadbury Schweppes, JD Wetherspoon and so on) are listed companies.

Activity 4.2

If, as has been pointed out earlier, the change in ownership of shares does not directly affect the particular company, why do many public companies actively seek to have their shares traded in a recognised market?

The main reason is that investors are generally very reluctant to pledge their money unless they can see some way in which they can turn their investment back into cash. In theory, the shares of a particular company may be very valuable because it has bright prospects, However, unless this value is capable of being realised in cash, the benefit to the shareholders is dubious. After all, we cannot spend shares; we generally need cash.

This means that potential shareholders are much more likely to be prepared to buy new shares from the company (thereby providing the company with new finance) where they can see a way of liquidating their investment (turning it into cash), as and when they wish. Stock exchanges provide the means of liquidation.

Though the buying and selling of 'second-hand' shares does not provide the company with cash, the fact that the buying and selling facility exists will make it easier for the company to raise new share capital when it needs to do so.

Managing a company – corporate governance and the role of directors

A limited company may have legal personality, but it is not a human being capable of making decisions and plans about the business and exercising control over it. People must undertake these management tasks. The most senior level of management of a company is the board of directors.

The shareholders elect **directors** (by law there must be at least one director) to manage the company on a day-to-day basis on behalf of those shareholders. In a small company, the board may be the only level of management and consist of all of the shareholders. In larger companies, the board may consist of ten or so directors out of many thousands of shareholders. Indeed, directors are not even required to be shareholders. Below the board of directors of the typical large company could be several layers of management comprising thousands of people.

In recent years, the issue of **corporate governance** has generated much debate. The term is used to describe the ways in which companies are directed and controlled. The issue of corporate governance is important because, in companies of any size, those who own the company (that is, the shareholders) are usually divorced from the day-to-day control of the business. The shareholders employ the directors to manage the company for them. Given this position, it may seem reasonable to assume that the best interests of shareholders will guide the directors' decisions. However, in practice this does not always occur. The directors may be more concerned with pursuing their own interests, such as increasing their pay and 'perks' (such as expensive motor cars, overseas visits and so on) and improving their job security and status. As a result, a conflict can occur between the interests of shareholders and the interests of directors.

Where directors pursue their own interests at the expense of the shareholders, there is clearly a problem for the shareholders. However, it may also be a problem for society as a whole. If shareholders feel their funds are likely to be mismanaged, they will be reluctant to invest. A shortage of funds will mean fewer investments can be made and the costs of funds will increase as businesses compete for what funds are available. Thus, a lack of concern for shareholders can have a profound effect on the performance of the economy. To avoid these problems, most competitive market economies have a framework of rules to help monitor and control the behaviour of directors.

These rules are usually based around three guiding principles:

- *Disclosure*. This lies at the heart of good corporate governance. An OECD report (see reference at end of chapter for details) summed up the benefits of disclosure as follows:

  > Adequate and timely information about corporate performance enables investors to make informed buy-and-sell decisions and thereby helps the market reflect the value of a corporation under present management. If the market determines that present management is not performing, a decrease in stock [share] price will sanction management's failure and open the way to management change.

- *Accountability*. This involves defining the roles and duties of the directors and establishing an adequate monitoring process. In the UK, company law requires that directors of a business act in the best interests of shareholders. This means, among other things, that they must not try to use their position and knowledge to make gains at the expense of the shareholders. The law also requires larger companies to have their annual financial statements independently audited. The purpose of an independent audit is to lend credibility to the financial statements prepared by the directors.

● *Fairness.* Directors should not be able to benefit from access to 'inside' information that is not available to shareholders. As a result, both the law and the Stock Exchange place restrictions on the ability of directors to deal in the shares of the business. One example of these restrictions is that the directors cannot buy or sell shares immediately before the announcement of the final results of the business for a year or before the announcement of a significant event such as a planned merger or the loss of the chief executive.

Strengthening the framework of rules

The number of rules designed to safeguard shareholders has increased considerably over the years. This has been in response to weaknesses in corporate governance procedures, which have been exposed through well-publicised business failures and frauds, excessive pay increases to directors and evidence that some financial reports were being 'massaged' so as to mislead shareholders. However, some believe that the shareholders must shoulder some of the blame for any weaknesses. Not all shareholders in large companies are private individuals owning just a few shares each. In fact, 80 per cent, by market value, of the shares listed on the London Stock Exchange are owned by the investing 'institutions'. These include insurance businesses, pension funds and so on. These are often massive operations, owning large quantities of the shares of the companies in which they invest. The institutional investors employ specialist staff to manage their portfolios of shares in other companies. It is often argued that these large institutional shareholders, despite their size and relative expertise, are not very active in corporate governance matters. Thus there has been little monitoring of directors. However, things are changing.

The codes of practice

During the 1990s there was a real effort by the accountancy profession and the London Stock Exchange to address the problems mentioned above. A Code of Best Practice on Corporate Governance emerged in 1992. This was concerned with accountability and financial reporting. In 1995, a separate code of practice emerged. This dealt with directors' pay and conditions. These two codes were revised, 'fine tuned' and amalgamated to produce the **Combined Code**, which was issued in 1998.

The Combined Code was revised in 2003, following the recommendations of the Higgs Report. These recommendations were mainly concerned with the roles of the company chairman (senior director) and the other directors. It was particularly concerned with the role of 'non-executive' directors. These are directors who do not work full time in the company, but act solely in the role of director. This contrasts with 'executive' directors who are salaried employees. For example, the finance director of most large companies is a full-time employee. This person is a member of the board of directors and, as such, takes part in the key decision making at board level. At the same time, s/he is also responsible for managing the departments of the company that act on those board decisions as far as finance is concerned.

The view reflected in the 2003 Combined Code is that executive directors can become too embroiled in the day-to-day management of the company to be able to take a broad view. It also reflects the view that, for executive directors, conflicts can arise between their own interests and those of the shareholders. The advantage of non-executive directors can be that they are much more independent of the company than their executive colleagues. Non-executive directors are remunerated by the company for their work, but this would normally form only a small proportion of their total income. This gives them an independence that the executive directors may not have. Non-executive directors are often senior managers in other businesses or people who have had good experience of such roles.

Both the 1998 and 2003 Combined Codes received the backing of the London Stock Exchange. This means that companies listed on the London Stock Exchange are expected to comply with the requirements of the Code or must give their shareholders good reason why they do not. Failure to do one or other of these can lead to the company's shares being suspended from listing. This is an important sanction against non-compliant directors.

The Combined Code sets out a number of principles relating to such matters as the role of the directors, their relations with shareholders, and their accountability. **Real World 4.3** outlines some of the more important of these.

REAL WORLD 4.3

The Combined Code

Some of the key elements of the Combined Code are as follows:

- Every listed company should have a board of directors to lead and control the company.
- There should be a clear division of responsibilities between the chairman and the chief executive officer of the company to ensure that a single person does not have unbridled power.
- There should be a balance between executive and non-executive (who are often part-time and independent) members of the board, to ensure that small groups of individuals cannot dominate proceedings.
- The board should receive timely information that is of sufficient quality to enable them to carry out their duties.
- Appointments to the board should be the subject of rigorous, formal and transparent procedures. All directors should submit themselves for re-election by the shareholders within a maximum period of three years.
- Boards should use the annual general meeting to communicate with private investors and to encourage their participation.
- The board should publish a balanced and understandable assessment of the company's position and performance.
- Internal controls should be in place to protect the shareholders' wealth.
- The board should set up an audit committee of non-executive directors to oversee the internal controls and financial reporting principles that are being applied, and to liaise with the external auditors.

Strengthening the framework of rules has improved the quality of information available to shareholders, resulted in better checks on the powers of directors, and provided greater transparency in corporate affairs. However, rules can only be a partial answer. A balance must be struck between the need to protect shareholders and the need to encourage the entrepreneurial spirit of directors – which could be stifled under a welter of rules. This implies that rules should not be too tight and so unscrupulous directors may still find ways around them.

Activity 4.3

Can you think of ways in which the shareholders themselves may try to ensure that the directors act on their behalf?

Two ways are commonly used in practice:

- The shareholders may insist on monitoring closely the actions of the directors and the way in which they use the resources of the company.
- The shareholders may introduce incentive plans for directors that link their pay to the share performance of the company. In this way, the interests of the directors and shareholders will become more closely aligned.

Real World 4.4 shows an extract from the statement on corporate governance made by the directors of Kingfisher plc, the retail business that owns B&Q and Comet, in the UK, and a number of other chains in various European countries, particularly in France. Note how much emphasis is placed on the distinction between executive and non-executive directors in the membership of the various committees. The committees operated by Kingfisher are broadly as recommended by the Combined Code. The last committee mentioned by Kingfisher, the Share Option Committee, arises because many senior managers and directors are awarded bonuses in the form of 'share options'. These are, in effect, the right to buy shares at a price that may well be below their current Stock Exchange price. This is an area where directors of some companies have been criticised for being overgenerous to themselves.

REAL WORLD 4.4

Corporate governance at Kingfisher

The following extract from the 2003 annual review of Kingfisher plc starts with a general statement that the directors have complied with the Combined Code during the year in question. It then goes on to detail how they complied in the specific context of board meetings and the establishment of committees to deal with sensitive issues.

Corporate governance – Combined Code statement

Kingfisher recognises the importance of, and is committed to, high standards of corporate governance. The principles of good governance adopted by the Group have been applied in the following way:

Main board

The Kingfisher Board currently comprises the Chairman, the Chief Executive, the Deputy Chairman, five other non-executive directors and four other executive directors.

Their biographies illustrate the directors' range of experience, which ensures an effective Board to lead and control the Group. All directors have access to the Company Secretary and may take independent professional advice at the Group's expense. Non-executive directors are appointed for an initial term of three years and each director receives appropriate training as necessary. Since April 2002 the Company has complied with the Combined Code requirement to have an identified senior independent director, namely John Nelson.

During the year ended 1 February 2003, the Board met on 24 occasions: 12 of these meetings were held principally to deal with regular business and the remaining 12 meetings were convened to approve the periodic trading statements or in connection with the Castorama transaction. The

Real World 4.4 continued

Board has adopted a schedule of matters reserved for its decision and is primarily responsible for the strategic direction of the Group. All directors have full and timely access to information. The Board has successfully completed a further independent evaluation of the performance through the service provided by the Institute of Chartered Secretaries and Administrators. These evaluations, the first of which was undertaken in 2001, examine the operation of the Board in practice including its corporate governance and the operation and content of its meetings.

The Board has established six standing committees with defined terms of reference as follows:

- The Audit Committee is chaired by Phillip Bentley and includes three other independent non-executive directors. This committee is responsible for providing an independent oversight of the Group's systems of internal control and financial reporting processes. Each of our major operating businesses has its own audit committee, meetings of which are attended by both Kingfisher's Head of Internal Audit and the external auditors.
- The Nomination Committee is chaired by Francis Mackay and includes two other independent non-executive directors and the Chief Executive. The committee is responsible for the consideration and recommendation of the appointment of new directors. It met on one occasion during 2002 to consider the selection of the new Chief Executive and the two new non-executive directors. Specialist recruitment consultants were engaged to assist with this process.
- The Remuneration Committee is chaired by John Nelson and includes three other independent non-executive directors. The committee is responsible for advising the Board on the Company's executive remuneration policy and its costs, and for the application of this policy to the remuneration and benefits of executive directors and certain senior executives. The Remuneration Report contains a more detailed description of the Group's policy and procedures in relation to directors' and officers' remuneration.
- The Social Responsibility Committee is chaired by Margaret Salmon and includes the Chief Executive, three other executive directors and representatives of the operating companies. The committee is responsible for discussing and developing a general policy relating to environmental, community and equal opportunities matters. The main Board director with overall responsibility for environmental matters is Gerry Murphy.
- The Finance Committee comprises the Chairman of the Board, the Chief Executive and two executive directors. The committee is responsible for the approval and authorisation of financing documents within its terms of reference and the authority limits laid down by the Board. On behalf of the Board, it reviews borrowing arrangements and other financial transactions, and makes appropriate recommendations. It also allots new shares in the Company to Group employees following the exercise of share options.
- The Share Option Committee comprises any two directors or any one director and the Company Secretary. Its role is to consider the Group's share funding policy in respect of share incentive awards and to decide upon the level of contributions of ESOP and QUEST in respect of the dilution cost when new shares are issued. The Committee also considers the making of loans to the ESOP in respect of grants that are hedged with existing shares. It has no authority in respect of the making of awards which is a matter reserved to the Remuneration Committee.

Source: Kingfisher plc Annual Review 2003.

Financing limited companies

Capital (owners' claim) of limited companies

The owner's claim of a sole proprietorship is normally encompassed in one figure on the balance sheet, usually labelled 'capital'. With companies, this is usually a little more complicated, though in essence the same broad principles apply. With a company, the owners' claim is divided between shares – for example, the original investment – on

→ the one hand and **reserves** – that is, profits and gains subsequently made – on the other. There is also the possibility that there will be more than one type of shares and of reserves. Thus, within the basic divisions of share capital and reserves, there might well be further subdivisions. This might seem quite complicated, but we shall shortly consider the reasons for these subdivisions and all should become clearer. The sum of → share capital and reserves is commonly known as **equity**.

The basic division

When a company is first formed, those who take steps to form it (the promoters) will decide how much needs to be raised by the potential shareholders to set the company up with the necessary assets to operate. Example 4.1 acts as a basis for illustration.

Example 4.1

Let us imagine that several people get together and decide to form a company to operate a particular business. They estimate that the company will need £50,000 to obtain the necessary assets to operate. Between them, they raise the cash which they use to buy shares in the company, on 31 March 2004, with a → **nominal** (or **par**) **value** of £1 each.

At this point the balance sheet of the company would be thus:

Balance sheet as at 31 March 2004

	£
Net assets (all in cash)	50,000
Equity	
Share capital	
50,000 shares of £1 each	50,000

The company now buys the necessary non-current assets and stock-in-trade (inventories) and starts to trade. During the first year, the company makes a profit of £10,000. This, by definition, means that the owners' claim expands by £10,000. During the year, the shareholders (owners) make no drawings of their capital, so at the end of the year the summarised balance sheet looks like this:

Balance sheet as at 31 March 2005

	£
Net assets (various assets less liabilities)	60,000
Equity	
Share capital	
50,000 shares of £1 each	50,000
Reserves (revenue reserve)	10,000
	60,000

→ The profit is shown in a reserve, known as a **revenue reserve**, because it arises from generating revenue (making sales). Note that we do not simply merge the profit with the share capital: we must keep the two amounts separate (to satisfy company law). The reason for this is that there is a legal restriction on the maximum drawings of capital → (or payment of a **dividend**) that the owners can make. This is defined by the amount of revenue reserves, and so it is helpful to show these separately. We shall look at why there is this restriction, and how it works, a little later in the chapter.

Share capital

Shares represent the basic units of ownership of a business. All companies issue **ordinary shares**. Ordinary shares are often known as *equities*. The nominal value of such shares is at the discretion of the people that start up the company. For example, if the initial capital is to be £50,000, this could be two shares of £25,000 each, 5 million shares of one penny each or any other combination that gives a total of £50,000. Each share must have equal value.

Activity 4.4

The initial capital requirement for a new company is £50,000. There are to be two equal shareholders. Would you advise them to issue two shares of £25,000 each? Why?

Such large denomination shares tend to be unwieldy. Suppose that one of the shareholders wanted to sell his or her shares. S/he would have to find one buyer. If there were shares of smaller denomination, it would be possible to sell part of the shareholding to various potential buyers. Furthermore, it would be possible to sell just part of the holding and retain a part.

In practice, £1 is the normal maximum nominal value for shares. Shares of 25 pence each and 50 pence each are probably the most common.

Some companies also issue other classes of shares, **preference shares** being the most common. Preference shares guarantee that *if a dividend is paid*, the preference shareholders will be entitled to the first part of it up to a maximum value. This maximum is normally defined as a fixed percentage of the nominal value of the preference shares. If, for example, a company issues 10,000 preference shares of £1 each with a dividend rate of 6 per cent, this means that the preference shareholders are entitled to receive the first £600 (that is, 6 per cent of £10,000) of any dividend that is paid by the company for a year. The excess over £600 goes to the ordinary shareholders. Normally, any undistributed profits and gains accrue to the ordinary shareholders.

The ordinary shareholders are the primary risk-takers as they are entitled to share in the profits of the company only after other claims have been satisfied, and their potential rewards reflect this risk. There are no upper limits, however, on the amount by which they may benefit. The potential rewards available to ordinary shareholders reflect the risks that they are prepared to take. Since ordinary shareholders take most of the risks, power normally resides in their hands. Usually, only the ordinary shareholders are able to vote on issues that affect the company, such as who the directors should be.

It is open to the company to issue shares of various classes – perhaps with some having unusual and exotic conditions – but in practice it is rare to find other than straightforward ordinary and preference shares. Though a company may have different classes of shares whose holders have different rights, within each class all shares must be treated equally. The rights of the various classes of shareholders, as well as other matters relating to a particular company, are contained in that company's set of rules, known as the 'articles and memorandum of association'. A copy of these rules must be lodged with the Registrar of Companies, who makes it available for inspection by the general public.

Reserves

Reserves are profits and gains that have been made by a company and that still form part of the shareholders' (owners') claim or equity because they have not been paid out to the shareholders. Profits and gains tend to lead to assets flowing into the company. In Example 4.1 we came across one type of reserve, the revenue reserve. We should recall that this reserve represents the company's retained trading profits and gains on the disposal of non-current assets.

It is worth mentioning that retained profits represent overwhelmingly the largest source of new finance for UK companies – amounting for most companies to more than share issues and borrowings combined. These ploughed-back profits create most of a typical company's reserves. The shareholders' claim normally consists of share capital and reserves.

Activity 4.5

Are reserves amounts of cash? Can you think of a reason why this is an odd question?

To deal with the second point first, it is an odd question because reserves are a claim, or part of one, on the assets of the company, whereas cash is an asset. So reserves cannot be cash.

Reserves are classified as either revenue reserves or capital reserves. As we have already seen, revenue reserves arise from trading profit. They also arise from gains made on the disposal of non-current assets.

→ **Capital reserves** arise for two main reasons:

1 issuing shares at above their nominal value (for example, issuing £1 shares at £1.50); and
2 revaluing (upwards) non-current assets.

Where a company issues shares at above their nominal value, UK law requires that the excess of the issue price over the nominal value be shown separately.

Activity 4.6

Can you think why shares might be issued at above their nominal value? *Hint*: This would not usually happen when a company is first formed and the initial shares are being issued.

Once a company has traded and has been successful, the shares would normally be worth more than the nominal value at which they were issued. If additional shares are to be issued to new shareholders to raise finance for further expansion, unless they are issued at a value higher than the nominal value, the new shareholders will be gaining at the expense of the original ones.

Now let us consider another example.

Example 4.2

Based on future prospects, the net assets of a company are worth £1.5m. There are currently 1m ordinary shares in the company, each with a face (nominal) value of £1. The company wishes to raise an additional £0.6m of cash for expansion and has decided to raise it by issuing new shares. If the shares are issued for £1 each (that is 600,000 shares), the total number of shares will be:

$$1.0m + 0.6m = 1.6m$$

and their total value will be the value of the existing net assets plus the new injection of cash:

$$£1.5m + £0.6m = £2.1m$$

This means that the value of each share after the new issue will be:

$$£2.1m/1.6m = £1.3125$$

The current value of each share is:

$$£1.5m/1.0m = £1.50$$

So the original shareholders will lose:

$$£1.50 - £1.3125 = £0.1875 \text{ a share}$$

and the new shareholders will have gained

$$£1.3125 - £1.0 = £0.3125 \text{ a share}$$

The new shareholders will, no doubt, be delighted with this outcome; the original ones will not.

Things could be made fair between the two sets of shareholders described in Example 4.2 by issuing the new shares at £1.50 each. In this case it would be necessary to issue 400,000 shares to raise the necessary £0.6m. £1 a share of the £1.50 is the nominal value and will be included with share capital in the balance sheet (£400,000 in total). The remaining £0.50 is a share premium, which will be shown as a capital reserve known as the **share premium account** (£200,000 in total).

It is not clear why UK company law insists on the distinction between nominal share values and the premium. Certainly, other countries (for example, the US) with a similar set of laws governing the corporate sector do not see the necessity of distinguishing between share capital and share premium. Instead, the total value at which shares are issued is shown as one comprehensive figure on the company balance sheet.

Real World 4.5 shows the capital of one well-known business.

REAL WORLD 4.5

How Tesco is funded

Tesco plc, the UK and international supermarket business, had the following share capital and reserves as at 22 February 2003:

	£m
Share capital (5p ordinary shares)	362
Share premium account	2,465
Other reserves (capital)	40
Profit and loss account (income statement)	3,649
	6,516

Tesco is typical of many companies that refer to their retained profit as 'profit and loss account'.

Note how the nominal share capital is tiny compared with the share premium account figure. This implies that Tesco has issued shares at much higher prices than the 5p a share nominal value. This reflects Tesco's trading success since the company was first formed. Note also how, at balance sheet values, retained profit makes up more than half of the total for share capital and reserves.

Source: Tesco plc Annual Report and Financial Statements 2003.

Altering the nominal value of shares

The point has already been made that the promoters of a new company may make their own choice of the nominal or par value of the shares. This value need not be permanent. At a later date the shareholders can decide to change it.

For example, a company has at issue 1 million ordinary shares of £1 each. A decision is made to change the nominal value of the shares from £1 to £0.50, in other words to halve the value. As a result, the company would issue each shareholder with a new share certificate (the shareholders' evidence of ownership of their shareholding) for exactly twice as many shares, each with half the nominal value. This would leave each shareholder with a holding of the same total nominal value. This process is known, not surprisingly, as splitting the shares. The opposite, reducing the number of shares and increasing their nominal value per share to compensate, is known as **consolidating**.

Since each shareholder would be left, after a split or consolidation, with exactly the same proportion of ownership of the company's assets as before, the process should not increase the value of the total shares held.

Activity 4.7

Why might the shareholders want to split their shares in the manner described above?

The answer is probably to avoid individual shares becoming too valuable and making them a bit unwieldy, in the way discussed in the answer to Activity 4.4. If a company trades successfully, the value of each share is likely to rise, and in time could increase to a level that is considered unwieldy. Splitting would solve this problem.

Real World 4.6 gives an example of a share split by a well-known UK company.

REAL WORLD 4.6

Share split at Enterprise Inns

In January 2004, Enterprise Inns plc split its ordinary shares' nominal value of 10p per share to 5p per share. This meant that each ordinary shareholder became the owner of twice as many new shares, with each share having a market value of one half of each of the old ones. The reason given by the company was that it would increase the liquidity of the shares.

Enterprise Inns plc is the UK's second largest operator of pubs.

Bonus shares

It is always open to a company to take reserves of any kind (capital or revenue) and turn them into share capital. This will involve transferring the desired amount from the reserve concerned to share capital and then distributing the appropriate number of new shares to the existing shareholders. New shares arising from such a conversion are known as **bonus shares**. Issues of bonus shares are quite frequently encountered in practice. Example 4.3 illustrates this aspect of share issues.

Example 4.3

The summary balance sheet of a company is as follows:

Balance sheet as at 31 March 2005

	£
Net assets (various assets less liabilities)	128,000
Equity	
Share capital	
50,000 shares of £1 each	50,000
Reserves	78,000
	128,000

The company decides that it will issue, to existing shareholders, one new share for every share owned by each shareholder. The balance sheet immediately following this will appear as follows:

Balance sheet as at 31 March 2005

	£
Net assets (various assets less liabilities)	128,000
Equity	
Share capital	
100,000 shares of £1 each (50,000 + 50,000)	100,000
Reserves (78,000 − 50,000)	28,000
	128,000

We can see that the reserves have decreased by £50,000 and share capital has increased by the same amount. Share certificates for the 50,000 ordinary shares of £1 each, that have been created from reserves, will be issued to the existing shareholders to complete the transaction.

Activity 4.8

A shareholder of the company in Example 4.3 owned 100 shares before the bonus issue. How will things change for this shareholder as regards the number of shares owned and the value of the shareholding?

The answer should be that the number of shares will double, from 100 to 200. Now the shareholder owns one five-hundredth of the company (that is, 200/100,000). Before the bonus issue, the shareholder also owned one five-hundredth of the company (that is, 100/50,000). The company's assets and liabilities have not changed as a result of the bonus issue and so, logically, one five-hundredth of the value of the company should be identical to what it was before. Thus each share is worth half as much.

A bonus issue simply takes one part of the owners' claim (part of a reserve) and puts it into another part of the owners' claim (share capital). The transaction has no effect on the company's assets or liabilities, so there is no effect on shareholders' wealth.

Note that a bonus issue is not the same as a share split. A split does not affect the reserves.

Activity 4.9

Can you think of any reasons why a company might want to make a bonus issue if it has no economic consequence?

We think that there are three possible reasons:

- *Share price.* To lower the value of each share without reducing the shareholders' collective or individual wealth. This is the same effect as splitting and may be seen as an alternative to splitting.
- *Shareholder confidence.* To provide the shareholders with a 'feel-good factor'. It is believed that shareholders like bonus issues because it seems to make them better off, though in practice it should not affect their wealth.
- *Lender confidence.* Where reserves arising from operating profits and/or realised gains on the sale of non-current assets are used to make the bonus issue, it has the effect of taking part of that portion of the owners' claim that could be drawn by the shareholders, as drawings (or dividends), and locking it up. The amount transferred becomes part of the permanent capital base of the company. (We shall see, a little later in this chapter, that there are severe restrictions on the extent to which shareholders may make drawings from their capital.) An individual or organisation contemplating lending money to the company may insist that the dividend payment possibilities are restricted as a condition of making the loan. This point will be explained shortly.

Real World 4.7 is an example of a bonus share issue by a well-known UK retailer.

REAL WORLD 4.7

Bonus on the cards

In October 2003, Clinton Cards plc announced a one-for-two bonus issue. The company said that the objective of this was to increase the liquidity/marketability of the shares, by reducing the market price per share. This is the first of the three reasons mentioned above for making bonus issues. The company's share price had increased strongly on the back of strong past, and expected future, profit growth.

Clinton Cards plc is the UK's largest specialist greetings card retailer.

Source: Based on information from FT Money – Markets week world: Clinton Cards, *Financial Times*, 4 October 2003, FT.com.

Share capital – some expressions used in company law

Before leaving our detailed discussion of share capital, it might be helpful to clarify some of the jargon relating to shares that is used in company financial statements.

When a company is first formed, the shareholders give the directors an upper limit on the amount of nominal value of the shares that can be issued. This is known as the **authorised share capital**. This value can easily be revised upwards, but only if the shareholders agree. That part of the authorised share capital that has been issued to shareholders is known as the **issued** (or **allotted**) **share capital**.

Sometimes, but not very commonly, a company may not require shareholders to pay the whole amount that is due to be paid for the shares at the time of issue. This may happen where the company does not need the money all at once. Some money would normally be paid at the time of issue and the company would 'call' for further instalments until the shares were **fully paid**. That part of the total issue price that has been 'called' is known as the **called-up share capital**. That part that has been called and paid is known as the **paid-up share capital**.

Real World 4.8 shows the share capital of a well-known UK business.

REAL WORLD 4.8

Glass maker's capital

The following extract shows the called up share capital section of the balance sheet of Pilkington plc as at 31 March 2003. Pilkington is a major UK glass manufacturer. Note that the company has just one class of share.

	2003
Share capital	£m
Authorised: 1,670,000,000 (2002 – 1,500,000,000) ordinary 50p shares	835
Allotted, called up and paid: 1,260,220,500 (2002 – 1,253,801,444) ordinary 50p shares	630

Source: Pilkington plc Annual Report, 2003.

Raising share capital

Once the company has made its initial share issue to start business, usually soon after the company is first formed, it may decide to make further issues of new shares. These may be:

- Rights issues, that is issues made to existing shareholders, in proportion to their existing shareholding.
- Public issues, that is issues made to the general investing public.
- Private placings, that is issues made to selected individuals who are usually approached and asked if they would be interested in taking up new shares.

During its lifetime a company may use all three of these approaches to raising funds through issuing new shares (although only public companies can make appeals to the general public).

Loans and other sources of finance

Many companies borrow money to supplement that raised from share issues and ploughed-back profits. Company borrowing is often on a long-term basis, perhaps on a ten-year contract. Lenders may be banks and other professional providers of loan finance. Many companies raise loan finance in such a way that small investors, including private individuals, are able to lend small amounts. This is particularly the case with the larger, Stock Exchange listed, companies and involves their making a **loan stock** or **debenture** issue, which, though large in total, can be taken up in small slices by individual investors, both private individuals and investing institutions, such as pension funds and insurance companies. In some cases, these slices of loans can be bought and sold through the Stock Exchange. This means that investors do not have to wait the full term of the loan to obtain repayment, but can sell their slice of the loan to another would-be lender at intermediate points in the term of the loan.

Some of the features of loan-stock financing, particularly the possibility that the loan stock may be traded on the Stock Exchange, can lead to a confusion that loan stock is shares by another name. We should be clear that this is not the case. It is the shareholders who own the company and, therefore, who share in its losses and profits. Loan stockholders lend money to the company under a legally binding contract that normally specifies the rate of interest, the interest payment dates and the date of repayment of the loan itself. Usually, long-term loans are secured on assets of the company.

Long-term financing of companies can be depicted as in Figure 4.1.

Companies may also borrow finance on a short-term basis, perhaps from a bank as an overdraft. Most companies buy goods and services on a month or two's credit, as is normal in business-to-business transactions. This is, in effect, an interest-free loan.

It is important to the prosperity and stability of a company that it strikes a suitable balance between finance provided by the shareholders (equity) and loan financing. This topic will be explored in Chapter 7.

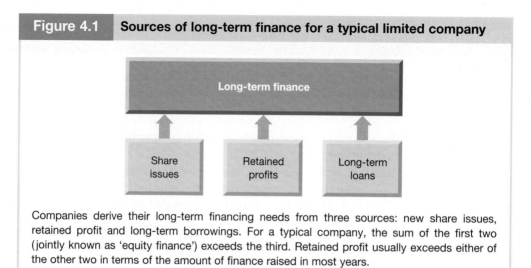

Figure 4.1   **Sources of long-term finance for a typical limited company**

Companies derive their long-term financing needs from three sources: new share issues, retained profit and long-term borrowings. For a typical company, the sum of the first two (jointly known as 'equity finance') exceeds the third. Retained profit usually exceeds either of the other two in terms of the amount of finance raised in most years.

Real World 4.9 shows the long-term borrowings of Rolls-Royce plc, the engine-building business, at 31 December 2002. Note the large number of sources from which the company borrows. This is typical of most large companies and probably reflects a desire to exploit all available means of raising finance, each of which may have some advantages and disadvantages. 'Secured' in this context means that the lender would have the right, should Rolls-Royce fail to meet its interest and/or capital repayment obligations, to seize a specified asset of the business (probably some land) and use it to raise the sums involved. Normally, a lender would accept a lower rate of interest where the loan is secured in this way as there is less risk involved. It should be said that whether a loan to a company like Rolls-Royce is secured or unsecured is usually pretty academic. It is unlikely that such a large and profitable company would fail to meet its obligations.

'Finance leases' are, in effect, arrangements where Rolls-Royce needs the use of a non-current asset (such as an item of machinery) and, instead of buying the asset itself, it arranges for a financier to buy the asset. The financier then leases it to the business, probably for the entire economic life of the asset. Though legally it is the financier who owns the asset, from an accounting point of view the essence of the arrangement is that, in effect, Rolls-Royce has borrowed cash from the financier to buy the asset. Thus, the asset appears among the business's non-current assets and the financial obligation to the financier is shown here as a long-term loan. This is a good example of how accounting tries to report the economic *substance* of a transaction, rather than its strict legal *form*. Finance leasing is a fairly popular means of raising long-term funds.

REAL WORLD 4.9

Borrowing at Rolls-Royce

The following extract from the annual financial statements of Rolls-Royce plc sets out the sources of the company's long-term borrowing as at 31 December 2002.

	2002 £m
Unsecured	
Bank loans	213
$4^{1}/_{2}$% Notes 2005	177
$6^{3}/_{8}$% Notes 2007	310
$7^{3}/_{8}$% Notes 2016	200
Other loans 2009 (interest rates nil)	4
Secured	
Bank loans	14
Obligations under finance leases payable:	
Between one and two years	7
Between two and five years	70
Zero-coupon bonds 2005/2007 (including 9.0% interest accretion)	43
	1,038
Repayable	
Between one and two years – by instalments	92
– otherwise	59
Between two and five years – by instalments	121
– otherwise	546
After five years – by instalments	20
– otherwise	200
	1,038

Source: Rolls-Royce plc Annual Financial Statements, 2002.

Restriction on the right of shareholders to make drawings of capital

Limited companies are required by law to distinguish between that part of their capital (shareholders' claim) or equity which may be withdrawn by the shareholders and that part which may not. The withdrawable part is that which has arisen from trading profits and from realised profits on the disposal of non-current assets (to the extent that tax payments on these profits and gains, as well as previous drawings, have not extinguished this part of the capital). This withdrawable element of the capital is *revenue reserves*.

The non-withdrawable part normally consists of that which has arisen from funds injected by shareholders buying shares in the company and that which came from upward revaluations of company assets that still remain in the company – that is, *share capital and capital reserves*.

Activity 4.10

Can you think of the reason why limited companies are required to distinguish different parts of their capital, whereas sole proprietorship businesses are not required to do so?

The reason for this situation is the limited liability, which company shareholders enjoy but which owners of unincorporated businesses do not. If a sole proprietor withdraws all of the owner's claim, or even an amount in excess of this, the position of the creditors of the business is not weakened since they can legally enforce their claims against the sole proprietor as an individual. With a limited company, where the business and the owners are legally separated, such a legal right to enforce claims against individuals does not exist. To protect the company's creditors, however, the law insists that a specific part of the company's capital cannot legally be withdrawn by the shareholders.

The law does not specify how large the non-withdrawable part of a particular company's capital should be, but simply that anyone dealing with the company should be able to tell from looking at the company's balance sheet how large it is. In the light of this, a particular prospective lender, or supplier of goods or services on credit, can make a commercial judgement as to whether to deal with the company or not. The larger it is, however, the easier the company is likely to find it to persuade potential lenders to lend and suppliers to supply goods and services on credit.

Let us now look at another example.

Example 4.4

The summary balance sheet of a company at a particular date is as follows:

Balance sheet

	£
Total assets less current liabilities	43,000
Equity	
Share capital	
20,000 shares of £1 each	20,000
Reserves (revenue)	23,000
	43,000

A bank has been asked to make a £25,000 long-term loan to the company. If the loan were to be made, the balance sheet immediately following would appear as follows:

Balance sheet (after the loan)

	£
Total assets less current liabilities (£43,000 + £25,000)	68,000
Less Non-current liability	
Long-term loan	25,000
	43,000
Equity	
Share capital	
20,000 shares of £1 each	20,000
Reserves (revenue)	23,000
	43,000

As things stand, there are total assets less current liabilities to a total balance sheet value of £68,000 to meet the bank's claim of £25,000. It would be possible and perfectly legal, however, for the company to pay a dividend (withdraw capital) of £23,000. The balance sheet would then appear as follows:

Balance sheet

	£
Total assets less current liabilities (£68,000 – £23,000)	45,000
Less **Non-current liabilities**	
Long-term loan	25,000
	20,000
Equity	
Share capital	
20,000 shares of £1 each	20,000
Reserves (revenue (£23,000 – £23,000))	–
	20,000

This leaves the bank in a very much weaker position, in that there are now total assets less current liabilities with a balance sheet value of £45,000 to meet a claim of £25,000. Note that the difference between the amount of the bank loan and the total assets less current liabilities always equals the capital and reserves total. Thus, the capital and reserves represent a **margin of safety** for creditors. The larger the amount of the owners' claim withdrawable by the shareholders, the smaller is the potential margin of safety for creditors.

As we have already seen, company law says nothing about how large the margin of safety must be. It is up the company concerned to do what is desirable.

Perhaps it is worth noting, as a practical footnote to Example 4.4, that most potential long-term lenders would seek to have the loan secured against a particular asset of the company, particularly an asset such as freehold property. This, as we have seen, would give the lender the right to seize the asset concerned, sell it and satisfy the repayment obligation, should the company default.

Activity 4.11

Would you expect a company to pay all of its revenue reserves as a dividend? What factors might be involved with a dividend decision?

It would be rare for a company to pay all of its revenue reserves as a dividend: a legal right to do so does not necessarily make it a good idea. Most companies see ploughed-back profits as a major – usually *the* major – source of new finance.

The factors that influence the dividend decision are likely to include:

● the availability of cash to pay a dividend. It would not be illegal to borrow to pay a dividend, but it would be unusual and, possibly, imprudent;
● the needs of the business for finance for new investment; and
● the expectations of shareholders concerning the amount of dividends to be paid.

You might have thought of others.

The law is adamant, however, that it is illegal, under normal circumstances, for shareholders to withdraw that part of their claim that is represented by shares and capital reserves. This means that potential creditors of the company know the maximum amount of the shareholders' claim that can be drawn by the shareholders. Figure 4.2 shows the important division between that part of the shareholders' claim that can be withdrawn as a dividend and that part that cannot.

Figure 4.2	Availability for dividends of various parts of the shareholders' claim

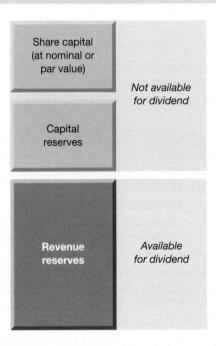

Total equity finance of limited companies consists of share capital, capital reserves and revenue reserves. Only the revenue reserves (which arise from realised profits and gains) can be used to fund a dividend. In other words, the maximum legal dividend is the amount of the revenue reserves.

Earlier in this chapter, the point was made that a potential creditor may insist that some revenue reserves are converted to bonus shares (or capitalised) so as to increase the margin of safety as a condition of granting the loan.

Activity 4.12

Can you think of any circumstances where the non-withdrawable part of a company's capital could be reduced without contravening the law?

It can be reduced, but only as a result of the company sustaining trading losses, or losses on disposal of non-current assets, that exceed the amount of the withdrawable portion of the company's capital. It cannot be reduced by shareholders making drawings.

Drawings are usually made in the form of a dividend paid by the company to the shareholders, in proportion to the number of shares owned by each one.

If we refer back to Real World 4.5, we can see that Tesco plc could legally have paid a dividend of £3,649 million on 22 February 2003, which is the amount of its revenue reserves. For several reasons, including the fact that this represented over half of the balance sheet value of the business's net assets, no such dividend was paid.

Accounting for limited companies

The main financial statements

As we might expect, the financial statements of a limited company are, in essence, identical to those of a sole proprietor. There are, however, some differences of detail, and we shall now consider these. Example 4.5 sets out the profit and loss account (income statement) and balance sheet of a limited company:

Example 4.5

Da Silva plc
Profit and loss account for the year ended 31 December 2005

	£m	£m
Revenue		840
Less Cost of sales		520
Gross profit		320
Less Operating expenses		
Wages and salaries	98	
Heat and light	18	
Rent and rates	24	
Motor-vehicle expenses	20	
Insurance	4	
Printing and stationery	12	
Depreciation	45	
Audit fee	4	
		225
Operating profit		95
Less Interest payable		10
Profit before tax		85
Less Tax on profit		24
Profit after tax		61
Less Transfer to general reserve	20	
Dividend paid	25	
		45
Unappropriated profit carried forward		16

→

Example 4.5 continued

Balance sheet as at 31 December 2005

	£m	£m
Non-current assets		
Property, plant and equipment		303
Current assets		
Stock (inventories)	65	
Trade debtors (receivables)	112	
Cash	36	
	213	
Less Current liabilities		
Trade creditors (payables)	99	
Corporation tax	12	
	111	
Net current assets (working capital)		102
Total assets less current liabilities		405
Less Non-current liabilities		
10% debentures		100
Net assets		305
Equity		
Share capital		
Ordinary shares of £0.50 each		200
Reserves		
Share premium account	30	
General reserve	50	
Profit and loss account	25	
		105
		305

Perhaps the most striking thing about these statements is the extent to which they look exactly the same as those that we have been used to with sole proprietors. This is correct; the differences are small. Let us go through and pick up these differences.

The profit and loss account (income statement)

There are several features in the profit and loss account that need consideration.

Profit

We can see that, following the calculation of gross profit, four further measures of profit are shown.

- The first of these is **operating profit**. This represents the profit achieved for the year before any financing expenses are taken into account. By excluding the financing expenses from the calculation of profit, a better idea of the operating performance for the year may be achieved.
- The second measure of profit is the net profit for the year (profit before tax). Interest charges are deducted from the operating profit to derive this figure. This measure is

already familiar to us, and in the case of a sole proprietor business, the profit and loss account (income statement) would end here.

● The third measure of profit is the net profit after tax. As the company is a separate legal entity, it is liable to pay tax (known as corporation tax) on the profits generated. (This contrasts with the sole proprietor business where it is the owner rather than the business that is liable for the tax on profits, as we saw earlier in the chapter.) This measure of profit represents the amount that is available for the shareholders.

● The final measure of profit is the unappropriated, or retained, profit for the year. We can see that most of the net profit after tax is appropriated, or allocated, to pay a dividend and to transfer to a general reserve (see below). Once these appropriations have been made we are left with the fourth measure of profit, which represents the unallocated profits. It is probably worth pointing out that the last part of the profit and loss account (income statement) dealing with appropriations for taxation, dividends and transfers to reserves is known as the 'appropriation account'.

Audit fee

As we shall see in Chapter 5, companies greater than a particular size are required to have their financial statements audited by an independent firm of auditors, for which a fee is charged. Though it is also open to sole proprietors to have their financial statements audited, very few do, so this is an expense that will normally be present in the profit and loss account of a company but not that of a sole proprietor.

Dividend

This represents the drawings of capital by the shareholders of the company. Only those dividends paid during the year and those approved by the shareholders before the year end, whether paid or not, appear in the profit and loss account. Sometimes shareholders receive a dividend before the end of the year. Companies may pay their shareholders an 'interim' dividend, part way through the year, and a 'final' dividend shortly after the year end. Had a dividend been approved before the year end, but not paid by the year end, it would appear on the balance sheet as a current liability. Where a dividend has been recommended by the directors, but not approved by the shareholders, it should be mentioned in a note to the financial statements.

Transfer to general reserve

After dividends have been deducted from the net profit after tax figure, the remaining profit is normally reinvested ('ploughed back') into the operations of the company. For this company, the amount reinvested is £36 million (that is, £61 million less £25 million). This amount could all have been unallocated and simply gone to increase the unappropriated profit figure. We can see, however, that an amount (£20 million for this company) has been transferred to a separate general reserve, which is quite common in practice.

It is not entirely clear why directors decide to make transfers to general reserves, since the funds concerned remain part of the revenue reserves, and are, therefore, still available for dividend. The most plausible explanation seems to be that directors feel that taking amounts out of the profit and loss account and placing them in a 'reserve' indicates an intention to retain the funds permanently in the company and not to use them to pay a dividend. Of course, the unappropriated profit is also a reserve, but that fact is not indicated in its title.

The balance sheet

The main points for consideration in the balance sheet are:

- *Corporation tax.* The amount that appears as part of the short-term liabilities represents 50 per cent of the tax on the profit for the year 2005. It is, therefore, 50 per cent of the charge that appears in the profit and loss account; the other 50 per cent will already have been paid. The unpaid 50 per cent will be paid shortly after the balance sheet date. These payment dates are set down by law.
- *Equity.* We have already discussed this area earlier in the chapter. The general reserve balance must have stood at £30 million before the year end as it was increased to its final level of £50 million by the transfer of £20 million of the year 2005 profit. Similarly, the profit and loss account balance must have been £9 million, just before the year end. As was mentioned above, the general reserve and the profit and loss account balance are identical in all respects; they both arise from retained profits, and are both available for dividend.

Self-assessment question 4.1

The summarised balance sheet of Dev Ltd is as follows:

Balance sheet as at 31 December 2005

	£
Net assets (various assets less liabilities)	235,000
Equity	
Share capital: 100,000 shares of £1 each	100,000
Share premium account	30,000
Revaluation reserve	37,000
Profit and loss account balance	68,000
	235,000

Required:

(a) Without any other transactions occurring at the same time, the company made a one-for-five rights share issue at £2 per share payable in cash. This means that each shareholder was offered one share for every five already held. All shareholders took up their rights. Immediately afterwards, the company made a one-for-two bonus issue. Show the balance sheet immediately following the bonus issue, assuming that the directors wanted to retain the maximum dividend payment potential for the future.

(b) Explain what external influence might cause the directors to choose not to retain the maximum dividend payment possibilities.

(c) Show the balance sheet immediately following the bonus issue, assuming that the directors wanted to retain the *minimum* dividend payment potential for the future.

(d) What is the maximum dividend that could be paid before and after the events described in (a) if the minimum dividend payment potential is achieved?

(e) Lee owns 100 shares in Dev Ltd before the events described in (a). Assuming that the net assets of the company have a value equal to their balance sheet value, show how these events will affect Lee's wealth.

(f) Looking at the original balance sheet of Dev Ltd, shown above, what four things do we know about the company's status and history that are not specifically stated on the balance sheet?

SUMMARY

The main points of this chapter may be summarised as follows:

The main features of a limited company

- It is an artificial person that has been created by law.
- It has a separate life from its owners and is granted a perpetual existence.
- It must take responsibility for its own debts and losses but its owners are granted limited liability.
- A public company can offer its shares for sale to the public; a private company cannot.
- It is governed by a board of directors, which is elected by the shareholders.
- Corporate governance is a major issue, various scandals have led to the emergence of the Combined Code.

Financing the limited company

- The share capital of a company can be of two main types – ordinary shares and preference shares.
- Ordinary shares (equities) are the main risk-takers and are given voting rights; they form the backbone of the company.
- Preference shares are given a right to a fixed dividend before ordinary shareholders receive a dividend.
- Reserves are profits and gains made by the company and form part of the ordinary shareholders' claim.
- Loan capital provides another major source of finance.

Share issues

- Bonus shares are issued to existing shareholders when part of the reserves of the company are converted into share capital.
- Rights share issues give existing shareholders the right to buy new shares in proportion to their existing holding.
- The shares of public companies may be bought and sold on a recognised stock exchange.

Reserves

- Reserves are of two types – revenue reserves and capital reserves.
- Revenue reserves arise from trading profits and from realised profits on the sale of non-current assets.
- Capital reserves arise from the issue of shares above their nominal value or from the upward revaluation of non-current assets.
- Revenue reserves can be withdrawn as dividends by the shareholders whereas capital reserves cannot.

Financial statements of limited companies

- The financial statements of limited companies are based on the same principles as those of sole proprietorship businesses. However, there are some differences in detail.

● The profit and loss account has four measures of profit displayed: operating profit, net profit for the year (profit before tax), net profit after tax and unappropriated profit.

● The profit and loss account also shows audit fees, transfers to reserves, corporation tax on profits for the year and dividends for the year.

● Any unpaid tax and unpaid, but authorised, dividends will appear in the balance sheet as current liabilities.

● The share capital plus the reserves will be shown as 'equity'.

→ Key terms

Limited company p. 101	**Preference shares** p. 112
Shares p. 101	**Capital reserves** p. 113
Limited liability p. 103	**Share premium account** p. 114
Public company p. 104	**Consolidating** p. 115
Private company p. 104	**Bonus shares** p. 116
Corporation tax p. 105	**Authorised share capital** p. 118
Director p. 106	**Issued (or allotted) share capital**
Corporate governance p. 106	p. 118
Combined Code p. 107	**Fully paid shares** p. 118
Reserves p. 111	**Called-up share capital** p. 118
Equity p. 111	**Paid-up share capital** p. 118
Nominal (or par) value p. 111	**Loan stock (debenture)** p. 119
Revenue reserve p. 111	**Margin of safety** p. 123
Dividend p. 111	**Operating profit** p. 126
Ordinary shares p. 112	

Further reading

If you would like to explore the topics covered in this chapter in more depth, we recommend the following books:

Financial Reporting, *Alexander D. and Britton A.*, 6th edn, International Thomson Business Press, 2001, chapter 12.

Financial Accounting and Reporting, *Elliott B. and Elliott J.*, 8th edn, Financial Times Prentice Hall, 2004, chapters 10 and 19.

Accounting Theory and Practice, *Glautier M. and Underdown B.*, 7th edn, Financial Times Prentice Hall, 2001, chapter 13.

Reference

Corporate Governance: Improving competitiveness and access to capital in global markets, an OECD report by Business Sector Advisory Group on Corporate Governance, Organisation for Economic Co-operation and Development, 1998, p. 14.

REVIEW QUESTIONS

Answers to these questions can be found on the students' side of the Companion Website at www.pearsoned.co.uk/atrillmclaney.

4.1 How does the liability of a limited company differ from the liability of a real person, in respect of amounts owed to others?

4.2 Some people are about to form a company, as a vehicle through which to run a new business. What are the advantages to them of forming a private limited company rather than a public one?

4.3 What is a reserve? Distinguish between a revenue reserve and a capital reserve.

4.4 What is a preference share? Compare the main features of a preference share with those of

(a) an ordinary share, and
(b) a debenture.

EXERCISES

Exercises 4.6 to 4.8 are more advanced than 4.1 to 4.5. Those with a coloured number have answers at the back of the book.

4.1 Comment on the following quotation:

> Limited companies can set a limit on the amount of debts that they will meet. They tend to have reserves of cash, as well as share capital and they can use these reserves to pay dividends to the shareholders. Many companies have preference as well as ordinary shares. The preference shares give a guaranteed dividend. The shares of many companies can be bought and sold on the Stock Exchange, and a shareholder selling his or her shares can represent a useful source of new capital to the company.

4.2 Comment on the following quotes:

(a) 'Bonus shares increase the shareholders' wealth because, after the issue, they have more shares, but each one of the same nominal value as they had before. Share splits, on the other hand, do not make the shareholders richer, because the total nominal value of their shareholding is the same before the issue as after it.'
(b) 'By law, once shares have been issued at a particular nominal value, they must always be issued at that value in any future share issues.'
(c) 'By law, companies can pay as much as they like by way of dividends on their shares, provided that they have sufficient cash to do so.'
(d) 'Companies do not have to pay tax on their profits because the shareholders have to pay tax on their dividends.'

4.3 Briefly explain each of the following expressions that you have seen in the financial statements of a limited company:

(a) Dividend
(b) Debenture
(c) Share premium account.

4.4   Iqbal Ltd started trading on 1 January 2002. During the first five years of trading, the following occurred:

Year ended 31 December	Trading profit (loss) £	Profit (loss) on sale of non-current assets £	Upward revaluation of non-current assets £
2002	(15,000)	–	–
2003	8,000	–	10,000
2004	15,000	5,000	–
2005	20,000	(6,000)	–
2006	22,000	–	–

Required:
Assuming that the company paid the maximum legal dividend each year, how much would each year's dividend be?

4.5   Da Silva plc's outline balance sheet as at a particular date was as follows:

	£m
Net assets	72
Equity:	
£1 ordinary shares	40
General reserve	32
	72

The directors made a one-for-four bonus issue, immediately followed by a one-for-four rights issue at a price of £1.80 per share.

Required:
Show the balance sheet of Da Silva plc immediately following the two share issues.

4.6   Presented below is a draft set of simplified financial statements for Pear Limited for the year ended 30 September 2005.

Profit and loss account for the year ended 30 September 2005

	£000	£000
Revenue		1,456
Costs of sales		(768)
Gross profit		688
Less Expenses:		
Salaries	220	
Depreciation	249	
Other operating costs	131	(600)
Operating profit		88
Interest payable		(15)
Profit before taxation		73
Taxation at 30%		(22)
Profit after taxation		51

Balance sheet as at 30 September 2005

	£000	£000
Non-current assets		
Property, plant and equipment		
Cost	1,570	
Depreciation	(690)	880
Current assets		
Stock (inventories)	207	
Trade debtors (receivables)	182	
Cash at bank	21	
	410	
Less **Current liabilities**		
Trade creditors (payables)	88	
Other creditors (payables)	20	
Taxation	22	
Bank overdraft	105	
	235	
Net current assets		175
Less **Non-current liabilities**		
10% debenture – repayable 2012		(300)
		755
Equity		
Share capital		300
Share premium account	300	
Retained profit at beginning of year	104	
Profit for year	51	455
		755

The following information is available:

(i) Depreciation has not been charged on office equipment with a written-down value of £100,000. This class of assets is depreciated at 12 per cent a year using the reducing-balance method.

(ii) A new machine was purchased, on credit, for £30,000 and delivered on 29 September 2005 but has not been included in the financial statements. (Ignore depreciation.)

(iii) A sales invoice to the value of £18,000 for September 2005 has been omitted from the financial statements. (The cost of sales figure is stated correctly.)

(iv) A dividend of £25,000 had been approved by the shareholders before 30 September 2005, but was unpaid at that date. This is not reflected in the financial statements.

(v) The interest payable on the debenture for the second half-year was not paid until 1 October 2005 and has not been included in the financial statements.

(vi) A general provision against bad debts is to be made at the level of 2 per cent of debtors (receivables).

(vii) An invoice for electricity to the value of £2,000 for the quarter ended 30 September 2005 arrived on 4 October and has not been included in the financial statements.

(viii) The charge for taxation will have to be amended to take account of the above information. Make the simplifying assumption that tax is payable shortly after the end of the year, at the rate of 30 per cent of the profit before tax.

Required:

Prepare a revised set of financial statements for the year ended 30 September 2005 incorporating the additional information in (i)–(viii) above. Note: work to the nearest £1,000.

4.7   Presented below is a draft set of financial statements for Chips Limited.

Chips Limited
Profit and loss account for the year ended 30 June 2005

	£000	£000
Revenue		1,850
Cost of sales		(1,040)
Gross profit		810
Less Depreciation	(220)	
Other operating costs	(375)	(595)
Operating profit		215
Interest payable		(35)
Profit before taxation		180
Taxation		(60)
Profit after taxation		120

Balance sheet as at 30 June 2005

	Cost	Depreciation	
	£000	£000	£000
Non-current assets			
Property, plant and equipment			
Buildings	800	(112)	688
Plant and equipment	650	(367)	283
Motor vehicles	102	(53)	49
	1,552	(532)	1,020
Current assets			
Stock (inventories)		950	
Trade debtors (receivables)		420	
Cash at bank		16	
		1,386	
Less **Current liabilities**			
Trade creditors (payables)		(361)	
Other creditors (payables)		(117)	
Taxation		(60)	
		(538)	
Net current assets			848
Less **Non-current liabilities**			
Secured 10% loan			(700)
			1,168
Equity			
Ordinary shares of £1, fully paid			800
Reserves at 1 July 2004		248	
Profit for the year		120	368
			1,168

The following additional information is available:

(i)   Purchase invoices for goods received on 29 June 2005 amounting to £23,000 have not been included. This means that the cost of sales figure in the profit and loss account has been understated.

(ii) A motor vehicle costing £8,000 with depreciation amounting to £5,000 was sold on 30 June 2005 for £2,100, paid by cheque. This transaction has not been included in the company's records.

(iii) No depreciation on motor vehicles has been charged. The annual rate is 20% of cost at the year end.

(iv) A sale on credit for £16,000 made on 1 July 2005 has been included in the financial statements in error. The cost of sales figure is correct in respect of this item.

(v) A half-yearly payment of interest on the secured loan due on 30 June 2005 has not been paid.

(vi) The tax charge should be 30% of the reported profit before taxation. Assume that it is payable, in full, shortly after the year end.

Required:

Prepare a revised set of financial statements incorporating the additional information in (i)–(vi) above. *Note*: Work to the nearest £1,000.

4.8 Rose Limited operates a small chain of retail shops that sell high-quality teas and coffees. Approximately half of sales are on credit. Abbreviated and unaudited financial statements are given below:

Profit and loss account for the year ended 31 March 2005

	£000	£000
Revenue		12,080
Cost of sales		(6,282)
Gross profit		5,798
Labour costs	(2,658)	
Depreciation	(625)	
Other operating costs	(1,003)	
		(4,286)
Net profit before interest		1,512
Interest payable		(66)
Net profit before tax		1,446
Tax payable		(434)
Net profit after tax		1,012
Dividend paid		(300)
Retained profit for year		712
Retained profit brought forward		756
Retained profit carried forward		1,468

(continued over)

Balance sheet as at 31 March 2005

	£000	£000
Non-current assets		2,728
Current assets		
Stock (inventories)	1,583	
Debtors (receivables)	996	
Cash	26	
	2,605	
Current liabilities		
Trade creditors (payables)	(1,118)	
Other creditors (payables)	(417)	
Tax	(434)	
Overdraft	(596)	
	(2,565)	
Net current assets		40
Non-current liabilities		
Secured loan (2010)		(300)
		2,468
Equity		
Share capital		
(50p shares, fully paid)		750
Share premium		250
Retained profit		1,468
		2,468

Since the unaudited financial statements for Rose Limited were prepared, the following information has become available:

(i)   An additional £74,000 of depreciation should have been charged on fixtures and fittings.
(ii) Invoices for credit sales on 31 March 2005 amounting to £34,000 have not been included; costs of sales is not affected.
(iii) Bad debts should be provided at a level of 2 per cent of debtors at the year end.
(iv) Stocks, which had been purchased for £2,000, have been damaged and are unsaleable. This is not reflected in the financial statements.
(v)   Fixtures and fittings to the value of £16,000 were delivered just before 31 March 2005, but these assets were not included in the financial statements and the purchase invoice had not been processed.
(vi) Wages for Saturday-only staff, amounting to £1,000, have not been paid for the final Saturday of the year. This is not reflected in the financial statements.
(vii) Tax is payable at 30 per cent of net profit before tax. Assume that it is payable shortly after the year end.

Required:
Prepare revised financial statements for Rose Limited for the year ended 31 March 2005, incorporating the information in (i) to (vii) above. *Note*: Work to the nearest £1,000.

5

Accounting for limited companies (2)

OBJECTIVES

When you have completed this chapter, you should be able to:

- Describe the responsibilities of directors and auditors concerning the annual financial statements provided to external users.

- Identify the main sources of regulation affecting the financial statements of limited companies.

- Discuss the framework of principles for accounting.

- Prepare a profit and loss account, balance sheet and statement of changes in equity for a limited company in accordance with international accounting standards.

- Explain the purpose of segmental reports and the operating and financial review and discuss the contents of these reports.

- Discuss the problem of creative accounting.

INTRODUCTION

In this chapter we continue our examination of the financial statements of limited companies. We begin by identifying the legal responsibilities of directors and then go on to discuss the main sources of accounting rules that govern the published financial statements. Although a detailed consideration of these accounting rules is beyond the scope of this book, the key rules that shape the form and content of the published financial statements are discussed along with the efforts that have been made to develop a framework of principles to underpin the accounting rules.

The increasing complexity of business and the increasing demands for information by users have led to the publication of a number of additional financial statements. We shall consider two of the more important, namely the segmental financial report and the operating and financial review. The aim of both these reports is to provide users with a more complete picture of financial performance and position.

Despite the proliferation of accounting rules, there are still concerns over the quality of published financial statements. The chapter ends by considering the problem of creative accounting and its impact on financial reporting.

The directors' duty to account

It is not usually possible for all of the shareholders to be involved in the general management of the company, nor do most of them wish to be involved. Instead, they elect directors to act on their behalf. It is both logical, and required by UK company law, that directors are accountable for their actions in respect of their stewardship (management) of the company's assets. In this context, directors are required by law:

● to maintain appropriate accounting records;
● to prepare annual financial statements and a directors' report, and to make these available to all shareholders and to the public at large.

The financial statements are made available to the general public by the company submitting a copy to the Companies Registry (Department of Trade and Industry), which allows anyone who wishes to do so to inspect these financial statements.

Activity 5.1

Can you think of any reasons why the law has decreed that companies must account in this way? We think there are broadly three reasons.

We thought of the following:

● *To inform and protect shareholders*. If shareholders do not receive a reasonable supply of information about the performance and position of their company, they will have problems in appraising their investment. Under these circumstances, they would probably be reluctant to invest and this, in turn, would affect the functioning of the private sector. Any society with a significant private sector needs to encourage equity investment.
● *To inform and protect suppliers of labour, goods, services and finance, particularly those supplying credit (loans) or goods and services on credit*. People and organisations would be reluctant to engage in commercial relationships, such as supplying goods or lending money, where a company does not provide information about its financial health. The fact that a company has limited liability increases the risks involved in dealing with the company. An unwillingness to engage in commercial relationships with limited companies will, once again, affect the functioning of the private sector.
● *To inform and protect society more generally*. Some companies exercise enormous power and influence in society generally, particularly on a geographically local basis. For example, a particular company may be the dominant employer and purchaser of commercial goods and services in a particular town or city. Legislators have tended to take the view that society has the right to information about the company and its activities.

The need for accounting rules

If we accept the need for directors of limited companies to prepare and publish financial statements, we must also accept the need for a framework of rules concerning how these statements are prepared and presented. A lack of regulation increases the risk that unscrupulous directors will use 'unacceptable' accounting practices when preparing the financial statements in order to portray a view of company performance that is not actually warranted. It also increases the risk that the financial statements of different companies will not be comparable, thereby making investment decisions difficult. These risks will, in turn, damage the integrity of the financial statements in the eyes of users.

Though the need for regulating the financial statements is widely accepted, users must be realistic about what can be achieved through regulation. Problems of manipulation and concealment can still occur, even in a highly regulated environment. However, regulation should reduce the scale of these problems, however. There are also limits to comparability between the financial statements of different companies. We have already seen that accounting is not a precise science and it will always be necessary for judgements and estimates to be made. In some cases, there may also be valid reasons for different companies to adopt different accounting methods.

The main sources of accounting rules

Before considering the particular rules to be followed by limited companies, we first need to be aware of the main sources of accounting rules. In the UK, we are currently going through a period of transition and the main sources of accounting rules are changing. In the following sections we provide some background to the changes.

The situation until January 2005

In the UK, company law has been the primary source of authority when preparing and presenting financial statements. The main body of law is set out in the Companies Act 1985, as amended by the Companies Act 1989. Company law incorporates the overriding requirement that the financial statements of limited companies show a true and fair view of the financial performance and position of the company. It also provides rules concerning the format (layout) of the financial statements as well as detailed disclosure requirements and valuation rules.

 To support the law, **financial reporting standards** (previously called **accounting standards**) have been issued by the Accounting Standards Board (ASB). The ASB was established by the UK accounting profession and the standards issued by the Board aim to improve the quality of the financial statements. These standards cover various aspects of preparing the financial statements including:

- what information should be disclosed;
- how information should be presented;
- how assets should be valued; and
- how profit should be measured.

Normally, companies must comply with ASB standards to ensure the financial statements provide a true and fair view. In essence, the law said that the financial statements should reflect a true and fair view, and the standards help to define what is meant by this expression. This gives accounting standards an important role in financial reporting.

Companies that are listed on the London Stock Exchange must adhere to further rules as a condition of having their shares traded there. These additional rules are imposed by the Financial Services Authority (FSA), in its role as the UK listing authority.

These rules include publication of summarised interim (half-year) financial statements, in addition to the annual financial statements, and disclosure of details of holdings of more than 20 per cent of the shares of other companies.

Figure 5.1 illustrates the sources of accounting rules with which larger UK companies must comply.

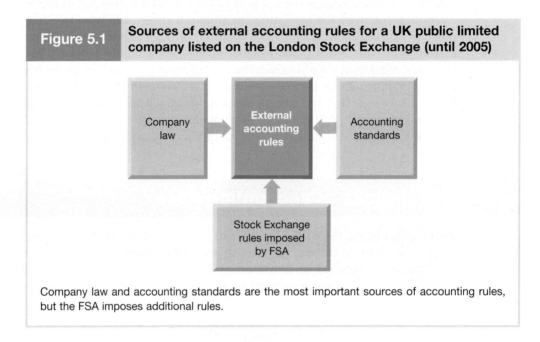

| Figure 5.1 | Sources of external accounting rules for a UK public limited company listed on the London Stock Exchange (until 2005) |

Company law and accounting standards are the most important sources of accounting rules, but the FSA imposes additional rules.

The situation from January 2005

There are significant changes to the sources of rules from January 2005. This reflects the growing momentum towards international harmonisation. Business has become more international in nature and so, it is argued, accounting has to become more international in nature in order to keep pace. If the accounting rules of different countries are harmonised, companies with an international reach should find it easier to make investment decisions and to raise capital. It can also help them to reduce the time and cost of producing financial statements as different sets of financial statements will no longer have to be prepared for the different countries in which these companies have a presence.

The potential benefits of internationalising accounting practice led to the creation of the International Accounting Standards Committee (IASC) in 1973. The IASC was set up with the aim of achieving improvement and harmonisation of accounting standards and during its life issued a number of **international accounting standards** (IASs). The IASC was restructured and renamed the International Accounting Standards Board (IASB) in 2001. The objectives of the IASB, which is an independent body funded by voluntary contributions, are to:

● develop a single set of high quality, global accounting standards that require transparent and comparable information in financial statements;
● promote the use and application of these standards; and
● work towards the convergence of national accounting standards.

The IASB's pronouncements are called **international financial reporting standards** (IFRSs) but the board has also adopted the international accounting standards (IASs) issued by the IASC. There are strong similarities between the standards issued, or adopted, by the IASB and those issued by the UK standard-setting body, the ASB. However, there are also important differences. The relationship between the two sets of standards has been described as that of 'cousins rather than siblings'. **Real World 5.1** provides a list of standards that have been issued, or adopted, by the IASB to give an idea of the range of topics that are covered.

REAL WORLD 5.1

International standards

The following is a list of the international accounting standards in force at the end of May 2004. Several standards have been issued and subsequently withdrawn, which explains the numerical gaps in the sequence. In addition, many of them have been revised and reissued.

IAS 1	Presentation of Financial Statements
IAS 2	Inventories
IAS 7	Cash Flow Statements
IAS 8	Net Profit or Loss for the Period, Fundamental Errors and Changes in Accounting Policies
IAS 10	Events After the Balance Sheet Date
IAS 11	Construction Contracts
IAS 12	Income Taxes
IAS 14	Segment Reporting
IAS 15	Information Reflecting the Effects of Changing Prices
IAS 16	Property, Plant and Equipment
IAS 17	Leases
IAS 18	Revenue
IAS 19	Employee Benefits
IAS 20	Accounting for Government Grants and Disclosure of Government Assistance
IAS 21	The Effects of Changes in Foreign Exchange Rates
IAS 23	Borrowing Costs
IAS 24	Related Party Transactions
IAS 26	Accounting and Reporting by Retirement Benefit Plans
IAS 27	Consolidated Financial Statements
IAS 28	Investments in Associates
IAS 29	Financial Reporting in Hyperinflationary Economies
IAS 30	Disclosures in the Financial Statements of Banks and Similar Financial Institutions
IAS 31	Financial Reporting of Interests in Joint Ventures
IAS 32	Financial Investments: Disclosure and Presentation
IAS 33	Earnings per Share
IAS 34	Interim Financial Reporting
IAS 35	Discontinuing Operations
IAS 36	Impairment of Assets
IAS 37	Provisions, Contingent Liabilities and Contingent Assets
IAS 38	Intangible Assets
IAS 39	Financial Instruments: Recognition and Measurement
IAS 40	Investment Property
IAS 41	Agriculture

→

Real World 5.1 continued

IFRS 1   First-time Adoption of International Financial Reporting Standards
IFRS 2   Share-based Payments
IFRS 3   Business Combinations
IFRS 4   Insurance Contracts

Key:
IAS = International accounting standard
IFRS = International financial reporting standard

Source: www.iasb.org.

The authority of the IASB was given a huge boost when the European Commission adopted a regulation requiring listed companies of EU Member States, to prepare their consolidated financial statements according to IASB standards as from January 2005. EU Member States have the power to extend this requirement to other companies and, in July 2003 the UK government announced that all companies would be allowed the option to adopt IASB standards. Non-listed companies can choose not to follow IASB standards, certainly for the immediate future. Many informed observers believe that once listed companies start to apply IASB standards, other companies will quickly follow, particularly larger and better-known non-listed companies. It seems likely that applying IASB standards will quickly become the norm.

The EU regulation overrides any laws in force in Member States that could either hinder or restrict compliance with IASB standards. However, those national laws that embody EU directives concerning the publication and audit of financial statements remain in force. The ultimate aim is to achieve a single framework of accounting rules for companies from all member countries. The EU recognises that this will only be achieved if governments of member countries do not add to the requirements imposed by the various IASB standards. Thus, it seems that accounting rules developed within individual EU Member States will eventually disappear.

For the time being, however, the EU accepts that the governments of Member States may need to impose additional disclosures for some corporate governance matters and regulatory requirements. In the UK, company law requires disclosure relating to various corporate governance issues. For example, there is a requirement to disclose details of directors' remuneration in the published financial statements. This requirement goes beyond that required by IASB standards.

This means that from 2005, the position shown in Figure 5.1 (see p. 140) remains valid, except that it is IASB, rather than UK, standards that provide that element. Company law and the FSA still play their part. It seems likely, that in the longer term, IASB standards will replace both company law and the FSA to become the sole source of company accounting requirements.

Presenting financial statements

Now that we have gained an insight to the sources of rules affecting limited companies, let us turn our attention to the main rules to be followed in the presentation of financial statements. We shall focus on the IASB rules and, in particular, those contained in IAS 1 *Presentation of Financial Statements*. This standard is very important as it sets out the structure and content of financial statements and the principles to be followed in preparing these statements.

According to IAS 1, the financial statements consist of:

- a profit and loss account (income statement)
- a balance sheet
- a statement of changes in equity
- a cash flow statement
- notes on accounting policies and other explanatory notes.

We shall discuss each of these below but, before doing so, we should be clear as to what is the main consideration when preparing these statements.

Fair representation

The overriding requirement is for the financial statements to provide a fair representation of the company's financial position, financial performance and cash flows. There is a presumption that this will be achieved where the financial statements are drawn up in accordance with the various IASB standards that have been issued. It is only in very rare circumstances that compliance with a standard would not result in a fair representation of the financial health of a company.

Activity 5.2

IAS 1 does not say that the overriding requirement is for the financial statements to show a 'correct' or an 'accurate' presentation of financial health. Why, in your opinion, does it not use those words?

Hint: Think of depreciation of fixed assets.

Accounting can never really be said to be 'correct' or 'accurate' as these words imply that there is a precise value that any asset, claim, revenue or expense could have. This is simply not true in many, if not most, cases.

Depreciation provides a good example. The annual depreciation expense is based on judgements about the future concerning the expected useful life and residual value. If all relevant factors are taken into account and reasonable judgements are applied, it may be possible to achieve a fair representation of the amount of the asset that is consumed for a particular period. However, a precise figure for depreciation for a period cannot be achieved.

The profit and loss account (income statement)

IAS 1 sets out the *minimum* information to be presented on the face of the profit and loss account, or income statement. These items include:

- revenue
- finance costs
- gains or losses on the sale of assets or settlement of liabilities arising from discontinued operations
- tax expense and
- profit or loss.

The standard makes it clear, however, that further items should be shown on the face of the profit and loss account where they are relevant to an understanding of performance. For example, if a business is badly affected by flooding, and stocks (inventories) are destroyed as a result, the cost of the flood damage should be shown.

As a further aid to understanding, all material expenses must be separately disclosed. However, they need not be shown on the face of the profit and loss account: they can appear in the notes to the financial statements. The sort of material items that may require separate disclosure include:

● write down of stocks to net realisable value
● write down or disposal of property, plant and equipment
● disposal of investments
● restructuring costs
● discontinuing operations and
● litigation settlements.

This is not an exhaustive list and, in practice, other material expenses may require separate disclosure.

The standard suggests two possible ways in which expenses can be presented on the face of the profit and loss account. The first is to analyse the expenses according to their nature, such as depreciation, employee expenses and so on. Example 5.1 below sets out how a profit and loss account analyses expenses in this way.

Example 5.1

Turner plc
Profit and loss account for the year ended 31 December 2005

	£000	£000
Revenue		576
Other income		107
		683
Changes in stocks	(65)	
Raw material and consumables used	(100)	
Employee expenses	(91)	
Depreciation and amortisation	(22)	
Impairment of property, plant and equipment	(25)	
Other expenses	(10)	
Finance costs	(8)	
Total expenses		(321)
Profit before tax		362
Corporation tax		(120)
Profit for the period		242

The second way to analyse expenses is according to business functions, such as administrative activities, distribution and finance. Example 5.2 below sets out a profit and loss account that analyses expenses in this way.

Example 5.2

Degas plc
Profit and loss account for the year ended 31 May 2005

	£000	£000
Revenue		690
Cost of sales		(350)
		340
Other income		20
		360
Distribution costs	(102)	
Administrative expenses	(115)	
Other expenses	(14)	
Finance costs	(20)	
Total expenses		(251)
Profit before tax		109
Corporation tax		(24)
Profit for the period		85

The choice between the two approaches will depend on which the directors believe will provide the more relevant and reliable information. This second form of presentation is potentially more relevant to users. It reveals how much of the revenue generated was absorbed by particular functions, which may provide a better insight to the efficiency of the business. However, it is not always easy to attribute costs to particular functional areas, particularly where facilities and other resources are being shared. If this second approach is adopted, additional information concerning the nature of the expenses, including depreciation charges and employee costs, must also be shown. This is because this kind of information can be useful in predicting future cash flows.

The balance sheet

IAS 1 prescribes the minimum information that should be presented on the face of the balance sheet. This includes the following:

- property, plant and equipment
- investment property
- intangible assets
- financial assets (such as shares and loans held)
- stocks (inventories)
- trade debtors and other receivables
- cash and cash equivalents
- trade creditors and other payables
- provisions
- financial liabilities (excluding payables and provisions shown above)
- tax liabilities and
- issued capital and reserves (equity).

Additional information should be also shown where it is relevant to an understanding of the financial position of the business.

The standard normally requires a distinction to be made on the balance sheet between current assets and non-current assets and between current liabilities and non-current liabilities. However, where a company considers that more reliable and relevant information will be presented by ordering the items according to their liquidity, it is permitted to do this. The standard does not prescribe a format for the balance sheet. Thus, the vertical format that we have been using so far in the book, and which has been almost universally adopted by UK companies to date, is acceptable. Example 5.3 below illustrates a balance sheet drawn up in accordance with IAS 1.

Example 5.3

Jhamna plc
Balance sheet as at 31 December 2005

	£m	£m	£m
Non-current assets			
Property, plant and equipment		420	
Goodwill		125	
Other intangible assets		40	585
Current assets			
Stocks (inventories)	41		
Trade debtors (receivables)	139		
Cash and cash equivalents	20	200	
Less **Current liabilities**			
Trade creditors (payables)	36		
Short-term borrowings	50		
Current portion of long-term borrowings	43		
Current corporation tax payable	12	141	
Net current assets			59
Total assets less current liabilities			644
Less **Non-current liabilities**			
Long-term borrowings	250		
Long-term provisions	83		
Total non-current liabilities			333
			311
Equity			
Share capital			150
Retained earnings			70
Other reserves			91
			311

The sub-classification of some of the items shown above may be necessary, either to comply with particular standards or because of their size or nature. For example, sub-classifications are required for certain assets such as property, plant and equipment and stocks as well as for provisions and reserves. In addition, details of share capital, such as the number of authorised and issued shares, and their par value, must also be shown. However, to avoid cluttering up the balance sheet, this additional information can be shown in the notes.

Statement of changes in equity

The **statement of changes in equity** aims to help users to understand the changes in share capital and reserves that took place during the period. It reconciles the capital and reserves figures at the beginning of the period with those at the end of the period.

This is achieved by showing the effect on the capital and reserves of all revenue and expenses, including gains and losses, as well as the effect of share issues and purchases during the period.

To show the effect on capital and reserves of gains and losses, we first need to understand how they are reported in the financial statements. The general rule is that the profit and loss account (income statement) should show all income and expenses, including gains and losses, for the period, that have already been realised. This contrasts with gains arising from an upward valuation of an asset that remains with the company. These do not affect the profit and loss account, but go directly to a revaluation reserve. We have seen in an earlier chapter, one example of where a gain, or loss, arising is not passed through the profit and loss account.

Activity 5.3

Can you think of this example?

It is where a business revalues its land and buildings, the gain, or loss, arising is not shown in the profit and loss account. It is transferred to a revaluation reserve, which forms part of the equity (capital and reserves). The rule does not just relate to land and buildings, but these types of asset are, in practice, far and away the most common examples of such unrealised gains.

Another exception to the general rule, which has not been mentioned so far, is exchange differences that arise when the results of foreign operations are translated into UK currency. Once again, any gain, or loss, bypasses the profit and loss account and is taken directly to a currency translation reserve. In the statement of changes in equity, we need to take account of *all* gains and losses that have arisen during the period. Thus, movements in the revaluation reserve and translation reserve must be identified in addition to profits (or losses) reported in the profit and loss account.

To see how a statement of changes in equity for a company may be prepared, let us consider Example 5.4 below.

Example 5.4

At 1 January 2005 Miro plc had the following share capital and reserves:

Miro plc

	£m
Share capital (£1 ordinary shares)	100
Revaluation reserve	20
Translation reserve	40
Retained earnings	150
	310

During 2005, the company made a profit after tax from normal business operations of £42m and reported a revaluation gain on freehold land and buildings of £120m. A loss on exchange differences on translating the results of foreign operations of £10m was also reported. To strengthen its balance sheet, the company

→

Example 5.4 continued

issued 50m new shares during the year at a premium of £0.40. The dividends for the year were £27m.

The above information for 2005 can be set out in a statement of changes in equity as follows:

Statement of changes in equity for the year ended 31 December 2005

	Share capital	Share premium	Revaluation reserve	Translation reserve	Retained earnings	Total
	£m	£m	£m	£m	£m	£m
Balance as at 1 January 2005	100	–	20	40	150	310
Changes in equity for 2005						
Gain on revaluation of properties	–	–	120	–	–	120
Exchange differences on translation of foreign operations	–	–	–	(10)	–	(10)
Net income recognised directly to equity	–	–	120	(10)	–	110
Profit for the period	–	–	–	–	42	42
Total recognised income and expense for the period	–	–	120	(10)	42	152
Dividends	–	–	–	–	(27)	(27)
Issue of share capital	50	20	–	–	–	70
Balance at 31 December 2005	150	20	140	30	165	505

It is probably worth mentioning the treatment of dividends at this point. We can see that, in the example above, dividends are shown separately in the statement of changes in equity. However, we may recall that, in Chapter 4, dividends were shown on the face of the profit and loss account when illustrating the format of this statement for limited companies. In fact, both approaches are equally acceptable. IAS 1 allows a choice as to the way in which the dividends for distribution are disclosed. They can be shown:

- on the face of the profit and loss account (income statement); or
- in the statement of changes in equity; or
- in the notes.

Dividends that are proposed during the year, but which are not recognised for distribution, must only be disclosed in the notes.

Cash flow statement

The cash flow statement tries to help users to assess the ability of a company to generate cash flows, also to assess the requirements for these cash flows. The presentation requirements for this statement are set out in IAS 7 *Cash Flow Statements*, which we shall consider in some detail in Chapter 6.

Explanatory notes

The notes play an important role in helping users to understand the financial statements. They will normally contain the following information:

- a statement that the financial statements comply with relevant IFRSs;

- a summary of the measurement bases used and other significant accounting policies applied (for example, the basis of stock valuation);
- supporting information relating to items appearing on the profit and loss account, balance sheet, statement of changes in equity or cash flow statement (as mentioned above); and
- other disclosures such as future contractual commitments that have not been recognised and management's objectives and policies.

General points

The standard requires that the financial statements be prepared annually, as a minimum, and that comparative figures be provided for the previous period. The standard provides support for three key accounting conventions when preparing the financial statements. These are:

- going concern
- accruals (except for the cash flow statement)
- consistency.

These conventions were covered in Chapters 2 and 3.

To improve the transparency of financial statements, the standard states that:

- offsetting liabilities against assets, or expenses against income, is not allowed. Thus, it is not acceptable, for example, to offset a bank overdraft against a positive bank balance; and
- material items must be shown separately.

Directors' report

In addition to preparing the financial statements discussed above, the law requires the directors to prepare an annual report to shareholders and other interested parties. This report contains information of both a financial and a non-financial nature and goes beyond that which is contained in the financial statements. The information disclosed covers a variety of topics including details of share ownership, details of directors and their financial interests in the company, employment policies, and charitable and political donations. The auditors do not carry out an audit of the **directors' report**. However, they will check to see that the information in the report is consistent with that contained within the audited financial statements.

Auditors

Shareholders are required to elect a qualified and independent person or, more usually, a firm, to act as **auditors**. The auditors' main duty is to make a report as to whether, in their opinion, the financial statements do what they are supposed to do, namely show a true and fair view of the financial performance, position and cash flows of the company by complying with relevant accounting standards and statutory requirements. To be in a position to form such an opinion, auditors must scrutinise both the annual financial statements prepared by the directors and the evidence on which they are based. The auditors' opinion must be included with the accounting statements that are sent to the shareholders and to the Registrar of Companies.

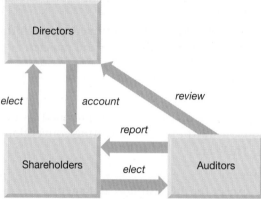

Figure 5.2	The relationship between the shareholders, the directors and the auditors

The directors are appointed by the shareholders to manage the company on the shareholders' behalf. The directors are required to report each year to the shareholders, principally by means of accounting statements, on the company's performance, position and cash flows. To give greater confidence in the statements, the shareholders also appoint auditors to investigate the reports and to express an opinion on their reliability.

The relationship between the shareholders, the directors and the auditors is illustrated in Figure 5.2. This shows that the shareholders elect the directors to act on their behalf, in the day-to-day running of the company. The directors are required to 'account' to the shareholders on the performance, position and cash flows of the company, on an annual basis. The shareholders also elect auditors, whose role it is to give the shareholders an impression of the extent to which they can regard as reliable the accounting statements prepared by the directors.

The framework of principles

In Chapters 2 and 3, we came across various accounting conventions such as prudence, historic cost, going concern and so on. These conventions were developed as a practical response to particular problems that were confronted when preparing financial statements. They have stood the test of time and are still of value to preparers today. However, they do not provide, and were never designed to provide, a framework of principles to guide the development of financial statements. As we grapple with increasingly complex financial reporting problems, the need to have a sound understanding of *why* we account for things in a particular way becomes more and more pressing. Knowing *why* we account, rather than simply *how* we account, is vitally important if we are to improve the quality of financial statements.

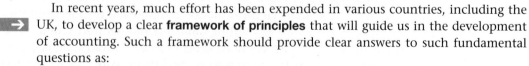 In recent years, much effort has been expended in various countries, including the UK, to develop a clear **framework of principles** that will guide us in the development of accounting. Such a framework should provide clear answers to such fundamental questions as:

● Who are the main users of financial statements?
● What is the purpose of financial statements?

- What qualities should financial information possess?
- What are the main elements of financial statements?
- How should these elements be defined, recognised and measured?

If these questions can be answered, accounting rule makers (including the IASB) will be in a stronger position to identify best practice and to develop more coherent rules. This should, in turn, increase the credibility of financial reports in the eyes of users. It may even help reduce the possible number of rules, because some issues may be resolved by reference to the application of general principles rather than the generation of further rules.

The IASB framework

The quest for a framework of accounting principles began in earnest in the 1970s when the Financial Accounting Standards Board (FASB) in the US devoted a very large amount of time and resources to this endeavour. The FASB's efforts resulted in a broad framework of principles that other rule-making bodies, including the IASB, have drawn upon when developing their own frameworks.

The IASB has produced a 'Framework for the Preparation and Presentation of Financial Statements', which begins by discussing the main user groups and their needs. This is well-trodden territory and the various groups and needs identified are broadly in line with those set out in the sections on this topic in Chapter 1. The framework goes on to identify the objective of financial statements, which is:

> to provide information about the financial position, performance and changes in financial position of an enterprise that is useful to a wide range of users in making economic decisions.

This reflects the mainstream view and is very similar to the objective of financial statements that others have developed in recent years.

The IASB framework sets out the qualitative characteristics that make financial statements useful. The main characteristics identified are relevance, reliability, comparability, and understandability, all of which were discussed in Chapter 1. The framework also identifies the main elements of financial statements. These are assets, liabilities, equity, income and expense, and definitions for each element are provided. The definitions adopted hold no surprises and are very similar to those adopted by other rule-making bodies and to those discussed earlier, in Chapters 2 and 3.

The IASB framework identifies different valuation bases in use but does not indicate a preference for a particular valuation method. It simply notes that historic cost is the most widely used method of valuation. Finally, the framework discusses the type of capital base that a business should try to maintain. It includes a discussion of the two main types of capital base – financial capital and physical capital – but, again, expresses no preference as to which should be maintained. The IASB framework does not have the same legal status as an IASB standard. Nevertheless, it should provide a basis for deciding on how to deal with accounting issues, particularly where there is no relevant accounting standard that can be used.

Overall, the IASB framework has provoked little debate and the principles and definitions adopted enjoy widespread acceptance. There has been some criticism, mainly from academics, that the framework is really a descriptive document and does not provide theoretical underpinning to the financial statements. There has also been some criticism of the definitions of the elements of the financial statements. However, these criticisms have not sparked a major controversy.

Segmental financial reports

Most large businesses are engaged in a number of different activities, with each activity having different levels of risk, growth and profitability. The problem for users of financial statements is that information relating to each type of activity will normally be aggregated in the financial statements to provide an overall picture of financial performance and position. This aggregation of information makes it difficult to undertake comparisons between businesses. The activities undertaken by a large business are likely to differ in range and/or scale from those of other businesses.

Where a business operates in different geographical markets, the same sort of arguments apply. The markets of different countries may well have different levels of risk, profitability and growth associated with them, and aggregation will obscure these differences. It will not be possible, for example, to assess the impact on a business of political changes, or changes in inflation or exchange rates that relate to a particular country, or geographical region, unless the degree of exposure to the country, or region, is known.

To undertake any meaningful analysis of financial performance and position, it is usually necessary to disaggregate the information contained within the financial statements. By breaking down the financial information according to business activities and/or geographical markets, we can evaluate the relative risks and profitability of each segment and make useful comparisons with other businesses or other business segments. We can also see the trend of performance for each segment over time and so determine more accurately the likely growth prospects for the business as a whole. We should also be able to assess more easily the impact on the overall business, of changes in market conditions relating to particular activities.

Disclosure of information relating to the performance of each segment may also help to improve the efficiency of the business by keeping managers on their toes. Business segments that are performing poorly will be revealed and this should put pressure on managers to take corrective action. In addition, where a business segment has been sold, the shareholders will be better placed to assess the wisdom of the managers' decision.

Segmental reporting: regulations and practice

An IASB standard (IAS 14 *Segment Reporting*) requires that large listed companies disclose segmental information according to each business segment *and* to each geographical region. Both forms of segmentation are regarded as important to users. A business segment, for the purposes of the standard, is a part of the business that can be separately identified and which provides an individual product or service, or a group of related products or services. A geographical segment is a part of the business that can be separately identified and which provides products or services within a particular economic environment. The environment may comprise a region within a country, a country or a group of countries. One problem that must be confronted when identifying geographical segments is whether the business should be segmented according to where the *operations* are located or where the *markets* are located. The relevant standard allows either approach to be used but states that the choice should be based on the way in which the business is organised and structured.

For reporting purposes, it is necessary to establish whether it is the products or services offered or the geographical regions in which the company operates that has the bigger impact on the risks and returns of the company. Whichever has the bigger impact will determine whether business segments or geographical segments are identified as the primary segments. This identification is important because the disclosure requirements are greater for the primary segments than for the secondary segments. The way in which a business is organised and structured should, again, provide a useful indicator.

The following are the main items of information that should be disclosed for the primary segments:

- revenue, distinguishing between revenue from external customers and revenue from other segments of the business;
- assets;
- capital expenditure for the period;
- depreciation and amortisation;
- segment result (that is, segment revenue less segment expenses); and
- liabilities.

For secondary segments, only the first three items identified above need be disclosed.

Example 5.5 provides an illustrative **segmental financial report** for a business where the business segments are the primary segments. Following the example, we shall discuss some of the key points that are raised.

Example 5.5

Goya plc
Segmental report for the year ended 30 June 2005

	Publishing	Film making	Eliminations	Consolidation (Total)
	£m	£m	£m	£m
Revenue				
External sales	150	200		350
Inter-segment sales	20	10	(30)	—
Total revenue	170	210	(30)	350
Result				
Segment result	15	19	(2)	32
Unallocated expenses				14
Operating profit				18
Interest expense				(6)
Net profit before tax				12
Corporation tax				(3)
Net profit				9
Other information				
Segment assets	74	86		160
Unallocated assets				32
Consolidated total assets				192
Segment liabilities	24	21		45
Unallocated liabilities				30
Consolidated total liabilities				75
Capital expenditure	10	8		
Depreciation	15	21		

We can see that information relating to each segment is shown as well as information relating to the business as a whole. External sales and inter-segment sales for each segment appear separately; however, only the combined external sales for the segments appear in the far right-hand column. This is because the inter-segment sales will cancel one another out when calculating the sales for the business as a whole. Similarly, the combined operating profit of each segment *less* the inter-segment profit will appear as the operating profit for the business as a whole.

Unallocated expenses appearing in the above report are those which are not attributable to a particular segment or which cannot be allocated to a segment on any reasonable basis. Note that these expenses have not been apportioned between the two segments but have been deducted from the results of the business as a whole.

Activity 5.4

What kind of items do you think may appear as unallocated expenses?

These items may include:

- head office expenses
- research and development costs
- marketing expenses
- finance charges.

You may have thought of others.

Unallocated assets and liabilities are those which are not attributable to a particular segment or which cannot be allocated to a particular segment on any reasonable basis. Head office buildings may provide an example of such an unallocated asset and loan capital may provide an example of an unallocated liability.

A similar layout to the report shown above can be used to show geographical segments, where they are regarded as the primary segments.

Problems of segmental reporting

There are various problems associated with preparing segmental reports, not least of which is the problem of identifying a segment. The relevant standard mentions some of the factors that should be taken into account when identifying segments; however, a fair amount of judgement by the directors will often be required. Although this may be the only sensible course of action, it does mean that comparisons between businesses may still be difficult because of different judgements being applied within different companies.

Many segments do not operate in a completely independent manner and there may be a significant amount of sales between segments. If this is the case, the **transfer price** of the goods or services between segments can have a substantial impact on the reported profits of each segment. Indeed, it may be possible to manipulate profit figures for each segment through the use of particular transfer pricing policies. For this reason, the international accounting standard requires that the basis for inter-segment transfers must be disclosed.

Finally, there may be problems where expenses incurred relate to more than one business segment. The way in which these costs are treated may vary between businesses and so may hinder comparisons.

Self-assessment question 5.1

Segmental information relating to J. Baxter plc, which has operations in three different countries, for the year to 30 April 2005 is shown below.

	UK £m	France £m	Italy £m	Eliminations £m	Consolidation £m
Revenue					
External sales	230	180	360		
Inter-segment sales	40	20	30	(90)	
Total revenue	270	200	390	(90)	770
Result					
Segment result	34	30	8	(6)	66
Unallocated expenses					18
Operating profit					48
Interest expense					(16)
Corporation tax					(6)
Net profit					26
Other information					
Segment assets	129	150	116		395
Unallocated assets					36
Consolidated total assets					431
Segment liabilities	35	28	22		85
Unallocated liabilities					40
Consolidated total liabilities					125
Capital expenditure	20	15	35		
Depreciation	28	35	11		

Required:
Analyse the performance of each of the business segments for the year and comment on your results.

Operating and financial review

Businesses have become more complex over time and, as a consequence, their financial statements have become more difficult to understand. Businesses can organise themselves in different ways, engage in a variety of financial and investing activities and enter into different types of trading relationships with both customers and other businesses. This can make it very difficult for users to interpret the figures set out in annual financial statements. As a result, there is now a need for a supplementary report to be provided, in narrative form, to help users to get to grips with the financial statements. This narrative report should provide a commentary from the directors on the performance and position of the business and it is likely to be of particular value when looking at the financial statements of large businesses.

 In the UK, the Accounting Standards Board (ASB) has recognised the need for such a report and has recommended that large businesses prepare an **operating and financial review (OFR)** each year. This report should contain a discussion of the:

- nature of the business, its objectives and how it seeks to achieve those objectives;
- performance of the business during the period under review and the factors affecting performance, including risks facing the business; and
- financial position of the business and the factors that affect it or are likely to affect it.

Each of these elements is discussed in more detail below.

Activity 5.5

What characteristics should the information contained within the OFR possess?

To be useful, the information should contain the characteristics for accounting information in general, which we identified in Chapter 1. Thus, the information should be relevant, understandable, reliable and comparable. The fact that we are dealing with a narrative report does not alter the need for these characteristics to be present.

We shall now look at the main elements of the OFR.

The business, its objectives and strategy

The OFR should identify and discuss the nature of the business to help set the context within which the financial statements are considered. This may include a discussion of the industries in which it operates, the products or services provided, the structure of the business, and so on. The OFR should also discuss the financial and non-financial objectives of the business, how these objectives will be achieved and how this achievement will be measured. **Real World 5.2** provides an example of how one well-known company discussed its objectives.

REAL WORLD 5.2

What's brewing at S&N?

Scottish and Newcastle plc (S and N) is a large brewer. In its OFR for 2003, the company states its objective as follows:

> S and N's ultimate objective is sustained value creation. We shall focus on driving value from our existing business, maximising growth and operational efficiencies. We shall apply rigorous criteria to possible developments into carefully selected markets.

The company then goes on to state how this objective will be measured.

> In a business environment where capital is rationed, the level of return on invested capital is the key measurement. S and N monitors its return on capital rigorously and evaluates all budget and capital expenditure against the cost of capital with the aim of maximising economic profit.

Finally, the company indicates how this objective will be achieved.

> The key value drivers in the brewing industry are organic sales growth, brand development and operational excellence in brewing and distribution. We will focus more aggressively on these through sales growth and improved margins.

Source: Scottish and Newcastle plc Annual Report and Accounts 2003.

The operating review

The operating review is designed to help explain to the user the main influences on the performance of the business. It should discuss the main factors that underlie the business and any changes that have occurred, or are likely to occur, to these factors. The following areas have been identified as providing a framework for the operating review.

Performance in the period

This section should discuss the significant features of the performance of the various business segments in relation to the business as a whole. It should cover all relevant aspects of performance and should include an analysis of the effect on current and future performance of significant changes within the industry or in the environment, such as changes in market conditions, new products, fluctuations in exchange rates, and so on.

Real World 5.3 provides an example of how one company discussed its performance.

REAL WORLD 5.3

Brandon Hire not much higher

Brandon Hire plc operates tool hire and lifting equipment branches in England and Wales. In its operating review for 2002, the company discussed its performance for the year as follows:

> Brandon Tool Hire had a mildly disappointing year. Turnover increased by 10% but this was largely attributable to new and acquired branches. In 2001 we achieved organic growth of 14%. In 2002 we anticipated organic growth of 6% but realised a much smaller increase and were too slow in adjusting our cost base. This was the primary contributor to our fall in operating profits.
>
> Trading reflected our usual seasonality with a stronger second half. We experienced two particularly poor months during the year: June was exceptionally weak due to the Jubilee and the World Cup which disrupted many of our customers' work patterns, while December was also poor with many customers starting their Christmas break much earlier than usual. Encouragingly, there was a return to organic growth of year-on-year turnover in the second half.

Source: Brandon Hire plc Annual Report and Accounts 2002.

Returns to shareholders

This section should include a discussion of earnings per share, profits for the year and dividends. It should also indicate the dividend policy that has been adopted. Where a discussion of changes in the share price is included, a comparison of these changes in relation to those of similar businesses should be provided.

Dynamics of the business

This section should include a discussion of the main factors that are likely to influence future results. It will also consider the main risks facing the business and indicate how they are managed. These risks and uncertainties may cover a wide range of matters and could include inflation, skills shortages, product liability, scarcity of raw materials, and so on. There should also be some discussion of the strengths and resources of the business that are not shown in the balance sheet such as market position, customer relationships, business reputation, research and development, and so on.

Real World 5.4 continues with the example of Brandon Hire plc by showing how the company discussed its customer strengths.

REAL WORLD 5.4

Brandon Hire customer strengths

In its operating review for 2002, Brandon Hire plc outlines its customer strengths as follows:

Our proposition for our customers is strong:

● we have a good reputation for service
● we have a full range of well-maintained equipment
● we have high density of coverage in the areas where we operate
● we have invested heavily in reducing our customers' administration costs.

Like many businesses we have a lot of customer data and we are now in a position to use that data to generate more business from existing customers, to target specific areas for new customers, and to assess the profitability to us of individual customers.

Source: Brandon Hire plc Annual Report and Accounts 2002.

Investment for the future

This section should include commentary on how the directors plan to maintain or improve the business through investment. This investment may take various forms, such as building brands through marketing and advertising campaigns, staff development, research, and so on. Current and planned levels of capital expenditure should also be discussed. The benefits from these investments should be explained in relation to the objectives of the business.

Real World 5.5 reveals how Brandon Hire plc seeks to expand its business in the future.

REAL WORLD 5.5

Expanding the business

In its operating review for 2002, Brandon Hire plc includes a section on the expansion of its network of branches and states:

We expect to continue our strategy of using a combination of acquisitions and new branches to strengthen our position in areas where we currently operate and to increase the geographical area that we cover.

Source: Brandon Hire plc Annual Report and Accounts 2002.

The financial review

The second part of the OFR, the financial review, is concerned with explaining the capital structure of the business, its treasury policy and the influences on its financial position. The following areas have been identified as providing a framework for the review.

Capital structure and treasury policy

This should involve a discussion of the capital structure policies of the business (that is, the mix of share capital, reserves and long-term borrowing) along with any relevant ratios. Treasury policy is concerned with such matters as managing cash, obtaining finance and managing relationships with financial institutions. Possible areas for discussion in the financial review include the ways in which treasury activities are managed, the currencies in which borrowings are made and the way in which currency risk and interest rate risk is managed.

Real World 5.6 reveals how Brandon Hire plc disclosed information relating to interest rate risk.

 REAL WORLD 5.6

Interest rate risk

Brandon Hire plc included the following statement on interest rate risk in its 2002 financial review:

> The company finances its operations through a mixture of retained profits, bank borrowings and hire purchase borrowings. . . . The Board considers that these arrangements provide an appropriate blend of certainty and flexibility in respect of interest rate risk. At the year end, 48% of the gross borrowings were at fixed rates and 52% at variable rates.

Source: Brandon Hire plc Annual Report and Accounts 2002.

Cash flows

This section should include a discussion of the cash inflows either from customers or from other sources and the special factors, if any, that influenced these. The main cash outflows for the period should also be identified and discussed. **Real World 5.7** reveals how one major company disclosed information concerning cash flows for the period.

 REAL WORLD 5.7

Cash flows at GUS

GUS plc, which owns a number of major businesses including Argos and Homebase, included the following statement on cash flows in its 2003 financial review:

> Cash flow before acquisitions, disposals and dividends amounted to £616m compared to £478m in the previous year. Cash flow benefited from the growth in profits in the year and from tight control over working capital which was £201m lower despite the growth in the Argos store card loan book. Capital expenditure grew by £7m to £329m and was equivalent to 134% of the depreciation charge in 2003.
>
> With the £902m purchase of Homebase, there was a net cash outflow of £802m for the year after the payment of dividends, the repayment of securitised loans and acquisitions and disposals.

Source: GUS plc Annual Report 2003.

Current liquidity

The liquidity at the end of the accounting period should be discussed, along with comments on the level of borrowing at the end of the period. The amounts required to meet future investment commitments should be mentioned. Furthermore, any loan conditions or restrictions on the ability to transfer funds within the business should be mentioned.

Going concern

The OFR should contain a confirmation, if appropriate, that the business is a going concern.

We can see from the list of headings above that the OFR can be quite a long report – often between five and ten pages in length. However, for many large businesses, the OFR is really an incremental rather than a radical change in reporting practice. The OFR builds on best practice, as many of the topics identified were previously contained within the chairman's report or directors' report.

Summary financial statements

Though directors of all companies are required to make a set of the company financial statements available to each shareholder, these statements can be a summarised version of the full version that follows the complete legal requirements. The reasons for not requiring that the full version be sent to all shareholders are broadly that:

- many shareholders do not wish to receive the full version, because they may not have the time, interest or skill necessary to be able to gain much from it;
- directors could improve their communication with their shareholders by providing something closer to the needs of many shareholders;
- reproducing and posting copies of the full version is expensive and a waste of resources where particular shareholders do not wish to receive it.

 Many companies send all of their private shareholders a copy of the **summary financial statements**, with a clear message that the full versions are available on request. Each full version is, however, required for filing with the Registrar of Companies.

Accounting rules and creative accounting

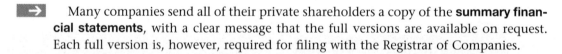

Despite the proliferation of accounting rules and the independent checks that are imposed, there are still concerns over the quality of company financial statements. There is evidence that the directors of some companies have employed particular accounting policies or structured particular transactions in such a way that portrays a picture of financial health that is in line with what they would like users to see rather than what is a true and fair view of financial position and performance. This practice is referred to as **creative accounting** and it poses a major problem for accounting rulemakers and for society generally.

Activity 5.6

Why might the directors of a company engage in creative accounting?

There are many reasons and these include:

- to get around restrictions (for example, to report sufficient profit to pay a dividend);
- to avoid government action (for example, the taxation of excessive profits);
- to hide poor management decisions;
- to achieve sales or profit targets, thereby ensuring that performance bonuses are paid to the directors;
- to attract new share capital or loan capital by showing a healthy financial position; and
- to satisfy the demands of major investors concerning levels of return.

Creative accounting methods

The particular methods that unscrupulous directors use to manipulate the financial statements are many and varied. Some of these methods concern the overstatement of revenue. These methods often involve the early recognition of sales income or the reporting of sales transactions that have no real substance. **Real World 5.8** provides examples of both types of revenue.

REAL WORLD 5.8

Overstating revenue

Hollow swaps: telecoms companies sell useless fibre optic capacity to each other in order to generate revenues on their income statements.

Channel stuffing: a company floods the market with more products than its distributors can sell, artificially boosting its sales. An international condom maker shifted £60 million in excess stock on to trade customers. Also known as 'trade loading'.

Round tripping: also known as 'in-and-out trading'. Used to notorious effect by Enron. Two or more traders buy and sell energy among themselves for the same price and at the same time. Inflates trading volumes and makes participants appear to be doing more business than they really are.

Pre-despatching: goods such as carpets are marked as 'sold' as soon as an order is placed. . . . This inflates sales and profits.

Note that some of the techniques used, such as round tripping, may inflate the sales for a period but do not inflate reported profits. Nevertheless, this may still benefit the company. Sales growth has become an important yardstick of performance for some investors and can affect the value they place on the company.

The revenue figure in the profit and loss account seems to be a popular target for creative accounting practices. It has been claimed that more than half the accounting irregularities investigated have been concerned with the overstatement of revenue. **Real World 5.9** provides an example of the impact of the early recognition of revenue on the measurement of performance.

REAL WORLD 5.9

Not to be copied

One case of overstating revenue is alleged to have been carried out by the Xerox Corporation, a large US company and a leading player in the photocopying business. It is alleged that the company brought forward revenues in order to improve profits as its fortunes declined in the late 1990s. These revenues related to copier equipment sales, particularly in Latin America. To correct for the overstatement of revenues, Xerox had to restate its equipment sales figures for a five-year period. The result was a reversal in reported revenues of a staggering $6.4bn, although $5.1bn was reallocated to other revenues as a result. This restatement was one of the largest in US corporate history.

In June 2002 the company paid a fine of $10m but denied any wrongdoing.

Sources: Based on information from 'Can't tell the scandals without a scorecard', *The Wall Street Journal Europe*, 3–5 October 2003, p. A5; 'Xerox acts to put itself on a firmer footing', FT.com, 28 June 2002.

Some creative accounting methods focus on the manipulation of expenses, and certain types of expenses are particularly vulnerable. These are expenses that rely heavily on the judgement of directors concerning estimates of the future or concerning the most suitable accounting policy to adopt.

Activity 5.7

Can you identify the kind of expenses where the directors must use judgement in the ways described?

These include certain expenses that we discussed in Chapter 3, such as:

● depreciation of property, plant and equipment;
● amortisation of intangible assets, such as goodwill;
● stock costing methods; and
● provisions for doubtful debts.

By changing estimates about the future (for example, the useful life or residual value of an asset), or by changing accounting policies (for example, switching from FIFO to AVCO) it may be possible to derive an expense figure, and consequently a profit figure, that suits the directors.

The incorrect capitalisation of expenses may also be used as a means of manipulation. Expenses may be treated as if they were amounts incurred to acquire or develop non-current assets, rather than amounts consumed during the period. Companies that build their own assets are often best placed to undertake this form of malpractice.

Activity 5.8

What would be the effect on the profits and total assets of a business of incorrectly capitalising expenses?

Both would be artificially inflated. Reported profits would increase because expenses would be reduced. Total assets would be increased because the expenses would be incorrectly treated as non-current assets.

REAL WORLD 5.10

Sorry – wrong numbers

One particularly notorious case of capitalising expenses is alleged to have occurred in the financial statements of WorldCom (now renamed MCI). This company, which is a large US telecommunications business, is alleged to have overstated profits by treating certain operating expenses, such as basic network maintenance, as capital expenditure. This happened over a fifteen-month period during 2001 and 2002. To correct for this over-statement, net profits had to be reduced by a massive $3.8bn.

Source: Based on Two personal views on WorldCom FT.com, 27 June 2002.

Some creative accounting methods focus on the concealment of losses or liabilities. The financial statements can look much healthier if these can somehow be eliminated. One way of doing this is to create a 'separate' entity that will take over the losses or liabilities.

REAL WORLD 5.11

For a very special purpose

Perhaps the most well-known case of concealment of losses and liabilities concerned the Enron Corporation. This was a large US energy business that used 'special purpose entities' (SPEs) as a means of concealment. SPEs were used by Enron to rid itself of problem assets that were falling in value, such as its broadband operations. In addition, liabilities were transferred to these entities to help Enron's balance sheet look healthier. The company had to keep its gearing ratios (the relationship between borrowing and equity) within particular limits to satisfy credit-rating agencies, and SPEs were used to achieve this. The SPEs used for concealment purposes were not independent of the company and should have been consolidated in the balance sheet of Enron, along with their losses and liabilities.

When these, and other accounting irregularities, were discovered in 2001, there was a restatement of Enron's financial performance and position to reflect the consolidation of the SPEs, which had previously been omitted. As a result of this restatement, the company recognised $591m in losses over the preceding four years and an additional $628m worth of liabilities at the end of 2000.

The company collapsed at the end of 2001.

Source: 'The rise and fall of Enron', C. W. Thomas, *Journal of Accountancy*, Vol. 194, no. 3, April 2002. This article represents the opinions of the author(s) and are not necessarily those of the Texas Society of Certified Public Accountants.

Finally, creative accounting may involve the overstatement of asset values. This may involve revaluing the assets using figures that do not correspond to their fair market values. It may also involve the capitalising of costs that should have been written off as expenses, as described earlier.

Checking for creative accounting

When examining the financial statements of a business, a number of checks may be carried out on the financial statements to help gain a 'feel' for their reliability. These can include checks to see whether:

- the reported profits are significantly higher than the operating cash flows for the period, which may suggest that profits have been overstated;
- the corporation tax charge is low in relation to reported profits, which may suggest, again, that profits are overstated, although there may be other, more innocent explanations;
- the valuation methods used for assets held are based on historic cost or current values, and if the latter approach has been used why and how the current values were determined;
- there have been any changes in accounting policies over the period, particular in key areas such as revenue recognition, stock valuation and depreciation;
- the accounting policies adopted are in line with those adopted by the rest of the industry;
- the auditors' report gives a 'clean bill of health' to the financial statements; and
- the 'small print', that is the notes to the financial statements, is not being used to hide significant events or changes.

Although such checks are useful, they are not guaranteed to identify creative accounting practices, some of which may be very deeply seated.

Creative accounting and economic growth

A few years ago, there was a wave of creative accounting scandals in both the US and Europe but this now appears to have subsided. It seems that accounting scandals are becoming less frequent and that the quality of financial statements is improving. It is to be hoped that trust among users in the integrity of financial statements will soon be restored. As a result of the actions taken by various regulatory bodies and by accounting rule-makers, creative accounting has become a more risky and difficult process for those who attempt it. However, it will never disappear completely and a further wave of creative accounting scandals may occur in the future. The recent wave coincided with a period of strong economic growth, and during good economic times, investors and auditors become less vigilant. Thus, the opportunity to manipulate the figures becomes easier. We must not, therefore, become too complacent. Things may change again when we next experience a period of strong growth.

SUMMARY

The main points of this chapter may be summarised as follows:

The directors' have a duty to

● Maintain accounting records.

● Prepare and publish financial statements and a directors' report.

Accounting rules are necessary to

● Avoid unacceptable accounting practices.

● Improve comparability of financial statements.

Accounting rules in the UK

● Until January 2005, the main sources of accounting rules were company law, the Accounting Standards Board and the Financial Services Authority.

● Since January 2005, the International Accounting Standards Board has become an important source of rules.

Presenting financial statements

● IAS 1 sets out the structure and content of financial statements.

● It identifies five financial statements: the profit and loss account (income statement), balance sheet, statement of changes in equity, cash flow statement and explanatory notes.

● The overriding consideration is to provide a fair representation of the financial health of a company and this will normally be achieved by adherence to relevant IASB standards.

● IAS 1 identifies information to be shown in the various financial statements.

● It also identifies some of the principles to be followed in preparing the statements.

Other statutory reports

● The directors' report contains information of a financial and a non-financial nature, which goes beyond that contained in the financial statements.

● The auditors' report provides an opinion by an independent auditor concerning whether the financial statements provide a true and fair view of the financial health of a business.

Framework of principles

● Helps to underpin accounting rules.

● The IASB framework identifies and discusses the users of financial statements, the objective of financial statements, the qualitative characteristics of financial statements, the elements of financial statements, different valuation bases, and different capital maintenance bases.

● The IASB framework draws on earlier work by other rule-making bodies.

Additional financial reports

● Segmental reports disaggregate information on the financial statements to help achieve a better understanding of financial health.

- Companies can be segmented according to products or services and according to geographical operations.
- An IASB standard requires certain information relating to each segment to be shown.
- Identifying a segment and allocating costs between segments can raise problems.
- An operating and financial review (OFR) discusses the nature of the business and its objectives, the performance of the business for the period and the financial position of the business.
- In the UK, the ASB has produced guidelines on the preparation of an OFR.
- Summary financial statements are available to investors who do not require the full set of financial statements.

Creative accounting

- Despite the accounting rules in place there have been recent examples of creative accounting by directors.
- This involves using accounting practices to show what the directors would like users to see rather than what is a fair representation of reality.
- There are various checks that can be carried out to the financial statements to see whether creative accounting practices may have been used.

Key terms

Accounting (financial reporting) standards p. 139	**Framework of principles** p. 150
International accounting (financial reporting) standards p. 140	**Segmental financial report** p. 153
	Transfer price p. 154
Statement of changes in equity p. 146	**Operating and financial review (OFR)** p. 155
Directors' report p. 149	**Summary financial statement** p. 160
Auditor p. 149	**Creative accounting** p. 160

Further reading

If you would like to explore the topics covered in this chapter in more depth, we recommend the following books:

Corporate Financial Accounting and Reporting, *Sutton T.*, 2nd edn, Financial Times Prentice Hall, 2004, chapters 6 and 7.

International Accounting, *Walton P., Haller A. and Raffournier B. (eds)*, 2nd edn, Thomson, 2003, chapter 19.

Improvements to International Accounting Standards, *International Accounting Standards Board*, IASB, 2003.

Operating and Financial Review, *Accounting Standards Board*, ASB, January 2003.

REVIEW QUESTIONS

Answers to these questions can be found on the students' side of the Companion Website at www.pearsoned.co.uk/atrillmclaney.

5.1 'Searching for an agreed framework of principles for accounting rules is likely to be a journey without an ending.' Discuss.

5.2 The size of annual financial reports published by limited companies has increased steadily over the years. Can you think of any reasons, apart from the increasing volume of accounting regulation, why this has occurred?

5.3 What problems does a user of segmental financial statements face when seeking to make comparisons between businesses?

5.4 'An OFR should not be prepared by accountants but should be prepared by the board of directors.' Why should this be the case?

EXERCISES

Exercises 5.6 to 5.8 are more advanced than 5.1 to 5.5. Those with a coloured number have answers at the back of the book.

5.1 It has been suggested that too much information might be as bad as too little information for users of annual reports. Explain.

5.2 What problems are likely to be encountered when preparing summary financial statements for shareholders?

5.3 The following information was extracted from the financial statements of I. Ching (Booksellers) plc for the year to 31 December 2005:

	£m
Interest payable	40
Cost of sales	460
Distribution costs	110
Income from investments	42
Revenue	943
Administration expenses	314
Other expenses	25

Note: Corporation tax is calculated at 25 per cent of the profit on ordinary activities.

Required:
Prepare a profit and loss account for the year ended 31 December 2005 that is set out in accordance with the requirements of IAS 1 *Presentation of Financial Statements*.

5.4   Manet plc had the following share capital and reserves as at 30 June 2004:

	£m
Share capital (£0.25 ordinary shares)	250
Share premium account	50
Revaluation reserve	120
Currency translation reserve	15
Retained earnings	380
	815

During the year to 30 June 2005, the company revalued its freehold land upwards by £30m and made a loss on foreign exchange translation of £5m. The company made a profit after tax from operations of £160m during the year and the dividend payout ratio was 50 per cent.

Required:

Prepare a statement of changes in equity in accordance with the requirements of IAS 1, *Presentation of Financial Statements*.

5.5   Professor Myddleton argues that accounting standards should be limited to disclosure requirements and should not impose rules on companies as to how to measure particular items in the financial statements. He states:

> The volume of accounting instructions is already high. If things go on like this, where will we be in 20 or 30 years' time? On balance I conclude we would be better off without any standards on accounting measurement. There could still be some disclosure requirements for listed companies, though probably less than now.

Do you agree with this idea? Discuss. (*Note*: This issue has not been directly covered in the chapter, but you should be able to use your knowledge to try to come up with some points on both sides of the argument.)

5.6   The following is the segment reports of Tora plc, which manufactures and sells three main classes of product, for the year ended 31 December 2005.

	Paper £m	Plastic £m	Metal £m	Eliminations £m	Consolidation £m
Revenue					
External sales	420	280	140		
Inter-segment sales	20	10	15	(45)	
Total revenue	440	290	155	(45)	840
Result					
Segment result	80	65	45	(6)	184
Unallocated expenses					38
					146
Interest expense					(14)
Corporation tax					(26)
Net profit					106
Other information					
Segment assets	350	650	226		1,226
Unallocated assets					146
Consolidated total assets					1,372
Segment liabilities	55	150	42		247
Unallocated liabilities					60
Consolidated total liabilities					307
Capital expenditure	10	–	15		25
Depreciation	72	130	70		272

Required:

Analyse the performance of each of the business segments for the year and comment on your results.

5.7 Obtain a copy of an operating and financial review of two companies within the same industry. Compare the usefulness of each. In answering this question, you should consider the extent to which the OFRs incorporate the recommendations made by the Accounting Standards Board.

5.8 The following information has been extracted from the segmental report for 2002 of Unilever plc, a large Anglo-Dutch company that sells a variety of foods, home- and personal-care products under a variety of well-known brand names such as Flora, Ben & Jerry's, Surf, Comfort, Sunsilk, Dove and Calvin Klein.

Segment (see key below)	A €m	B €m	C €m	D €m	E €m	F €m	G €m	Total €m
Analysis by operation 2002								
Group turnover	9,272	6,145	4,064	7,456	8,565	12,236	532	48,270
Trading result	1,362	834	504	704	725	1,976	27	6,132
Amortisation of goodwill and intangibles								(1,245)
Other adjustments								154
Group operating profit								5,041
Depreciation and amortisation	1,291	204	220	315	437	252	83	2,802
Capital expenditure	202	166	167	270	215	251	27	1,298
Total assets by operation	19,717	3,610	4,095	3,851	3,581	4,066	2,662	41,582
Corporate assets								3,778
Other adjustments								(762)
Total assets								44,598

	United Kingdom & Netherlands €m	United States €m	Other €m	Total €m
Additional geographic analysis 2002				
Group turnover	5,406	11,421	31,443	48,270
Property, plant and equipment	979	1,564	4,893	7,436

Key to segments
A = Savoury and dressings
C = Health and wellness and beverages
E = Home care and professional cleaning
G = Other operations

B = Spreads and cooking products
D = Ice cream and frozen foods
F = Personal care

Source: Unilever plc.

Required:

(a) Analyse the performance of each of the major segments in so far as the information allows.

(b) State what additional information would be useful to help in your analysis of segmental performance.

6

Measuring and reporting cash flows

OBJECTIVES

When you have completed this chapter, you should be able to:

- Discuss the crucial importance of cash to a business.

- Explain the nature of the cash flow statement and discuss how it can be helpful in identifying cash flow problems.

- Prepare a cash flow statement.

- Interpret a cash flow statement.

INTRODUCTION

This chapter is devoted to the third major financial statement identified in Chapter 2 – the cash flow statement. This statement reveals the movements of cash over a period and the effect of these movements on the cash position of the business. It is an important financial statement because cash is important to the survival of a business. Without cash, no business can operate.

In this chapter, we shall see how the cash flow statement is prepared and how the information that it contains may be interpreted. We shall also see why the deficiencies of the profit and loss account (income statement) in revealing cash flows over time make a separate cash flow statement necessary.

The cash flow statement is being considered after the chapters on limited companies because the format of the statement requires an understanding of this type of business. Limited companies are required to provide a cash flow statement, as well as the more traditional profit and loss account and balance sheet, for shareholders and other interested parties.

The cash flow statement

The cash flow statement is a fairly recent addition to the set of financial statements sent to shareholders and to others. There used to be no regulation requiring companies to produce more than a profit and loss account (income statement) and balance sheet. The prevailing view seemed to have been that any financial information required would be contained within these two statements. This view may have been based partly on the assumption that if a business were profitable, it would also have plenty of cash. Though in the very long run this is likely to be true, it is not necessarily true in the short to medium term.

We have already seen in Chapter 3 that the profit and loss account sets out the revenue and expenses, rather than the cash receipts and cash payments, for the period. Thus, profit (loss), which represents the difference between the revenue and expenses for the period, may have little or no relation to the cash generated for the period. To illustrate this point, let us take the example of a business making a sale (a revenue). This may well lead to an increase in wealth and will be reflected in the profit and loss account. However, if the sale is made on credit, no cash changes hands – not at the time of sale at least. Instead, the increase in wealth is reflected in another asset – an increase in trade debtors (receivables). Furthermore, if an item of stock (inventory) is the subject of the sale, wealth is lost to the business through the reduction in the stock. This means an expense is incurred in making the sale, which will be shown in the profit and loss account. Once again, however, no cash has changed hands at the time of sale. For such reasons, the profit and the cash generated for a period will rarely go hand in hand.

The following Activity helps to underline how profit and cash for a period may be affected differently by particular transactions or events.

Activity 6.1

The following is a list of business/accounting events. In each case, state the effect (increase, decrease or no effect) on both cash and profit:

		Effect	
		on profit	on cash
1	Repayment of a loan	_____	_____
2	Making a sale on credit	_____	_____
3	Buying a non-current asset for cash	_____	_____
4	Receiving cash from a trade debtor (receivable)	_____	_____
5	Depreciating a non-current asset	_____	_____
6	Buying some stock (inventory) for cash	_____	_____
7	Making a share issue for cash	_____	_____

You should have come up with the following:

		Effect	
		on profit	on cash
1	Repayment of a loan	none	decrease
2	Making a sale on credit	increase	none
3	Buying a non-current asset for cash	none	decrease
4	Receiving cash from a trade debtor (receivable)	none	increase
5	Depreciating a non-current asset	decrease	none
6	Buying some stock (inventory) for cash	none	decrease
7	Making a share issue for cash	none	increase

Activity 6.1 continued

The reasons for these answers are as follows:

1 Repaying the loan requires that cash be paid to the lender. Thus two figures in the balance sheet will be affected, but not the profit and loss account.
2 Making a sale on credit will increase the sales figure and probably profit or loss (unless the sale was made for a price that precisely equalled the expenses involved). No cash will change hands, however, at this point.
3 Buying a non-current asset for cash obviously reduces the cash balance of the business, but the profit figure is not affected.
4 Receiving cash from a debtor increases the cash balance and reduces the debtor's balance. Both of these figures are on the balance sheet. The profit and loss account is unaffected.
5 Depreciating a non-current asset means that an expense is recognised. This causes the value of the asset, as it is recorded on the balance sheet, to fall by an amount equal to the amount of the expense. No cash is paid or received.
6 Buying some stock for cash means that the value of the stock will increase and the cash balance will decrease by a similar amount. Profit is not affected.
7 Making a share issue for cash increases the owners' claim and increases the cash balance; profit is unaffected.

It is clear from the above that if we are to gain an insight to cash movements over time, the profit and loss account is not the answer. Instead we need a separate financial statement. This fact has become widely recognised in recent years and in 1991 a UK financial reporting standard, FRS 1, emerged that requires all but the smallest companies to produce and publish a cash flow statement. This standard has been superseded for many companies from 2005 by the international accounting standard IAS 7. The two standards have broadly similar requirements. This chapter follows the provisions of IAS 7.

Why is cash so important?

It is worth asking why is cash so important? After all, cash is just an asset that a business needs to help it to function. In that sense, it is no different from stock (inventory) or non-current assets.

The reason for the importance of cash is that people and organisations will not normally accept other than cash in settlement of their claims against the business. If a business wants to employ people it must pay them in cash. If it wants to buy a new non-current asset to exploit a business opportunity, the seller of the asset will normally insist on being paid in cash, probably after a short period of credit. When businesses fail, it is their inability to find the cash to pay the amounts owed that really pushes them under.

These factors lead to cash being the pre-eminent business asset. It is the one that analysts tend to watch most carefully when trying to assess the ability of businesses to survive and/or to take advantage of commercial opportunities as they arise. The fact that cash and profits do not always go hand in hand is illustrated in **Real World 6.1**. This explains how Eurotunnel, the cross-channel business, continues to struggle to achieve profit, yet generates positive cash flows.

REAL WORLD 6.1

Cash flows under the channel   **FT**

'Richard Shirrefs [Eurotunnel's chief executive] called for a shift from "a stable equilibrium of failure to a stable equilibrium of success".'

'The company, which last restructured its long term debt in 2003, proposes to shift to a lower price, higher volume model for tunnel usage. Access rates for train operators would be reduced to entice them to introduce more services to more destinations, such as Amsterdam, and to encourage greater freight traffic.'

'Eurotunnel progressed its own plans for freight on Monday, announcing it expected to start a traction business in 2005 and that a platform designed to accept continental gauge freight trains would begin operations at Folkestone in the same year.'

'Mr Shirrefs said taxpayers had invested £10bn and industry £15bn in the tunnel and associated infrastructure and: "We need to get all that infrastructure working . . . neither investor nor taxpayer is getting value".'

'Last year was a difficult one for Eurotunnel with reduced cross channel passenger flows bringing fare competition from ferry operators.'

'The company's operating revenue was down 5 per cent at £566m and its operating profit down 18 per cent at £170m. With interest payments of £318m, the underlying loss was up 40 per cent at £148m. However, it maintained a positive cash flow of £290m, down from £307m in 2002.'

Source: Extracts from 'Eurotunnel takes £1.3bn impairment charge', Toby Shelley, FT.com , 9 February 2004.

The main features of the cash flow statement

The cash flow statement is, in essence, a summary of the cash receipts and payments over the period concerned. All payments of a particular type for example, cash payments to acquire additional non-current assets or other investments, are added together to give just one figure that appears in the statement. The net total of the statement is the net increase or decrease of the cash (and cash equivalents) of the business over the period. The statement is basically an analysis of the business's cash movements for the period.

The definition of cash and cash equivalents

IAS 7 defines cash as notes and coins in hand and deposits in banks and similar institutions that are accessible to the business on demand. Cash equivalents are short-term highly liquid investments that are readily convertible to known amounts of cash and which are subject to an insignificant risk of changes of value. Cash equivalents are held for the purpose of meeting short-term cash commitments rather than for investment or other purposes.

Activity 6.2 should clarify the types of items that fall within the definition of 'cash equivalents'.

Activity 6.2

At the end of its accounting period, Zeneb plc's balance sheet included the following items:

1 *A bank deposit account where one month's notice of withdrawal is required.* This deposit was made because the business has a temporary cash surplus that it will need to use in the short term for operating purposes;
2 *Ordinary shares in Jones plc (a Stock Exchange listed business).* These were acquired because the business has a temporary cash surplus and Zeneb plc's directors believed that the share represented a good short-term investment. The funds invested will need to be used in the short term for operating purposes.
3 *A bank deposit account that is withdrawable instantly.* This represents an investment of surplus funds that are not seen as being needed in the short term.
4 *An overdraft on the business's bank current account.*

Which (if any) of these four items would be included in the figure for cash and cash equivalents?

....

Your response should have been as follows:

1 A cash equivalent, because the deposit is part of the business's normal cash management activities and there is little doubt about how much cash will be obtained when the deposit is withdrawn.
2 Not a cash equivalent. Although the investment was made as part of normal cash management, there is a significant risk that the amount expected (hoped for!) when the shares are sold may not actually be forthcoming.
3 Not a cash equivalent, because this represents an investment, rather than a short-term surplus amount of cash.
4 This is cash itself, though a negative amount of it. The only exception to this classification would be where the business is financed in the longer term by an overdraft, when it would be part of the financing of the business.

As can be seen from the responses to Activity 6.2, whether a particular item falls within the definition of cash and cash equivalent depends on two factors:

1 the nature of the item
2 why it has arisen.

In practice, it is not usually difficult to decide whether an item is a cash equivalent.

The cash flow statement, the profit and loss account (income statement) and the balance sheet

The cash flow statement is now accepted, along with the profit and loss account and balance sheet, as a primary financial statement. The relationship between the three statements is shown in Figure 6.1. The balance sheet reflects the combination of assets (including cash) and claims (including the owners' capital) of the business *at a particular point in time*. Both the cash flow statement and the profit and loss account explain the *changes over a period* to two of the items in the balance sheet, namely cash and owners' claim respectively. In practice, this period is typically the business's accounting year.

Figure 6.1	The relationship between the balance sheet, the profit and loss account and the cash flow statement

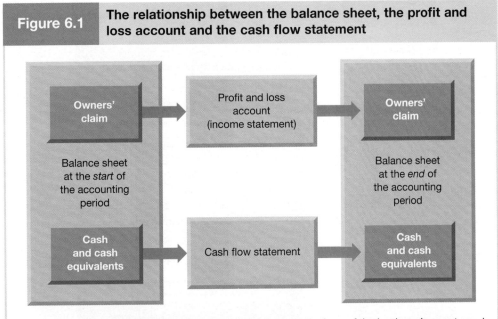

The balance sheet shows the position, at a particular point in time, of the business's assets and claims. The profit and loss account explains how, over a period between two balance sheets, the owners' claim figure in the first balance sheet has altered as a result of trading operations to become the figure in the second balance sheet. The cash flow statement also looks at changes over the accounting period, but this statement explains the alteration in the cash (and cash equivalent) balances shown in the two consecutive balance sheets.

The form of the cash flow statement

The standard layout of the cash flow statement is summarised in Figure 6.2 (see p. 176).
Explanations of the terms used in the cash flow statement are as follows.

→ Cash flows from operating activities

This is the net inflow or outflow from trading operations, after tax and financing costs. It is equal to the sum of cash receipts from trade debtors (receivables), and cash receipts from cash sales where relevant, less the sums paid to buy stock, to pay rent, to pay wages and so on. From this are also deducted payments for interest on the business's borrowings, corporation tax and dividends paid.

Note that it is the amounts of cash received and paid during the period that feature in the cash flow statement, not the revenue and expenses for that period. It is, of course, the profit and loss account that deals with the revenue and expenses. Similarly the tax and dividend payments that appear in the cash flow statement are those made in the period of the statement. Companies normally pay tax on their profits in four equal instalments. Two of these are during the year concerned, and the other two are during the following year. Thus by the end of each accounting year, one half of the tax will have been paid and the remainder will be a current liability at the end of the year, to be paid off during the following year. During any particular year, therefore, the tax payment would normally equal 50 per cent of the previous year's tax charge and 50 per cent of that of the current year.

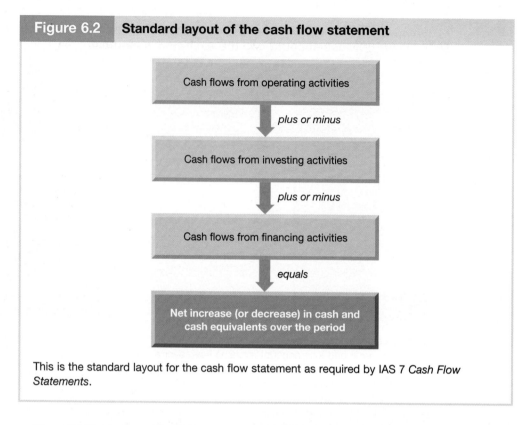

Figure 6.2 Standard layout of the cash flow statement

This is the standard layout for the cash flow statement as required by IAS 7 *Cash Flow Statements*.

The net figure for this section is intended to indicate the net cash flows for the period that arose from normal day-to-day trading activities after taking account of the tax that has to be paid on them and the cost of servicing the finance (equity and loans) needed to support them.

Cash flows from investing activities

This section of the statement is concerned with cash payments made to acquire additional non-current assets and with cash receipts from the disposal of non-current assets. These non-current assets could be loans made by the business or shares in another business bought by the business, as well as the more usual non-current assets such as buildings, machinery and so on.

This section also includes receipts from investments (loans and equity investments) made outside the business. These receipts are interest on loans made by the business and dividends from shares in other businesses that are owned by the business.

This section shows the net cash flows from making new investments and/or disposing of existing ones.

Cash flows from financing activities

This part of the statement is concerned with the long-term financing of the business. So we are considering borrowings (other than very short term) and finance from share issues. This category is concerned with repayment/redemption of finance as well as with the raising of it. It is permissible under IAS 7 to include dividend payments made by the business here, as an alternative to including them in 'Cash flows from operating activities' (above).

This section shows the net cash flows from raising and/or paying back long-term finance.

Net increase or decrease in cash and cash equivalents

The total of the statement must, of course, be the net increase or decrease in cash and cash equivalents over the period covered by the statement.

The effect on a business's cash and cash equivalents of its various activities is shown in Figure 6.3. The activities that affect cash are analysed in the same way as is required by IAS 7. As explained below, the arrows in the figure show the *normal* direction of cash flow for the typical healthy, profitable business in a typical year.

Figure 6.3	Diagrammatical representation of the cash flow statement

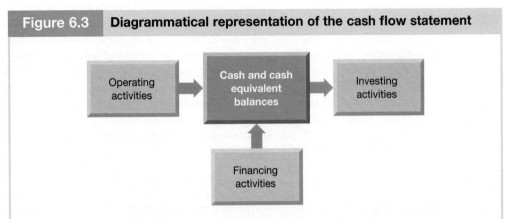

Various activities of the business each have their own effect on its cash and cash equivalent balances, either positive (increasing them) or negative (reducing them). The net increase or decrease in the cash and cash equivalent balances over a period will be the sum of these individual effects, taking account of the direction (cash in or cash out) of each activity.

Note that the direction of the arrow shows the *normal* direction of the cash flow in respect of each activity. In certain circumstances, each of these arrows could be reversed in direction.

The normal direction of cash flows

Normally 'operating activities' provide positive cash flows: that is, they help to increase the business's cash resources. In fact, for most UK businesses, cash generated from day-to-day trading, even after deducting tax, interest and dividends, is overwhelmingly the most important source of new finance in most time periods.

Activity 6.3

Last year's cash flow statement for Angus plc showed a negative cash flow from operating activities. What could be the reason for this, and should the business's management be alarmed by it? (*Hint*: We think that there are two broad possible reasons for a negative cash flow.)

The two reasons are:

- The business is unprofitable. This leads to more cash being paid out to employees, suppliers of goods and services, interest and so on, than is received from debtors in respect of sales. This would be particularly alarming, because a major expense for most businesses is depreciation of non-current assets. Since depreciation does not lead to

Activity 6.3 continued

a cash flow, it is not considered in 'net cash inflows from operating activities'. Thus, a negative operating cash flow might well indicate a very much larger trading loss – in other words, a significant loss of the business's wealth.

● The other reason might be less alarming. A business that is expanding its activities (level of sales) would tend to spend quite a lot of cash, relative to the amount of cash coming in from sales. This is because it will probably be expanding its assets (non-current and current) to accommodate the increased demand. In the first instance, it would not necessarily benefit, in cash flow terms, from all of the additional sales. For example, a business may well have to have stock-in-trade (inventory) in place before additional sales can be made. Even when the additional sales are made, the sales would normally be made on credit, with the cash inflow lagging behind the sale. This would be particularly likely to be true of a new business, which would be expanding stocks and other assets from zero. Expansion typically causes cash flow strains for the reasons just explained. This can be a particular problem because the business's increased profitability might encourage a feeling of optimism, which could lead to lack of concern for the cash flow problem.

Investing activities can give rise to positive cash flows when a business sells some non-current assets. However, because most types of non-current asset wear out, and because businesses tend to seek to expand their asset base, the normal direction of cash in this area is out of the business: that is, negative.

Financing can go in either direction, depending on the financing strategy at the time. Since businesses seek to expand, there is a general tendency for this area to lead to cash coming into the business rather than leaving it.

Preparing the cash flow statement

Deducing net cash flows from operating activities

The first section of the cash flow statement, and the one that is typically the most important for most businesses, is the cash flows from operations. There are two methods that can be used to derive the figure in the statement: the direct method and the indirect method.

The direct method

→ The **direct method** involves an analysis of the cash records of the business for the period, picking out all payments and receipts relating to operating activities. These are summarised to give the total figures for inclusion in the cash flow statement. This could be a time-consuming and laborious activity, though a computer could do it. Not many businesses adopt this approach.

The indirect method

→ The **indirect method** is the more popular method. It relies on the fact that, broadly, sales give rise to cash inflows, and expenses give rise to outflows. Broadly, therefore, the net profit figure will be closely linked to the net cash inflows from operating activities.

Since businesses have to produce a profit and loss account (income statement) in any case, information from it can be used as a starting point to deduce the cash inflows from operating activities.

Of course, within a particular accounting period, net profit will not normally equal the net cash inflows from operating activities. We saw in Chapter 3 that, when sales are made on credit, the cash receipt occurs some time after the sale. This means that sales made towards the end of an accounting year will be included in that year's profit and loss account, but most of the cash from those sales will flow into the business, and should be included in the cash flow statement, in the following year. Fortunately it is easy to deduce the cash received from sales if we have the relevant profit and loss account and balance sheets, as we shall see in Activity 6.4.

Activity 6.4

How can we deduce the cash inflows from sales using the profit and loss account and balance sheet for the business?

The balance sheet will tell us how much was owed in respect of credit sales at the beginning and end of the year (trade debtors (trade accounts receivable)). The profit and loss account tells us the sales figure. If we adjust the sales figure by the increase or decrease in trade debtors over the year, we deduce the cash from sales for the year.

Example 6.1

The sales figure for a business for the year was £34m. The trade debtors were £4m at the beginning of the year, but had increased to £5m by the end of the year.

Basically, the debtors figure is affected by sales and cash receipts. It is increased when a sale is made and decreased when cash is received from a debtor. If, over the year, the sales and the cash receipts had been equal, the beginning-of-year and end-of-year debtors figures would have been equal. Since the debtors figure increased, it must mean that less cash was received than sales were made. Thus the cash receipts from sales must be £33m (34 – (5 – 4)).

Put slightly differently, we can say that as a result of sales, assets of £34m flowed into the business during the year. If £1m of this went to increasing the asset of trade debtors, this leaves only £33m that went to increase cash.

The same general point is true in respect of nearly all of the other items that are taken into account in deducing the operating profit figure. The exception is depreciation. This is not necessarily associated with any movement in cash during the accounting period.

All of this means we can take the operating profit (that is, the profit after interest but before tax) for the year, add back the depreciation and interest expense charged in arriving at that profit, and adjust this total by movements in stock (inventories), trade debtors and creditors (trade accounts payable). If we then go on to deduct payments made during the accounting period for corporation tax, loan interest and dividends, we have the net cash from operating activities.

Example 6.2

The relevant information from the financial statements of Dido plc for last year is as follows:

	£m
Net profit, after interest, before taxation	122
Depreciation charged in arriving at net operating profit	34
Interest expense	6
At the beginning of the year	
Stock	15
Trade debtors	24
Trade creditors	18
At the end of the year	
Stock	17
Trade debtors	21
Trade creditors	19

The following further information is available about payments during last year:

	£m
Corporation tax paid	32
Interest paid	5
Dividends paid	9

The cash flows from operating activities is derived as follows:

	£m	£m
Net profit, after interest, before taxation		122
Add Depreciation	34	
Interest expense	6	40
		162
Less Increase in stock (17 – 15)		(2)
Add Decrease in trade debtors (21 – 24)	3	
Increase in trade creditors (19 – 18)	1	4
Cash generated from operations		164
Less Interest paid	5	
Corporation tax paid	32	
Dividends paid	9	46
Net cash from operating activities		118

Thus the net increase in working capital, as a result of trading, was £162m. Of this, £2m went into increased stocks. More cash was received from trade debtors than sales were made, and less cash was paid to trade creditors than purchases of goods and services on credit. Both of these had a favourable effect on cash, which increased by £164m. When account was taken of the payments for interest, tax and dividends, the net cash flows from operating activities was £118m (inflow).

Note that we needed to adjust the net profit, after interest, before taxation by the depreciation and interest expenses to derive the profit before depreciation and interest.

The indirect method of deducing the net cash flow from operating activities is summarised in Figure 6.4 on p. 182.

Figure 6.4	The indirect method of deducing the net cash flows from the operating activities

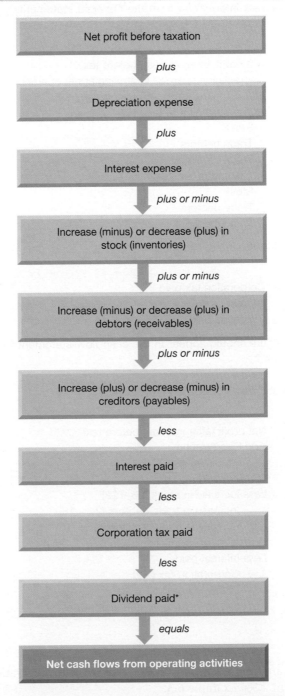

Determining the net cash flows from operating activities firstly involves adding back the depreciation and the interest expense to the net profit for the period. Next, adjustment is made for increases or decreases in stock, debtors and creditors. Lastly, cash paid for interest, tax and dividends is deducted.

* Note that dividends could alternatively be included under the heading 'Cash flows from financing activities'.

Activity 6.5

The relevant information from the financial statements of Pluto plc for last year is as follows:

	£m
Net profit, after interest, before tax	165
Depreciation charged in arriving at net operating profit	41
Interest expense	21
At the beginning of the year	
Stock	22
Trade debtors	18
Trade creditors	15
At the end of the year	
Stock	23
Trade debtors	21
Trade creditors	17

The following further information is available about payments during last year:

	£m
Corporation tax paid	49
Interest paid	25
Dividends paid	28

What figure should appear in the cash flow statement for 'Cash flows from operating activities'?

Net cash inflows from operating activities:

	£m	£m
Net profit (after interest, before tax)		165
Add Depreciation	41	
Interest expense	21	62
		227
Less Increase in stock (23 – 22)	1	
Increase in trade debtors (21 – 18)	3	(4)
Add Increase in trade creditors (17 – 15)		2
Cash generated from operations		225
Less Interest paid	25	
Corporation tax paid	49	
Dividends paid	28	(102)
Net cash flows from operating activities		123

We can now go on to take a look at the preparation of a complete cash flow statement – see Example 6.3.

Example 6.3

Torbryan plc's profit and loss account for the year ended 31 December 2005 and the balance sheets as at 31 December 2004 and 2005 are as follows:

Profit and loss account for the year ended 31 December 2005

	£m	£m
Revenue		576
Less Cost of sales		307
Gross profit		269
Less Distribution costs	65	
Administrative expenses	26	91
		178
Other operating income		21
Operating profit		199
Interest receivable		17
		216
Less Interest payable		23
Profit on ordinary activities before taxation		193
Less Tax on profit (or loss) on ordinary activities		46
Profit on ordinary activities after taxation		147
Retained profit brought forward from last year		26
		173
Less Dividend paid on ordinary shares		50
Retained profit carried forward		123

Balance sheets as at 31 December 2004 and 2005

	2004 £m	2005 £m
Non-current assets		
Property, plant and equipment		
Land and buildings	241	241
Plant and machinery	309	325
	550	566
Current assets		
Stock	44	41
Trade debtors	121	139
	165	180
Less Current liabilities		
Bank overdraft	68	56
Trade creditors	55	54
Corporation tax	16	23
	139	133
Net current assets	26	47
Total assets less current liabilities	576	613
Less Non-current liabilities		
Debenture loans	400	250
	176	363
Equity		
Called-up ordinary share capital	150	200
Share premium account	–	40
Profit and loss account	26	123
	176	363

Example 6.3 continued

During 2005, the business spent £95 million on additional plant and machinery. There were no other non-current-asset acquisitions or disposals. The interest receivable revenue and the interest payable expenses for the year were equal to the cash inflow and outflow respectively.

The cash flow statement would be as follows:

Torbryan plc
Cash flow statement for the year ended 31 December 2005

	£m	£m
Cash flows from operating activities		
Net profit, after interest, before taxation		
(see Note 1 below)		193
Adjustments for:		
Depreciation (Note 2)		79
Investment income (Note 3)		(17)
Interest expense (Note 4)		23
		(278)
Increase in trade debtors (139 – 121)		(18)
Decrease in trade creditors (55 – 54)		(1)
Decrease in stocks (44 – 41)		3
Cash generated from operations		262
Interest paid		(23)
Corporation tax paid (Note 5)		(39)
Dividend paid		(50)
Net cash from operating activities		150
Cash flows from investing activities		
Payments to acquire tangible non-current assets	(95)	
Interest received (Note 3)	17	
Net cash used in investing activities		(78)
Cash flows from financing activities		
Repayments of debenture stock (Note 7)	(150)	
Issue of ordinary shares (Note 8)	90	
Net cash used in financing activities		(60)
Net increase in cash and cash equivalents		12
Cash and cash equivalents at 1 January 2005 (Note 9)		(68)
Cash and cash equivalents at 31 December 2005		(56)

To see how this relates to the cash of the business at the beginning and end of the year it can be useful to provide a reconciliation as follows:

Analysis of cash and cash equivalents during the year ended 31 December 2005

	£m
Overdraft balance at 1 January 2005	(68)
Net cash inflow	12
Overdraft balance at 31 December 2005	(56)

Notes

1 This is simply taken from the profit and loss account for the year.
2 Since there were no disposals, the depreciation charges must be the difference between the start and end of the year's plant and machinery (non-current assets) values, adjusted by the cost of any additions.

	£m
Book value, at 1 January 2005	309
Add Additions	(95)
	404
Less Depreciation (balancing figure)	79
Book value, at 31 December 2005	325

(handwritten annotations: 347, 35, 312)

3   Interest receivable must be taken away to work towards the profit before crediting it, because it is not part of operations, but of investing activities. The cash inflow from this source appears under the 'Cash flows from investing activities' heading.

4   Interest payable expense must be taken out, by adding it back to the profit figure. We subsequently deduct the cash paid for interest payable during the year. In this case the two figures are identical.

5   Tax is paid by companies 50 per cent during their accounting year and the other 50 per cent in the following year. Thus the 2005 payment would have been half the tax on the 2004 profit (that is, the figure that would have appeared in the current liabilities at the end of 2004), plus half of the 2005 tax charge (that is, $16 + (^{1}/_{2} \times 46) = 39$). Probably the easiest way to deduce the amount paid during the year to 31 December 2005 is by following this approach:

	£m
Tax owed at start of the year (from the balance sheet as at 31 December 2004)	16
Add Tax charge for the year (from the profit and loss account)	46
	62
Less Tax owed at the end of the year (from the balance sheet as at 31 December 2005)	23
Tax paid during the year	39

This follows the logic that if we start with what the business owed at the beginning of the year, add on the increase in what was owed as a result of the current year's tax and then deduct what was owed at the end, the resulting figure must be what was paid during the year.

7   It has been assumed that the debentures were redeemed for their balance sheet value. This is not, however, always the case.

8   The share issue raised £90m, of which £50m went into the share capital total on the balance sheet and £40m into share premium.

9   There were no 'cash equivalents', just cash (though negative).

What does the cash flow statement tell us?

The cash flow statement tells us how the business has generated cash during the period and where that cash has gone. Since cash is properly regarded as the lifeblood of just about any business, this is potentially very useful information.

Tracking the sources and uses of cash over several years could show financing trends that a reader of the statements could use to help to make predictions about the likely future behaviour of the company.

Looking specifically at the cash flow statement for Torbryan plc, in Example 6.3, we can see the following:

● Net cash flows from operations was strong, much larger than the profit figure, after taking account of the dividend paid. This would be expected because depreciation is deducted in arriving at profit. There was a general tendency for working capital to absorb some cash. This would not be surprising had there been an expansion of activity (sales output) over the year. From the information supplied, we do not know whether there was an expansion or not. (We have only one year's profit and loss account.)

- There were net outflows of cash for investing activities, but this would not be unusual. Many items of property, plant and equipment have limited lives and need to be replaced with new ones. The expenditure during the year was not out of line with the depreciation expense for the year, which is what we might expect.
- There was a fairly major outflow of cash to redeem some debt finance, partly offset by the proceeds of a share issue. This presumably represents a change of financing strategy. Together with the ploughed-back profit from trading, there has been a significant shift in the equity/debt balance.

Self-assessment question 6.1

Touchstone plc's profit and loss accounts for the years ended 31 December 2004 and 2005 and the balance sheets as at 31 December 2004 and 2005 are as follows:

Profit and loss accounts for the years ended 2004 and 2005

	2004	2005
	£m	£m
Revenue	173	207
Cost of sales	(96)	(101)
Gross profit	77	106
Distribution costs	(18)	(20)
Administrative expenses	(24)	(26)
	35	60
Other operating income	3	4
Operating profit	38	64
Interest payable	(2)	(4)
Profit on ordinary activities before taxation	36	60
Tax on profit on ordinary activities	(8)	(16)
Profit on ordinary activities after taxation	28	44
Retained profit brought forward from last year	16	30
	44	74
Dividend paid on ordinary shares	(14)	(18)
Retained profit carried forward	30	56

Balance sheets as at 31 December 2004 and 2005

	2004	2005
	£m	£m
Non-current assets		
Property, plant and equipment:		
Land and buildings	94	110
Plant and machinery	53	62
	147	172
Current assets		
Stock	25	24
Treasury bills (short-term investments)	–	15
Trade debtors	16	26
Cash at bank and in hand	4	4
	45	69
Less **Current liabilities**		
Trade creditors (payables)	38	37
Corporation tax	4	8
	42	45

	2004	2005
	£m	£m
Net current assets	3	24
Total assets less current liabilities	150	196
Less Non-current liabilities		
Debenture loans (10%)	20	40
	130	156
Equity		
Called-up ordinary share capital	100	100
Profit and loss account	30	56
	130	156

Included in 'cost of sales', 'distribution costs' and 'administration expenses', depreciation was as follows:

	2004	2005
	£m	£m
Land and buildings	5	6
Plant and machinery	6	10

There were no non-current asset disposals in either year.

In the cases of both interest payable and receivable, the cash outflow/inflow equalled the expense/revenue.

The Treasury bills represent a short-term investment of funds that will be used shortly in operations. There is insignificant risk that this investment will lose value.

Required:
Prepare a cash flow statement for the business for 2005.

SUMMARY

The main points of this chapter may be summarised as follows:

The need for a cash flow statement
- Cash is important because no business can operate without it.
- The cash flow statement is specifically designed to reveal movements in cash over a period.
- Cash movements cannot be readily detected from the profit and loss account, which focuses on revenue and expenses rather than on cash receipts and cash payments.
- Profit (loss) and cash generated for the period are rarely equal.
- The cash flow statement is a primary financial statement, along with the profit and loss account and the balance sheet.

Preparing the cash flow statement
- The layout of the statement contains three categories of cash movement:
  - cash flows from operating activities;
  - cash flows from investing activities; and
  - cash flows from financing activities.

● The total of the cash movements under these three categories will provide the net increase or decrease in cash and cash equivalents for the period.

● A reconciliation can be undertaken to check that the opening balance of cash and cash equivalents plus the net increase (decrease) for the period equals the closing balance.

Calculating the cash generated from operations

● The net cash flows from operating activities can be derived from either the direct method or the indirect method.

● The direct method is based on an analysis of the cash records for the period, whereas the indirect method uses information contained within the profit and loss account and balance sheets of the business.

● The indirect method takes the net operating profit for the period, adds back any depreciation charge and then adjusts for changes in stocks, debtors and creditors during the period.

Interpreting the cash flow statement

● The cash flow statement shows the main sources and uses of cash.

● Tracking the cash movements over several periods may reveal financing and investing patterns and may help predict future management action.

→ Key terms

Cash flows from operating activities
p. 175
Cash flows from investing activities
p. 176

Cash flows from financing activities
p. 176
Direct method p. 178
Indirect method p. 178

Further reading

If you would like to explore the topics covered in this chapter in more depth, we recommend the following books:

Financial Reporting, *Alexander D. and Britton A.*, 6th edn, International Thomson Business Press, 2001, chapter 27.

Students' Guide to Accounting and Financial Reporting Standards, *Black G.*, 9th edn, Financial Times Prentice Hall, 2003, chapter 12.

Financial Accounting and Reporting, *Elliott B. and Elliott J.*, 8th edn, Financial Times Prentice Hall, 2004, chapter 24.

REVIEW QUESTIONS

Answers to these questions can be found on the students' side of the Companion Website at **www.pearsoned.co.uk/atrillmclaney**.

6.1 The typical business outside the service sector has about 50 per cent more of its resources tied up in stock (inventories) than in cash, yet there is no call for a 'stock flow statement' to be prepared. Why is cash regarded as more important than stock?

6.2 What is the difference between the direct and indirect methods of deducing cash generated from operations?

6.3 Taking each of the categories of the cash flow statement in turn, in which direction would you normally expect the cash flow to be? Explain your answer.

(a) Cash flows from operating activities.
(b) Cash flows from investing activities.
(c) Cash flows from financing activities.

6.4 What causes the net profit for the year not to equal the net cash inflow?

EXERCISES

Exercises 6.3 to 6.8 are more advanced than 6.1 and 6.2. Those with a coloured number have answers at the back of the book.

6.1 How will each of the following events ultimately affect the amount of cash?

(a) An increase in the level of stock-in-trade (inventories).
(b) A rights issue of ordinary shares.
(c) A bonus issue of ordinary shares.
(d) Writing off the value of some stock-in-trade.
(e) The disposal of a large number of the business's shares by a major shareholder.
(f) Depreciating a non-current asset.

6.2 The following information has been taken from the financial statements of Juno plc for last year and the year before last:

	Year before last £m	Last year £m
Net operating profit	156	187
Depreciation charged in arriving at net operating profit	47	55
Stock held at the end of:	27	31
Debtors at the end of:	24	23
Creditors at the end of:	15	17

Required:
What is the cash generated from operations figure for Juno plc for last year?

6.3   Torrent plc's profit and loss account for the year ended 31 December 2005 and the balance sheets as at 31 December 2004 and 2005 are as follows:

Profit and loss account

	£m	£m
Revenue		623
Less Cost of sales		353
Gross profit		270
Less Distribution costs	71	
Administrative expenses	30	101
		169
Rental income		27
Operating profit		196
Less Interest payable		26
Profit on ordinary activities before taxation		170
Less Tax on profit on ordinary activities		36
Profit on ordinary activities after taxation		134
Retained profit brought forward from last year		123
		257
Less Dividend paid on ordinary shares		60
Retained profit carried forward		197

Balance sheets as at 31 December 2004 and 2005

	2004	2005
	£m	£m
Non-current assets		
Property, plant and equipment		
Land and buildings	310	310
Plant and machinery	325	314
	635	624
Current assets		
Stock	41	35
Trade debtors	139	145
	180	180
Current liabilities		
Bank overdraft	56	89
Trade creditors	54	41
Corporation tax	23	18
	133	148
Net current assets	47	32
Total assets less current liabilities	682	656
Less **Non-current liabilities**		
Debenture loans	250	150
	432	506
Equity		
Called-up ordinary share capital	200	300
Share premium account	40	–
Revaluation reserve	69	9
Profit and loss account	123	197
	432	506

During 2005, the business spent £67 million on additional plant and machinery. There were no other non-current asset acquisitions or disposals.

There was no share issue for cash during the year.

The interest payable expense was equal in amount to the cash outflow.

Required:

Prepare the cash flow statement for Torrent plc for the year ended 31 December 2005.

6.4 Chen plc's profit and loss accounts for the years ended 31 December 2004 and 2005 and the balance sheets as at 31 December 2004 and 2005 are as follows:

Profit and loss account

	2004	2005
	£m	£m
Revenue	207	153
Cost of sales	(101)	(76)
Gross profit	106	77
Distribution costs	(22)	(20)
Administrative expenses	(20)	(28)
Operating profit	64	29
Interest payable	(4)	(4)
Profit on ordinary activities before taxation	60	25
Tax on profit (or loss) on ordinary activities	(16)	(6)
Profit on ordinary activities after taxation	44	19
Retained profit brought forward from last year	30	56
	74	75
Dividends paid on ordinary shares	(18)	(18)
Retained profit carried forward	56	57

Balance sheets as at 31 December 2004 and 2005

	2004	2005
	£m	£m
Non-current assets		
Property, plant and equipment		
Land and buildings	110	130
Plant and machinery	62	56
	172	186
Current assets		
Stock	24	25
Trade debtors	26	25
Cash at bank and in hand	19	–
	69	50
Less Current liabilities		
Bank overdraft	–	2
Trade creditors	37	34
Corporation tax	8	3
	45	39
Net current assets	24	11
Total assets less current liabilities	196	197
Less Non-current liabilities		
Debenture loans (10%)	40	40
	156	157
Equity		
Called-up ordinary share capital	100	100
Profit and loss account	56	57
	156	157

Included in 'cost of sales', 'distribution costs' and 'administrative expenses', depreciation was as follows:

	2004	2005
	£m	£m
Land and buildings	6	10
Plant and machinery	10	12

There were no non-current asset disposals in either year.

The amount of cash paid for interest equalled the expense in both years.

Required:

Prepare a cash flow statement for the business for 2005.

6.5 The following are the financial statements for Nailsea plc for the years ended 30 June 2004 and 2005:

Profit and loss accounts for years ended 30 June

	2004		2005	
	£m	£m	£m	£m
Revenue		1,230		2,280
Less Operating costs	722		1,618	
Depreciation	270	992	320	1,938
Operating profit		238		342
Less Interest payable		–		27
Profit before tax		238		315
Less Tax		110		140
Profit after tax		128		175
Less Dividend paid		40		45
Retained profit for year		88		130

Balance sheets as at 30 June

	2004		2005	
	£m	£m	£m	£m
Non-current assets				
Property, plant and equipment (at net book value)				
Land and buildings		1,500		1,900
Plant and machinery		810		740
		2,310		2,640
Current assets				
Stock	275		450	
Trade debtors	100		250	
Bank	–		118	
	375		818	
Less **Current liabilities**				
Bank overdraft	32		–	
Trade creditors	170		230	
Taxation	55		70	
	257		300	
Net current assets		118		518
		2,428		3,158
Less **Non-current liabilities**				
9% debentures (repayable 2009)		–		300
		2,428		2,858
Equity				
Share capital (fully paid £1 shares)		1,400		1,600
Share premium account		200		300
Retained profits		828		958
		2,428		2,858

There were no disposals of non-current assets in either year.

Required:

Prepare a cash flow statement for Nailsea plc for the year ended 30 June 2005.

6.6   The following financial statements for Blackstone plc are a slightly simplified set of published accounts. Blackstone plc is an engineering business that developed a new range of products in 2003; these now account for 60 per cent of its turnover.

Profit and loss account for the years ended 31 March

	notes	2004 £m	2005 £m
Revenue		7,003	11,205
Cost of sales		(3,748)	(5,809)
Gross profit		3,255	5,396
Operating costs	1	(2,205)	(3,087)
Operating profit		1,050	2,309
Interest payable	2	(216)	(456)
Profit before taxation		834	1,853
Taxation		(210)	(390)
Profit after taxation		624	1,463
Dividend paid		(300)	(400)
Retained profit for the year		324	1,063
Retained profit brought forward		361	685
Retained profit carried forward		685	1,748

Balance sheets as at 31 March

	notes	2004 £m	2004 £m	2005 £m	2005 £m
Non-current assets					
Intangible assets	3		–		700
Property, plant and equipment	4		4,300		7,535
			4,300		8,235
Current assets					
Stock		1,209		2,410	
Trade debtors		641		1,173	
Cash at bank		123		–	
		1,973		3,583	
Current liabilities					
Trade creditors		(931)		(1,507)	
Taxation		(105)		(195)	
Bank overdraft		–		(1,816)	
		(1,036)		(3,518)	
Net current assets			937		65
Non-current liabilities					
Bank loan (repayable 2010)			(1,800)		(3,800)
			3,437		4,500
Equity					
Share capital			1,800		1,800
Share premium			600		600
Capital reserves			352		352
Retained profits			685		1,748
			3,437		4,500

Notes to the accounts

1   Operating costs include the following items:

	£m
Exceptional items	203
Depreciation	1,251
Administrative expenses	427
Marketing expenses	385

2   The expense and the cash outflow for interest payable are equal.

3   Intangible assets represent the amounts paid for the goodwill of another engineering business acquired during the year.

4   The movements in property, plant and equipment during the year are set out below.

	Land and buildings £m	Plant and machinery £m	Fixtures and fittings £m	Total £m
Cost				
At 1 April 2004	4,500	3,850	2,120	10,470
Additions	–	2,970	1,608	4,578
Disposals	–	(365)	(216)	(581)
At 31 March 2005	4,500	6,455	3,512	14,467
Depreciation				
At 1 April 2004	1,275	3,080	1,815	6,170
Charge for year	225	745	281	1,251
Disposals	–	(305)	(184)	(489)
At 31 March 2005	1,500	3,520	1,912	6,932
Net book value				
At 31 March 2005	3,000	2,935	1,600	7,535

Proceeds from the sale of non-current assets in the year ended 31 March 2005 amounted to £54 million.

Required:

Prepare a cash flow statement for Blackstone plc for the year ended 31 March 2005. *Hint*: A loss (deficit) on disposal of non-current assets is simply an additional amount of depreciation and should be dealt with as such in preparing the cash flow statement.

6.7   Simplified financial statements for York plc are set out below.

York plc
Profit and loss account for the year ended 30 September 2005

	£m
Revenue	290.0
Cost of sales	(215.0)
Gross profit	75.0
Operating expenses (note 1)	(62.0)
Operating profit	13.0
Interest payable (note 2)	(3.0)
Profit before taxation	10.0
Taxation	(2.6)
Profit after taxation	7.4
Dividends paid	(3.5)
Retained profit	3.9

Balance sheet at 30 September

	2004		2005	
	£m	£m	£m	£m
Non-current assets (note 3)		80.0		85.0
Current assets				
Stock and debtors	119.8		122.1	
Cash at bank	9.2		16.6	
	129.0		138.7	
Current liabilities				
Trade creditors	(80.0)		(82.5)	
Taxation	(1.0)		(1.3)	
	(81.0)		(83.8)	
Net current assets		48.0		54.9
Non-current liabilities		(32.0)		(35.0)
		96.0		104.9
Equity				
Share capital		35.0		40.0
Share premium account		30.0		30.0
Reserves		31.0		34.9
		96.0		104.9

Notes to the accounts

1 Operating expenses include depreciation of £13m and a surplus of £3.2m on the sale of non-current assets.
2 The expense and the cash outflow for interest payable are equal.
3 Non-current asset costs and depreciation:

	Cost	Accumulated depreciation	Net book value
	£m	£m	£m
At 1 October 2004	120.0	40.0	80.0
Disposals	(10.0)	(8.0)	(2.0)
Additions	20.0		20.0
Depreciation		13.0	(13.0)
At 30 September 2005	130.0	45.0	85.0

Required:
Prepare a cash flow statement for York plc for the year ended 30 September 2005 using the data above.

6.8 The balance sheets of Axis plc as at 31 December 2004 and 2005 and the summary profit and loss account for the year ended 31 December 2005 were as follows:

(continued over)

Balance sheet as at 31 December

	2004		2005	
	£m	£m	£m	£m
Non-current assets				
Property, plant and equipment				
Land and building at cost	130		130	
Less Accumulated depreciation	30	100	32	98
Plant and machinery at cost	70		80	
Less Accumulated depreciation	17	53	23	57
		153		155
Current assets				
Stock	25		24	
Trade debtors	16		26	
Short-term investments	–		12	
Cash at bank and in hand	–		7	
	41		69	
Current liabilities				
Trade creditors	31		36	
Taxation	7		8	
	38		44	
Net current assets		3		25
		156		180
Non-current liabilities				
10% debentures		(20)		(40)
		136		140
Equity				
Share capital		100		100
Revenue reserves		36		40
		136		140

Profit and loss account for the year ended 31 December 2005

	£m	£m
Revenue		173
Less Cost of sales		(96)
Gross profit		77
Interest receivable		2
		79
Less		
Sundry expenses	24	
Interest payable	2	
Deficit on sale of non-current asset	1	
Depreciation – buildings	2	
– plant	16	(45)
Net profit before tax		34
Corporation tax		(16)
Net profit after tax		18
Dividend paid		(14)
Unappropriated profit added to revenue reserves		4

During the year, plant (a non-current asset) costing £15m and with accumulated depreciation of £10m was sold.

The short-term investments were government securities, where there was little or no risk of loss of value.

The expense and the cash outflow for interest payable were equal.

Required:

Prepare a cash flow statement for Axis plc for the year ended 31 December 2005.

7

Analysing and interpreting financial statements

OBJECTIVES

When you have completed this chapter, you should be able to:

● Identify the major categories of ratios that can be used for analysis purposes.

● Calculate important ratios for assessing the financial performance and position of a business, and explain the significance of the ratios calculated.

● Discuss the limitations of ratios as a tool of financial analysis.

● Discuss the use of ratios in helping to predict financial failure.

INTRODUCTION

In this chapter we shall consider the analysis and interpretation of the financial statements discussed in Chapters 2, 3 and 6. We shall see how financial (or accounting) ratios can help in assessing the financial health of a business. We shall also consider the problems that are encountered when applying this technique.

Financial ratios can be used to examine various aspects of financial position and performance and are widely used for planning and control purposes. They can be very helpful to managers in a wide variety of decision areas, such as profit planning, pricing, working-capital management, financial structure and dividend policy.

Financial ratios

Financial ratios provide a quick and relatively simple means of assessing the financial health of a business. A ratio simply relates one figure appearing in the financial statements to some other figure appearing there (for example, net profit in relation to capital employed) or, perhaps, to some resource of the business (for example, net profit per employee, sales revenue per square metre of counter space and so on).

Ratios can be very helpful when comparing the financial health of different businesses. Differences may exist between businesses in the scale of operations, and so a direct comparison of, say, the profits generated by each business may be misleading. By expressing profit in relation to some other measure (for example, sales revenue), the problem of scale is eliminated. A business with a profit of, say, £10,000 and sales revenue of £100,000 can be compared with a much larger business with a profit of, say, £80,000 and sales revenue of £1,000,000 by the use of a simple ratio. The net profit to sales revenue ratio for the smaller business is 10 per cent ([10,000/100,000] × 100%) and the same ratio for the larger business is 8 per cent ([80,000/1,000,000] × 100%). These ratios can be directly compared whereas comparison of the absolute profit figures would be less meaningful. The need to eliminate differences in scale through the use of ratios can also apply when comparing the performance of the same business over time.

By calculating a relatively small number of ratios, it is often possible to build up a good picture of the position and performance of a business. Thus, it is not surprising that ratios are widely used by those who have an interest in businesses and business performance. Though ratios are not difficult to calculate, they can be difficult to interpret and so it is important to appreciate that they are really only the starting point for further analysis.

Ratios help to highlight the financial strengths and weaknesses of a business, but they cannot, by themselves, explain why certain strengths or weaknesses exist, or why certain changes have occurred. Only a detailed investigation will reveal these underlying reasons.

Ratios can be expressed in various forms, for example as a percentage or as a proportion. The way that a particular ratio is presented will depend on the needs of those who will use the information. Though it is possible to calculate a large number of ratios, only a relatively few based on key relationships tend to be helpful to a particular user. Many ratios that could be calculated from the financial statements (for example, rent payable in relation to current assets) may not be considered because there is no clear or meaningful relationship between the two items.

There is no generally accepted list of ratios that can be applied to the financial statements, nor is there a standard method of calculating many ratios. Variations in both the choice of ratios and their calculation will be found in practice. However, it is important to be consistent in the way in which ratios are calculated for comparison purposes. The ratios discussed below are those that are widely used because many consider them to be among the more important for decision-making purposes.

Financial ratio classification

Ratios can be grouped into categories, each of which relates to a particular aspect of financial performance or position. The following broad categories provide a useful basis for explaining the nature of the financial ratios to be dealt with. There are five of them:

● *Profitability*.   Businesses generally exist with the primary purpose of creating wealth for their owners. Profitability ratios provide an insight to the degree of success in achieving this purpose. They express the profits made (or figures bearing on profit, such as overheads) in relation to other key figures in the financial statements or to some business resource.

● *Efficiency*.   Ratios may be used to measure the efficiency with which particular resources have been used within the business. These ratios are also referred to as *activity* ratios.

● *Liquidity*.   It is vital to the survival of a business for there to be sufficient liquid resources available to meet maturing obligations (that is, debts that must be paid in the relatively near future). Some liquidity ratios examine the relationship between liquid resources held and creditors (payables) due for payment in the near future.

● *Financial gearing*.   This is the relationship between the contribution to financing the business made by the owners of the business and the amount contributed by others, in the form of loans. The level of gearing has an important effect on the degree of risk associated with a business, as we shall see. Gearing is, therefore, something that managers must consider when making financing decisions. Gearing ratios tend to highlight the extent to which the business uses loan finance.

● *Investment*.   Certain ratios are concerned with assessing the returns and performance of shares held in a particular business from the perspective of shareholders who are not involved with the management of the business.

The analyst must be clear *who* the target users are and *why* they need the information.

Different users of financial information are likely to have different information needs, which will in turn determine the ratios that they find useful. For example, shareholders are likely to be interested in their returns in relation to the level of risk associated with their investment. Thus profitability, investment and gearing ratios will be of particular interest. Long-term lenders are concerned with the long-term viability of the business and to help them to assess this, the profitability and gearing ratios of the business are also likely to be of particular interest. Short-term lenders, such as suppliers of goods and services on credit, may be interested in the ability of the business to repay the amounts owing in the short term. As a result, the liquidity ratios should be of interest.

We shall consider ratios falling into each of the five categories (profitability, efficiency, liquidity, gearing and investment) a little later in the chapter.

The need for comparison

Merely calculating a ratio will not tell us very much about the position or performance of a business. For example, if a ratio revealed that the business was generating £100 in sales revenue per square metre of counter space, it would not be possible to deduce from this information alone whether this particular level of performance was good, bad or indifferent. It is only when we compare this ratio with some 'benchmark' that the information can be interpreted and evaluated.

Activity 7.1

Can you think of any bases that could be used to compare a ratio you have calculated from the financial statements of a particular period?

In answering this activity you may have thought of the following bases:

- *Past periods*. By comparing the ratio we have calculated with the same ratio, but for a previous period, it is possible to detect whether there has been an improvement or deterioration in performance. Indeed, it is often useful to track particular ratios over time (say, five or ten years) to see whether it is possible to detect trends. The comparison of ratios from different time periods brings certain problems, however. In particular, there is always the possibility that trading conditions may have been quite different in the periods being compared. There is the further problem that, when comparing the performance of a single business over time, operating inefficiencies may not be clearly exposed. For example, the fact that net profit per employee has risen by 10 per cent over the previous period may at first sight appear to be satisfactory. This may not be the case, however, if similar businesses have shown an improvement of 50 per cent for the same period. Finally, there is the problem that inflation may have distorted the figures on which the ratios are based. Inflation can lead to an overstatement of profit and an understatement of asset values.
- *Similar businesses*. In a competitive environment, a business must consider its performance in relation to that of other businesses operating in the same industry. Survival may depend on the ability to achieve comparable levels of performance. Thus a very useful basis for comparing a particular ratio is the ratio achieved by similar businesses during the same period. This basis is not, however, without its problems. Competitors may have different year ends, and therefore trading conditions may not be identical. They may also have different accounting policies, which can have a significant effect on reported profits and asset values (for example, different methods of calculating depreciation or valuing stock (inventory)). Finally, it may be difficult to obtain the financial statements of competitor businesses. Sole proprietorships and partnerships, for example, are not obliged to make their financial statements available to the public. In the case of limited companies, there is a legal obligation to do so. However, a diversified business may not provide a breakdown of activities that is sufficiently detailed that analysts can compare the activities with those of other businesses.
- *Planned performance*. Ratios may be compared with the targets that management developed before the start of the period under review. The comparison of planned performance with actual performance may therefore be a useful way of revealing the level of achievement attained. However, the planned levels of performance must be based on realistic assumptions if they are to be useful for comparison purposes.

Planned performance is likely to be the most valuable benchmark for the managers to assess their own business. Businesses tend to develop planned ratios for each aspect of their activities. When formulating its plans, a business may usefully take account of its own past performance and that of other businesses. There is no reason, however, why a particular business should seek to achieve either its own previous performance or that of other businesses. Neither of these may be seen as an appropriate target.

Analysts outside the business do not normally have access to the business's plans. For these people, past performance and the performances of other, similar, businesses may be the only practical benchmarks.

Key steps in financial ratio analysis

When undertaking a ratio analysis, analysts follow a sequence of steps. The first step involves identifying the key indicators and relationships that require examination. In carrying out this step, the analyst must be clear *who* the target users are and *why* they need the information. We saw earlier that different types of users of financial information are likely to have different information needs that will, in turn, determine the ratios that they find useful.

The next step in the process is to calculate ratios that are considered appropriate for the particular users and the purpose for which they require the information.

The final step is interpretation and evaluation of the ratios. Interpretation involves examining the ratios in conjunction with an appropriate basis for comparison and any other information that may be relevant. The significance of the ratios calculated can then be established. Evaluation involves forming a judgement concerning the value of the information uncovered in the calculation and interpretation of the ratios. Whilst calculation is usually straightforward, and can be easily carried out by computer, the interpretation and evaluation are more difficult and often require high levels of skill. This skill can only really be acquired through much practice. The three steps described are shown in Figure 7.1.

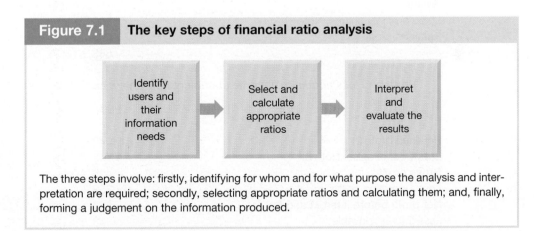

| Figure 7.1 | **The key steps of financial ratio analysis** |

The three steps involve: firstly, identifying for whom and for what purpose the analysis and interpretation are required; secondly, selecting appropriate ratios and calculating them; and, finally, forming a judgement on the information produced.

Calculating the ratios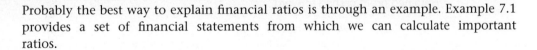

Probably the best way to explain financial ratios is through an example. Example 7.1 provides a set of financial statements from which we can calculate important ratios.

Example 7.1

The following financial statements relate to Alexis plc, which operates a whole-sale carpet business:

Balance sheets as at 31 March

	2004		2005	
	£m	£m	£m	£m
Non-current assets				
Property, plant and equipment (at cost less depreciation)				
Freehold land and buildings	381		427	
Fixtures and fittings	129		160	
		510		587
Current assets				
Stock at cost	300		406	
Trade debtors	240		273	
Bank	4		–	
	544		679	
Current liabilities				
Trade creditors	(221)		(314)	
Dividends approved, but unpaid	(40)		(40)	
Corporation tax due	(30)		(2)	
Bank overdraft	–		(76)	
	(291)	253	(432)	247
		763		834
Non-current liabilities				
9% debentures (secured)		(200)		(300)
		563		534
Equity				
£0.50 ordinary shares (Note 1)		300		300
Retained profit		263		234
		563		534

Profit and loss accounts (income statements) for the year ended 31 March

	2004	2005
	£m	£m
Revenue (Note 2)	2,240	2,681
Less Cost of sales (Note 3)	1,745	2,272
Gross profit	495	409
Less Operating costs	252	362
Net profit before interest and tax	243	47
Less Interest payable	18	32
Net profit before tax	225	15
Less Corporation tax	60	4
Net profit after tax	165	11
Add Retained profit brought forward	138	263
	303	274
Less Dividends approved, but unpaid (Note 4)	40	40
Retained profit carried forward	263	234

Cash flow statement for the year ended 31 March

	2004		2005	
Cash flows from operating activities	£m	£m	£m	£m
Net profit, after interest, before taxation	225		15	
Adjustments for:				
Depreciation	26		33	
Interest expense	18		32	
	269		80	
Increase in stocks	(22)		(106)	
Increase in trade debtors	(17)		(33)	
Increase in trade creditors	21		93	
Cash generated from operations	251		34	
Interest paid	(18)		(32)	
Corporation tax paid	(63)		(32)	
Dividend paid	(40)		(40)	
Net cash from/(used in) operating activities		130		(70)
Cash flows from investing activities				
Payments to acquire property, plant and equipment	(77)		(110)	
Net cash used in investing activities		(77)		(110)
Cash flows from financing activities				
Issue of debenture stock	–		100	
Net cash from financing activities		–		100
Net increase in cash and cash equivalents		53		(80)
Cash and cash equivalents at start of year				
Cash/(overdraft)		(49)		4
Cash and cash equivalents at end of year				
Cash/(overdraft)		4		(76)

Notes

1 The market value of the shares of the business at the end of the year was £2.50 for 2004 and £1.50 for 2005.
2 All sales and purchases are made on credit.
3 The cost of sales figure can be analysed as follows:

	2004	2005
	£m	£m
Opening stock	241	300
Purchases (Note 2)	1,804	2,378
	2,045	2,678
Less Closing stock	300	406
Cost of sales	1,745	2,272

4 The dividend had been approved by the shareholders before the end of the accounting year (in both years), but not paid until after then.
5 The business employed 13,995 staff at 31 March 2004 and 18,623 at 31 March 2005.
6 The business expanded its capacity during 2005 by setting up a new warehouse and distribution centre in the north of England.
7 At 1 April 2003, the total of equity stood at £438m and the total of equity and non-current liabilities stood at £638m.

A brief overview

Before we start our detailed look at the ratios for Alexis plc (in Example 7.1), it is helpful to take a quick look at what information is obvious from the financial statements. This will usually pick up some issues that the ratios may not be able to identify. It may also highlight some points that could help us in our interpretation of the ratios. Starting at the top of the balance sheet, the following points can be noted:

- *Expansion of non-current assets.* These have increased by about 15 per cent (from £510m to £587m). This would appear not entirely (if at all) to be from any upward revaluation in assets existing in 2004, because the cash flow statement makes clear that £110m was spent on new non-current assets during 2005. The reason that the non-current assets in 2005 did not total £620m (that is, £510m plus £110m) is presumably that depreciation will have been charged. Note 5 mentions a new warehouse and distribution centre, which may account for much of the additional investment in non-current assets. We are not told when this new facility was established, but it is quite possible that it was well into the year. This could mean that not much benefit was reflected in terms of additional sales revenue or cost saving during 2005. Sales revenue, in fact, expanded by about 20 per cent (from £2,240m to £2,681m), greater than the expansion in non-current assets.

- *Major expansion in the elements of working capital.* Stock (inventory) increased by about 35 per cent, trade debtors (receivables) by about 14 per cent and trade creditors (payables) by about 33 per cent between 2004 and 2005. These are major increases, particularly in stock and creditors (which are linked because the stock is all bought on credit – see Note 2).

- *Reduction in the cash balance.* The cash balance fell from £4m (in funds) to a £76m overdraft, between 2004 and 2005. The bank may be putting the business under pressure to reverse this, which could raise difficulties.

- *Apparent debt capacity.* Comparing either the non-current assets or the net assets with the long-term borrowings implies that the business may well be able to offer security on further borrowing. This is because potential lenders usually look at the value of assets that can be offered as security, when assessing loan requests. Lenders seem particularly attracted to freeholds as security. For example, at 31 March 2005, non-current assets had a balance sheet value of £587m, but long-term borrowing was only £300m (though there was also an overdraft of £76m). Balance sheet values are not normally, of course, market values. On the other hand, freeholds tend to have a market value higher than their balance sheet value due to inflation in land values.

- *Lower profit.* Though sales revenue expanded by 20 per cent between 2004 and 2005, both cost of sales and operating costs rose by a greater percentage, leaving both gross profit and, particularly, net profit massively reduced. The level of staffing, which increased by about 33 per cent (from 13,995 to 18,623), may have greatly affected the operating costs. (Without knowing when the additional employees were recruited during 2005, we cannot be sure of the effect on operating costs.) Increasing staffing by 33 per cent must put an enormous strain on management, at least in the short term. It is not surprising, therefore that 2005 was not successful for the business.

Having had a quick look at what is fairly obvious without calculating the normal ratios, we shall now go on to do so.

Profitability

The following ratios may be used to evaluate the profitability of the business:

- return on ordinary shareholders' funds;
- return on capital employed;
- net profit margin; and
- gross profit margin.

We shall now look at each of these in turn.

Return on ordinary shareholders' funds (ROSF)

The **return on ordinary shareholders' funds** compares the amount of profit for the period available to the owners, with the owners' average stake in the business during that same period. The ratio (which is normally expressed in percentage terms) is as follows:

$$ROSF = \frac{\text{Net profit after taxation and preference dividend (if any)}}{\text{Ordinary share capital plus reserves}} \times 100$$

The net profit after taxation and any preference dividend is used in calculating the ratio, as this figure represents the amount of profit that is left for the owners.

In the case of Alexis plc, the ratio for the year ended 31 March 2004 is:

$$ROSF = \frac{165}{(438 + 563)/2} \times 100 = 33.0\%$$

Note that, when calculating the ROSF, the average of the figures for ordinary shareholders' funds as at the beginning and at the end of the year has been used. It is preferable to use an average figure, as this might be more representative. This is because the shareholders' funds did not have the same total throughout the year, yet we want to compare it with the profit earned during the whole period. We know, from Note 7, that the total of the shareholders' funds at 1 April 2003 was £438m. By a year later, however, it had risen to £563m, according to the balance sheet as at 31 March 2004.

The easiest approach to calculating the average amount of shareholders' funds is to take a simple average based on the opening and closing figures for the year. This is often the only information available, as is the case with Example 7.1. Where not even the beginning-of-year figure is available, it is usually acceptable to use just the year-end figure, provided that this approach is consistently adopted. This is generally valid for all ratios that combine a figure for a period (such as net profit) with one taken at a point in time (such as shareholders' funds).

Activity 7.2

Calculate the ROSF for Alexis plc for the year to 31 March 2005.

The ROSF for 2005 is:

$$ROSF = \frac{11}{(563 + 534)/2} \times 100 = 2.0\%$$

Broadly, businesses seek to generate as high a value as possible for this ratio, provided that it is not achieved at the expense of potential future returns by, for example, taking on more risky activities. In view of this, the 2005 ratio is very poor by any standard; a bank deposit account will yield a better return than this. We need to try to find out why things went so badly wrong in 2005. As we look at other ratios, we should find some clues.

Return on capital employed (ROCE)

The **return on capital employed** is a fundamental measure of business performance. This ratio expresses the relationship between the net profit generated during a period and the average long-term capital invested in the business during that period.

The ratio is expressed in percentage terms and is as follows:

$$\text{ROCE} = \frac{\text{Net profit before interest and taxation}}{\text{Share capital} + \text{Reserves} + \text{Long-term loans}} \times 100$$

Note, in this case, that the profit figure used is the net profit *before* interest and taxation, because the ratio attempts to measure the returns to all suppliers of long-term finance before any deductions for interest payable to lenders or payments of dividends to shareholders are made.

For the year to 31 March 2004, the ratio for Alexis plc is:

$$\text{ROCE} = \frac{243}{(638 + 763)/2} \times 100 = 34.7\%$$

ROCE is considered by many to be a primary measure of profitability. It compares inputs (capital invested) with outputs (profit). This comparison is vital in assessing the effectiveness with which funds have been deployed. Once again, an average figure for capital employed may be used where the information is available.

Activity 7.3

Calculate the ROCE for Alexis plc for the year to 31 March 2005.

For 2005, the ratio is:

$$\text{ROCE} = \frac{47}{(763 + 834)/2} \times 100 = 5.9\%$$

This ratio tells much the same story as ROSF: namely a poor performance, with the return on the assets being less than the rate that the business has to pay for most of its borrowed funds (that is, 9 per cent for the debentures). See **Real World 7.2** (p. 223) for how Tesco plc, the well-known supermarket chain, has been able to use loan financing to increase its ROSF ratios, despite a decline in ROCE.

Net profit margin

The **net profit margin ratio** relates the net profit for the period to the sales revenue during that period. The ratio is expressed as follows:

$$\text{Net profit margin} = \frac{\text{Net profit before interest and taxation}}{\text{Sales revenue}} \times 100$$

The net profit before interest and taxation is used in this ratio as it represents the profit from trading operations before the interest costs are taken into account. This is often regarded as the most appropriate measure of operational performance, when used as a basis of comparison, because differences arising from the way in which the business is financed will not influence the measure.

For the year ended 31 March 2004, Alexis plc's net profit margin ratio is:

$$\text{Net profit margin} = \frac{243}{2,240} \times 100 = 10.8\%$$

This ratio compares one output of the business (profit) with another output (sales revenue). The ratio can vary considerably between types of business. For example, supermarkets tend to operate on low prices and, therefore, low profit margins in an attempt to stimulate sales and thereby increase the total amount of profit generated. Jewellers, on the other hand, tend to have high net profit margins but have much lower levels of sales volume. Factors such as the degree of competition, the type of customer, the economic climate and industry characteristics (such as the level of risk) will influence the net profit margin of a business.

Activity 7.4

Calculate the net profit margin for Alexis plc for the year to 31 March 2005.

The net profit margin for 2005 is:

$$\text{Net profit margin} = \frac{47}{2,681} \times 100 = 1.8\%$$

Once again a very weak performance compared with that of 2004. Whereas in 2004 for every £1 of sales revenue an average of 10.8 pence (that is, 10.8%) was left as profit, after paying the cost of the carpets sold and other expenses of operating the business, for 2005 this had fallen to only 1.8 pence for every £1. Thus the reason for the poor ROSF and ROCE ratios was partially, perhaps wholly, a high level of expenses relative to sales revenue. The next ratio should provide us with a clue as to how the sharp decline in this ratio occurred.

Gross profit margin

The **gross profit margin ratio** relates the gross profit of the business to the sales revenue generated for the same period. Gross profit represents the difference between sales revenue and the cost of sales. The ratio is therefore a measure of profitability in buying (or producing) and selling goods before any other expenses are taken into account. As cost of sales represents a major expense for many businesses, a change in this ratio can have a significant effect on the 'bottom line' (that is, the net profit for the year). The gross profit margin ratio is calculated as follows:

$$\text{Gross profit margin} = \frac{\text{Gross profit}}{\text{Sales revenue}} \times 100$$

For the year to 31 March 2004, the ratio for Alexis plc is:

$$\text{Gross profit margin} = \frac{495}{2{,}240} \times 100 = 22.1\%$$

Activity 7.5

Calculate the gross profit margin for Alexis plc for the year to 31 March 2005.

The gross profit margin for 2005 is:

$$\text{Gross profit margin} = \frac{409}{2{,}681} \times 100 = 15.3\%$$

The decline in this ratio means that gross profit was lower *relative* to sales revenue in 2005 than it had been in 2004. Bearing in mind that:

Gross profit = Sales revenue − Cost of sales (or cost of goods sold)

this means that cost of sales was higher *relative* to sales revenue in 2005 than in 2004. This could mean that sales prices were lower and/or that the purchase cost of goods sold had increased. It is possible that both sales prices and goods sold prices had reduced, but the former at a greater rate than the latter. Similarly they may both have increased, but with sales prices having increased at a lesser rate than costs of the goods sold.

Clearly, part of the decline in the net profit margin ratio is linked to the dramatic decline in the gross profit margin ratio. Whereas, after paying for the carpets sold, for each £1 of sales revenue 22.1 pence was left to cover other operating expenses and leave a profit in 2004, this was only 15.3 pence in 2005.

The profitability ratios for the business over the two years can be set out as follows:

	2004	2005
	%	%
ROSF	33.0	2.0
ROCE	34.7	5.9
Net profit margin	10.8	1.8
Gross profit margin	22.1	15.3

Activity 7.6

What do you deduce from a comparison of the declines in the net profit and gross profit margin ratios?

It occurs to us that the decline in the net profit margin was 9% (that is, 10.8% to 1.8%), whereas that of the gross profit margin was only 6.8% (that is, from 22.1% to 15.3%). This can only mean that operating expenses were greater, compared with sales revenue in 2005, than they had been in 2004. Thus, the declines in both ROSF and ROCE were caused partly by the business incurring higher stock purchasing costs relative to sales revenue and partly through higher operating expenses to sales revenue. We should need to compare these ratios with the planned levels for them before we could usefully assess the business's success.

The analyst must now try to discover what caused the increases in both cost of sales and operating costs, relative to sales revenue, from 2004 to 2005. This will involve checking on what has happened with sales and stock prices over the two years. Similarly, it will involve looking at each of the individual expenses that make up operating costs to discover which ones were responsible for the increase, relative to sales revenue. Here, further ratios, for example staff costs (wages and salaries) to sales revenue, could be calculated in an attempt to isolate the cause of the change from 2004 to 2005. In fact, as we discussed when we took an overview of the financial statements, the increase in staffing may well account for most of the increase in operating costs.

Real World 7.1 shows how one well-known business is seeking to improve its ROCE.

REAL WORLD 7.1

Lazy assets raise the ROCE at Shell   **FT**

During 2003, Shell, the oil business (The 'Shell' Transport and Trading Company plc) disposed of $4bn of what it called 'lazy assets'. These are assets that the business felt were not earning their keep and were holding the ROCE below the target range of 13 to 15%. The business had also identified a further $3bn of assets that could be 'improved', so that they could also boost the business's ROCE.

Source: 'Shell disposals of $4 billion double initial estimate', Toby Shelley, FT.com, 22 December 2003.

Efficiency

Efficiency ratios examine the ways in which various resources of the business are managed. The following ratios consider some of the more important aspects of resource management:

● average stock (inventory) turnover period;
● average settlement period for debtors (receivables);
● average settlement period for creditors (payables);
● sales revenue to capital employed; and
● sales revenue per employee.

We shall now look at each of these in turn.

Average stock (inventory) turnover period

Stocks often represent a significant investment for a business. For some types of business (for example, manufacturers), stocks may account for a substantial proportion of the total assets held (see Real World 7.7, p. 237). The **average stock turnover period** measures the average period for which stocks are being held. The ratio is calculated as follows:

$$\text{Average stock turnover period} = \frac{\text{Average stock held}}{\text{Cost of sales}} \times 365$$

The average stock for the period can be calculated as a simple average of the opening and closing stock levels for the year. However, in the case of a highly seasonal business, where stock levels may vary considerably over the year, a monthly average may be more appropriate.

In the case of Alexis plc, the stock turnover period for the year ended 31 March 2004 is:

$$\text{Average stock turnover period} = \frac{(241 + 300)/2}{1,745} \times 365 = 56.6 \text{ days}$$

This means that, on average, the stock held is being 'turned over' every 56.6 days. So, a carpet bought by the business on a particular day would, on average, have been sold about eight weeks later. A business will normally prefer a short stock turnover period to a long one, as funds tied up in stocks cannot be used for other purposes. When judging the amount of stock to carry, the business must consider such things as the likely demand for the stock, the possibility of supply shortages, the likelihood of price rises, the amount of storage space available and the perishability of the stock.

This ratio is sometimes expressed in terms of months rather than days. Multiplying by 12 rather than 365 will achieve this.

Activity 7.7

Calculate the average stock turnover period for Alexis plc for the year ended 31 March 2005.

The average stock turnover period for 2005 is:

$$\text{Average stock turnover period} = \frac{(300 + 406)/2}{2,272} \times 365 = 56.7 \text{ days}$$

Thus the stock turnover period is virtually the same in both years.

Average settlement period for debtors

A business will usually be concerned with how long it takes for customers to pay the amounts owing. The speed of payment can have a significant effect on the business's cash flow. The **average settlement period for debtors** calculates how long, on average, credit customers take to pay the amounts that they owe to the business. The ratio is as follows:

$$\text{Average settlement period for debtors} = \frac{\text{Trade debtors}}{\text{Credit sales revenue}} \times 365$$

A business will normally prefer a shorter average settlement period to a longer one as, once again, funds are being tied up that may be used for more profitable purposes. Though this ratio can be useful, it is important to remember that it produces an *average* figure for the number of days for which debts are outstanding. This average may be badly distorted by, for example, a few large customers who are very slow or very fast payers.

Since all sales made by Alexis plc are on credit, the average settlement period for debtors for the year ended 31 March 2004 is:

$$\text{Average settlement period for debtors} = \frac{240}{2{,}240} \times 365 = 39.1 \text{ days}$$

Since no figures for opening debtors are available, the year-end debtors figure only is used. This is common practice.

Activity 7.8

Calculate the average settlement period for Alexis plc's debtors for the year ended 31 March 2005. (In the interests of consistency, use the year-end debtors figure rather than an average figure.)

The average settlement period for 2005 is:

$$\text{Average settlement period for debtors} = \frac{273}{2{,}681} \times 365 = 37.2 \text{ days}$$

On the face of it, this reduction in the settlement period is welcome. It means that less cash was tied up in debtors for each £1 of sales revenue in 2005 than in 2004. Only if the reduction were achieved at the expense of customer goodwill or a high direct financial cost, might the desirability of the reduction be questioned. For example, the reduction may have been due to chasing customers too vigorously or as a result of incurring higher costs, such as discounts allowed to customers who pay quickly.

Average settlement period for creditors

→ The **average settlement period for creditors** measures how long, on average, the business takes to pay its trade creditors. The ratio is calculated as follows:

$$\text{Average settlement period for creditors} = \frac{\text{Trade creditors}}{\text{Credit purchases}} \times 365$$

This ratio provides an average figure, which, like the average settlement period for debtors ratio, can be distorted by the payment period for one or two large suppliers.

As trade creditors provide a free source of finance for the business, it is perhaps not surprising that some businesses attempt to increase their average settlement period for trade creditors. However, such a policy can be taken too far and result in a loss of goodwill of suppliers.

For the year ended 31 March 2004, Alexis plc's average settlement period for creditors is:

$$\text{Average settlement period for creditors} = \frac{221}{1{,}804} \times 365 = 44.7 \text{ days}$$

Once again, the year-end figure rather than an average figure for creditors has been used in the calculations.

Activity 7.9

Calculate the average settlement period for creditors for Alexis plc for the year ended 31 March 2005. (For the sake of consistency, use a year-end figure for creditors.)

The average settlement period for creditors is:

$$\text{Average settlement period for creditors} = \frac{314}{2,378} \times 365 = 48.2 \text{ days}$$

There was an increase, between 2004 and 2005, in the average length of time that elapsed between buying stock and paying for it. On the face of it, this is beneficial because the business is using free finance provided by suppliers. If, however, this is leading to a loss of supplier goodwill that could have adverse consequences for Alexis plc, it is not necessarily advantageous.

Sales revenue to capital employed

The **sales revenue to capital employed ratio** (or asset turnover ratio) examines how effectively the assets of the business are being used to generate sales revenue. It is calculated as follows:

$$\frac{\text{Sales revenue to}}{\text{capital employed ratio}} = \frac{\text{Sales revenue}}{\text{Share capital} + \text{Reserves} + \text{Non-current liabilities}}$$

Generally speaking, a higher asset turnover ratio is preferred to a lower one. A higher ratio will normally suggest that assets are being used more productively in the generation of revenue. However, a very high ratio may suggest that the business is 'overtrading on its assets', that is, it has insufficient assets to sustain the level of sales revenue achieved. (Overtrading will be discussed in more detail later in the chapter.) When comparing this ratio for different businesses, factors such as the age and condition of assets held, the valuation bases for assets and whether assets are rented or purchased outright can complicate interpretation.

A variation of this formula is to use the total assets less current liabilities (which is equivalent to long-term capital employed) in the denominator (lower part of the fraction) – the identical result is obtained.

For the year ended 31 March 2004, this ratio for Alexis plc is as follows:

$$\text{Sales revenue to capital employed} = \frac{2,240}{(638 + 763)/2} = 3.19 \text{ times}$$

Activity 7.10

Calculate the sales revenue to capital employed ratio for Alexis plc for the year ended 31 March 2005.

The sales revenue to capital employed ratio for 2005 is:

$$\text{Sales revenue to capital employed} = \frac{2{,}681}{(763 + 834)/2} = 3.36 \text{ times}$$

This seems to be an improvement, since in 2005 more sales revenue was being generated for each £1 of capital employed (£3.36) than was the case in 2004 (£3.19). Provided that overtrading is not an issue, this is to be welcomed.

Sales revenue per employee

→ The **sales revenue per employee ratio** relates sales revenue generated to a particular business resource, that is, labour. It provides a measure of the productivity of the workforce. The ratio is:

$$\textbf{Sales revenue per employee} = \frac{\textbf{Sales revenue}}{\textbf{Number of employees}}$$

Generally, businesses would prefer to have a high value for this ratio, implying that they are using their staff efficiently.

For the year ended 31 March 2004, the ratio for Alexis plc is:

$$\text{Sales revenue per employee} = \frac{£2{,}240m}{13{,}995} = £160{,}057$$

Activity 7.11

Calculate the sales revenue per employee for Alexis plc for the year ended 31 March 2005.

The ratio for 2005 is:

$$\text{Sales revenue per employee} = \frac{£2{,}681m}{18{,}623} = £143{,}962$$

This represents a fairly significant decline and probably one that merits further investigation. As we discussed previously, the number of employees had increased quite notably (by about 33 per cent) during 2005 and the analyst will probably try to discover why this had not generated sufficient additional sales revenue to maintain the ratio at its 2004 level. It could be that the additional employees were not appointed until late in the year ended 31 March 2005.

The efficiency, or activity, ratios may be summarised as follows:

	2004	2005
Average stock turnover period	56.6 days	56.7 days
Average settlement period for debtors	39.1 days	37.2 days
Average settlement period for creditors	44.7 days	48.2 days
Sales revenue to capital employed (asset turnover)	3.19 times	3.36 times
Sales revenue per employee	£160,057	£143,962

Activity 7.12

What do you deduce from a comparison of the efficiency ratios over the two years?

We feel that maintaining the stock turnover period at the 2004 level seems reasonable, though whether this represents a satisfactory period can probably only be assessed by looking at the business's planned stock period. The stockholding period for other businesses operating in carpet retailing, particularly those regarded as the market leaders, may have been helpful in formulating the plans. On the face of things, a shorter debtor collection period and a longer creditor payment period are both desirable. On the other hand, these may have been achieved at the cost of a loss of the goodwill of customers and suppliers, respectively. The increased asset turnover ratio seems beneficial, provided that the business can manage this increase. The decline in the sales revenue per employee ratio is undesirable but, as we have already seen, is probably related to the dramatic increase in the level of staffing. As with the stock turnover period, these other ratios need to be compared with the planned standard of efficiency.

The relationship between profitability and efficiency

In our earlier discussions concerning profitability ratios on page 206, we saw that return on capital employed (ROCE) is regarded as a key ratio by many businesses. The ratio is:

$$\text{ROCE} = \frac{\text{Net profit before interest and taxation}}{\text{Long-term capital employed}} \times 100$$

(where long-term capital comprises share capital plus reserves plus long-term loans). This ratio can be broken down into two elements, as shown in Figure 7.2. The first ratio

Figure 7.2   The main elements comprising the ROCE ratio

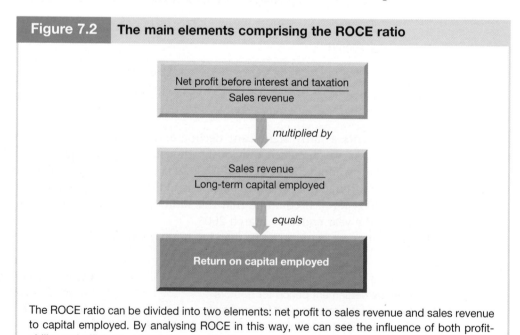

The ROCE ratio can be divided into two elements: net profit to sales revenue and sales revenue to capital employed. By analysing ROCE in this way, we can see the influence of both profitability and efficiency on this important ratio.

is the net profit margin ratio, and the second is the sales revenue to capital employed (asset turnover) ratio, which we discussed earlier.

By breaking down the ROCE ratio in this manner, we highlight the fact that the overall return on funds employed within the business will be determined both by the profitability of sales and by efficiency in the use of capital.

Example 7.2

Consider the following information concerning two different businesses operating in the same industry:

	Antler plc	Baker plc
Profit before interest and tax	£20m	£15m
Long-term capital employed	£100m	£75m
Sales revenue	£200m	£300m

The ROCE for each business is identical (20%). However, the manner in which the return was achieved by each business was quite different. In the case of Antler plc, the net profit margin is 10% and the sales revenue to capital employed ratio is 2 times (so, ROCE = 10% × 2 = 20%). In the case of Baker plc, the net profit margin is 5% and the sales revenue to capital employed ratio is 4 times (and so, ROCE = 5% × 4 = 20%).

Example 7.2 demonstrates that a relatively low net profit margin can be compensated for by a relatively high sales revenue to capital employed ratio, and a relatively low sales revenue to capital employed ratio can be compensated for by a relatively high net profit margin. In many areas of retail and distribution (for example, supermarkets and delivery services), the net profit margins are quite low but the ROCE can be high, provided that the assets are used productively.

Activity 7.13

Show how the ROCE ratio for Alexis plc can be analysed into the two elements for each of the years 2004 and 2005.
 What conclusions can you draw from your figures?

	ROCE	=	Net profit margin	×	Sales revenue to capital employed
2004	34.7%		10.8%		3.19
2005	5.9%		1.8%		3.36

Thus the relationship between the three ratios holds for Alexis plc, for both years. The small apparent differences arise because the three ratios are stated above only to one or two decimal places.

 Though the business was more effective at generating sales (sales revenue to capital employed ratio increased) from 2004 to 2005, it fell well below the level necessary to compensate for the sharp decline in the effectiveness of each sale (net profit margin). As a result, the 2005 ROCE was well below the 2004 value.

Liquidity

Liquidity ratios are concerned with the ability of the business to meet its short-term financial obligations. The following ratios are widely used:

- current ratio;
- acid test ratio; and
- cash generated from operations to maturing obligations ratio.

These three will now be considered.

Current ratio

The **current ratio** compares the 'liquid' assets (that is, cash and those assets held that will soon be turned into cash) of the business with the current liabilities. The ratio is calculated as follows:

$$\text{Current ratio} = \frac{\text{Current assets}}{\text{Current liabilities}}$$

Some people seem to suggest that there is an 'ideal' current ratio (usually 2 times or 2:1) for all businesses. However, this fails to take into account the fact that different types of business require different current ratios. For example, a manufacturing business will often have a relatively high current ratio because it is necessary to hold stocks of finished goods, raw materials and work in progress. It will also normally sell goods on credit, thereby incurring debtors. A supermarket chain, on the other hand, will have a relatively low ratio, as it will hold only fast-moving stocks of finished goods and will generate mostly cash sales revenue. (See Real World 7.7 on p. 237.)

The higher the ratio, the more liquid the business is considered to be. As liquidity is vital to the survival of a business, a higher current ratio might be thought to be preferable to a lower one. If a business has a very high ratio, however, it may be that funds are tied up in cash or other liquid assets and are not, therefore, being used as productively as they might otherwise be.

As at 31 March 2004, the current ratio of Alexis plc is:

$$\text{Current ratio} = \frac{544}{291} = 1.9 \text{ times (or 1.9:1)}$$

Activity 7.14

Calculate the current ratio for Alexis plc as at 31 March 2005.

....

The current ratio as at 31 March 2005 is:

$$\text{Current ratio} = \frac{679}{432} = 1.6 \text{ times (or 1.6:1)}$$

Though this is a decline from 2004 to 2005, it is not necessarily a matter of concern. The next ratio may provide a clue as to whether there seems to be a problem.

Acid test ratio

→ The **acid test ratio** is very similar to the current ratio, but it represents a more stringent test of liquidity. It can be argued that, for many businesses, stock cannot be converted into cash quickly. (Note that, in the case of Alexis plc, the stock turnover period was about 57 days in both years (see p. 210).) As a result, it may be better to exclude this particular asset from any measure of liquidity. The acid test ratio is a variation of the current ratio, but excluding stock.

The minimum level for this ratio is often stated as 1.0 times (or 1:1 – that is, current assets (excluding stock) equals current liabilities). In many highly successful businesses that are regarded as having adequate liquidity, however, it is not unusual for the acid test ratio to be below 1.0 without causing particular liquidity problems. (See Real World 7.7 on p. 237.)

The acid test ratio is calculated as follows:

$$\text{Acid test ratio} = \frac{\text{Current assets (excluding stock)}}{\text{Current liabilities}}$$

The acid test ratio for Alexis plc as at 31 March 2004 is:

$$\text{Acid test ratio} = \frac{544 - 300}{291} = 0.8 \text{ times (or 0.8:1)}$$

We can see that the 'liquid' current assets do not quite cover the current liabilities, and so the business may be experiencing some liquidity problems.

Activity 7.15

Calculate the acid test ratio for Alexis plc as at 31 March 2005.

The acid test ratio as at 31 March 2005 is:

$$\text{Acid test ratio} = \frac{679 - 406}{432} = 0.6 \text{ times}$$

The 2005 ratio is significantly below that for 2004. The 2005 level may well be a cause for concern. The rapid decline in this ratio should lead to steps being taken, at least, to stop further decline.

Cash generated from operations to maturing obligations

→ The **cash generated from operations to maturing obligations ratio** compares the cash generated from operations (taken from the cash flow statement) with the current liabilities of the business. It provides a further indication of the ability of the business to meet its maturing obligations. The ratio is expressed as:

$$\frac{\text{Cash generated from operations}}{\text{to maturing obligations}} = \frac{\text{Cash generated from operations}}{\text{Current liabilities}}$$

The higher this ratio, the better the liquidity of the business. This ratio has the advantage over the current ratio that the operating cash flows for a period usually provide a more reliable guide to the liquidity of a business than the current assets held at the balance sheet date. Alexis plc's ratio for the year ended 31 March 2004 is:

$$\text{Cash generated from operations to maturing obligations} = \frac{251}{291} = 0.9 \text{ times}$$

This ratio indicates that the operating cash flows for the period are just sufficient to cover the current liabilities at the end of the period.

Activity 7.16

Calculate the cash generated from operations to maturing obligations ratio for Alexis plc for the year ended 31 March 2005.

The ratio is:

$$\text{Cash generated from operations to maturing obligations} = \frac{34}{432} = 0.1 \text{ times}$$

This ratio shows an alarming decline in the ability of the business to meet its maturing obligations from its operating cash flows. This confirms that liquidity is a real cause for concern for the business.

The liquidity ratios for the two-year period may be summarised as follows:

	2004	2005
Current ratio	1.9	1.6
Acid test ratio	0.8	0.6
Cash generated from operations to maturing obligations	0.9	0.1

Activity 7.17

What do you deduce from the liquidity ratios set out above?

Though it is probably not really possible to make a totally valid judgement without knowing the planned ratios, there appears to have been an alarming decline in liquidity. This is indicated by all three of these ratios. The most worrying is in the last ratio because it shows that the ability of the business to generate cash from trading operations has declined, relative to the short-term debts, from 2004 to 2005. The apparent liquidity problem may, however, be planned, short-term and linked to the expansion in non-current assets and staffing. It may be that when the benefits of the expansion come on stream, liquidity will improve. On the other hand, short-term creditors may become anxious when they see signs of weak liquidity. This anxiety could lead to steps being taken to press for payment and this could cause problems for Alexis plc.

Gearing

→ **Financial gearing** occurs when a business is financed, at least in part, by borrowing, instead of by finance provided by the owners (the shareholders). A business's level of gearing (that is, the extent to which it is financed from sources that require a fixed return) is an important factor in assessing risk. Where a business borrows heavily, it takes on a commitment to pay interest charges and make capital repayments. This can be a significant financial burden; it can increase the risk of the business becoming insolvent. Nevertheless, most businesses are geared to some extent.

Given the risks involved, we may wonder why a business would want to take on gearing (that is, to borrow). One reason may be that the owners have insufficient funds, so the only way to finance the business adequately is to borrow from others. Another reason is that gearing can be used to increase the returns to owners. This is possible provided the returns generated from borrowed funds exceed the cost of paying interest. Example 7.3 illustrates this point.

Example 7.3

The long-term capital structures of two new businesses, Lee Ltd and Nova Ltd, are as follows:

	Lee Ltd	Nova Ltd
	£	£
£1 ordinary shares	100,000	200,000
10% loan	200,000	100,000
	300,000	300,000

In their first year of operations, they each make a profit before interest and taxation of £50,000. The tax rate is 30% of the net profit after interest.

Lee Ltd would probably be considered relatively highly geared, as it has a high proportion of borrowed funds in its long-term capital structure. Nova Ltd is much lower geared. The profit available to the shareholders of each business in the first year of operations will be:

	Lee Ltd	Nova Ltd
	£	£
Profit before interest and taxation	50,000	50,000
Interest payable	(20,000)	(10,000)
Profit before taxation	30,000	40,000
Taxation (30%)	(9,000)	(12,000)
Profit available to ordinary shareholders	21,000	28,000

The return on ordinary shareholders' funds (ROSF) for each business will be:

Lee Ltd	Nova Ltd

$$\frac{21,000}{100,000} \times 100 = 21\% \qquad \frac{28,000}{200,000} \times 100 = 14\%$$

We can see that Lee Ltd, the more highly geared business, has generated a better ROSF than Nova Ltd. This is despite the fact that the ROCE (return on capital employed) is identical for both businesses (that is (£50,000/£300,000) × 100 = 16.7%).

An effect of gearing is that returns to shareholders become more sensitive to changes in profits. For a highly geared business, a change in profits can lead to a proportionately greater change in the ROSF ratio.

Activity 7.18

Assume that the profit before interest and tax was 20% higher for each business than stated above (that is, a profit of £60,000). What would be the effect of this on ROSF?

The revised profit available to the shareholders of each business in the first year of operations will be:

	Lee Ltd	Nova Ltd
	£	£
Profit before interest and taxation	60,000	60,000
Interest payable	(20,000)	(10,000)
Profit before taxation	40,000	50,000
Taxation (30%)	(12,000)	(15,000)
Profit available to ordinary shareholders	28,000	35,000

The ROSF for each business will now be:

Lee Ltd

$$\frac{28,000}{100,000} \times 100 = 28\%$$

Nova Ltd

$$\frac{35,000}{200,000} \times 100 = 17.5\%$$

We can see that for Lee Ltd, the higher-geared business, the returns to shareholders have increased by a third (from 21 to 28 per cent), whereas for the lower-geared business, Nova Ltd, the benefits of gearing are less pronounced, increasing by only a quarter (from 14 to 17.5 per cent). The effect of gearing, of course, can work in both directions. Thus, for a highly geared business, a small decline in profits may bring about a much greater decline in the returns to shareholders.

The reason that gearing tends to be beneficial to shareholders is that loan interest rates are relatively low, compared with the returns that the typical business can earn. On top of this, interest costs are tax deductible, in the way shown in Example 7.3 and Activity 7.18, making the effective cost of borrowing quite cheap. It is debatable whether the apparent low interest rates really are beneficial to the shareholders. Some argue that since borrowing increases the risk to shareholders, there is a hidden cost of borrowing. What are not illusory, however, are the benefits to the shareholders of the tax deductibility of loan interest.

The effect of gearing is like that of two intermeshing cogwheels of unequal size (see Figure 7.3). The movement in the larger cog (profit before interest and tax) causes a more than proportionate movement in the smaller cog (returns to ordinary shareholders).

Real World 7.2, which appears later in this section on gearing ratios, provides an example of the effective use of gearing by a well-known business (Tesco plc).

Figure 7.3 The effect of financial gearing

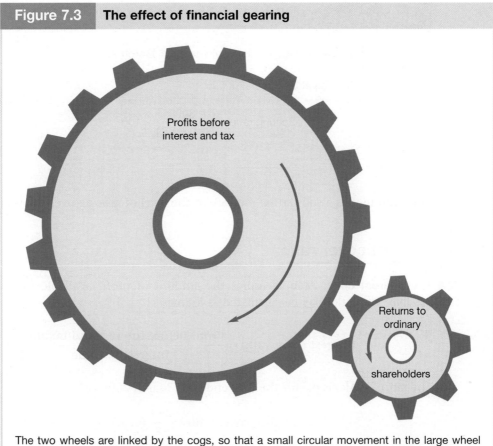

The two wheels are linked by the cogs, so that a small circular movement in the large wheel (profit before interest and tax) leads to a relatively large circular movement in the small wheel (returns to ordinary shareholders).

There are two ratios that are widely used to assess gearing:

- gearing ratio
- interest cover ratio.

Gearing ratio

The **gearing ratio** measures the contribution of long-term lenders to the long-term capital structure of a business:

$$\text{Gearing ratio} = \frac{\text{Long-term (non-current) liabilities}}{\text{Share capital} + \text{Reserves} + \text{Long-term (non-current) liabilities}} \times 100$$

The gearing ratio for Alexis plc, as at 31 March 2004, is:

$$\text{Gearing ratio} = \frac{200}{(563 + 200)} \times 100 = 26.2\%$$

This ratio reveals a level of gearing that would not normally be considered to be very high.

Activity 7.19

Calculate the gearing ratio of Alexis plc as at 31 March 2005.

The gearing ratio as at 31 March 2005 is:

$$\text{Gearing ratio} = \frac{300}{(534 + 300)} \times 100 = 36.0\%$$

This ratio reveals a substantial increase in the level of gearing over the year.

 ## Interest cover ratio

→ The **interest cover ratio** measures the amount of profit available to cover interest payable. The ratio may be calculated as follows:

$$\text{Interest cover ratio} = \frac{\textbf{Profit before interest and taxation}}{\textbf{Interest payable}}$$

The ratio for Alexis plc for the year ended 31 March 2004 is:

$$\text{Interest cover ratio} = \frac{243}{18} = 13.5 \text{ times}$$

This ratio shows that the level of profit is considerably higher than the level of interest payable. Thus a significant fall in profits could occur before profit levels failed to cover interest payable. The lower the level of profit coverage, the greater the risk to lenders that interest payments will not be met, and the greater the risk to the shareholders that the lenders will take action against the business to recover the interest due.

Activity 7.20

Calculate the interest cover ratio of Alexis plc for the year ended 31 March 2005.

The interest cover ratio for 2005 is:

$$\text{Interest cover ratio} = \frac{47}{32} = 1.5 \text{ times}$$

Real World 7.2 shows how Tesco plc, the UK and, increasingly, international supermarket chain, has been able to use increasing loan financing to boost ROSF in the early 2000s.

REAL WORLD 7.2

Tesco gears up for shareholders' returns

The following information relates to Tesco plc for its accounting years to the end of February, from 1999 to 2003:

	1999	2000	2001	2002	2003
ROCE (%)	17.2	16.1	16.6	16.1	15.3
Interest cover (times)	10.7	10.5	9.4	8.7	8.4
ROSF (%)	21.3	20.9	22.7	23.2	23.3

Over the five years there was a decline in ROCE, but a steady increase in gearing (as measured by a decline in the interest cover ratio) which had the effect of broadly increasing ROSF. The business must have been able to borrow at a lower rate of interest than its rate of ROCE. This boosted the returns to shareholders.

There is absolutely no suggestion here that Tesco's increased gearing was unwise. This is an extremely well-managed and successful business.

Source: Tesco plc Annual Report and Financial Statements 2003.

Alexis plc's gearing ratios are:

	2004	2005
Gearing ratio	26.2%	36.0%
Interest cover ratio	13.5 times	1.5 times

Activity 7.21

What do you deduce from a comparison of Alexis plc's gearing ratios over the two years?

The gearing ratio altered significantly. This is mainly due to the substantial increase in the long-term loan during 2005, which has had the effect of increasing the relative contribution of long-term lenders to the financing of the business.

The interest cover ratio has declined dramatically from a position where profit covered interest 13.5 times in 2004, to one where profit covered interest only 1.5 times in 2005. This was partly caused by the increase in borrowings in 2005, but mainly caused by the dramatic decline in profitability in that year. The later situation looks hazardous; only a small decline in future profitability in 2005 would leave the business with insufficient profit to cover the interest payments. The gearing ratio at 31 March 2005 would not necessarily be considered to be very high for a business that was trading successfully. It is the low profitability that is the problem.

Without knowing what the business planned these ratios to be, it is not possible to reach a totally valid conclusion on Alexis plc's gearing.

Real World 7.3 below provides some evidence concerning the gearing of listed businesses.

REAL WORLD 7.3

The gearing of listed businesses   **FT**

Larger listed businesses tend to have higher levels of gearing than smaller ones. A Bank of England report on the financing of small businesses found that the average level of gearing among smaller listed businesses was 27 per cent compared with 37 per cent for the top 350 listed businesses. Over recent years the level of borrowing by larger listed businesses has risen steadily (Tesco – Real World 7.2 – provides an example of this) whereas the level of borrowing for smaller listed businesses has remained fairly stable. This difference in gearing levels between larger and smaller businesses flies in the face of conventional wisdom.

Recent government investigations have found that smaller listed businesses often find it hard to attract the interest of investors. Many large institutional investors, who dominate the stock market, are not interested in the shares of smaller listed businesses because the amount of investment required is too small. As a result, shares in smaller businesses are less marketable. In such circumstances, it may be imagined that smaller businesses would become more reliant on loan financing and so would have higher levels of gearing than larger businesses. However, this is clearly not the case.

Although smaller businesses increase the level of shareholder funds by issuing relatively low dividends and therefore retaining more profits, they tend to be less profitable than larger businesses. Thus, higher retained profits do not seem to explain satisfactorily this phenomenon.

The only obvious factors that could explain this difference between smaller and larger businesses are the level of tax relief on loan interest and borrowing capacity. Broadly, larger businesses pay tax at a higher rate than their smaller counterparts. This means that the tax benefits of borrowing tend to be greater per £ of interest paid for larger businesses than for smaller ones. It may well be that larger businesses can borrow at lower interest rates than smaller ones, if only because they tend to borrow larger sums and so the economies of scale may apply. Also larger businesses tend to be less likely to get into financial difficulties than smaller ones, so they may be able to borrow at lower interest rates.

Source: Adapted from 'Small companies surprise on lending', *Financial Times*, 25 April 2003.

Investment ratios

There are various ratios available that are designed to help investors assess the returns on their investment. The following are widely used:

- dividend payout ratio;
- dividend yield ratio;
- earnings per share;
- operating cash flow per share; and
- price/earnings ratio.

Dividend payout ratio

 The **dividend payout ratio** measures the proportion of earnings that a business pays out to shareholders in the form of dividends. The ratio is calculated as follows:

$$\text{Dividend payout ratio} = \frac{\text{Dividends announced for the year}}{\text{Earnings for the year available for dividends}} \times 100$$

In the case of ordinary shares, the earnings available for dividend will normally be the net profit after taxation and after any preference dividends announced during the period. This ratio is normally expressed as a percentage.

The dividend payout ratio for Alexis plc for the year ended 31 March 2004 is:

$$\text{Dividend payout ratio} = \frac{40}{165} \times 100 = 24.2\%$$

The information provided by this ratio is often expressed slightly differently as the **dividend cover ratio**. Here the calculation is:

$$\text{Dividend cover ratio} = \frac{\text{Earnings for the year available for dividend}}{\text{Dividend announced for the year}}$$

In the case of Alexis plc, for 2004 it would be 165/40 = 4.1 times. That is to say, the earnings available for dividend cover the actual dividend by just over four times.

Activity 7.22

Calculate the dividend payout ratio of Alexis plc for the year ended 31 March 2005.

The ratio for 2005 is:

$$\text{Dividend payout ratio} = \frac{40}{11} \times 100 = 363.6\%$$

This would normally be considered to be a very alarming decline in the ratio over the two years. Paying a dividend of £40m in 2005 would probably be regarded as very imprudent.

Dividend yield ratio

The **dividend yield ratio** relates the cash return from a share to its current market value. This can help investors to assess the cash return on their investment in the business. The ratio, expressed as a percentage, is:

$$\text{Dividend yield} = \frac{\text{Dividend per share}/(1 - t)}{\text{Market value per share}} \times 100$$

where t is the 'lower' rate of income tax. This requires some explanation. In the UK, investors who receive a dividend from a business also receive a tax credit. This tax credit is equal to the amount of tax that would be payable on the dividends received by a lower-rate taxpayer. As this tax credit can be offset against any tax liability arising from the dividends received, the dividends are in effect issued net of tax to lower-rate income tax payers.

Investors may wish to compare the returns from shares with the returns from other forms of investment. As these other forms of investment are often quoted on a 'gross' (that is, pre-tax) basis it is useful to 'gross up' the dividend to make comparison easier. We can achieve this by dividing the **dividend per share** by $(1 - t)$, where t is the 'lower' rate of income tax.

Assuming a lower rate of income tax of 10 per cent, the dividend yield for Alexis plc for the year ended 31 March 2004 is:

$$\text{Dividend yield} = \frac{0.067^*/(1 - 0.10)}{2.50} \times 100 = 3.0\%$$

* Dividend proposed/number of shares = 40/(300 × 2) = £0.067 dividend per share (the 300 is multiplied by 2 because they are £0.50 shares).

Activity 7.23

Calculate the dividend yield for Alexis plc for the year ended 31 March 2005.

Your answer to this activity should be as follows:

$$\text{Dividend yield} = \frac{0.067^*/(1 - 0.10)}{1.50} \times 100 = 5.0\%$$

* 40/(300 × 2) = £0.067

Earnings per share

The **earnings per share (EPS) ratio** relates the earnings generated by the business, and available to shareholders, during a period to the number of shares in issue. For equity (ordinary) shareholders, the amount available will be represented by the net profit after tax (less any preference dividend). The ratio for equity shareholders is calculated as:

$$\text{Earnings per share} = \frac{\text{Earnings available to ordinary shareholders}}{\text{Number of ordinary shares in issue}}$$

In the case of Alexis plc, the earnings per share for the year ended 31 March 2004 is:

$$\text{EPS} = \frac{165}{600} = 27.5\text{p} \quad 0.0375$$

Many investment analysts regard the EPS ratio as a fundamental measure of share performance. The trend in earnings per share over time is used to help assess the investment potential of a business's shares. Though it is possible to make total profits rise through ordinary shareholders investing more in the business, this will not necessarily mean that the profitability *per share* will rise as a result.

It is not usually very helpful to compare the earnings per share of one business with those of another. Differences in capital structure (for example, in the nominal value of shares issued) can render any such comparison meaningless. However, it can be very useful to monitor the changes that occur in this ratio for a particular business over time.

Activity 7.24

Calculate the earnings per share of Alexis plc for the year ended 31 March 2005.

The earnings per share for 2005 is:

$$\text{EPS} = \frac{£11}{600} = 1.8\text{p}$$

Cash generated from operations per share

It can be argued that, in the short run at least, cash generated from operations (found in the cash flow statement) provides a betters guide to the ability of a business to pay dividends and to undertake planned expenditures than the earnings per share figure. The **cash generated from operations (CGO) per ordinary share** is calculated as follows:

$$\text{Cash generated from operations per share} = \frac{\text{Cash generated from operations less preference dividend (if any)}}{\text{Number of ordinary shares in issue}}$$

The ratio for Alexis plc for the year ended 31 March 2004 is as follows:

$$\text{CGO per share} = \frac{£251}{600} = 41.8\text{p}$$

Activity 7.25

Calculate the CGO per ordinary share for Alexis plc for the year ended 31 March 2005.

The CGO per share for 2005 is:

$$\text{CGO per share} = \frac{£34}{600} = 5.7\text{p}$$

There has been a dramatic decrease in this ratio over the two-year period.

Note that, for both years, the CGO per share for Alexis plc is higher than the earnings per share. This is not unusual. The effect of adding back depreciation to derive the CGO figures will often ensure that a higher figure is derived.

Price/earnings (P/E) ratio

The **price/earnings ratio** relates the market value of a share to the earnings per share. This ratio can be calculated as follows:

$$\text{P/E ratio} = \frac{\text{Market value per share}}{\text{Earnings per share}}$$

The P/E ratio for Alexis plc as at 31 March 2004 is:

$$\text{P/E ratio} = \frac{£2.50}{27.5p^*} = 9.1 \text{ times}$$

* The EPS figure (27.5p) was calculated on p. 226.

This ratio reveals that the capital value of the share is 9.1 times higher than its current level of earnings. The ratio is a measure of market confidence in the future of a business. The higher the P/E ratio, the greater the confidence in the future earning power of the business and, consequently, the more investors are prepared to pay in relation to the earnings stream of the business.

P/E ratios provide a useful guide to market confidence concerning the future and they can, therefore, be helpful when comparing different businesses. However, differences in accounting policies between businesses can lead to different profit and earnings per share figures, and this can distort comparisons.

Activity 7.26

Calculate the P/E ratio of Alexis plc as at 31 March 2005.

Your answer to this activity should be as follows:

$$\text{P/E ratio} = \frac{£1.50}{1.8p} = 83.3 \text{ times}$$

The investment ratios for Alexis plc over the two-year period are as follows:

	2004	2005
Dividend payout ratio	24.2%	363.6%
Dividend yield ratio	3.0%	5.0%
Earnings per share	27.5p	1.8p
Cash generated from operations per share	41.8p	5.7p
P/E ratio	9.1 times	83.3 times

Activity 7.27

What do you deduce from the investment ratios set out above?
   Can you offer an explanation why the share price has not fallen as much as it might have done, bearing in mind the very poor (relative to 2004) trading performance in 2005?

We thought that, though:

● the EPS and the CGO per share figures have both fallen dramatically, and
● the dividend payment for 2005 seems very imprudent,

the share price seems to have held up remarkably well (fallen from £2.50 to £1.50, see p. 203). This means that dividend yield and P/E value for 2005 look better than those for 2004. This is an anomaly of these two ratios, which stems from using a forward-looking value (the share price) in conjunction with historic data (dividends and earnings). Share prices are based on investors' assessments of the business's future. It seems with Alexis plc that, at the end of 2005, the 'market' was not happy with the business, relative to 2004. This is evidenced by the fact that the share price had fallen by £1 a share. On the other hand, the share price has not fallen as much as profits. It appears that investors believe that the business will perform better in the future than it did in 2005. This may well be because they believe that the large expansion in assets and employee numbers that occurred in 2005 will yield benefits in the future; benefits that the business was not able to generate during 2005.

Real World 7.4 gives some information about the shares of several large, well known UK businesses. This type of information is provided on a daily basis by several newspapers, notably the *Financial Times*.

REAL WORLD 7.4

Market statistics for some well-known businesses   FT

The following information was extracted from the *Financial Times* on 3 January 2004, relating to the previous day's trading of the shares of some well-known businesses on the London Stock Exchange:

Share	Price	(+/−)	52 week High	Low	Y'ld Gr's	P/E	Volume 000s
BP	$454^3/_4$	$+1^3/_4$	$459^1/_2$	$348^3/_4$	3.4	20.1	21,113
JD Wetherspoon	286	+6	290	158	1.2	16.8	784
Manchester United	264	$+6^1/_2$	275	103	0.9	43.3	153
Marks and Spencer	$289^1/_4$	$+^1/_4$	339	$258^1/_2$	3.8	13.6	7,243
Rolls-Royce	178	$+^3/_4$	194	$64^1/_4$	4.6	19.4	5,170
Vodafone	$139^1/_4$	$+1^1/_4$	$140^1/_2$	$100^3/_4$	1.3	28.5	81,870

The column headings are as follows:

Price   Mid-market price (that is, the price midway between buying and selling price) of the shares at the end of 2 January 2004.

(+/−)   Gain or loss (usually stated in pence) from the previous day's mid-market price.

High/Low   Highest and lowest prices reached by the share during the year (stated in pence).

Y'ld gr's   Gross dividend yield, based on the most recent year's dividend and the current share price.

P/E   Price/earnings ratio, based on the most recent year's after-tax profit and the current share price.

Volume   The number of shares (in thousands) that were bought and sold on 2 January 2004.

Real World 7.5 shows how investment ratios can vary between different industry sectors.

REAL WORLD 7.5

How investment ratios vary between industries

Investment ratios can vary significantly between businesses and between industries. To give some indication of the range of variations that occur, the average dividend yield ratios and average P/E ratios for listed businesses in 12 different industries are shown in Figures 7.4 and 7.5 respectively.

These ratios are calculated from the current market value of the shares and the most recent year's dividend paid (dividend yield) or earnings per share (P/E).

Some industries tend to pay out lower dividends than others, leading to lower dividend yield ratios. Pharmaceutical businesses tend to invest heavily in developing new drugs, hence their tendency to pay low dividends compared with their share prices. Electricity businesses probably tend to invest less heavily than pharmaceuticals, hence their rather higher level of dividend yields. Some of the inter-industry differences in the dividend yield ratio can be explained by the nature of the calculation of the ratio. The prices of shares at any given moment are based on expectations of their economic futures; dividends are actual past events. A business that had a good trading year recently may have paid a dividend that, in the light of investors' assessment on the business's economic future, may be high (a high dividend yield).

Businesses that have a high share price relative to their recent historic earnings have high P/E ratios. This may be because their future is regarded as economically bright, which may be the result of investing heavily in the future at the expense of current profits (earnings).

| Figure 7.4 | Average dividend yield ratios for businesses in a range of industries |

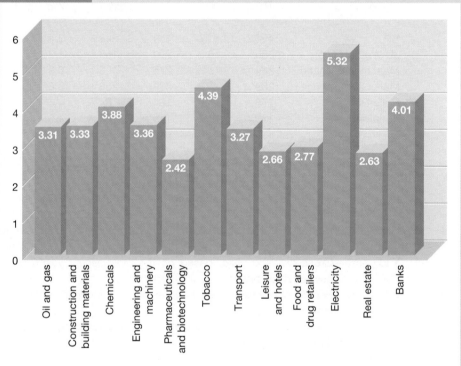

Average levels of dividend yield tend to vary from one industry to the next.

Source: Constructed from data appearing in *Financial Times*, 3 January 2004.

| Figure 7.5 | Average price/earnings ratios for businesses in a range of industries |

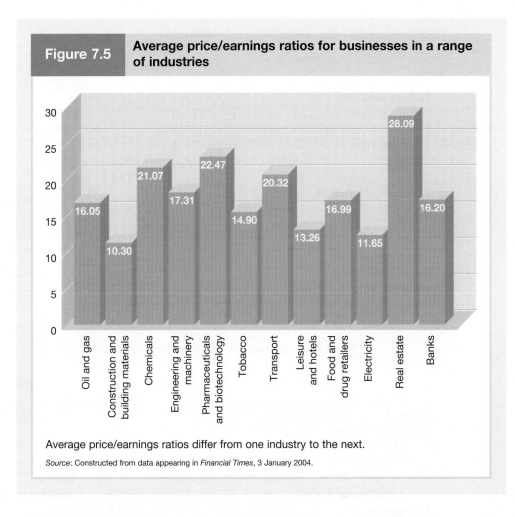

Average price/earnings ratios differ from one industry to the next.

Source: Constructed from data appearing in *Financial Times*, 3 January 2004.

Self-assessment question 7.1

Both Ali plc and Bhaskar plc operate electrical stores throughout the UK. The financial statements of each business for the year ended 30 June 2005 are as follows:

Balance sheets as at 30 June 2005

	Ali plc		Bhaskar plc	
	£000	£000	£000	£000
Non-current assets				
Property, plant and equipment (cost less depreciation)				
Freehold land and buildings at cost		360.0		510.0
Fixtures and fittings at cost		87.0		91.2
		447.0		601.2
Current assets				
Stock at cost	592.0		403.0	
Debtors	176.4		321.9	
Cash at bank	84.6		91.6	
	853.0		816.5	

Self-assessment question 7.1 continued

	Ali plc £m	Ali plc £m	Bhaskar plc £m	Bhaskar plc £m
Current liabilities				
Trade creditors	(271.4)		(180.7)	
Dividends (approved, but unpaid)	(135.0)		(95.0)	
Corporation tax	(16.0)		(17.4)	
	(422.4)	430.6	(293.1)	523.4
		877.6		1,124.6
Non-current liabilities				
Debentures		(190.0)		(250.0)
		687.6		874.6
Equity				
£1 ordinary shares		320.0		250.0
General reserves		355.9		289.4
Retained profit		11.7		335.2
		687.6		874.6

Profit and loss accounts for the year ended 30 June 2005

	Ali plc £000	Ali plc £000	Bhaskar plc £000	Bhaskar plc £000
Revenue		1,478.1		1,790.4
Less Cost of sales				
Opening stock	480.8		372.6	
Purchases	1,129.5		1,245.3	
	1,610.3		1,617.9	
Less Closing stock	592.0	1,018.3	403.0	1,214.9
Gross profit		459.8		575.5
Less Operating expenses		308.5		408.6
Net profit before interest and tax		151.3		166.9
Less Interest payable		19.4		27.5
Net profit before tax		131.9		139.4
Less Corporation tax		32.0		34.8
Net profit after taxation		99.9		104.6
Add Retained profit brought forward		46.8		325.6
		146.7		430.2
Less Dividends approved, but unpaid		135.0		95.0
Retained profit carried forward		11.7		335.2

All purchases and sales were on credit. The dividends for both years had been approved by the shareholders before the respective year ends, but were paid after those times. The market values of a share in each business at the end of the year were £6.50 and £8.20 respectively.

Required:

For each business, calculate two ratios that are concerned with liquidity, gearing and investment (six ratios in total). What can you conclude from the ratios that you have calculated?

Financial ratios and the problem of overtrading

→ **Overtrading** occurs where a business is operating at a level of activity that cannot be supported by the amount of finance that has been committed. For example, the business has inadequate finance to fund the level of debtors and stocks necessary for the level of sales revenue that it is achieving. This situation usually reflects a poor level of financial control over the business. The reasons for overtrading are varied. It may occur:

- in young, expanding businesses that fail to prepare adequately for the rapid increase in demand for its goods or services,
- in businesses where the managers may have miscalculated the level of expected sales demand or have failed to control escalating project costs,
- as a result of a fall in the value of money (inflation), causing more finance to be committed to stock-in-trade and debtors, even where there is no expansion in the real volume of trade,
- where the owners are unable both to inject further funds into the business and to persuade others to invest in the business.

Whatever the reason for overtrading, the problems that it brings must be dealt with if the business is to survive over the longer term.

Overtrading results in liquidity problems such as exceeding borrowing limits, or slow repayment of lenders and creditors. It can also result in suppliers withholding supplies, thereby making it difficult to meet customer needs. The managers of the business might be forced to direct all their efforts to dealing with immediate and pressing problems, such as finding cash to meet interest charges due or paying wages. Longer-term planning becomes difficult and managers may spend their time going from crisis to crisis. At the extreme, a business may fail because it cannot meet its maturing obligations.

Activity 7.28

If a business is overtrading, do you think the following ratios would be higher or lower than normally expected?

(a) Current ratio.
(b) Average stock turnover period.
(c) Average settlement period for debtors.
(d) Average settlement period for creditors.

Your answer should be as follows:

(a) The current ratio would be lower than normally expected. This is a measure of liquidity, and lack of liquidity is an important symptom of overtrading.
(b) The average stock turnover period would be lower than normally expected. Where a business is overtrading, the level of stocks held will be low because of the problems of financing stocks. In the short term, sales revenue may not be badly affected by the low stock levels and therefore stocks will be turned over more quickly.
(c) The average settlement period for debtors may be lower than normally expected. Where a business is suffering from liquidity problems it may chase debtors more vigorously so as to improve cash flows.
(d) The average settlement period for creditors may be higher than normally expected. The business may try to delay payments to creditors because of the liquidity problems arising.

To deal with the overtrading problem, a business must ensure that the finance available is commensurate with the level of operations. Thus, if a business that is overtrading is unable to raise new finance, it should cut back its level of operations in line with the finance available. Although this may mean lost sales and lost profits in the short term, it may be necessary to ensure survival over the longer term.

Trend analysis

It is often helpful to see whether ratios are indicating trends. Key ratios can be plotted on a graph to provide a simple visual display of changes occurring over time. The trends occurring within a business may, for example, be plotted against trends for the industry as a whole for comparison purposes. An example of trend analysis is shown in Figure 7.6. Here the current ratio of a particular business (XYZ Ltd) at various dates is plotted against the average current ratio for other businesses in the same industry as XYZ Ltd. This enables a comparison of the business and similar businesses to be tracked over time.

Figure 7.6	Graph plotting current ratio against time

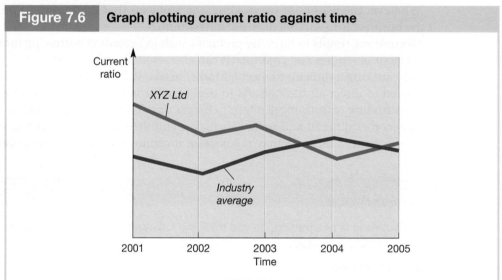

The current ratio for a particular business (XYZ Ltd) is plotted over time. On the same graph the same ratio for the average of businesses in the same industry is also plotted, enabling comparison to be made between the ratio for the particular business and the industry average.

Many larger businesses publish certain key financial ratios as part of their annual reports to help users identify significant trends. These ratios typically cover several years' activities. **Real World 7.6** shows part of the table of 'key performance measures' of Marks and Spencer plc (M&S), the well-known UK high street store. After many years of profitable growth, M&S suffered a decline in its fortunes during the late 1990s. This was seen by the directors, and by many independent commentators, as arising from the business allowing itself to be drawn away from its traditional areas of strength into such activities as operating overseas businesses. Steps were taken to deal with the problem and the business seemed to have 'turned the corner'. M&S seems to have reached its low point in the year ended March 2001 when it incurred a significant overall loss, with a trading profit only about 40 per cent of what had been achieved in 1998. We can see from the table that the gross profit margin seemed not to be the cause of the problem. In fact, turnover was down in 2001 and expenses were up. The improvements in 2002 and 2003 are very clear. The return on equity (return on shareholders funds) in 2003 is significantly better than for any others of the five years. Also in 2003, both the gross (profit) and net (profit) margins are the best of the five years.

REAL WORLD 7.6

Key performance measures of Marks and Spencer plc

		2003 52 weeks	2002 52 weeks	2001 52 weeks	2000 53 weeks	1999 52 weeks
Gross margin	$\dfrac{\text{Gross profit}}{\text{Turnover}}$	36.4%	35.8%	34.3%	31.8%	31.1%
Net margin	$\dfrac{\text{Operating profit}}{\text{Turnover}}$	8.9%	8.3%	6.2%	6.6%	8.0%
Net margin excluding exceptional items		9.4%	8.3%	6.5%	7.5%	8.4%
Profitability	$\dfrac{\text{Profit before tax}}{\text{Turnover}}$	8.4%	9.0%	5.2%	6.3%	8.6%
Profitability excluding exceptional items		8.9%	8.5%	6.7%	7.3%	8.8%
Earnings per share	$\dfrac{\text{Standard earnings}}{\substack{\text{Weighted average ordinary} \\ \text{shares in issue}}}$	20.7p	5.4p	(0.2)p	9.6p	13.0p
Earnings per share adjusted for exceptional items		22.2p	16.3p	11.2p	13.8p	15.6p
Dividend per share		10.5p	9.5p	9.0p	9.0p	14.4p
Dividend cover	$\dfrac{\substack{\text{Profit attributable to} \\ \text{shareholders}}}{\text{Dividends}}$	2.0x	2.2x	n/a	1.1x	0.9x
Return on equity	$\dfrac{\substack{\text{Profit after tax and} \\ \text{minority interests}}}{\text{Average shareholders' funds}}$	16.5%	11.1%	(0.1)%	5.7%	7.8%

Source: Marks and Spencer plc Annual Report 2003. Reproduced by kind permission of Marks and Spencer plc.

Common-size financial statements

→ **Common-size financial statements** are normal financial statements (such as the profit and loss account (income statement), balance sheet and cash flow statement), which are expressed in terms of some base figure. The objective of presenting financial statements in this way is to help make better comparisons. The detection of differences and trends is often more obvious than may be the case when examining the original statements, which are expressed in financial values.

Vertical analysis

One approach to common-size statements is to express all the figures in a particular statement in terms of one of the figures in that statement. This 'base' figure is typically chosen because it is a key figure in the statement, such as revenue in a profit and loss account, total long-term funds in a balance sheet and the cash flow from operating activities in the cash flow statement.

Example 7.4 is a common-size profit and loss account that uses revenue as the base figure. Note the base figure is set at 100 and all other figures are expressed as a percentage of this.

Example 7.4

The common-size profit and loss account of Alexis plc (see Example 7.1 on p. 202) for 2004 in abbreviated form, and using revenue as the base figure, will be as follows:

Common-size profit and loss account for the year ended 31 March 2004

		Calculation of figures
Revenue	100.0	Base figure
Cost of sales	(77.9)	(1,745/2,240) × 100%
Gross profit	22.1	(495/2,240) × 100%
Operating expenses	(11.3)	(252/2,240) × 100%
Net profit before interest and tax	10.8	(243/2,240) × 100%
Less Interest payable	0.8	(18/2,240) × 100%
Net profit before tax	10.0	(225/2,240) × 100%
Less Corporation tax	2.7	(60/2,240) × 100%
Net profit after tax	7.3	(165/2,240) × 100%

Each of the figures in the profit and loss account is simply the original financial figure divided by the revenue figure and then expressed as a percentage.

Of course, not much can be discerned from looking at just one common-size statement. We need some benchmark for comparison, and this could be other accounting periods for the same business.

Activity 7.29

The following is a set of common-size profit and loss accounts for a major high street department store for five consecutive accounting periods:

	Year 1	*Year 2*	*Year 3*	*Year 4*	*Year 5*
Revenue	100.0	100.0	100.0	100.0	100.0
Cost of sales	(68.9)	(68.5)	(67.2)	(66.5)	(66.3)
Gross profit	31.1	31.5	32.8	33.5	33.7
Other operating expenses	(28.1)	(28.4)	(27.6)	(29.2)	(30.2)
Operating profit	3.0	3.1	5.2	4.3	3.5
Interest	(1.1)	(1.2)	(1.6)	(2.1)	(1.3)
Profit before tax	1.9	1.9	3.6	2.2	2.2

What significant features are revealed by the common-size profit and loss accounts?

Operating profit, relative to revenue, rose in Year 3 but fell back again in Years 4 and 5 to end the five-year period at much the same level as it had been in Years 1 and 2. Although the gross profit margin rose steadily over the five-year period, so did the operating expenses, with the exception of Year 3. Clearly, the fall in operating expenses to revenue in Year 3 led to the improvement in operating profit to revenue.

The common-size financial statements being compared do not have to be for the same business. They can be for different businesses. **Real World 7.7** gives common-size balance sheets for five UK businesses that are either very well-known by name, or whose products are everyday commodities for most of us. For each business the major balance sheet items are expressed as a percentage of the total investment by the providers of long-term finance.

 REAL WORLD 7.7

A summary of the balance sheets of five UK businesses

Business	The Boots Company plc	Go-Ahead Group plc	Rolls-Royce plc	Tesco plc	United Utilities plc
Balance sheet date	31.3.03	28.6.03	31.12.02	22.2.03	31.3.03
	%	%	%	%	%
Non-current assets	74	126	70	126	104
Current assets					
Stock	25	2	27	10	–
Trade debtors	13	23	23	–	3
Other debtors	12	29	33	6	4
Cash and near cash	19	16	17	6	10
	69	70	100	22	17
Current liabilities					
Trade creditors	14	25	11	20	1
Tax and dividends	12	15	9	6	5
Other short-term liabilities	12	55	44	10	12
Overdrafts and short-term loans	5	1	6	12	3
	43	96	70	48	21
Working capital	26	(26)	30	(26)	(4)
Total long-term investment	100	100	100	100	100

Source: The table was constructed from information appearing in the annual reports of the five businesses concerned.

The non-current assets, current assets and current liabilities are expressed as a percentage of the total net investment (equity plus non-current liabilities) of the business concerned. The businesses were randomly selected, except that they were deliberately taken from different industries. Boots is a major UK health-care manufacturer that operates a chain of high-street retail stores. Go-Ahead is a major passenger transport provider, principally through buses and trains. It runs much of the Central London bus service and owns South Central and Thames Trains. Rolls-Royce builds engines for aircraft and for other purposes. Tesco is one of the major UK supermarkets. United Utilities is a major distributor of electricity and water, particularly in the north west of England.

It is quite striking, in Real World 7.7, how different the make-up of the balance sheet is from one business to the next. Take working capital, for example. Though the percentages for current assets are generally pretty large in relation to the total long-term investment, these percentages vary considerably from one type of business to the next. The totals for current assets are pretty large when compared with the total long-term investment. This is particularly true of Boots, Go-Ahead and Rolls-Royce. The amounts vary considerably from one type of business to the next. Rolls-Royce is the only one of the five businesses that is solely a manufacturer. Boots and Tesco are both retailers, though Boots is also a manufacturer. These three are the only ones that hold significant amounts of stock. The other two are service providers. Tesco does not sell on credit and little of United Utilities' sales are on credit, so they have little or nothing invested in trade debtors. It is interesting to note that Tesco's trade creditors are much higher than its stock. Since most of these creditors will be suppliers of stock, it means that the business is able, on average, to have the cash from a particular sale in the bank before it needs to pay for the goods concerned.

So far we have been considering what is known as **vertical analysis**. That is, we have been treating all of the figures in each statement as a percentage of a figure in that statement – the sales revenue figure, in the case of the profit and loss account, and the total long-term investment in the case of the balance sheet. Note that common-size statements do not have to be expressed in terms of any particular factor; it is up to the individual carrying out the analysis. It seems, however, that revenue and long-term investment are popular bases for vertically analysed common-size profit and loss accounts and balance sheets, respectively.

Horizontal analysis

Horizontal analysis is an alternative to the vertical analysis that we have seen so far. Here the figures appearing in a particular financial statement are expressed as a base figure (that is, 100) and the equivalent figures appearing in similar statements are expressed as a percentage of this base figure. So, for example, the stock figure appearing in a particular balance sheet may be set as the base figure (that is, set at 100) and then the stock (inventory) figures appearing in successive balance sheets could each be expressed as a percentage of this base stock figure. The 'base' statement would normally be the earliest (or latest) of a set of statements for the same business. Where the analysis was between businesses, as in Real World 7.7 (above), selecting which business should be the base one is not so obvious, unless one of the businesses is the one of most interest, perhaps because the objective is to compare a particular business with each of the others in turn.

Example 7.5 shows a horizontally analysed common-size profit and loss account for the business, a department store, that was the subject of Activity 7.29.

Example 7.5

The following is a set of common-size profit and loss accounts for a major high street department store for five consecutive accounting periods, using horizontal analysis and making Year 1 the base year:

	Year 1	Year 2	Year 3	Year 4	Year 5
Revenue	100.0	104.3	108.4	106.5	108.9
Cost of sales	(100.0)	(103.7)	(105.7)	(102.9)	(104.8)
Gross profit	100.0	105.5	114.4	114.5	118.0
Other operating expenses	(100.0)	(105.4)	(106.7)	(110.4)	(117.2)
Operating profit	100.0	106.6	185.9	153.3	125.6
Interest	(100.0)	(111.9)	(157.1)	(202.4)	(127.4)
Profit before tax	100.0	103.5	202.8	124.5	124.5

Year 1 is the base year so all of the figures in the Year 1 profit and loss account are 100.0. All of the figures for the other years are that year's figure divided by the Year 1 figure for the same item and then expressed as a percentage. For example, the Year 4 profit before tax, divided by the profit before tax for Year 1 was 124.5 or the profit was 24.5% greater in Year 4 than it had been for Year 1. (By coincidence, the profits for Years 4 and 5 were identical.)

Activity 7.30

What are the significant features revealed by the common-size profit and loss accounts in Example 7.5?

Revenue did not show much of an increase over the five years, particularly if these figures are not adjusted for inflation. Years 2 and 3 saw increases, but Years 4 and 5 were less impressive. The rate of increase in the cost of sales was less, and, therefore, the gross profit growth was greater, than the rate of increase of revenue. Other operating expenses showed fairly steady growth over the years. Interest increased strongly during the first four years of the period, but then fell back significantly in Year 5.

Activity 7.31

The vertical approach to common-size financial statements has the advantage of enabling the analyst to see each figure expressed in terms of the same item (revenue, long-term finance and so on). What are the disadvantages of this approach and how do horizontally analysed common-sized statements overcome any problems, and what problems do they bring?

The problem with the horizontal approach is that it is not possible to see, for example, that revenue values are different from one year or business to the next. Normally, a vertically analysed common-size profit and loss account shows the revenue figure as 100 for all years or businesses. This is, of course, a problem of all approaches to ratio analysis.

Horizontally analysed common-size statements overcome this problem because, say, revenue figures are expressed in terms of one year or one particular business. This makes differences in revenue levels crystal clear. Unfortunately, such an approach makes comparison within each year's, or within a particular business's, statement rather difficult.

Perhaps the answer is to produce two sets of common-size statements, one analysed vertically and the other horizontally.

Using ratios to predict financial failure

Financial ratios, based on current or past performance, are often used to help predict the future. However, both the choice of ratios and the interpretation of results are normally dependent on the judgement and opinion of the analyst. In recent years, however, attempts have been made to develop a more rigorous and systematic approach to the use of ratios for prediction purposes. In particular, researchers have shown an interest in the ability of ratios to predict the financial failure of a business.

By financial failure, we mean a business either going out of business or being severely adversely affected by its inability to meet its financial obligations. It is often referred to as 'going bust' or 'going bankrupt'. This, of course, is an area with which all those connected with the business are likely to be concerned.

Using single ratios

Many methods and models employing ratios have now been developed that claim to predict future financial failure. Early research focused on the examination of ratios on an individual basis to see whether they were good or bad predictors of financial failure. Here a particular ratio (for example, the current ratio), for a business that had failed, were tracked over several years leading up to the date of the failure. This was to see if it were possible to say that the ratio had showed a trend that could have been taken as a warning sign.

Beaver (see reference 1 at the end of the chapter) carried out the first research in this area. He calculated the average (mean) of various ratios for 79 businesses that had actually failed, over the ten-year period leading up to their failure. Beaver then compared these average ratios with similarly derived ratios for a sample of 79 businesses that did not fail over this period. (The research used a matched-pair design, where each failed business was matched with a non-failed business of similar size and industry type.) Beaver found that some ratios exhibited a marked difference between the failed and non-failed businesses for up to five years prior to failure. This is shown in Figure 7.7.

To explain Figure 7.7, let us take a closer look at graph (a). This plots the ratio, cash flow (presumably the operating cash flow figure, taken from the cash flow statement) divided by total debt. For the non-failed businesses this stayed fairly steady at about +0.45 over the period. For the failed businesses, however, this was already well below the non-failed businesses at about +0.15 even five years before those businesses eventually failed. It then declined steadily until, by one year before the failure, it was less than −0.15. Note that the scale of the horizontal axis shows the most recent year (Year 1) on the left and the earliest one (Year 5) on the right. The other graphs ((b) to (f)) show a similar picture for five other ratios. In each case there is a deteriorating average ratio for the failed businesses, as the time of failure approaches.

What is shown in Figure 7.7 implied that failure could be predicted by careful assessment of the trend shown by particular key ratios.

Research by Zmijewski (see reference 2 at the end of the chapter), using a sample of 72 failed and 3,573 non-failed businesses over a six-year period, found that failed businesses were characterised by lower rates of return, higher levels of gearing, lower levels of coverage for their fixed interest payments and more variable returns on shares. Whilst we may not find these results very surprising, it is interesting to note that Zmijewski, like a number of other researchers in this area, did not find liquidity ratios particularly useful in predicting financial failure. Intuition might have led us

Figure 7.7   Average (mean) ratios of failed and non-failed businesses

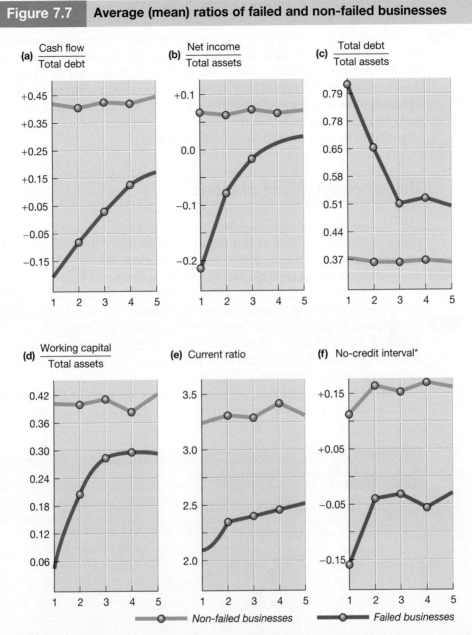

(a) Cash flow / Total debt

(b) Net income / Total assets

(c) Total debt / Total assets

(d) Working capital / Total assets

(e) Current ratio

(f) No-credit interval*

Non-failed businesses   Failed businesses

Each of the ratios (a) to (f) above indicates a marked difference in the average ratio between the sample of failed businesses and a matched sample of non-failed businesses. The vertical scale of each graph is the average value of the particular ratio for each group of businesses (failed and non-failed). The horizontal axis is the number of years before failure. Thus Year 1 is the most recent year and Year 5 the earliest of the years. For each of the six ratios, the difference between the average for the failed and the non-failed businesses can be detected five years prior to the failure of the former group. (From Beaver – see reference 1 at the end of the chapter.)

* The no-credit interval is the same as the cash generated from operations to maturing obligations ratio discussed earlier in the chapter.

Source: Beaver (see reference 1 at the end of the chapter).

(wrongly it seems) to believe that the liquidity ratios would have been particularly helpful in this context.

The approach adopted by Beaver and Zmijewski is referred to as **univariate analysis**, because it looks at one ratio at a time. Though this approach can produce interesting results, there are practical problems associated with its use. Let us say for example, that past research has identified two ratios as being good predictors of financial failure. When applied to a particular business, however, it may be found that one ratio predicts financial failure whereas the other does not. Given these conflicting signals, how should the decision maker interpret the results?

Using combinations of ratios

The weaknesses of univariate analysis have led researchers to develop models that combine ratios in such a way as to produce a single index that can be interpreted more clearly. One approach to model development, much favoured by researchers, applies **multiple discriminate analysis (MDA)**. This is, in essence, a statistical technique that is similar to regression analysis and which can be used to draw a boundary between those businesses that fail and those businesses that do not. This boundary is referred to as the **discriminate function**. In this context, MDA attempts to identify those factors likely to influence financial failure. However, unlike regression analysis, MDA assumes that the observations come from two different populations (for example, failed and non-failed businesses) rather than from a single population.

To illustrate this approach, let us assume that we wish to test whether two ratios (say, the current ratio and the return on capital employed) can help to predict failure.

Figure 7.8	Scatter diagram showing the distribution of failed and non-failed businesses

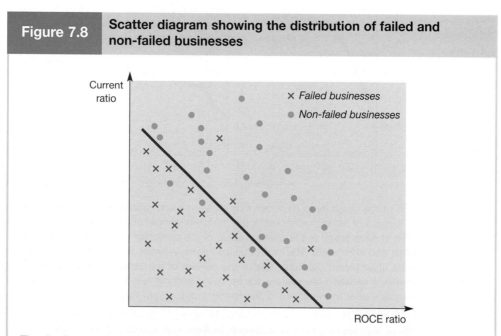

The distribution of failed and non-failed businesses is based on two ratios. The line represents a boundary between the samples of failed and non-failed businesses. Although there is some crossing of the boundary, the boundary represents the line that minimises the problem of mis-classifying particular businesses.

To do this, we can calculate these ratios first for a sample of failed businesses and then for a matched sample of non-failed businesses. From these two sets of data we can produce a scatter diagram that plots each business according to these two ratios to produce a single coordinate. Figure 7.8 illustrates this approach. Using the observations plotted on the diagram, we try to identify the boundary between the failed and the non-failed businesses. This is the diagonal line in Figure 7.8.

We can see that those businesses that fall to the left of the line are predominantly failed ones and those that fall to the right are predominantly non-failed ones. Note that there is some overlap between the two populations. The boundary produced is unlikely, in practice, to eliminate all errors. Some businesses that fail may fall on the side of the boundary with non-failed businesses, and the other way round as well. However, it will *minimise* the misclassification errors.

The boundary shown in Figure 7.8 can be expressed in the form:

$$Z = a + (b \times \text{Current ratio}) + (c \times \text{ROCE})$$

where *a* is a constant and *b* and *c* are weights to be attached to each ratio. A weighted average or total score (*Z*) is then derived. The weights given to the two ratios will depend on the slope of the line and its absolute position.

Z score models

Altman (see reference 3 at the end of the chapter) was the first to develop a model using financial ratios that was able to predict financial failure. His model, the *Z* score model, is based on five financial ratios and is as follows:

$$Z = 1.2a + 1.4b + 3.3c + 0.6d + 1.0e$$

where *a* = Working capital/Total assets
       b = Accumulated retained profits/Total assets
       c = Profit before interest and taxation/Total assets
       d = Market value of ordinary and preference shares/Total liabilities at book value
       e = Sales revenue/Total assets

In developing this model, Altman carried out experiments using a paired sample of failed businesses and non-failed businesses and collected relevant data for each business for five years prior to failure. He found that the model represented by the formula above was able to predict failure for up to two years before it occurred. However, the predictive accuracy of the model became weaker the further the period from failure.

The ratios used in this model were identified by Altman through a process of trial and error, as there is no underlying theory of financial failure to help guide researchers in their selection of appropriate ratios. According to Altman, those businesses with a *Z* score of less than 1.81 tend to fail, and the lower the score the greater the probability of failure. Those with a *Z* score greater than 2.99 tended not to fail. Those businesses with a *Z* score between 1.81 and 2.99 occupied a 'zone of ignorance' and were difficult to classify. However, the model was able overall to classify 95 per cent of the businesses correctly. Altman based his model on US businesses.

In recent years, this model has been updated and other models, using a similar approach, have been developed throughout the world. In the UK, Taffler (see reference 4 at the end of the chapter) has developed separate *Z* score models for different types of business.

The prediction of financial failure is not the only area where research into the predictive ability of ratios has taken place. Researchers have also developed ratio-based models that claim to assess the vulnerability of a business to takeover by another. This is another area that is of vital importance to all those connected with the business.

Limitations of ratio analysis

Though ratios offer a quick and useful method of analysing the position and performance of a business, they are not without their problems and limitations. Some of the more important limitations are as follows:

- *Quality of financial statements*. It must always be remembered that ratios are based on financial statements, and the results of ratio analysis are dependent on the quality of these underlying statements. Ratios will inherit the limitations of the financial statements on which they are based. A significant example of this arises from the application of the prudence convention to internally generated intangible non-current assets (as compared with purchased ones). This convention tends to lead to assets of considerable value, such as goodwill and brand names, being excluded from the balance sheet. This can mean that ratios, such as ROSF, ROCE and the gearing ratio, fail to take account of these assets.

    There is also the problem of deliberate attempts to make the financial statements misleading. We discussed this problem of *creative accounting* in Chapter 5.
- *Inflation*. A persistent, though recently less severe, problem, in most western countries is that the financial results of businesses can be distorted as a result of inflation. One effect of inflation is that the values of assets held for any length of time may bear little relation to current values. Generally speaking, the value of assets will be understated in current terms during a period of inflation as they are usually recorded at their original cost (less any amounts written off for depreciation). This means that comparisons, either between businesses or between periods, will be hindered. A difference in, say, return on capital employed may simply be owing to the fact that assets in one of the balance sheets being compared were acquired more recently (ignoring the effect of depreciation on the asset values). Another effect of inflation is to distort the measurement of profit. Sales revenue for a period is often matched against costs from an earlier period, because there is often a time lag between acquiring a particular resource and using it in the business. For example, stocks may be acquired in one period and sold in a later period. During a period of inflation, this will mean that the costs do not reflect current prices. The cost of goods sold figure is usually based on the historic cost of the stock concerned. As a result, costs will be understated in the current profit and loss account and this, in turn, means that profit will be overstated. One effect of this will be to distort the profitability ratios discussed earlier.
- *The restricted vision of ratios*. It is important not to rely exclusively on ratios, thereby losing sight of information contained in the underlying financial statements. As we saw earlier in the chapter, some items reported in these statements can be vital in assessing position and performance. For example, the total sales revenue, capital employed and profit figures may be useful in assessing changes in absolute size that occur over time, or differences in scale between businesses. Ratios do not provide such information. When comparing one figure with another, ratios measure *relative*

performance and position, and therefore provide only part of the picture. Thus, when comparing two businesses, it will often be useful to assess the absolute size of profits, as well as the relative profitability of each business. For example, Business A may generate £1 million profit and have a ROCE of 15 per cent, and Business B may generate £100,000 profit and have a ROCE of 20 per cent. Although Business B has a higher level of *profitability*, as measured by ROCE, it generates lower total profits.

● *The basis for comparison.* We saw earlier that for ratios to be useful they require a basis for comparison. Moreover, it is important that the analyst compares like with like. When comparing businesses, however, no two businesses will be identical, and the greater the differences between the businesses being compared, the greater the limitations of ratio analysis. Also, when comparing businesses, differences in such matters as accounting policies, financing methods (gearing levels) and financial year ends will add to the problems of evaluation.

● *Balance sheet ratios.* Because the balance sheet is only a 'snapshot' of the business at a particular moment in time, any ratios based on balance sheet figures, such as the liquidity ratios above, may not be representative of the financial position of the business for the year as a whole. For example, it is common for a seasonal business to have a financial year end that coincides with a low point in business activity. Thus stocks and debtors may be low at the balance sheet date, and the liquidity ratios may also be low as a result. A more representative picture of liquidity can only really be gained by taking additional measurements at other points in the year.

Real World 7.8 points out another way in which ratios are limited.

 REAL WORLD 7.8

Remember, it's people that really count . . .

Lord Weinstock (1924–2002) was an influential industrialist whose management style and philosophy helped to shape management practice in many UK businesses. During his long and successful reign at GEC plc, a major engineering business, Lord Weinstock relied heavily on financial ratios to assess performance and to exercise control. In particular, he relied on ratios relating to sales revenue, costs, debtors, profit margins and stock turnover. However, he was keenly aware of the limitations of ratios and recognised that, ultimately, people produce profits.

In a memo written to GEC managers he pointed out that ratios are an aid to good management, rather than a substitute for it. He wrote:

> The operating ratios are of great value as measures of efficiency but they are only the measures and not efficiency itself. Statistics will not design a product better, make it for a lower cost or increase sales. If ill-used, they may so guide action as to diminish resources for the sake of apparent but false signs of improvement.
>
> Management remains a matter of judgement, of knowledge of products and processes and of understanding and skill in dealing with people. The ratios will indicate how well all these things are being done and will show comparison with how they are done elsewhere. But they will tell us nothing about how to do them. That is what you are meant to do.

Source: Extract from *Arnold Weinstock and the Making of GEC* by S. Aris (Aurum Press, 1998), published in *The Sunday Times*, 22 February 1998, p. 3.

SUMMARY

The main points of this chapter may be summarised as follows:

Ratio analysis

- Compares two related figures, usually both from the same set of financial statements.
- Is an aid to understanding what the financial statements say.
- Is an inexact science so results must be interpreted cautiously.
- Past periods – the performance of similar businesses and planned performance are often used to provide benchmark ratios.
- A brief overview of the financial statements can often provide insights that may not be revealed by ratios and/or may help in the interpretation of them.

Profitability ratios – concerned with effectiveness at generating profit

- Return on ordinary shareholders' funds (ROSF).
- Return on capital employed (ROCE).
- Net profit margin.
- Gross profit margin.

Efficiency ratios – concerned with efficiency of using assets/resources

- Average stock turnover period.
- Average settlement period for debtors.
- Average settlement period for creditors.
- Sales revenue to capital employed.
- Sales revenue per employee.

Liquidity ratios – concerned with the ability to meet short-term obligations

- Current ratio.
- Acid test ratio.
- Cash generated from operations to maturing obligations.

Gearing ratios – concerned with relationship between equity and debt financing

- Gearing ratio.
- Interest cover ratio.

Investment ratios – concerned with returns to shareholders

- Dividend payout ratio.
- Dividend yield ratio.
- Earnings per share.
- Cash generated from operations per share.
- Price/earnings ratio.

Overtrading = trading at a level of activity that the business is insufficiently funded to sustain.

Individual ratios can be tracked (for example, plotted on a graph) to detect trends.

Common-size financial statements (P and L, BS and CFS) can be produced.

- All of the figures in the statement can be expressed as a percentage of one of the key figures (revenue, long-term finance, cash flow from operations and so on).
- Enables a comparison across time or businesses.
- Common-size statements can be prepared vertically (basing the other figures on a figure in the same statement) or horizontally (basing the figures in each of a set of statements on those in a particular one of the statements).

Ratios can be used to predict financial failure.

- Univariate analysis – looking at just one ratio over time in an attempt to predict financial failure.
- Multiple discriminate analysis – looking at several ratios, put together in a model, over time in an attempt to predict financial failure – Z scores.

Limitations of ratio analysis

- Ratios are only as reliable as the financial statements from which they derive.
- Inflation can distort the information.
- Ratios have restricted vision.
- It can be difficult to find a suitable benchmark (for example, another business) to compare with.
- Some ratios could mislead due to the 'snapshot' nature of the balance sheet.

→ **Key terms**

Further reading

If you would like to explore the topics covered in this chapter in more depth, we recommend the following books:

Financial Accounting and Reporting, *Elliott B. and Elliott J.*, 8th edn, Financial Times Prentice Hall, 2004, chapters 25 and 26.

International Financial Reporting and Analysis, *Alexander D., Britton A. and Jorissen A.*, Prentice Hall, 2003, chapters 26 and 27.

Financial Analysis, *Rees B.*, 2nd edn, Prentice Hall International, 1995, chapters 1–3.

The Analysis and Use of Financial Statements, *White G., Sondhi A. and Fried D.*, 3rd edn, Wiley, 2003, chapter 4.

References

1 'Financial ratios as predictors of failure', *Beaver W. H.*, in **Empirical Research in Accounting: Selected studies**, 1966, pp. 71–111.

2 'Predicting corporate bankruptcy: an empirical comparison of the extent of financial distress models', *Zmijewski M. E.*, Research Paper, State University of New York, 1983.

3 'Financial ratios, discriminant analysis and the prediction of corporate bankruptcy', *Altman E. I.*, in **Journal of Finance**, September 1968, pp. 589–609.

4 'The assessment of company solvency and performance using a statistical model: a comparative UK-based study', *Taffler, R.*, in **Accounting and Business Research**, Autumn 1983, pp. 295–307.

REVIEW QUESTIONS

Answers to these questions can be found on the students' side of the Companion Website at www.pearsoned.co.uk/atrillmclaney.

7.1 Some businesses operate on a low net profit margin (for example, a supermarket chain). Does this mean that the return on capital employed from the business will also be low?

7.2 What potential problems arise for the external analyst from the use of balance sheet figures in the calculation of financial ratios?

7.3 Two businesses operate in the same industry. One has a stock turnover period that is higher than the industry average. The other has a stock turnover period that is lower than the industry average. Give three possible explanations for each business's stock turnover period ratio.

7.4 Identify and discuss three reasons why the P/E ratio of two businesses operating within the same industry may differ.

EXERCISES

Exercises 7.5 to 7.8 are more advanced than 7.1 to 7.4. Those with a coloured number have an answer at the back of the book.

7.1 Jiang Ltd has recently produced its financial statements for the current year. The directors are concerned that the return on capital employed (ROCE) had decreased from 14 per cent last year to 12 per cent for the current year.

The following reasons were suggested as to why this reduction in ROCE had occurred:

(i) an increase in the gross profit margin;
(ii) a reduction in sales revenue;
(iii) an increase in overhead expenses;
(iv) an increase in amount of stock held;
(v) the repayment of a loan at the year end; and
(vi) an increase in the time taken for debtors to pay.

Required:
Taking each of these six suggested reasons in turn, state, with reasons, whether each of them could lead to a reduction in ROCE.

7.2 Amsterdam Ltd and Berlin Ltd are both engaged in retailing, but they seem to take a different approach to it according to the following information:

Ratio	Amsterdam Ltd	Berlin Ltd
Return on capital employed (ROCE)	20%	17%
Return on ordinary shareholders' funds (ROSF)	30%	18%
Average settlement period for debtors	63 days	21 days
Average settlement period for creditors	50 days	45 days
Gross profit margin	40%	15%
Net profit margin	10%	10%
Stock turnover period	52 days	25 days

Required:
Describe what this information indicates about the differences in approach between the two businesses. If one of them prides itself on personal service and one of them on competitive prices, which do you think is which and why?

7.3 Conday and Co. Ltd has been in operation for three years and produces antique reproduction furniture for the export market. The most recent set of financial statements for the business is set out as follows:

Balance sheet as at 30 November

	£000	£000	£000
Non-current assets			
Property, plant and equipment			
Freehold land and buildings at cost			228
Plant and machinery at cost		942	
Less Accumulated depreciation		180	762
			990
Current assets			
Stocks		600	
Trade debtors		820	
		1,420	
Less **Current liabilities**			
Trade creditors	665		
Taxation	48		
Bank overdraft	432	1,145	275
			1,265
Less **Non-current liabilities**			
9% debentures (Note 1)			200
			1,065
Equity			
Ordinary shares of £1 each			700
Retained profits			365
			1,065

Profit and loss account for the year ended 30 November

	£000	£000
Revenue		2,600
Less Cost of sales		1,620
Gross profit		980
Less Selling and distribution expenses (Note 2)	408	
Administration expenses	194	
Finance expenses	58	660
Net profit before taxation		320
Less Corporation tax		95
Net profit after taxation		225
Less Dividend paid		160
Retained profit for the year		65

Notes
1 The debentures are secured on the freehold land and buildings.
2 Selling and distribution expenses include £170,000 in respect of bad debts.

The directors have invited an investor to take up a new issue of ordinary shares in the business at £6.40 each making a total investment of £200,000. The directors wish to use the funds to finance a programme of further expansion.

Required:

(a) Analyse the financial position and performance of the business and comment on any features that you consider to be significant.

(b) State, with reasons, whether or not the investor should invest in the business on the terms outlined.

7.4 The directors of Helena Beauty Products Ltd have been presented with the following abridged financial statements:

Helena Beauty Products Ltd
Profit and loss account for the year ended 30 September

	2004		2005	
	£000	£000	£000	£000
Revenue		3,600		3,840
Less Cost of sales				
Opening stock	320		400	
Purchases	2,240		2,350	
	2,560		2,750	
Less Closing stock	400	2,160	500	2,250
Gross profit		1,440		1,590
Less Expenses		1,360		1,500
Net profit		80		90

Balance sheet as at 30 September

	2004		2005	
	£000	£000	£000	£000
Non-current assets		1,900		1,860
Current assets				
Stock	400		500	
Debtors	750		960	
Bank	8		4	
	1,158		1,464	
Less Current liabilities	390	768	450	1,014
		2,668		2,874
Equity				
£1 ordinary shares		1,650		1,766
Reserves		1,018		1,108
		2,668		2,874

Required:

Using six ratios, comment on the profitability (three ratios) and efficiency (three ratios) of the business as revealed by the statements shown above.

7.5 Threads Limited manufactures nuts and bolts, which are sold to industrial users. The abbreviated financial statements for 2004 and 2005 are as follows:

(continued over)

Profit and loss account for the year ended 30 June

	2004		2005	
	£000	£000	£000	£000
Revenue		1,180		1,200
Cost of sales		(680)		(750)
Gross profit		500		450
Operating expenses	(200)		(208)	
Depreciation	(66)		(75)	
Interest	–		(8)	
		(266)		(291)
Profit before tax		234		159
Tax		(80)		(48)
Profit after tax		154		111
Dividend – paid		(70)		(72)
Retained profit for year		84		39

Balance sheet as at 30 June

	2004		2005	
	£000	£000	£000	£000
Non-current assets		702		687
Current assets				
Stocks	148		236	
Debtors	102		156	
Cash	3		4	
	253		396	
Current liabilities				
Trade creditors	(60)		(76)	
Other creditors and accruals	(18)		(16)	
Tax	(40)		(24)	
Bank overdraft	(81)		(122)	
	(199)		(238)	
Net current assets		54		158
Non-current liabilities				
Bank loan		–		(50)
		756		795
Equity				
Ordinary share capital of £1 (fully paid)		500		500
Retained profits		256		295
		756		795

Required:

(a) Calculate the following financial ratios for *both* 2004 and 2005 (using year-end figures for balance sheet items):

  (i)   return on capital employed;
  (ii)   net profit margin;
  (iii) gross profit margin;
  (iv)   current ratio;
  (v)   acid test ratio;
  (vi)   settlement period for debtors;
  (vii) settlement period for creditors; and
  (viii) stock turnover period.

(b) Comment on the performance of Threads Limited from the viewpoint of a business considering supplying a substantial amount of goods to Threads Limited on usual trade credit terms.

7.6   Bradbury Ltd is a family-owned clothes manufacturer based in the south west of England. For a number of years the chairman and managing director was David Bradbury. During his period of office, sales revenue had grown steadily at a rate of 2 to 3 per cent each year. David Bradbury retired on 30 November 2004 and was succeeded by his son Simon. Soon after taking office, Simon decided to expand the business. Within weeks he had successfully negotiated a five-year contract with a large clothes retailer to make a range of sports and leisurewear items. The contract will result in an additional £2 million in sales revenue during each year of the contract. To fulfil the contract, Bradbury Ltd acquired new equipment and premises.

Financial information concerning the business is given below.

Profit and loss account for the year ended 30 November

	2004	2005
	£000	£000
Turnover	9,482	11,365
Profit before interest and tax	914	1,042
Interest charges	(22)	(81)
Profit before tax	892	961
Taxation	(358)	(386)
Profit after tax	534	575
Dividend paid	(120)	(120)
Retained profit	414	455

Balance sheet as at 30 November

	2004		2005	
	£000	£000	£000	£000
Non-current assets				
Property, plant and equipment				
Freehold premises at cost		5,240		7,360
Plant and equipment (net)		2,375		4,057
		7,615		11,417
Current assets				
Stock	2,386		3,420	
Trade debtors	2,540		4,280	
	4,926		7,700	
Current liabilities				
Trade creditors	(1,157)		(2,245)	
Taxation	(179)		(193)	
Bank overdraft	(172)		(2,736)	
	(1,508)		(5,174)	
Net current assets		3,418		2,526
		11,033		13,943
Non-current liabilities				
Loans		(1,220)		(3,674)
Total net assets		9,813		10,269
Equity				
Share capital		2,000		2,000
Reserves		7,813		8,269
		9,813		10,269

Required:

(a) Calculate, for each year (using year-end figures for balance sheet items), the following ratios:
   (i)   net profit margin;
   (ii)   return on capital employed;

(iii) current ratio;

(iv) gearing ratio;

(v) days debtors (settlement period); and

(vi) sales revenue to capital employed.

(b) Using the above ratios, and any other ratios or information you consider relevant, comment on the results of the expansion programme.

7.7 The financial statements for Harridges Limited are given below for the two years ended 30 June 2004 and 2005. Harridges Limited operates a department store in the centre of a small town.

Harridges Limited
Profit and loss account for the years ended 30 June

	2004		2005	
	£000	£000	£000	£000
Revenue		2,600		3,500
Cost of sales		(1,560)		(2,350)
Gross profit		1,040		1,150
Expenses: Wages and salaries	(320)		(350)	
Overheads	(260)		(200)	
Depreciation	(150)		(250)	
		(730)		(800)
Operating profit		310		350
Interest payable		(50)		(50)
Profit before taxation		260		300
Taxation		(105)		(125)
Profit after taxation		155		175
Dividend (approved, but unpaid at the year end)		(65)		(75)
Profit retained for the year		90		100

Balance sheet as at 30 June

	2004		2005	
	£000	£000	£000	£000
Non-current assets		1,265		1,525
Current assets				
Stocks	250		400	
Debtors	105		145	
Cash at bank	380		115	
	735		660	
Current liabilities				
Trade creditors	(235)		(300)	
Dividend (approved, but unpaid)	(65)		(75)	
Other	(100)		(110)	
	(400)		(485)	
Net current assets		335		175
Total assets less current liabilities		1,600		1,700
Non-current liabilities				
10% loan stock		(500)		(500)
		1,100		1,200
Equity				
Share capital: £1 shares fully paid		490		490
Share premium		260		260
Profit and loss account		350		450
		1,100		1,200

Required:

(a) Choose and calculate eight ratios that would be helpful in assessing the performance of Harridges Limited. Use end-of-year values and calculate ratios for both 2004 and 2005.

(b) Using the ratios calculated in (a) and any others you consider helpful, comment on the business's performance from the viewpoint of a prospective purchaser of a majority of shares.

7.8 Genesis Ltd was incorporated in 2001 and has grown rapidly over the past three years. The rapid rate of growth has created problems for the business, which the directors have found difficult to deal with. Recently, a firm of management consultants has been asked to help the directors to overcome these problems.

In a preliminary report to the board of directors, the management consultants state: 'Most of the difficulties faced by the business are symptoms of an underlying problem of overtrading.'

The most recent financial statements of the business are set out below:

Balance sheet as at 31 October 2004

	£000	£000	£000
Non-current assets			
Property, plant and equipment			
Freehold land and buildings at cost		530	
Less Accumulated depreciation		88	442
Fixtures and fittings at cost		168	
Less Accumulated depreciation		52	116
Motor vans at cost		118	
Less Accumulated depreciation		54	64
			622
Current assets			
Stock-in-trade		128	
Trade debtors		104	
		232	
Less **Current liabilities**			
Trade creditors	184		
Taxation	8		
Bank overdraft	358	550	(318)
			304
Less **Non-current liabilities**			
10% debentures (secured)			(120)
			184
Equity			
Ordinary £0.50 shares			60
General reserve			50
Retained profit			74
			184

(continued over)

Profit and loss account for the year ended 31 October 2004

	£000	£000
Revenue		1,640
Less Cost of sales		
Opening stock	116	
Purchases	1,260	
	1,376	
Less Closing stock	128	(1,248)
Gross profit		392
Less Selling and distribution expenses	204	
Administration expenses	92	
Interest expenses	44	(340)
Net profit before taxation		52
Corporation tax		(16)
Net profit after taxation		36
Dividends paid		(4)
Retained profit for the year		32

All purchases and sales were on credit.

Required:

(a) Explain the term 'overtrading' and state how overtrading might arise for a business.
(b) Discuss the kinds of problem that overtrading can create for a business.
(c) Calculate and discuss *five* financial ratios that might be used to establish whether or not the business is overtrading.
(d) State the ways in which a business may overcome the problem of overtrading.

8

Reporting the financial results of groups of companies

OBJECTIVES

When you have completed this chapter, you should be able to:

- Discuss the nature of groups, and explain why they exist and how they are formed.

- Prepare a group balance sheet and profit and loss account.

- Explain the nature of associate company status and its accounting implications.

- Explain and interpret the contents of a set of group financial statements.

INTRODUCTION

Many larger businesses, including virtually all of those that are household names in the UK, consist not just of one single company but of a group of companies. Here one company (the parent company) controls one or more other companies (the subsidiary companies). This usually arises because the parent owns the majority of the shares of the subsidiaries.

In this chapter we shall look at groups and, more particularly, at the accounting treatment that they usually receive. This will draw heavily on what has already been covered, particularly in Chapters 2, 3, 4 and 5. Associate companies are briefly considered.

What is a group of companies?

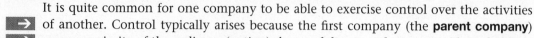
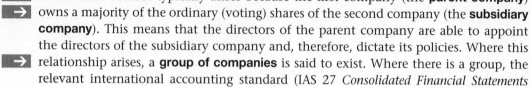

It is quite common for one company to be able to exercise control over the activities of another. Control typically arises because the first company (the **parent company**) owns a majority of the ordinary (voting) shares of the second company (the **subsidiary company**). This means that the directors of the parent company are able to appoint the directors of the subsidiary company and, therefore, dictate its policies. Where this relationship arises, a **group of companies** is said to exist. Where there is a group, the relevant international accounting standard (IAS 27 *Consolidated Financial Statements and Accounting for Investments in Subsidiaries*) requires that a set of financial statements is drawn up annually not only for each individual company, but also for the group taken as a whole. Before we go on to consider how the **group financial statements** (that is, the financial statements of a group of companies) are prepared, we shall look at the reasons why groups exist at all and at the types of group relationships that can exist.

Why do groups exist?

Companies have subsidiaries where the parent company:

- creates a new company to operate some part of its business, perhaps a new activity;
- buys a majority, perhaps all, of the shares of some other existing company; that is, a **takeover**.

Many companies have subsidiaries as a result of both of these reasons.

Newly created companies

It is very common for large businesses to be made up of, and to operate through, a number, often a large number, of individual companies. All of these subsidiaries are wholly owned by the parent company, sometimes known as the **holding company**. In some cases, the only assets of the parent company are the shares that it owns in the subsidiary companies. Strictly speaking, it is the subsidiary companies that own the land, buildings, machinery, stocks, and so on that are used to generate profit. However, since the parent owns the subsidiaries, in effect, it owns the individual 'real' assets of those companies.

An obvious question is, why do businesses operate through subsidiaries? To put it another way, why do the parent companies not own all of the assets of the business directly, instead of through the subsidiaries? The answers to these questions are probably:

- *Limited liability.* Each individual company has individual limited liability. This means that if there is a financial failure of one subsidiary, neither the assets of other subsidiaries nor of the parent could be legally demanded by any unsatisfied creditors of the failed company. Thus the group can 'ring fence' each part of the business by having separate companies, each with its own limited liability.
- *Individual identity.* A sense of independence and autonomy may be created that could, in turn, increase levels of commitment among staff. It may also help to develop, or perpetuate, a market image of a smaller, independent business.

Customers, as well as staff, may prefer to deal with what they see as a smaller, specialist business than with a division of a large diversified business.

To create a subsidiary, the would-be parent may simply form a new company in the normal way. The new company would then issue shares to the parent, in exchange for some asset or assets of the parent. Where the new subsidiary has been formed to undertake a completely new activity the asset may well be cash. If the subsidiary is to carry on some activity which the parent had undertaken directly up to that point, the assets are likely to be such things as the non-current and current assets associated with the particular activity.

Example 8.1

The summarised balance sheet of Baxter plc is as follows:

Balance sheet as at 31 December

Non-current assets	£m	£m	£m
Property, plant and equipment			
Land			43
Plant			15
Vehicles			8
			66
Current assets			
Stock	15		
Debtors	23		
Cash	13		
		51	
Less **Current liabilities**			
Creditors		11	
Net current assets			40
Total assets less current liabilities			106
Less **Non-current liabilities**			
Debentures			40
			66
Equity			
Called-up share capital:			
ordinary shares of £1 each, fully paid			50
Profit and loss account			16
			66

Baxter plc has recently formed a new company, Nova Ltd, which is to undertake the work that has previously been done by the industrial fibres division of Baxter plc. The following assets are to be transferred to Nova Ltd at the values that currently are shown in the balance sheet of Baxter plc:

	£m
Land	10
Plant	5
Vehicles	3
Stock	6
Cash	3
	27

Example 8.1 continued

Nova Ltd is to issue £1 ordinary shares at the nominal or par value (that is, £1) to Baxter plc in exchange for these assets.

Baxter plc's balance sheet immediately after these transfers will be:

Balance sheet as at 31 December

Non-current assets	£m	£m	£m
Property, plant and equipment			
Land (43 – 10)			33
Plant (15 – 5)			10
Vehicles (8 – 3)			5
Investments			48
27 million ordinary £1 shares of Nova Ltd			27
			75
Current assets			
Stocks (15 – 6)	9		
Debtors	23		
Cash (13 – 3)	10		
		42	
Less **Current liabilities**			
Creditors		11	
Net current assets			31
Total assets less current liabilities			106
Less **Non-current liabilities**			
Debentures			40
			66
Equity			
Called-up share capital:			
ordinary shares of £1 each, fully paid			50
Profit and loss account			16
			66

As you have probably noted, the individual assets have simply been replaced by the asset, shares in Nova Ltd.

Activity 8.1

Try to prepare the balance sheet of Nova Ltd immediately following the transfers of the assets and the shares being issued.

It should look something like this:

Balance sheet as at 31 December

Non-current assets	£m	£m
Property, plant and equipment (at transfer value)		
Land		10
Plant		5
Vehicles		3
		18

Current assets	£m	£m
Stocks	6	
Cash	3	
		9
Total assets		27
Equity		
Called-up share capital: ordinary shares of £1 each, fully paid		27

Takeovers

A would-be parent company may also create a subsidiary by taking over an existing company. Here it buys enough of the shares of a hitherto unconnected **target company** to enable it to exercise control over the target company, thereby making the target a new subsidiary company. The shares are, of course, bought from the existing shareholders of the target company.

The shares may be bought through the stock exchange or an approach may be made directly to the individual shareholders of the target company. This second course is feasible because all companies are required by law to provide the names and addresses of their shareholders to any interested party. In many takeovers, the parent offers to the target company shareholders shares in the parent as all, or part of, the bid consideration. This means the target company shareholders who accept the offer will exchange their shares in the target for shares in the parent. Thus, they cease to be shareholders of the target company and become shareholders in the parent. The parent company simply replaces them as shareholders in the target.

Example 8.2

The summarised balance sheet of Adams plc is as follows:

Balance sheet as at 31 March

Non-current assets	£m	£m	£m
Property, plant and equipment			
Land			35
Plant			21
Vehicles			12
			68
Current assets			
Stocks	25		
Debtors	28		
Cash	22		
		75	
Less Current liabilities			
Creditors	23		
Net current assets			52
Total assets less current liabilities			120
Less Non-current liabilities			
Debentures			50
			70

Example 8.2 continued

	£m	£m	£m
Equity			
Called-up share capital:			
ordinary shares of £1 each, fully paid			50
Share premium account			5
Profit and loss account			15
			70

Adams plc has recently made an offer of £1 a share for all the share capital of Beta Ltd (20m shares of 50p each). This is to be met by issuing the appropriate number of new ordinary shares of Adams plc at an issue value of £2 a share.

All the Beta Ltd shareholders accepted the offer. This means that to meet the required consideration, Adams plc will need to issue shares to the value of £20m (that is, 20m × £1). Since the Adams plc shares are to be issued at £2 each, 10m shares will need to be issued, at a share premium of £1 each.

Following the takeover, the balance sheet of Adams plc will look as follows:

Balance sheet as at 31 March

	£m	£m	£m
Non-current assets			
Property, plant and equipment			
Land			35
Plant			21
Vehicles			12
Investments			68
Shares in Beta Ltd			20
			88
Current assets			
Stocks		25	
Debtors		28	
Cash		22	
			75
Less **Current liabilities**			
Creditors			23
Net current assets			52
Total assets less current liabilities			140
Less **Non-current liabilities**			
Debentures			50
			90
Equity			
Called-up share capital:			
ordinary shares of £1 each, fully paid			60
Share premium account			15
Profit and loss account			15
			90

Note that the assets have increased by £20m and that this is balanced by the value of the shares issued (£10m share capital and £10m share premium).

Activity 8.2

If, instead of the consideration offered being in shares, the offer had been 50 per cent in cash and 50 per cent in Adams plc shares, what would the balance sheet of Adams plc have looked like after the takeover?

The total offer value would still be £20m, but this would be met by paying cheques totalling £10m and by issuing shares worth £10m (£5m share capital and £5m share premium). So the balance sheet would be:

Balance sheet as at 31 March

Non-current assets	£m	£m	£m
Property, plant and equipment			
Land			35
Plant			21
Vehicles			12
Investments			68
Shares in Beta Ltd			20
			88
Current assets			
Stocks	25		
Debtors	28		
Cash	12		
		65	
Less **Current liabilities**			
Creditors		23	
Net current assets			42
Total assets less current liabilities			130
Less **Non-current liabilities**			
Debentures			50
			80
Equity			
Called-up share capital:			
ordinary shares of £1 each, fully paid			55
Share premium account			10
Profit and loss account			15
			80

Activity 8.3

How would the takeover affect the balance sheet of Beta Ltd?

The balance sheet of Beta Ltd would not be affected at all. A change of shareholders does not affect the financial statements of a company.

It is not necessary that the parent company should retain the target/subsidiary as a separate company following the takeover. The latter could be wound up and its assets owned directly by the parent. Normally this would not happen, however, for the reasons that we considered above: namely, limited liability and individual identity. The latter may be particularly important in the case of a takeover. The new parent company may be very keen to retain the name and identity of its new subsidiary where the subsidiary has a good marketing image.

Types of group relationship

So far we have considered a situation where there is the simple relationship between a parent and its subsidiary or subsidiaries that is shown in Figure 8.1.

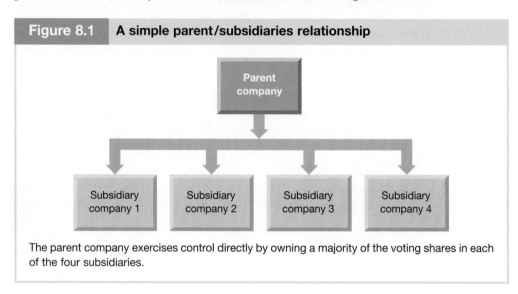

Figure 8.1   A simple parent/subsidiaries relationship

The parent company exercises control directly by owning a majority of the voting shares in each of the four subsidiaries.

A slightly more complex relationship is shown in Figure 8.2. Here Subsidiary 2 is a subsidiary by virtue of being controlled by another company (Subsidiary 1), which is, in turn, a subsidiary of the parent. In these circumstances, Subsidiary 2 is usually called a 'sub-subsidiary' of the parent. Subsidiary 3 is a straightforward subsidiary. The parent company here is sometimes known as the 'ultimate' parent company of Subsidiary 2.

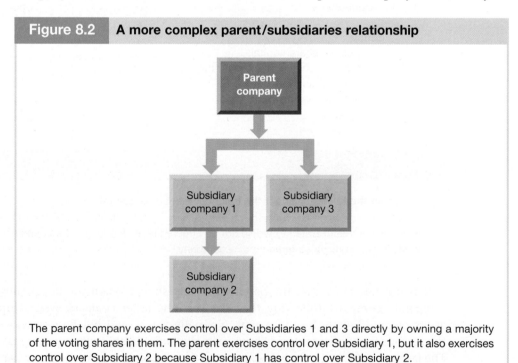

Figure 8.2   A more complex parent/subsidiaries relationship

The parent company exercises control over Subsidiaries 1 and 3 directly by owning a majority of the voting shares in them. The parent exercises control over Subsidiary 1, but it also exercises control over Subsidiary 2 because Subsidiary 1 has control over Subsidiary 2.

Earlier in this chapter, it was pointed out that one company is a subsidiary of another because the latter *controls* the former. This is usually as a result of the latter owning a majority of the voting shares of the other, but this does not need to be the case. Consider Figure 8.2 and suppose that the parent owns 60 per cent of the voting shares of Subsidiary 1 and that Subsidiary 1 owns 60 per cent of the shares of Subsidiary 2. In effect, the parent only owns 36 per cent of the shares of Subsidiary 2 (that is, 60 per cent of 60 per cent), yet the latter is a subsidiary of the former. This is because the parent has complete control over (though not total ownership of) Subsidiary 1, which in turn has complete control over (though again not total ownership of) Subsidiary 2.

Activity 8.4

Company A owns 40 per cent of the voting shares of both Company B and Company C. The other 60 per cent of the voting shares of Company C are owned by Company B. Is Company C a subsidiary of Company A?

The answer is no. This is despite the fact that Company A can be seen to own 64 per cent of the shares of Company C; 40 per cent directly and 24 per cent (that is, 40 per cent × 60 per cent) through Company B. Since A does not control B, it cannot control B's shares in C.

Though ownership and control do not necessarily go hand-in-hand, in practice this tends to be the case.

The reason that we are concerned as to whether one company is a subsidiary of another is, of course, that group financial statements must be prepared where there is a parent/subsidiary relationship, but not otherwise.

Real World 8.1 shows the subsidiaries of the Go-Ahead Group plc. Many of us in the UK use the services of at least one of the subsidiaries, some of us on a daily basis. Most of the tangible assets of the group are owned by the subsidiaries, rather than directly by the parent company. Note that Go-Ahead uses the word 'group' in its official name. This is not unusual, but not a legal requirement. Many companies that operate mainly through subsidiaries do not indicate this in the company name.

REAL WORLD 8.1

Going ahead with subsidiaries

Go-Ahead Group plc

PRINCIPAL SUBSIDIARY UNDERTAKINGS as at 28 June 2003

Name	*Principal activity*
Brighton & Hove Bus and Coach Company Limited	Bus and coach operator
City of Oxford Motor Services Limited	Bus and coach operator
Go Gateshead Limited	Bus operator
London Central Bus Company Limited	Bus and coach operator
Mokett Limited	Intermediate holding co.

Real World 8.1 continued

Name		Principal activity
London General Transport Services Limited	(a)	Bus and coach operator
Go Northern Limited		Bus and coach operator
Go Wear Buses Limited		Bus operator
Go Coastline Limited		Bus operator
MetroCity (Newcastle) Limited	(a)	Taxi operator
Metrobus Limited		Bus operator
Victory Railway Holdings Limited		Intermediate holding co.
ThamesTrains Limited	(a)	Train operator
Govia Limited	(b)	Intermediate holding co.
Thameslink Rail Limited	(a)	Train operator
South Central Limited	(a)	Train operator
Abingdon Bus Company Limited		Intermediate holding co.
Aviance UK Limited	(a)	Aviation Services
Reed Aviation Limited	(a)	Aviation services
Meteor Parking Limited		Aviation services

Notes
1 All the principal subsidiary undertakings are incorporated and operate in Great Britain.
2 The above are subsidiary undertakings by virtue of the majority voting rights being held by the immediate parent undertaking.
3 Subsidiary undertakings held indirectly are marked (a). Thameslink Rail Limited and South Central Limited are owned 100% by Govia Limited, and therefore 65% by the Go-Ahead Group plc.
4 The proportion of nominal value of ordinary share capital held in each company is 100%, except companies marked (b), where the proportion is 65%.
5 All subsidiary undertakings are included in the consolidated accounts.
6 The year end of Plane Handling Limited is not co-terminus with the group, being 30 September.

Source: Go-Ahead Group plc Annual Review 2003.

Preparation of a group balance sheet

We are now going to look at the preparation of a **group balance sheet**. We shall do this by considering a series of examples, starting with the simplest possible case and gradually building in more and more of the complexities found in real life.

Each company within the group will prepare its own balance sheet, which considers things from the perspective of that particular company. As well as this, the parent company will produce a balance sheet that reflects the assets and claims of the group as a whole. In effect, the group balance sheet looks at the group as if the parent company owned the assets and, therefore, was responsible for the outside liabilities of all the group members. This means, among other things, that whereas the *parent company* balance sheet will include the assets of investments in the shares of the subsidiary companies, in the *group* balance sheet, this will be replaced by the net assets (assets less claims of non-group liabilities). In other words, the group balance sheet looks behind the subsidiary company shares to see what they represent, in terms of assets and liabilities. The assets and liabilities of subsidiaries are **consolidated** into the balance sheet of the parent company. This point should become clearer as we look at some examples.

Example 8.3

The balance sheets of Parent plc and of Subsidiary Ltd, on the date that the former bought the shares in the latter, were as follows:

Balance sheet as at 31 May

	Parent plc		Subsidiary Ltd	
	£m	£m	£m	£m
Non-current assets				
Property, plant and equipment				
Land		40		5
Plant		30		2
Vehicles		20		2
		90		9
Investment				
5 million shares of Subsidiary Ltd		10		–
		100		9
Current assets				
Stocks	20		3	
Debtors	30		2	
Cash	10		2	
	60		7	
Less **Current liabilities**				
Creditors	20		6	
Net current assets		40		1
Total assets less current liabilities		140		10
Less **Non-current liabilities**				
Debentures		30		–
		110		10
Equity				
Called-up share capital:				
ordinary shares of £1 each, fully paid		70		5
Share premium account		10		–
Profit and loss account		30		5
		110		10

To deduce the group balance sheet, we simply combine each of the like items by adding them together. For example, the group investment in land is £45m, representing £40m invested by Parent plc and £5m invested by Subsidiary Ltd.

The only exceptions to the rule that we simply add like items together, lies with the investment in the shares of Subsidiary Ltd, in the balance sheet of Parent plc, and with the equity (share capital plus reserves) in the balance sheet of Subsidiary Ltd. In effect, these are two sides of the same coin, since Parent plc is the owner of Subsidiary Ltd. For this reason, it is logical simply to add these two items together, and since one is an asset and the other is a claim and they are equal in amount, they will cancel each other out.

→

Example 8.3 continued

The group balance sheet will be as follows:

Balance sheet as at 31 May

	£m	£m
Non-current assets		
Property, plant and equipment		
Land (40 + 5)		45
Plant (30 + 2)		32
Vehicles (20 + 2)		22
		99
Current assets		
Stocks (20 + 3)	23	
Debtors (30 + 2)	32	
Cash (10 + 2)	12	
	67	
Less Current liabilities		
Creditors (20 + 6)	26	
Net current assets		41
Total assets less current liabilities		140
Less Non-current liabilities		
Debentures (30 + 0)		30
		110
Equity		
Called-up share capital:		
ordinary shares of £1 each, fully paid		70
Share premium account		10
Profit and loss account		30
		110

The equity section of the group balance sheet is simply that of Parent plc. The £10m equity for Subsidiary Ltd cancels out the £10m '5 million shares of Subsidiary Ltd' in the non-current assets section of the parent company's balance sheet.

Activity 8.5

The balance sheets of Large plc and of Small plc, on the date that Large plc bought the shares in Small plc, were as follows:

Balance sheet as at 30 June

	Large plc		Small plc	
	£m	£m	£m	£m
Non-current assets				
Property, plant and equipment				
Land		55		–
Plant		43		21
Vehicles		25		17
		123		38
Investment				
20 million shares of Small plc		32		–
		155		38

Current assets	£m	£m	£m	£m
Stocks	42		18	
Debtors	18		13	
Cash	24		13	
	84		44	
Less Current liabilities				
Creditors	25		20	
Net current assets		59		24
Total assets less current liabilities		214		62
Less Non-current liabilities				
Debentures		50		30
		164		32
Equity				
Called-up share capital:				
ordinary shares of £1 each, fully paid		100		20
Share premium account		–		5
Profit and loss account		64		7
		164		32

Have a try at deducing the group balance sheet.
The group balance sheet will be as follows:

Balance sheet as at 30 June

Non-current assets	£m	£m
Property, plant and equipment		
Land (55 + 0)		55
Plant (43 + 21)		64
Vehicles (25 + 17)		42
		161
Current assets		
Stocks (42 + 18)	60	
Debtors (18 + 13)	31	
Cash (24 + 13)	37	
	128	
Less **Current liabilities**		
Creditors (25 + 20)	45	
Net current assets		83
Total assets less current liabilities		244
Less **Non-current liabilities**		
Debentures (50 + 30)		80
		164
Equity		
Called-up share capital:		
ordinary shares of £1 each, fully paid		100
Profit and loss account		64
		164

The equity section of the group balance sheet is simply that of Large plc. The £32m for the equity (share capital and reserves) of Small plc cancels out the £32m 'investment in 20m shares of Small plc' in the non-current assets section of the balance sheet of Large plc.

Example 8.3 and Activity 8.5 represent the simplest case because:

● the parent owns all of the shares of the subsidiary;
● the price paid for the shares (£10 million and £32 million) exactly equals the 'book' or balance sheet value of the net assets of the subsidiary; and
● no trading has taken place since the shares were purchased.

In practice, these three 'simplifications' frequently do not all exist; often none of them exists.

We shall now go on to look at the 'complications', firstly, one by one and then all together.

Less than 100 per cent ownership of the subsidiary by the parent

The problem here is that when we come to set the asset of 'shares of subsidiary', in the balance sheet of the parent, against the 'equity' (owners' claim) in the balance sheet of the subsidiary, they do not completely cancel one another.

Example 8.4

The balance sheets of Parent plc and of Subsidiary Ltd, on the date that the former bought the shares in the latter, are the same as in the previous example except that Parent plc owns only 4 million (of the 5 million) shares of Subsidiary Ltd. Thus the investment is only £8m, instead of £10m. As a result, Parent plc's cash balance is £2m greater than in the previous example.

The two balance sheets were as follows:

Balance sheets as at 30 September

	Parent plc		Subsidiary Ltd	
Non-current assets	£m	£m	£m	£m
Property, plant and equipment				
Land		40		5
Plant		30		2
Vehicles		20		2
		90		9
Investment				
4 million shares of Subsidiary Ltd		8		–
		98		9
Current assets				
Stocks	20		3	
Debtors	30		2	
Cash	12		2	
	62		7	
Less **Current liabilities**				
Creditors	20		6	
Net current assets		42		1
Total assets less current liabilities		140		10
Less **Non-current liabilities**				
Debentures		30		–
		110		10
Equity				
Called-up share capital:				
ordinary shares of £1 each, fully paid		70		5
Share premium account		10		–
Profit and loss account		30		5
		110		10

As before, to prepare the group balance sheet, we simply add like items together. The problem is that when we come to set the £8 million investment made by Parent plc against the £10 million equity of Subsidiary Ltd, they do not cancel. There is an owners' claim of £2 million in the balance sheet of Subsidiary Ltd that has not been cancelled out.

Activity 8.6

Can you puzzle out what the £2m represents?

It represents the extent to which Parent plc does not own all of the shares of Subsidiary Ltd. Parent plc only owns 80 per cent of the shares, and therefore others must own the rest. Since we are including all of the assets and liabilities of Subsidiary Ltd as being those of the group, the group balance sheet needs to acknowledge that there is another source of equity finance, as well as Parent plc.

→ This £2 million owners' claim is known as **minority interests** or 'outsiders' interests'. It is shown in the group balance sheet as an addition to, but not part of, the equity. The group balance sheet will be as follows:

Balance sheet as at 30 September

Non-current assets	£m	£m
Property, plant and equipment		
Land (40 + 5)		45
Plant (30 + 2)		32
Vehicles (20 + 2)		22
		99
Current assets		
Stocks (20 + 3)	23	
Debtors (30 + 2)	32	
Cash (12 + 2)	14	
	69	
Less **Current liabilities**		
Creditors (20 + 6)	26	
Net current assets		43
Total assets less current liabilities		142
Less **Non-current liabilities**		
Debentures (30 + 0)		30
		112
Equity		
Called-up share capital: ordinary shares of £1 each, fully paid		70
Share premium account		10
Profit and loss account		30
		110
Minority or outsiders' interests		2
		112

This balance sheet can be interpreted as the group having control over net assets totalling £112 million. Of this, £110 million is financed by the shareholders of the parent company and £2 million by others.

It may have occurred to you that an alternative approach to dealing with less than 100 per cent ownership is to scale down the assets and liabilities, to reflect this, before carrying out the 'consolidation' of the two sets of financial statements. Since Parent plc owns only 80 per cent of Subsidiary Ltd, we could multiply all of the figures in Subsidiary Ltd's balance sheet by 0.8 before preparing the group financial statements. If we did this, the owners' claim would be reduced to £8 million, which would exactly cancel with the asset (shares of Subsidiary Ltd) in the balance sheet of Parent plc.

Activity 8.7

Can you think of the (logical) reason why we do not 'scale down' for less than 100 per cent owned subsidiaries when preparing the group balance sheet?

The reason that all of the assets and liabilities of the subsidiary are included in the group balance sheet, in these circumstances, is that the parent company *controls* all of the subsidiaries' assets, even though it may not strictly own them all. Control is the key issue in group financial statements.

Activity 8.8

The balance sheets of Large plc and of Small plc, on the date that Large plc bought the shares in Small plc, were as follows:

Balance sheets as at 30 June

	Large plc £m	Large plc £m	Small plc £m	Small plc £m
Non-current assets				
Property, plant and equipment				
Land		55		–
Plant		43		21
Vehicles		25		17
		123		38
Investment				
15 million shares of Small plc		24		–
		147		38
Current assets				
Stocks	42		18	
Debtors	18		13	
Cash	32		13	
	92		44	
Less **Current liabilities**				
Creditors	25		20	
Net current assets		67		24
Total assets less current liabilities		214		62
Less **Non-current liabilities**				
Debentures		50		30
		164		32
Equity				
Called-up share capital:				
ordinary shares of £1 each, fully paid		100		20
Share premium account		–		5
Profit and loss account		64		7
		164		32

Have a go at preparing the group balance sheet.

The group balance sheet will be as follows:

Balance sheet as at 30 June

	£m	£m
Non-current assets		
Property, plant and equipment		
Land (55 + 0)		55
Plant (43 + 21)		64
Vehicles (25 + 17)		42
		161
Current assets		
Stocks (42 + 18)	60	
Debtors (18 + 13)	31	
Cash (32 + 13)	45	
	136	
Less **Current liabilities**		
Creditors (25 + 20)	45	
Net current assets		91
Total assets less current liabilities		252
Less **Non-current liabilities**		
Debentures (50 + 30)		80
		172
Equity		
Called-up share capital:		
ordinary shares of £1 each, fully paid		100
Profit and loss account		64
		164
Minority interests		8
		172

The £8m for minority interests represents the 25 per cent of the Small plc shares owned by the 'outside' shareholders (that is, 25 per cent of £32m).

Paying more or less than the underlying net asset value for the shares

Here the problem is that, even where the subsidiary is 100 per cent owned, the asset of 'shares of the subsidiary', in the balance sheet of the parent, will not exactly cancel against the equity figure in the balance sheet of the subsidiary. Anything paid in excess of the underlying net asset value of the subsidiary's shares must represent an undisclosed asset, which is normally referred to as **goodwill arising on consolidation**. Any amount paid below the underlying net asset value is normally referred to as **capital reserve arising on consolidation**.

For the sake of simplicity, we shall assume that the asset values reported in the balance sheet of a subsidiary reflect their fair values. We shall, however, consider the situation where this assumption is not made later in the chapter.

Example 8.5

We are returning to the original balance sheets of Parent plc and Subsidiary Ltd, on the date that the former bought the shares in the latter. So Parent plc owns all of the shares in Subsidiary Ltd, but we shall assume that they were bought for £15m rather than £10m. Parent plc's cash balance reflects the higher amount paid. The balance sheets are as follows:

Balance sheets as at 30 September

	Parent plc		Subsidiary Ltd	
Non-current assets	£m	£m	£m	£m
Property, plant and equipment				
Land		40		5
Plant		30		2
Vehicles		20		2
		90		9
Investment				
5 million shares of Subsidiary Ltd		15		–
		105		9
Current assets				
Stocks	20		3	
Debtors	30		2	
Cash	5		2	
	55		7	
Less Current liabilities				
Creditors	20		6	
Net current assets		35		1
Total assets less current liabilities		140		10
Less Non-current liabilities				
Debentures		30		–
		110		10
Equity				
Called-up share capital:				
ordinary shares of £1 each, fully paid		70		5
Share premium account		10		–
Profit and loss account		30		5
		110		10

The normal routine of adding like items together and cancelling the investment in Subsidiary Ltd shares against the equity of that company is followed, except that the last two do not exactly cancel. The difference is, of course, goodwill arising on consolidation.

The group balance sheet will be as follows:

Balance sheet as at 30 September

Non-current assets	£m	£m
Property, plant and equipment		
Land (40 + 5)		45
Plant (30 + 2)		32
Vehicles (20 + 2)		22
		99

	£m	£m
Intangible asset		
Goodwill arising on consolidation (15 – 10)		5
		104
Current assets		
Stocks (20 + 3)	23	
Debtors (30 + 2)	32	
Cash (5 + 2)	7	
	62	
Less **Current liabilities**		
Creditors (20 + 6)	26	
Net current assets		36
Total assets less current liabilities		140
Less **Non-current liabilities**		
Debentures (30 + 0)		30
		110
Equity		
Called-up share capital:		
ordinary shares of £1 each, fully paid		70
Share premium account		10
Profit and loss account		30
		110

The goodwill represents the excess of what was paid by Parent plc for the shares over their underlying net asset value, according to Subsidiary Ltd's balance sheet.

Activity 8.9

The balance sheets of Large plc and of Small plc, on the date that Large plc bought the shares in Small plc, were as follows:

Balance sheets at 30 June

	Large plc		Small plc	
	£m	£m	£m	£m
Non-current assets				
Property, plant and equipment				
Land		55		–
Plant		43		21
Vehicles		25		17
		123		38
Investment				
20 million shares of Small plc		28		–
		151		38
Current assets				
Stocks		42		18
Debtors		18		13
Cash		28		13
		88		44
Less **Current liabilities**				
Creditors		25		20

	Large plc		Small plc	
	£m	£m	£m	£m
Net current assets		63		24
Total assets less current liabilities		214		62
Less Non-current liabilities				
Debentures		50		30
		164		32
Equity				
Called-up share capital:				
ordinary shares of £1 each, fully paid		100		20
Share premium account		–		5
Profit and loss account		64		7
		164		32

Have a go at preparing the group balance sheet.

The group balance sheet will be as follows:

Balance sheet as at 30 June

	£m	£m
Non-current assets		
Property, plant and equipment		
Land (55 + 0)		55
Plant (43 + 21)		64
Vehicles (25 + 17)		42
		161
Current assets		
Stocks (42 + 18)	60	
Debtors (18 + 13)	31	
Cash (28 + 13)	41	
	132	
Less Current liabilities		
Creditors (25 + 20)	45	
Net current assets		87
Total assets less current liabilities		248
Less Non-current liabilities		
Debentures (50 + 30)		80
		168
Equity		
Called-up share capital:		
ordinary shares of £1 each, fully paid		100
Capital reserve arising on		
consolidation (32 – 28)		4
Profit and loss account		64
		168

In effect, the capital reserve arising on consolidation represents the apparent gain that has been made by Large plc as a result of buying assets for less than they are worth (according to the fair values reflected in Small plc's balance sheet).

We shall now take a look at how we cope with a situation where the parent owns less than all of the shares of its subsidiary, and it has paid more or less than the underlying net asset value of the shares.

Example 8.6

Again we shall look at Parent plc and Subsidiary Ltd on the date that the former bought the shares in the latter. This time we shall combine both of the 'complications' that we have already met. Thus, Parent plc now only owns 80 per cent of the shares of Subsidiary Ltd, for which it paid £3 a share, that is, £1 above their underlying net asset value.

Balance sheets as at 30 September

	Parent plc £m	Parent plc £m	Subsidiary Ltd £m	Subsidiary Ltd £m
Non-current assets				
Property, plant and equipment				
Land		40		5
Plant		30		2
Vehicles		20		2
		90		9
Investment				
4 million shares of Subsidiary Ltd		12		–
		102		9
Current assets				
Stocks	20		3	
Debtors	30		2	
Cash	8		2	
	58		7	
Less **Current liabilities**				
Creditors	20		6	
Net current assets		38		1
Total assets less current liabilities		140		10
Less **Non-current liabilities**				
Debentures		30		–
		110		10
Equity				
Called-up share capital:				
ordinary shares of £1 each, fully paid		70		5
Share premium account		10		–
Profit and loss account		30		5
		110		10

The normal routine still applies. This means adding like items together and cancelling the investment in Subsidiary Ltd shares against the equity of that

→

Example 8.6 continued

company. Again they will not cancel, but this time for a combination of two reasons; minority interests *and* goodwill arising on consolidation.

We need to separate out the two issues before we go on to prepare the group financial statements.

To establish the minority interests element, we need simply to calculate the part of the owners' claim of Subsidiary Ltd that is not owned by Parent plc. Parent plc owns 80 per cent of the shares, so others own 20 per cent. 20 per cent of the equity of Subsidiary Ltd is £2m (that is, 20 per cent × £10m).

To discover the appropriate goodwill figure (or capital reserve), we need to compare what Parent plc paid and what it got, in terms of the fair values reflected in the balance sheet. It paid £12m and got net assets with a fair value of £8m (that is, 80 per cent × £10m). Thus, goodwill is £4m (that is, 12 − 8).

The group balance sheet will be as follows:

Balance sheet as at 30 September

	£m	£m
Non-current assets		
Property, plant and equipment		
Land (40 + 5)		45
Plant (30 + 2)		32
Vehicles (20 + 2)		22
		99
Intangible asset		
Goodwill arising on consolidation		
(12 − (80% × 10))		4
		103
Current assets		
Stocks (20 + 3)	23	
Debtors (30 + 2)	32	
Cash (8 + 2)	10	
	65	
Less **Current liabilities**		
Creditors (20 + 6)	26	
Net current assets		39
Total assets less current liabilities		142
Less **Non-current liabilities**		
Debentures (30 + 0)		30
		112
Equity		
Called-up share capital:		
ordinary shares of £1 each, fully paid		70
Share premium account		10
Profit and loss account		30
		110
Minority interests		2
		112

Activity 8.10

The balance sheets of Large plc and Small plc, on the date that Large plc bought the shares in Small plc, were as follows:

Balance sheets as at 30 June

	Large plc £m	Large plc £m	Small plc £m	Small plc £m
Non-current assets				
Property, plant and equipment				
Land		55		–
Plant		43		21
Vehicles		25		17
		123		38
Investment				
15 million shares of Small plc		21		–
		144		38
Current assets				
Stocks	42		18	
Debtors	18		13	
Cash	35		13	
	95		44	
Less **Current liabilities**				
Creditors	25		20	
Net current assets		70		24
Total assets less current liabilities		214		62
Less **Non-current liabilities**				
Debentures		50		30
		164		32
Equity				
Called-up share capital:				
ordinary shares of £1 each, fully paid		100		20
Share premium account		–		5
Profit and loss account		64		7
		164		32

Have a try at preparing the group balance sheet.

Activity 8.10 continued

The minority interest will be £8m (that is, 25 per cent of £32m).

To discover goodwill/capital reserve, we need to compare what was paid (£21m) with what was obtained (75 per cent of £32m = £24m). Thus, we have a capital reserve of £3m.

The group balance sheet will be as follows:

Balance sheet as at 30 June

	£m	£m
Non-current assets		
Property, plant and equipment		
Land (55 + 0)		55
Plant (43 + 21)		64
Vehicles (25 + 17)		42
		161
Current assets		
Stocks (42 + 18)	60	
Debtors (18 + 13)	31	
Cash (35 + 13)	48	
	139	
Less **Current liabilities**		
Creditors (25 + 20)	45	
Net current assets		94
Total assets less current liabilities		255
Less **Non-current liabilities**		
Debentures (50 + 30)		80
		175
Equity		
Called-up share capital:		
ordinary shares of £1 each, fully paid		100
Capital reserve arising on		
consolidation [(75% × 32) − 21]		3
Profit and loss account		64
		167
Minority interests (25% × 32)		8
		175

Trading has taken place since the shares were purchased

Except very rarely, most group balance sheets will be prepared some time after the parent company purchased the shares in the subsidiary. This does not in any way raise major difficulties, but we need to backtrack to the position at the time of the purchase to establish the goodwill/capital reserve.

We shall look at another example, this time a new one will be introduced, just to provide a little variety.

Example 8.7

The balance sheets of Mega plc and Micro plc, as at 31 December, are set out below. Mega plc bought its shares in Micro plc some time ago, at which time the latter's share capital was exactly as shown below and the profit and loss account balance stood at £30m.

Balance sheets as at 31 December

	Mega plc		Micro plc	
Non-current assets	£m	£m	£m	£m
Property, plant and equipment				
Land		53		18
Plant		34		11
Vehicles		24		9
		111		38
Investment				
6 million shares of Micro plc		33		–
		144		38
Current assets				
Stocks	27		10	
Debtors	29		11	
Cash	11		1	
	67		22	
Less **Current liabilities**				
Creditors	23		5	
Net current assets		44		17
Total assets less current liabilities		188		55
Less **Non-current liabilities**				
Debentures		50		10
		138		45
Equity				
Called-up share capital:				
ordinary shares of £1 each, fully paid		100		10
Profit and loss account		38		35
		138		45

We can see that the investment in the balance sheet of Mega plc (£33 million) comes nowhere near cancelling the £45 million owners' claim of Micro plc. We need to separate out the elements.

Let us start with minority interests. We are not concerned at all with the position at the date of the takeover. If the equity of Micro plc totals £45 million at the balance sheet date and the minorities own 4 million of the 10 million shares, their contribution to the financing of the group's assets must be £18 million (that is, 40% × £45m).

Next, let us ask ourselves what Mega plc got when it paid £33 million for the shares. At that time, the equity part of Micro plc's balance sheet looked like this:

	£m
Called-up share capital:	
ordinary shares of £1 each, fully paid	10
Profit and loss account	30
	40

This means that the net assets of Micro plc must have also been worth (in terms of fair values reflected in the balance sheet) £40 million; otherwise the balance sheet would not have balanced. Since Mega plc bought 6 million of 10 million shares, it paid £33 million for net assets worth £24 million (that is, 60% of £40 million). Thus, there is goodwill arising on consolidation of £9 million (that is, 33 – 24).

We shall assume that no steps have been taken since the takeover to alter this goodwill figure. We shall consider why such steps may have been taken a little later in this chapter.

In dealing with minority interests and goodwill we have, in effect, picked up the following parts of the owners' claim of Micro plc at 31 December:

- The minorities' share of both the equity (as the 'minority interests' figure).
- Mega plc's share of the share capital and its share of the reserves as they stood at the date of the takeover (in the calculation of the 'goodwill' figure).

The only remaining part of the owners' claim of Micro plc at 31 December is Mega plc's share of the reserves that have built up since the takeover, that is, its share of £35 million – £30 million = £5 million. This share is £3 million (that is, 60 per cent of £5 million). This is Mega plc's share of the profits that have been earned by its subsidiary since the takeover, to the extent that profits have not already been paid out as dividends. As such, it is logical for this £3 million to be added to the profit and loss account balance of the parent company in arriving at the group reserves.

This treatment of the equity of Micro plc can be represented in a tabular form as shown in Figure 8.3.

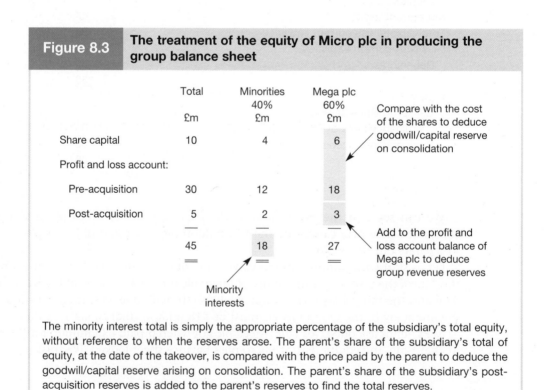

Figure 8.3 The treatment of the equity of Micro plc in producing the group balance sheet

	Total £m	Minorities 40% £m	Mega plc 60% £m	
Share capital	10	4	6	Compare with the cost of the shares to deduce goodwill/capital reserve on consolidation
Profit and loss account:				
Pre-acquisition	30	12	18	
Post-acquisition	5	2	3	
	45	18	27	Add to the profit and loss account balance of Mega plc to deduce group revenue reserves

Minority interests

The minority interest total is simply the appropriate percentage of the subsidiary's total equity, without reference to when the reserves arose. The parent's share of the subsidiary's total of equity, at the date of the takeover, is compared with the price paid by the parent to deduce the goodwill/capital reserve arising on consolidation. The parent's share of the subsidiary's post-acquisition reserves is added to the parent's reserves to find the total reserves.

The group balance sheet will be as follows:

Balance sheet as at 31 December

Non-current assets	£m	£m
Property, plant and equipment		
Land (53 + 18)		71
Plant (34 + 11)		45
Vehicles (24 + 9)		33
		149
Intangible asset		
Goodwill arising on consolidation (33 − (6 + 18))		9
		158
Current assets		
Stocks (27 + 10)	37	
Debtors (29 + 11)	40	
Cash (11 + 1)	12	
	89	
Less Current liabilities		
Creditors (23 + 5)	28	
Net current assets		61
Total assets less current liabilities		219
Less Non-current liabilities		
Debentures (50 + 10)		60
		159
Equity		
Called-up share capital:		
ordinary shares of £1 each, fully paid		100
Profit and loss account (38 + 3)		41
		141
Minority interests (40% × 45)		18
		159

Activity 8.11

The balance sheets of Grand plc and Petit Ltd, as at 30 June, are set out below. Grand plc bought its shares in Petit Ltd some time ago at which time the latter's share capital was the same as it is currently and the profit and loss account balance stood at £14m.

Balance sheets as at 30 June

	Grand plc		Petit Ltd	
Non-current assets	£m	£m	£m	£m
Property, plant and equipment				
Land		12		10
Plant		14		8
Vehicles		3		6
		29		24
Investment				
7.5 million shares of Petit Ltd		21		–
		50		24
Current assets				
Stocks	10		5	
Debtors	9		4	
Cash	2		2	
	21		11	
Less Current liabilities				
Creditors	7		3	
Net current assets		14		8
Total assets less current liabilities		64		32

Activity 8.11 continued

	Grand plc		Petit Ltd	
	£m	£m	£m	£m
Less **Non-current liabilities**				
Debentures		20		–
		44		32
Equity				
Called-up share capital:				
ordinary shares of £1 each, fully paid	30		10	
Profit and loss account	14		22	
	44		32	

Prepare the balance sheet for the group as at 30 June.

Your answer should be something like this:

> Minority interests
> 25% × £32m = £8m
> Goodwill arising on consolidation
> £21m − [75% × (£10m + £14m)] = £3m
> Grand plc's share of Petit Ltd's post-acquisition reserves
> 75% × (£22m − £14m) = £6m

Assuming that no steps have been taken since the takeover to alter the goodwill figure, the group balance sheet will be as follows:

Balance sheet as at 30 June

	£m	£m
Non-current assets		
Property, plant and equipment		
Land (12 + 10)		22
Plant (14 + 8)		22
Vehicles (3 + 6)		9
		53
Intangible asset		
Goodwill arising on consolidation		3
		56
Current assets		
Stocks (10 + 5)	15	
Debtors (9 + 4)	13	
Cash (2 + 2)	4	
	32	
Less **Current liabilities**		
Creditors (7 + 3)	10	
Net current assets		22
Total assets less current liabilities		78
Less **Non-current liabilities**		
Debentures (20 + 0)		20
		58
Equity		
Called-up share capital:		
ordinary shares of £1 each, fully paid		30
Profit and loss account (14 + 6)		20
		50
Minority interests		8
		58

Goodwill arising on consolidation and balance sheet values

 Goodwill on consolidation represents the difference between the cost of acquiring the shares in a subsidiary and the **fair value** of the net assets acquired. In the examples that we have considered so far, we have assumed that the balance sheet values are the same as the fair values of the assets of the subsidiary company. Thus, it has been possible to deduce goodwill by making a comparison of the cost of acquiring the subsidiary with the balance sheet values of the subsidiary. Unfortunately, things are not usually that simple.

Balance sheet values often differ from the fair values of assets. Generally speaking, balance sheet values are lower because accounting conventions, such as prudence and historic cost, conspire to produce a conservative bias. This means that, to calculate goodwill on consolidation, we cannot rely on balance sheet values. We must find out what the fair values of the assets acquired really are.

Example 8.8 seeks to illustrate this point.

Example 8.8

The balance sheets of Parent plc and of Subsidiary Ltd (which we last met in Example 8.6) on the date that the former bought the shares in the latter, were as follows:

Balance sheets as at 30 September

	Parent plc		Subsidiary Ltd	
	£m	£m	£m	£m
Non-current assets				
Property, plant and equipment				
Land		40		5
Plant		30		2
Vehicles		20		2
		90		9
Investment				
5 million shares of Subsidiary Ltd		15		–
		105		9
Current assets				
Stocks	20		3	
Debtors	30		2	
Cash	5		2	
	55		7	
Less **Current liabilities**				
Creditors	20		6	
Net current assets		35		1
Total assets less current liabilities		140		10
Less **Non-current liabilities**				
Debentures		30		–
		110		10
Equity				
Called-up share capital:				
ordinary shares of £1 each, fully paid		70		5
Share premium account		10		–
Profit and loss account		30		5
		110		10

Example 8.8 continued

When Parent plc was valuing the shares of Subsidiary Ltd, it was judged that most of the balance sheet values were in line with the fair values, but that the following values should be applied to the three categories of property, plant and equipment:

	£m
Land	7
Plant	3
Vehicles	3

In addition it was recognised that the subsidiary has a good reputation, which was valued at £1m. When these fair values are incorporated into the group balance sheet, it will be as follows:

Balance sheet as at 30 September

	£m	£m
Non-current assets		
Property, plant and equipment		
Land (40 + 7)		47
Plant (30 + 3)		33
Vehicles (20 + 3)		23
		103
Intangible asset		
Goodwill		1
		104
Current assets		
Stocks (20 + 3)	23	
Debtors (30 + 2)	32	
Cash (5 + 2)	7	
	62	
Less **Current liabilities**		
Creditors (20 + 6)	26	
Net current assets		36
Total assets less current liabilities		140
Less **Non-current liabilities**		
Debentures (30 + 0)		30
		110
Equity		
Called-up share capital:		
ordinary shares of £1 each, fully paid		70
Share premium account		10
Profit and loss account		30
		110

This example takes the simple case of no minority interests (that is, a 100 per cent subsidiary) and no post-acquisition trading (the balance sheets are at the date of acquisition), but these 'complications' would not alter the principles.

It should be noted that there is no need for the balance sheet of the subsidiary to be adjusted for fair values, just the group balance sheet. In fact, adjusting the subsidiary's balance sheet would contravene the historic cost convention since, as far as the subsidiary is concerned, no change occurs with the takeover except a change in the names on the list of shareholders. No transaction has occurred regarding its assets.

Goodwill arising on consolidation is simply the excess of what the parent company paid for the subsidiary company's shares over their fair value. This asset (goodwill) is seen as being the parent company's share of the value of the subsidiary company's goodwill. This goodwill may represent a loyal workforce, a regular and profitable customer base and so on, that a new business setting up could not have. These attributes could well be enduring, but they can be lost partially or completely. The appropriate international accounting standard (IAS 36) recognises this and asserts that the value of this goodwill needs to be revalued at the end of each accounting year. If its value has been impaired, it must be reduced to the lower value in the group financial statements. It should be noted that goodwill arising on consolidation does not appear in the balance sheets of either the parent or the subsidiary. It only appears on the group balance sheet.

Inter-company assets and claims

Though members of a group are separate legal entities, the element of control exercised by the parent, and generally close relations between them, tends to lead to inter-company trading and other inter-company transactions. This, in turn, means that a particular asset in one company's balance sheet could relate to an equally sized liability in the balance sheet of another member of the same group.

The principle underlying the group balance sheet is that it should represent the situation as if all the assets and claims of individual group members were directly the assets and claims of the parent company. Since the parent company cannot owe itself money, where there are inter-company balances these must be eliminated when preparing the group balance sheet.

Example 8.9

Delta plc and its subsidiary Gamma plc are the only members of a group. Delta plc sells goods on credit to Gamma plc. At the balance sheet date the following balances existed in the books of the companies:

	Debtors (receivables) £m	Creditors (payables) £m
Delta plc	34	26
Gamma plc	23	18

Included in the debtors of Delta plc, and the creditors of Gamma plc, is £5 million in respect of some recent inter-company trading.

In deducing the figures to be included in the group balance sheet, we have to eliminate the inter-company balance, as follows:

$$\text{Debtors} = 34 - 5 + 23 = £52 \text{ million}$$

$$\text{Creditors} = 26 + 18 - 5 = £39 \text{ million}$$

Note that these consolidated debtors and creditors figures represent what is, respectively, owed by and owed to individuals and organisations outside of the group. This is what they are intended to represent, according to the principles of group accounting.

Preparing the group profit and loss account (income statement)

The **group profit and loss account** follows very similar principles to those that apply to the balance sheet. These are:

- Like items are added together. For example, the revenue of each subsidiary is added to that of the parent company to discover group revenue.
- All the amounts appearing under each heading in the profit and loss accounts of subsidiaries are included in the total, even where it is not a wholly owned subsidiary. For example, the revenue of a subsidiary, say 60 per cent owned by the parent, is included in full.
- The interests of minorities are separately identified towards the bottom of the profit and loss account.

Example 8.10

Holder plc owns 75 per cent of the ordinary shares of Sub Ltd. At the date of the acquisition, Sub Ltd's profit and loss account balance stood at £7m. The outline profit and loss accounts of the two companies for the year ended on 31 December are as follows:

Profit and loss accounts for the year ended 31 December

	Holder plc		Sub Ltd	
	£m	£m	£m	£m
Revenue		83		40
Cost of sales		(41)		(15)
Gross profit		42		25
Administration expenses	(18)		(10)	
Distribution expenses	(6)	(24)	(3)	(13)
		18		12
Income from shares in group companies		3		–
Profit before tax		21		12
Taxation		(8)		(4)
Profit after tax		13		8
Profit and loss account balance				
brought forward from the previous year		25		19
		38		27
Dividend on ordinary shares		(6)		(4)
Profit and loss account balance				
carried forward to the following year		32		23

Preparing the group profit and loss account is a very simple matter of adding like items together, except for three issues:

- Dealing with the dividend paid by Sub Ltd to its parent. From Sub Ltd's point of view this is a normal dividend payment to a shareholder. Since Holder plc owns 75 per cent of the shares of Sub Ltd, it will be paid 75 per cent (£3m) of the dividend paid (£4m). From Holder plc's point of view, this dividend is part of its income and should be reflected in the profit and loss account as such. From a group point of view, however, it is simply a transfer of money from one member of the group to another and should not, therefore, appear in the group profit and loss account. We deal with this by ignoring both Sub Ltd's dividends and the income from dividends of Holder plc. The £1 million, which is the dividend entitlement of the minorities, is dealt with as part of the minority interests.

● Not all of the profit after tax of the subsidiary 'belongs' to the group. Twenty-five per cent (£2m) of it belongs to the minorities. We recognise this in the group profit and loss account by deducting the 25 per cent of the after-tax profit of the subsidiary from the combined after-tax profit. This also takes account of the minorities' entitlement to £1m dividend.

● Only the group's share of the post-acquisition reserves (that is, those that have arisen since Sub Ltd became a subsidiary of Holder plc) of Sub Ltd should be included in the group profit and loss account. This is exactly the same point as we encountered when considering the group balance sheet. The post-acquisition profit and loss account balance brought forward is £12m (that is, £19m – £7m). Of this, only £9m (75 per cent) 'belongs' to the group and should be added to Holder plc's reserves.

The group profit and loss account will be as follows:

Profit and loss account for the year ended 31 December

	£m	£m
Revenue (83 + 40)		123
Cost of sales (41 + 15)		(56)
Gross profit		67
Administration expenses (18 + 10)	(28)	
Distribution expenses (6 + 3)	(9)	(37)
Profit before tax		30
Taxation (8 + 4)		(12)
Profit after tax		18
Attributable to minorities		(2)
Profit after tax attributable to Holder plc shareholders		16
Profit and loss account balance brought forward from the previous year (25 + 9)		34
		50
Dividend on ordinary shares		(6)
Profit and loss account balance carried forward to the following year		44

This statement says that the assets under the control of the group generated net profit after tax of £18m. Of this, £2m is the share of the 'outside' shareholders of Sub Ltd. This follows the normal approach of group financial statements of treating all assets, claims, revenues and expenses of group companies as if they were those of the group. Where the subsidiaries are not 100 per cent owned by the parent, this fact is acknowledged by making an adjustment to reflect the minority interests.

Activity 8.12

Ajax plc owns 60 per cent of the ordinary shares of Exeter plc. At the date of the acquisition, Exeter plc's profit and loss account balance stood at £25m. The outline profit and loss accounts of the two companies for the year ended on 31 December are as follows:

Profit and loss accounts for the year ended 31 December

	Ajax plc		Exeter plc	
	£m	£m	£m	£m
Revenue		120		80
Cost of sales		(60)		(40)
Gross profit		60		40
Administration expenses	(20)		(5)	
Distribution expenses	(10)	(30)	(15)	(20)
		30		20
Income from shares in group companies		6		–
Profit before tax		36		20
Taxation		(12)		(10)
Profit after tax		24		10
Profit and loss account balance brought forward from the previous year		60		45
		84		55
Dividend on ordinary shares		(10)		(10)
Profit and loss account balance carried forward to the following year		74		45

Have a try at preparing a consolidated (group) profit and loss account.

Your answer should look something like this:

Group profit and loss account for the year ended 31 December

	£m	£m
Revenue (120 + 80)		200
Cost of sales (60 + 40)		(100)
Gross profit		100
Administration expenses (20 + 5)	(25)	
Distribution expenses (10 + 15)	(25)	(50)
Profit before tax		50
Taxation (12 + 10)		(22)
Profit after tax		28
Attributable to minorities (40% × 10)		(4)
Profit after tax attributable to Ajax plc shareholders		24
Profit and loss account balance brought forward from the previous year [60 + ((45 − 25) × 60%)]		72
		96
Dividend on ordinary shares		(10)
Profit and loss account balance carried forward to the following year		86

Group cash flow statements

Groups must normally prepare a cash flow statement that follows the same logic as the balance sheet and profit and loss account, that is, to show the movements in all of the cash that is in the control of the group, for the period under review.

The preparation of a **group cash flow statement** follows the same rules as apply to the preparation of the statement for individual companies. In view of this, we need not spend time looking separately at cash flow statements in a group context.

Self-assessment question 8.1

The balance sheets, as at 31 December last year, and profit and loss accounts, for the year ended last 31 December, of Great plc and Small plc are set out below. Great plc bought its shares in Small plc on 1 January last year at which time the latter's share capital was the same as it is currently and the profit and loss account balance stood at £35m.

At the time of the acquisition, the fair value of all the assets of Small plc was thought to be the same as their balance sheet values, except for land whose fair value was thought to be £5m more than the balance sheet value. It is believed that there has been no impairment in the value of the goodwill arising on consolidation since 1 January last year.

Balance sheets as at 31 December last year

	Great plc		Small plc	
	£m	£m	£m	£m
Non-current assets				
Property, plant and equipment				
Land		80		14
Plant		33		20
Vehicles		20		11
		133		45
Investment				
16 million shares of Small plc		53		–
		186		45
Current assets				
Stocks	20		9	
Debtors	21		6	
Cash	17		5	
	58		20	
Less **Current liabilities**				
Creditors	17		5	
Net current assets		41		15
Total assets less current liabilities		227		60
Less **Non-current liabilities**				
Debentures		50		–
		177		60
Equity				
Called-up share capital:				
ordinary shares of £1 each, fully paid		100		20
Profit and loss account		77		40
		177		60

Self-assessment question 8.1 continued

Profit and loss accounts for the year ended 31 December last year

	Great plc		Small plc	
	£m	£m	£m	£m
Revenue		91		53
Cost of sales		(46)		(24)
Gross profit		45		29
Administration expenses	(10)		(7)	
Distribution expenses	(7)	(17)	(4)	(11)
		28		18
Income from shares in group companies		4		–
Profit before tax		32		18
Taxation		(9)		(8)
Profit after tax		23		10
Profit and loss account balance brought forward from the previous year		65		35
		88		45
Dividend on ordinary shares		(11)		(5)
Profit and loss account balance carried forward to the following year		77		40

Required:

Prepare the balance sheet and profit and loss account for the group.

Accounting for less than a controlling interest – associate companies

What happens when one company makes a substantial investment in another company but this does not provide the investing company with a controlling interest? In other words, the company whose shares have been acquired does not become a subsidiary of the investing company. One approach would simply include the investment of shares in the company at cost in the investing company's balance sheet. Assuming that the shares are held on a long-term basis, they would be treated as a non-current asset. Any dividends received from the investment would be treated as income in the investing company's profit and loss account.

The problem with this approach, however, is that companies normally pay dividends of much less than the profits earned for the period. The profits that are not distributed, but are ploughed back to generate more profits for the future, still belong to the shareholders. From the perspective of the investing company, the treatment described would not, therefore, reflect fully the investment made. Where the investment made by the investing group does not involve the purchase of a substantial shareholding in the company, this problem is overlooked and so the treatment of the investment described above (that is, showing the investment, at cost, as a non-current asset and taking account only of any dividends received) is applied. Where, however, the investment involves the purchase of a significant number of voting shares in the company, a different kind of accounting treatment seems more appropriate.

Associate companies

To deal with the problem identified above, a particular type of relationship between the two companies has been defined. An **associate company** is one in which an investing company or group has a substantial, but not a controlling, interest. To be more precise, it is a company in which another company can exercise significant influence over its operating and financial policies. If a company holds 20 per cent or more of the voting shares of another company it is presumed to be able to exercise significant influence. This influence is usually demonstrated by representation on the board of directors of the company or participation in policy making. The relevant international accounting standard (IAS 28 *Investments in Associates*) provides the detailed guidelines concerning what constitutes an associate company.

The accounting treatment of an associate company falls somewhere between consolidation (as with group financial statements) and the treatment of small share investments, as described at the beginning of this section. Let us assume that a company invests in another company, so that the latter becomes an associate of the former. The accounting treatment will be as follows:

- The investing company will be required to produce consolidated financial statements that reflect not only its own performance and position but also those of its associated company (companies).
- In the consolidated profit and loss account, the investing company's share of the operating profit of the associate company (companies) will be shown and will be added to the operating profit of the investing company. As operating profit represents the profit before interest and tax, the investing company's share of any interest payable and tax relating to the associate company (companies) will also be shown. These will be deducted in deriving the net profit after tax for the investing company and its associate company (companies).
- In the consolidated balance sheet, the investment made in the associate company (companies) will be shown and the investing company's share of any post-acquisition reserves will be added to the investment. This will have the effect of showing more fully the investment made in the associate company (companies).
- Dividends received by the investing company from the associate company (companies) will not be included in the consolidated profit and loss account. This is because the investing company's share of the associate company's (companies') profit will already be fully reflected in the financial statements.
- If the investing company also has subsidiaries, their financial statements will also have to be incorporated, in the manner that we saw for groups earlier in the chapter. Thus a company that has both subsidiary companies and associate companies will prepare consolidated financial statements reflecting all of these.

To illustrate these points, let us take a simple example.

Example 8.11

A plc owns 25 per cent of the ordinary shares of B plc. The price paid for the shares was £26m. A plc bought its shares in B plc, when the latter's reserves stood at £24m. The reserves of B plc had increased to £40m by 31 March last year.

The profit and loss account for A plc and B plc for the year ended 31 March this year are as follows:

Profit and loss accounts for the year ended 31 March this year

	A plc	B plc
	£000	£000
Revenues	800,000	100,000
Cost of sales	(500,000)	(60,000)
Gross profit	300,000	40,000
Operating expenses	(120,000)	(12,000)
Operating profit	180,000	28,000
Dividend – B plc	10,000	
	190,000	
Interest payable	(30,000)	(8,000)
Profit from ordinary activities before tax	160,000	20,000
Corporation tax payable	(40,000)	(4,000)
Profit after tax	120,000	16,000
Dividends paid	(30,000)	(12,000)
Retained profit	90,000	4,000

To comply with the relevant standard (IAS 28), the dividend received from B plc will be eliminated from the consolidated profit and loss account of A plc. However, A plc's share of the operating profit of B plc as well as its share of interest payable and taxation relating to B plc will be incorporated within A plc's consolidated profit and loss account. A plc's consolidated profit and loss account will, therefore, be as follows:

A plc Consolidated profit and loss account

	£000	£000	
Revenues		800,000	
Cost of sales		(500,000)	
Gross profit		300,000	
Operating expenses		(120,000)	
Group operating profit		180,000	
Share of operating profit of associate – B plc		7,000	(25% × £28,000)
Total operating profit		187,000	
Interest payable			
A plc	(30,000)		
Associate – B plc	(2,000)	(32,000)	(25% × £8,000)
Profit on ordinary activities before tax		155,000	
Corporation tax payable			
A plc	(40,000)		
Associate – B plc	(1,000)	(41,000)	(25% × £4,000)
Profit after tax		114,000	
Dividends paid*		(30,000)	
Retained profit		84,000	

* The only dividends reflected are those of A plc.

The consolidated balance sheet of A plc, treating B plc as an associate company, would include an amount for the investment in B plc that is calculated as follows:

Extract from A plc's consolidated balance sheet as at 31 March this year

	£000	
Cost of investment in associate company	26,000	
Share of post-acquisition reserves	4,000	(that is, 25% × (40 − 24))
	30,000	

Activity 8.13

What is the crucial difference between the approach taken when consolidating sub-sidiary company results and incorporating the results of associate companies, as far as the balance sheet and profit and loss account are concerned?

In preparing group financial statements, all of the items in the statements are added together, as if the parent owned them all, even when the subsidiary is less than 100 per cent owned. For example, the revenue figure in the consolidated profit and loss account is the sum of all the revenues made by group companies, the stock (inventories) figure in the balance sheet is the sum of all the stock held by all members of the group.

When dealing with associate companies, we only deal with the shareholding company's share of the profit of the associate and its effect on the value of the shareholding.

Real World 8.2 is the list of the associate companies of Cadbury Schweppes plc, the confectionery and drinks manufacturer. Most of the business's associate companies are overseas companies that are involved in some aspect of confectionery and beverages, but they also include a stake in Camelot Group plc, the business that operates the UK national lottery.

REAL WORLD 8.2

A bit of a lottery

Details of principal associated undertakings

	Activities	Country of incorporation and operation	Proportion of issued share capital held if not 100%
Camelot Group plc	(c)	Great Britain	20%
L'Européenne D'Embouteillage SNC	(b)	France	50%
Dr Pepper/Seven Up Bottling Group, Inc	(b)	US	40.4%
Cadbury Nigeria PLC (listed)	(a)	Nigeria	46%
Crystal Candy (Private) Ltd	(a)	Zimbabwe	49%
Gumlink A/S	(a)	Denmark	25%

The nature of the activities of the individual companies is designated as follows:

(a) Confectionery
(b) Beverages
(c) Other

Source: Cadbury Schweppes plc Report and Accounts 2002.

The argument against consolidation

There seems to be a compelling logic for consolidating the results of subsidiaries controlled by a parent company, to reflect the fact that the shareholders of the parent company effectively control all of the assets of all of the companies in the group. There is also, however, a fairly strong argument against doing so.

Anyone reading the consolidated financial statements of a group of companies could be misled into believing that trading with any member of the group would, in effect, be the same as trading with the group as a whole. The person might imagine that all of the group's assets could be called upon to meet any amounts owed by any member of the group. This would be untrue. Only the assets owned by the particular group member would be accessible to any creditor of that group member. The reason for this is, of course, the legal separateness of the limited company from its shareholder(s), which in turn leads to limited liability of individual group members. There would be absolutely no legal obligation on a parent company, or a fellow subsidiary, to meet the debts of a struggling subsidiary. In fact this is a reason why some businesses operate through a series of subsidiaries, a point that was made early in this chapter.

Despite this criticism of consolidation, the method has been widely adopted as a legal requirement throughout the world.

SUMMARY

The main points of this chapter may be summarised as follows:

Groups

- A group exists where one company (parent) can exercise control over another (subsidiary), usually by owning more than 50 per cent of the voting shares.
- Groups arise by a parent setting up a new company or taking over an existing one.
- Businesses operate as groups:
  - to have limited liability for each part of the business; and
  - to give each part of the business an individual identity.
- Normally, parent companies are required to produce financial statements for the group as a whole, as if the parent company itself had all of the group members' assets, liabilities, revenues, expenses and cash flows.

Group balance sheets

- Derived by adding like items (assets and liabilities) together and setting the equity of each subsidiary (in the subsidiary's balance sheet) against the investment in subsidiary figure (in the parent's balance sheet).
- Where the equity of the subsidiary does not cancel the investment in the subsidiary, it will be for one (or more) of three possible reasons:
  - more, or less, was paid for the subsidiary shares than their 'fair value', leading to 'goodwill on consolidation' (an intangible non-current asset), or capital reserve on consolidation, in the group balance sheet;
  - the parent does not own all of the shares of the subsidiary, leading to 'minority (or outsiders') interests' (similar to equity in the group balance sheet), reflecting the fact that the parent's shareholders do not supply all of the equity finance for the group's assets;
  - the subsidiary has made profits or losses since it became a subsidiary.

- 'Goodwill arising on consolidation' represents the value of the ability of the subsidiary to generate additional profits as a result of a loyal workforce, established customer base and so on.
- Goodwill remains on the group balance sheet but is subject to an 'impairment review' annually and written down in value if this has diminished.

Group profit and loss account (income statement)

- Derived by adding like items (revenues and expenses) together and setting the dividends paid by each subsidiary to the parent (in the subsidiary's profit and loss account) against the dividends received from subsidiaries figure (in the parent's profit and loss account).
- The minority shareholders' share of the after-tax profit is deducted from the group total to reflect the fact that not all of the subsidiary's profit belongs to the group.

Group cash flow statement

- Derived by adding like items (cash flows) together.

Associate companies

- An 'associate company' is one where there is a second (investing) company that has less than a controlling interest, but yet is able to exert significant influence over the first (associate) company, often indicated by representation on the board of directors.
- The investing company will be required to produce consolidated financial statements that reflect not only its own performance and position but also those of its associate company (companies) as well.
- In the consolidated profit and loss account, the investing company's share of the operating profit of the associate company is added to the operating profit of the investing company. Any interest payable and tax relating to the associate company will also be shown.
- In the consolidated balance sheet, the investment made in the associate company will be shown and the investing company's share of any post-acquisition reserves will be added to the investment.
- Dividends received by the investing company from the associate company are not included in the consolidated profit and loss account.

→ **Key terms**

Further reading

If you would like to explore the topics covered in this chapter in more depth, we recommend the following books:

Financial Reporting, *Alexander D. and Britton A.*, 6th edn, Thomson Learning, 2001, chapter 24.

Financial Accounting and Reporting, *Elliott B. and Elliott J.*, 8th edn, Financial Times Prentice Hall, 2004, chapters 19–22.

Financial Accounting, *Melville A.*, 2nd edn, Financial Times Prentice Hall, 1999, chapter 18.

Corporate Financial Accounting and Reporting, *Sutton T.*, 2nd edn, Financial Times Prentice Hall, 2004, chapter 14.

REVIEW QUESTIONS

Answers to these questions can be found on the students' side of the Companion Website at **www.pearsoned.co.uk/atrillmclaney**.

8.1 When does a group relationship arise and what are its consequences for accounting?

8.2 What does a group balance sheet show?

8.3 Quite often, when an existing company wishes to start a new venture, perhaps to produce a new product or render a new service, it will form a subsidiary company as a vehicle for the new venture. Why is this, why not have the new venture conducted by the original company?

8.4 What is an associate company and what are the consequences for accounting of one company being the associate company of a group of companies?

EXERCISES

Exercises 8.5 to 8.8 are more advanced than 8.1 to 8.4. Those with a coloured number have answers at the back of the book.

8.1 Giant plc bought a majority shareholding in Jack Ltd, on the 31 March. On that date the balance sheets of the two companies were as follows:

Balance sheets as at 31 March

	Giant plc		Jack Ltd	
Non-current assets	£m	£m	£m	£m
Property, plant and equipment				
Land		27		12
Plant		55		8
Vehicles		18		7
		100		27
Investment				
10 million shares of Jack Ltd		30		–
		130		27
Current assets				
Stocks	33		13	
Debtors	42		17	
Cash	22		5	
	97		35	
Less **Current liabilities**				
Creditors	41		19	
Net current assets		56		16
Total assets *less* current liabilities		186		43
Less **Non-current liabilities**				
Debentures		50		13
		136		30
Equity				
Called-up share capital:				
ordinary shares of £1 each, fully paid		50		10
Share premium account		40		5
Revaluation reserve		–		8
Profit and loss account		46		7
		136		30

Required:

Assume that the balance sheet values of Jack Ltd's assets represent 'fair' values. Prepare the group balance sheet immediately following the takeover.

8.2 The balance sheets of Jumbo plc and of Nipper plc, on the date that Jumbo plc bought the shares in Nipper plc, were as follows:

Balance sheets as at 31 March

	Jumbo plc £m	Jumbo plc £m	Nipper plc £m	Nipper plc £m
Non-current assets				
Property, plant and equipment				
Land		84		18
Plant		34		33
Vehicles		45		12
		163		63
Investment				
12 million shares of Nipper plc		24		–
		187		63
Current assets				
Stocks	55		32	
Debtors	26		44	
Cash	14		10	
	95		86	
Less **Current liabilities**				
Creditors	41		39	
Net current assets		54		47
Total assets *less* current liabilities		241		110
Less **Non-current liabilities**				
Debentures		100		70
		141		40
Equity				
Called-up share capital:				
ordinary shares of £1 each, fully paid		100		20
Share premium account		–		12
Profit and loss account		41		8
		141		40

Required:

Assume that the balance sheet values of Nipper plc's assets represent fair values. Prepare the group balance sheet immediately following the share acquisition.

8.3 An abridged set of consolidated financial statements for Toggles plc is given below.

Toggles plc
Consolidated profit and loss account for the year ended 30 June

	£m
Revenue	172.0
Operating profit	21.2
Less Taxation	6.4
Profit after taxation	14.8
Less Minority interest	2.4
Profit for year	12.4
Less Dividends	8.5
Retained profit for year	3.9

Consolidated balance sheet as at 30 June

	£m	£m
Non-current assets		
Intangible asset		
Goodwill on consolidation		7.2
Property, plant and equipment		85.6
Current assets		92.8
Stock	21.8	
Debtors	16.4	
Cash	1.7	
	39.9	
Current liabilities		
Trade creditors	(15.3)	
Net current assets		24.6
		117.4
Equity		
Share capital		100.0
Retained profit		16.1
		116.1
Minority interest		1.3
		117.4

Required:

(a) Answer, briefly, the following questions:

   (i)   What is meant by 'minority interest' in both the profit and loss account and the balance sheet?

   (ii) What is meant by 'goodwill on consolidation'?

   (iii) Why will the 'retained profit' figure on the consolidated balance sheet usually be different from the 'retained profit' as shown in the parent company's balance sheet?

(b) Explain the purposes and advantages in preparing consolidated financial statements for the parent company's shareholders.

8.4 Arnold plc owns 75 per cent of the ordinary shares of Baker plc. At the date of the acquisition, Baker plc's profit and loss account balance stood at £17m. The outline profit and loss accounts of the two companies for the year ended on 31 December are as follows:

Profit and loss accounts for the year ended 31 December

	Arnold plc		Baker plc	
	£m	£m	£m	£m
Revenue		83		47
Cost of sales		(36)		(19)
Gross profit		47		28
Administration expenses	(14)		(7)	
Distribution expenses	(21)	(35)	(10)	(17)
		12		11
Income from shares in group companies		3		–
Profit before tax		15		11
Taxation		(4)		(3)
Profit after tax		11		8
Profit and loss account balance brought forward				
from the previous year		34		21
		45		29
Dividend on ordinary shares		(12)		(4)
Profit and loss account balance carried forward				
to the following year		33		25

Required:

Prepare the consolidated (group) profit and loss account for Arnold plc and its subsidiary for the year ended 31 December.

8.5 The summary balance sheets for Apple Limited and Pear Limited are set out below.

Balance sheets as at 30 September

	Apple Limited		Pear Limited	
	£000	£000	£000	£000
Non-current assets				
Property, plant and equipment		950		320
Investment				
Shares in Pear Limited		240		–
		1,190		320
Current assets				
Stocks	320		160	
Debtors	180		95	
Cash at bank	41		15	
	541		270	
Less **Current liabilities**				
Trade creditors	170		87	
Taxation	54		55	
	224		142	
Net current assets		317		128
Non-current liabilities				
Long-term loan		(500)		(160)
		1,007		288
Equity:				
£1 fully paid ordinary shares		700		200
Reserves		307		88
		1,007		288

Apple Ltd purchased 150,000 shares in Pear Ltd at a price of £1.60 per share on 30 September (the above balance sheet date).

Required:

Prepare a consolidated balance sheet for Apple Ltd as at 30 September.

8.6 Abridged statements for Harvest Limited and Wheat Limited as at 30 June this year are set out below. On 1 July last year Harvest Limited acquired 800,000 ordinary shares in Wheat Limited for a payment of £3,500,000. Wheat Ltd's share capital and share premium were each the same at both dates. At that date and at 30 June this year, the assets in the balance sheet of Wheat Limited were shown at fair market values.

Balance sheets as at 30 June this year

	Harvest Limited		Wheat Limited	
	£000	£000	£000	£000
Non-current assets				
Property, plant and equipment		10,850		4,375
Investment				
Shares of Wheat Limited		3,500		–
Current assets	3,775		1,470	
Current liabilities	(2,926)		(1,395)	
		849		75
Non-current liabilities				
Bank loans		(7,000)		(2,500)
		8,199		1,950
Equity				
Share capital (£1 shares)		2,000		1,000
Share premium account		3,000		500
Revenue reserves at				
1 July last year	2,800		375	
Profit for current year	399		75	
		3,199		450
		8,199		1,950

Required:

Prepare the consolidated balance sheet for Harvest Ltd as at 30 June this year, using the data given above.

8.7 On 1 July 2004, Pod Limited purchased 225,000 £1 fully paid ordinary shares of Pea Limited for a consideration of £500,000. Pea Limited's share capital and share premium were each the same at both dates. Simplified balance sheets for both companies as at 30 June 2005 are set out below.

Balance sheets as at 30 June 2005

	Pod Limited		Pea Limited	
	£	£	£	£
Non-current assets				
Property, plant and equipment		1,104,570		982,769
Investments				
Shares in Pea Limited		500,000		–
Current assets				
Stocks	672,471		294,713	
Debtors	216,811		164,517	
Amounts due from subsidiary company	76,000		–	
Cash	2,412		1,361	
	967,694		460,591	
Current liabilities				
Creditors	(184,719)		(137,927)	
Amounts owing to holding company	–		(76,000)	
Overdraft	(68,429)		(25,681)	
	(253,148)		(239,608)	
Net current assets		714,546		220,983
Non-current liabilities				
Bank loan		(800,000)		(750,000)
		1,519,116		453,752

	Pod Limited		Pea Limited	
	£	£	£	£
Equity				
Share capital: £1 ordinary shares		750,000		300,000
Share premium		250,000		50,000
Reserves at 1 July 2004	449,612		86,220	
Profit for year	69,504		17,532	
Reserves at 30 June 2005		519,116		103,752
		1,519,116		453,752

Required:

Prepare a consolidated balance sheet for Pod Ltd and its subsidiary company as at 30 June 2005.

8.8 The balance sheets for Maxi Limited and Mini Limited are set out below.

Balance sheets as at 31 March this year

	Maxi Limited		Mini Limited	
	£000	£000	£000	£000
Non-current assets				
Property, plant and equipment		23,000		17,800
Investment				
1,500,000 shares in Mini Limited		5,000		–
		28,000		17,800
Current assets				
Stocks	5,000		2,400	
Debtors	4,280		1,682	
Amounts owed by Maxi Limited	–		390	
Cash at bank	76		1,570	
	9,356		6,042	
Current liabilities				
Trade creditors	(3,656)		(2,400)	
Other creditors	(1,047)		(1,962)	
Amounts owed to Mini Limited	(390)		–	
Overdraft	(2,450)		–	
	(7,543)		(4,362)	
Net current assets		1,813		1,680
Non-current liabilities				
Bank loans		(13,000)		(14,000)
		16,813		5,480
Equity				
10,000,000 £1 ordinary shares fully paid		10,000		
2,000,000 50p ordinary shares fully paid				1,000
Share premium account		3,000		2,000
Profit and loss account at beginning of year		3,100		2,080
Profit for the year		713		400
		16,813		5,480

On 1 April last year, Maxi Limited purchased 1,500,000 shares of Mini Limited for a consideration of £5m. At that date Mini Limited's share capital and share premium were each the same as shown above.

Required:

Prepare a consolidated balance sheet for Maxi Limited at 31 March this year.

9

Reporting additional measures of performance

OBJECTIVES

When you have completed this chapter, you should be able to:

- Explain the nature and purpose of the value added statement and prepare a simple value added statement from available information.

- Describe the effect of inflation on the conventional financial statements and explain how the problem of inflation may be dealt with when reporting financial performance and position.

- Discuss the need for environmental and social reports and explain the key issues that confront a business seeking to publish such reports.

- Explain the concept of sustainable development and the nature of triple bottom line reporting.

INTRODUCTION

Over the years, there has been a trend towards greater disclosure of information relating to the performance of larger businesses. Various reasons can be cited for this trend. These include the increasing complexity of business, the increasing sophistication of users and an increasing recognition of the responsibilities of businesses towards a variety of stakeholder groups.

In this final chapter we consider some additional measures of performance that may be provided by businesses. We shall see that some of these measures, such as those relating to the environment, go beyond the conventional boundaries of accounting. This implies a rethinking of the way in which we define and measure business success.

The value added statement

The **value added statement (VAS)** came to prominence in the mid-1970s following publication of an influential discussion document entitled *The Corporate Report* (see reference 1 at the end of the chapter). This report argued that the VAS should be seen as an important financial statement that:

> elaborates on the profit and loss account and in time may come to be regarded as a preferable way of describing performance.

Following publication of *The Corporate Report*, two government reports lent further support for the inclusion of the VAS within the annual reports of limited companies.

The VAS is similar to the profit and loss account (income statement) in certain respects; indeed, it can be seen as a modified form of the profit and loss account. Both financial statements are concerned with measuring the operating performance of a business over a period of time. They are also both based on the matching convention, discussed in Chapter 3. However, the VAS differs from the profit and loss account in so far as it is concerned with measuring the *valued added* by a business rather than the *profit earned*.

A business can be viewed as buying in goods and/or services to which it then 'adds value'. The method of calculating value added is set out in Figure 9.1.

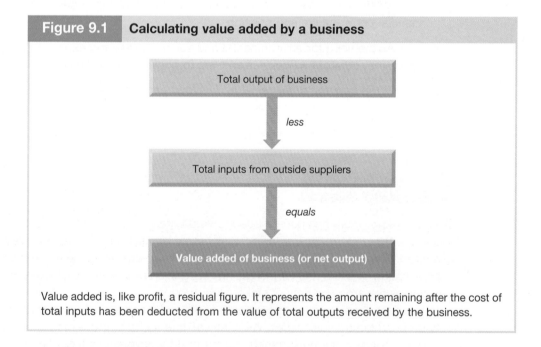

| Figure 9.1 | Calculating value added by a business |

Value added is, like profit, a residual figure. It represents the amount remaining after the cost of total inputs has been deducted from the value of total outputs received by the business.

The total output of the business will normally be the sales revenue for the period. The total inputs will be the bought-in materials and services such as stock purchases, rent, rates, electricity, telephone and so on. The resulting figure of net output, or value added, represents the income that has been generated from the collective effort of employees, suppliers of capital, and government.

The VAS is seen as providing a broader focus than the profit and loss account. The problem with the conventional profit and loss account, so it is argued, is that it takes an owner perspective. It is concerned only with measuring the income attributable to the shareholders of the business. However, there are other groups who contribute to, and have a stake in, the wealth generated by a business. These other stakeholders include the employees, government and lenders. The VAS provides a measure of income generated by all the stakeholders and shows how this income, or value added, is then distributed among them.

Example 9.1 shows a value added statement.

Example 9.1

Value added statement for the year ended 30 June

	£m	£m
Revenue		130.6
Less Bought-in materials and services		88.4
Value added		42.2
Applied in the following way:		
To employees		
Wages, pensions and fringe benefits		28.1
To suppliers of capital		
Interest payable on loans	2.6	
Dividends to shareholders	3.8	6.4
To pay government		
Corporation tax payable		3.2
To provide for maintenance and expansion of assets		
Depreciation of non-current assets	3.0	
Retained profits	1.5	4.5
		42.2

From Example 9.1 we can see that the value added statement consists of two elements. The first is concerned with deriving a measure of value added for the period (here £42.2 million), which is achieved by deducting the bought-in materials and services from sales revenue. The second element is concerned with showing how that value added is applied. That is, it shows how value added is divided among the various stakeholder groups and how much is retained within the business. The depreciation and profits retained within the business can be reinvested so as to maintain and expand the asset base.

An important point to note is that the VAS will not provide any information that is not already contained within the conventional profit and loss account. Rather, it rearranges this information so as to provide new insights concerning the performance of the business.

Activity 9.1

Ray Cathode (Lighting Supplies) plc has produced the following:

Profit and loss account for the year ended 31 December

	£m	£m
Revenue		198
Less Cost of sales		(90)
Gross profit		108
Salaries and wages	(35)	
Rent and rates	(18)	
Insurance	(3)	
Light and heat	(10)	
Interest payable	(6)	
Postage and stationery	(1)	
Advertising	(4)	
Depreciation	(19)	(96)
Net profit before taxation		12
Corporation tax payable		(4)
Net profit after taxation		8
Dividends paid		(3)
Retained profit for the year		5

From this information, see if you can produce a value added statement for the year. (Use the format in Example 9.1 above to guide you.)

Your answer should be as follows:

Value added statement for the year ended 31 December

	£m	£m
Revenue		198
Less Bought-in materials and services		
(90 + 18 + 3 + 10 + 1 + 4)		126
Value added		72
Applied in the following way:		
To employees		
Salaries and wages		35
To suppliers of capital		
Interest payable on loans	6	
Dividends to shareholders	3	9
To pay government		
Corporation tax payable		4
To provide for maintenance and		
** expansion of assets**		
Depreciation of non-current assets	19	
Retained profits	5	24
		72

What useful information can you glean from the VAS in Activity 9.1?

The VAS in Activity 9.1 reveals that nearly half of the value added generated by the business is distributed to employees in the form of salaries and wages. This proportion is much higher than that distributed to suppliers of capital. A relatively high proportion of value added being distributed to employees is not unusual (which may explain the enthusiasm among some managers for publishing this statement). The business retains one third of the value added to provide for maintenance and expansion of assets. A high proportion of value added retained may suggest a concern for growth to be financed through internally generated sources. The proportion of value added required to pay corporation tax is relatively small.

Advantages of the value added statement

A major advantage claimed for the VAS is that it can contribute towards better relations between employees, managers and shareholders. It is said to encourage a team spirit among those with a stake in the business. It reflects the view that the business is a coalition of interests and that business success depends on co-operation between the various stakeholders. By identifying employees as an important stakeholder, it is hoped that they will feel more a part of the team and will respond by showing greater co-operation and commitment. In addition, the VAS should emphasise to managers that employees are an important part of the team and not simply an expense, which is how they are portrayed in the conventional profit and loss account.

A second major advantage claimed is that a number of useful ratios can be derived from this statement. These include:

- value added to sales revenue (per cent);
- value added per £1 of wages and salaries (£);
- dividends to value added (per cent);
- tax to value added (per cent);
- depreciation and retentions to value added (per cent);
- value added to capital employed (per cent).

Calculate each of the above ratios using the information contained in the solution to Activity 9.1 above. How could these ratios be useful? (For purposes of calculation, assume that the business's capital employed is £80m.)

Your answer should be as follows:

$$\text{Value added to sales revenue} = \frac{72}{198} \times 100\%$$

$$= 36.4\%$$

Activity 9.3 continued

The lower this ratio, the greater the reliance of the business on outside sources of materials and services. For example, a wine retailer that purchases its wine from a wholesaler is likely to have a relatively low value added to sales revenue ratio whereas a wine retailer that owns its own vineyards and bottling facilities will have a much higher ratio. The lower the ratio the more vulnerable the business will be to difficulties encountered from external suppliers.

$$\text{Value added per £1 of wages} = \frac{72}{35}$$

$$= £2.10$$

This ratio is a measure of labour productivity. In this case, the employees are generating £2.10 of value added for every £1 of wages expended: the higher the ratio, the higher the level of productivity. This ratio may be useful when making comparisons between businesses. Normally, the ratio would be higher than 1.0. A ratio of less than 1.0 means that employees are earning more than the value of their output.

$$\text{Dividends to value added} = \frac{3}{72} \times 100\%$$

$$= 4.2\%$$

This ratio calculates that portion of value added which will be received in cash more or less immediately by shareholders. The trend of this ratio may provide an insight to the distribution policy of the business over time. It is important to remember, however, that shareholders also benefit, in the form of capital growth, from amounts reinvested in the business. Thus, the ratio is only a partial measure of the benefits received by shareholders.

$$\text{Tax to value added} = \frac{4}{72} \times 100\%$$

$$= 5.6\%$$

This ratio calculates that portion of the value added which is payable to government in the form of taxes. It may be useful in assessing whether or not the business has an unfair burden of taxation.

$$\text{Depreciation and retentions to value added} = \frac{24}{72} \times 100\%$$

$$= 33.3\%$$

This ratio may provide an insight to the ability or inclination of the business to raise finance for new investment from internal operations rather than from external sources. A high ratio may suggest a greater ability or inclination to raise finance internally than a low ratio.

$$\text{Value added to capital employed} = \frac{72}{80} \times 100\%$$

$$= 90\%$$

This ratio is a measure of the productivity of capital employed. A high ratio is, therefore, normally preferred to a low ratio. Once again, this may be a useful ratio for comparison between businesses.

Problems of the value added statement

The proposal to include a VAS as part of the annual report was, at first, greeted with enthusiasm, particularly among large UK businesses. At one time, almost one third of them included a VAS in their annual reports. However, it is now no longer popular. Although the VAS simply rearranges information contained in the conventional profit and loss account, the effect of this rearrangement is to raise a number of difficult measurement and reporting problems. Many of these problems have not really been resolved and this has undermined greater acceptance of the statement. The more important of these problems are:

- *The team concept.* Some dismiss the idea of a business being a team of stakeholders as no more than a public relations exercise. It has been argued that this is simply an attempt to obscure the underlying conflict between suppliers of capital and employees.
- *Team membership.* Others believe that the composition of the team is inappropriate. Why, for example, is government regarded as part of the team and yet suppliers of goods and services are not?
- *The classification of items.* The VAS is beset with classification problems. For example, gross wages to employees (that is, wages before tax and national insurance payments are deducted) are normally shown under the heading 'To employees'. However, it is the government that receives the taxation and National Insurance payments. Employees will receive their wages net of taxation.
- *The importance of profit.* Profit will remain of central importance within a capitalist economy and so the conventional profit and loss account is likely to remain the centrepiece of financial reports. Shareholders are concerned with the returns from their investment in a business. If the managers do not ensure that the shareholders receive adequate returns then they are likely to be replaced by managers who will.

There is a danger that if managers become overconcerned with the improvement of value added this will have an adverse effect on profit. To illustrate this point, consider Activity 9.4 below.

Activity 9.4

Ray Von (Manufacturers) plc is currently considering whether to make a particular component or to purchase the item from an outside supplier. The component can be sold by the business for £40. Making the component would involve a labour cost of £12 a unit and a material cost of £18. The cost of buying the item from an outside supplier would be £26. Calculate the value added and profit arising under each option.

Your answer should be as follows:

	Buy-in	Make
	£	£
Selling price	40	40
Less Bought-in materials	26	18
Value added	14	22
Less Labour costs	–	12
Profit	14	10

We can see that to make the item will provide the greater value added but the lower profit. Thus, a decision to maximise value added would be at the expense of profit.

Where a business has a high value added but a poor profit record, there is a danger that some users will be misled concerning the viability of the business.

It should be emphasised that the profit generated by a business is likely to be important to various stakeholders and not only the shareholders. Lenders will be interested in the profit generated to enable them to assess the riskiness of their investment; governments will be interested for taxation purposes; and employees will be interested for the assessment of likely future pay increases and job security. Those who support the VAS have failed to demonstrate that this statement is useful for decision-making purposes in the way that the profit and loss account is useful.

The VAS and employee reporting

Although the VAS now rarely appears in businesses' annual reports, many businesses continue to use this statement where they provide separate reports of business performance to employees. The VAS is then often portrayed in diagrammatic form for ease of understanding. For example, the application of total value added of Ray Cathode (Lighting Supplies) plc that we met earlier in Activity 9.1 (see p. 308) can be represented in the form of a pie chart, as in Figure 9.2.

| Figure 9.2 | Distribution of total value added by Ray Cathode (Lighting Supplies) plc |

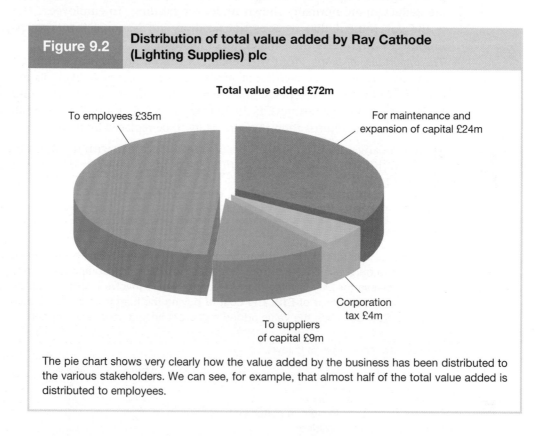

Total value added £72m

To employees £35m

For maintenance and expansion of capital £24m

Corporation tax £4m

To suppliers of capital £9m

The pie chart shows very clearly how the value added by the business has been distributed to the various stakeholders. We can see, for example, that almost half of the total value added is distributed to employees.

Reporting value added to employees alone, however, raises an issue of credibility. Employees may well ask why a financial report that is not regarded as being important to other users is being provided to them. They may feel the major motivation is to demonstrate the extent to which value added is taken up in salaries and wages. As mentioned earlier, a sizeable proportion of value added is often distributed to employees.

Self-assessment question 9.1

The data set out below have been extracted from the accounting records of Samodiva Limited for the year ended 30 September.

	£000
Revenue	6,252
Bad debts	254
Non-recoverable value added tax	62
Cost of goods sold	1,630
Payments to other suppliers	858
Wages	628
Employers' National Insurance	128
Corporation tax payable	244
Dividend to ordinary shareholders	500
Interest payable to debenture holders	320
Depreciation: plant and machines	632
office buildings and fittings	222
Cost of employees' benefit-in-kind	82
Retained profit for the year	692

Required:

(a) Prepare a value added statement for Samodiva Limited for the year ended 30 September.

(b) Calculate any ratios that you consider appropriate for a better understanding of the information contained within the value added statement and comment on your results.

Inflation accounting and reporting

We saw in Chapter 2 that accounting measures items in monetary terms and that there is an assumption that this unit of measurement will remain stable over time. However, this assumption does not hold in reality, as each year the value of money changes. Usually, this is owing to inflation (that is, when the general purchasing power of money is reduced because of a rise in prices). However, it is also possible for deflation to occur (that is, for the general purchasing power of money to increase because of a fall in prices). The measurement of performance and financial position, as reflected in the conventional financial statements, tends to be undermined by these changes in the value of money. In this section, we shall concentrate on the effect of inflation rather than deflation on the financial statements, as it is the former rather than the latter that has created problems for UK businesses over the years. We shall see that inflation tends to result in an overstatement of profit and an understatement of financial position. In a later section we shall consider **inflation accounting** methods that attempt to deal with these problems.

The impact of inflation on profit measurement

During a period of inflation, profits tend to be overstated because of the time period which will often elapse between buying a particular resource and its subsequent use. Stock-in-trade is a good illustration of this, as Example 9.2 demonstrates.

Example 9.2

Kostova Car Sales Ltd acquired a new Mercedes motor car for £25,000 as part of its showroom stock. The car was held for three months before being sold to a customer for £30,000. The cost of replacing the vehicle from the manufacturer increased during the three-month stockholding period to £26,250. This was in line with the general rate of inflation for that period. What is the profit made on the sale of the motor car?

The conventional approach to measuring profit involves matching the selling price of the vehicle to the original outlay cost. Thus, the profit will be calculated as follows:

	£
Sale of motor car	30,000
Less Cost of acquisition	25,000
Profit	5,000

Where the value of money is constant, this approach can produce a valid result. However, when prices are rising, we encounter a problem, as the original cost will be an understatement of the resources consumed. We are told that during the stockholding period the cost of replacing the car increased in line with the rate of inflation. This is to say that the *average* purchasing power, as measured by the general rate of inflation, and the *specific* purchasing power of money, as measured by changes in the cost of the car, decreased by the same amount during the stockholding period. In view of this loss of purchasing power, the original cost of the car ceases to be a meaningful measure of the resources consumed during the period. It can be argued that it would be more realistic to calculate the profit for the period by taking the difference between the selling price and cost of the new car *expressed in current terms*. This means the profit will be as follows:

	£
Sale of motor car	30,000
Less Current purchase cost of car	26,250
Profit	3,750

We can see from Example 9.2 that the effect of substituting the original cost of the car with that expressed in current terms is to reduce the level of profit for the period.

The problem of time elapsing between the acquisition of a resource and its ultimate use is even more acute in the case of non-current assets. A non-current asset may be held for many years and the profit and loss accounts for each of the years during which the asset is held will be charged with depreciation relating to the asset. We saw in Chapter 3 that this depreciation charge is meant to represent that portion of the cost of the asset that is consumed during the period. However, the depreciation charge is based on the original cost of the asset and, during a period of inflation, this cost-based figure will become increasingly out of date. In practice, therefore, the profit and loss account will often match current sales with depreciation charges based on costs incurred many years earlier. This failure to match current revenue with costs expressed in current terms will mean, once again, that profits are overstated.

The impact of inflation on financial position

Another problem of inflation is the risk that it may pose to the capital base of the business. Consider Example 9.3.

Example 9.3

Habbad Enterprises sells training videos to small businesses. The balance sheet of the business as at 31 March is as follows:

	£
Stock (20 videos @ £100)	2,000
Capital	2,000

Assume that, during the next period, the business managed to sell all of the videos for cash for £150 each. The reported profit for the period would be £1,000 (that is, 20 × £(150 − 100)) and the balance sheet at the end of the period would be as follows:

	£
Cash	3,000
Opening capital	2,000
Plus Profit for the period	1,000
	3,000

When prices are constant, it would be possible for Habbad Enterprises to pay a dividend equal to the whole of the reported profit for the period and still retain its capital base intact. That is, dividend distribution would not have an adverse effect on the purchasing power of the owners' investment in the business, or the ability of the business to maintain its scale of operations; there would still be the start-of-period £2,000.

Let us assume, however, that the general rate of inflation during the period was 10 per cent and the cost of the videos increased in line with this rate. To ensure that the owners' investment in the business is kept intact and the business is able to continue its current scale of operations, it would not now be possible to distribute all of the profits as conventionally measured.

Activity 9.5

What amount of profit do you think could be distributed to the owners of Habbad Enterprises without any adverse effect on the capital base?

As the general rate of inflation was 10 per cent during the period, and the cost of videos increased in line with this rate, the capital base must be increased by this amount to preserve the owners' investment and to ensure that the existing scale of operations can be maintained. The capital at the end of the period should, therefore, be:

$$£2,000 + (10\% × £2,000) = £2,200$$

Activity 9.5 continued

As the unadjusted capital at the end of the period is £3,000, the amount that can be distributed will be:

$$£3,000 - £2,200 = £800$$

Calculating profit by matching revenue with the cost of purchases expressed in current terms will also provide this measure of the amount that can be safely distributed to owners. Hence:

	£
Sales revenue (20 @ £150)	3,000
Less Cost of videos in current terms (20 @ £110)	2,200
Profit	800

During a period of inflation, the effect of reporting assets at their original cost on the balance sheet is also a problem as the cost or value of the asset expressed in current terms may be quite different. The higher the rate of inflation the greater this difference is likely to be. There is also the additional problem that the assets will normally be acquired at different dates. Thus, for example, the cost of plant purchased by a business on different dates, and appearing on the balance sheet, may be:

Plant at cost

	£
Acquired 31 March 1997	18,000
Acquired 30 June 2001	34,000
Acquired 20 September 2005	42,000
	94,000

During a period of inflation, the purchasing power of the pound will be quite different at each acquisition date. The sum total of this group of assets (£94,000) will, therefore, be meaningless. In effect, the pounds spent at the various dates represent different currencies, each with a different purchasing power.

Activity 9.6

Can you think what will be the effect of inflation on the calculation of profitability ratios such as net profit margin and ROCE?

As the net profit is overstated during a period of inflation, profitability ratios will tend to be higher. The problem will be more acute where profit is related to a measure of financial position such as the ROCE ratio. This is because the financial position of the business tends to be understated.

The problem of monetary items

Some items on the balance sheet have a fixed number of pounds assigned to them that cannot be changed as a result of inflation. These are known as **monetary items**.

Activity 9.7

Can you think of any items that would be categorised as monetary items?

Examples of monetary items on the asset side of the balance sheet would be trade debtors and cash. Examples on the liabilities side would be loans, overdrafts, trade creditors and tax owing.

The effect of holding monetary assets during a period of inflation will be to make a loss, whereas the effect of holding monetary liabilities will be to make a gain.

Activity 9.8

Explain the effects of holding £1,000 cash during a year when inflation was at the rate of 20 per cent.

The purchasing power of the cash held will be 20% lower at the end of the year than at the beginning.

Beginning of period	*End of period*
Cash	Cash
£1,000	£1,000

Purchasing power compared with beginning of period

$\longrightarrow \longrightarrow$ £800 (that is, £1,000 less 20%)

This loss of purchasing power will have a real effect on the business's ability to preserve the capital invested by the owners and on its ability to maintain its scale of operations.

The reverse situation will apply where a monetary liability is held during a period of inflation. In real terms, the liability will be reduced and so the owners will make a gain at the expense of the lenders. These monetary gains and losses may be significant for a business but they are not revealed in the conventional financial statements.

Reporting the effect of inflation

The problems caused by inflation over the years have led to calls for additional financial statements that will help users understand the impact of inflation on the financial performance and position of the business. These additional financial statements take the form of a profit and loss account and balance sheet but differ from the conventional statements in that they incorporate the effect of price-level changes.

There are two basic approaches to the problem of dealing with inflation. The first of these is concerned with ensuring that the *general purchasing power of owners* is maintained during a period of inflation. To do this, a general price index, such as the Retail Price Index, will be used to measure changes in the purchasing power of the pound. To maintain the owners' general purchasing power, the profit available for distribution must take account of price-level changes. As a result, profit will be deduced by matching the revenue for the period with the original cost of the goods expressed in terms of *current purchasing power*.

→   To illustrate how **current purchasing power (CPP) accounting** operates, let us look at Example 9.4.

Example 9.4

Konides and Co. purchased stock when the Retail Price Index was 100 and sold the stock ten months later when the index stood at 105. The goods were purchased for £2,000 and sold for £2,500.

To maintain the general purchasing power of the owners of the business, the profit for the period will be calculated as follows:

	£
Sales revenue	2,500
Less Cost of sales (2,000 × 105/100)	2,100
Profit	400

The alternative approach to maintaining capital intact is concerned with ensuring that the *business is able to maintain its scale of operations*. To do this, the specific price changes that affect the business must be taken into account when preparing the financial statements. Here, the profit available for distribution will be deduced by matching the revenue with the specific changes that arise in the cost of the goods acquired by the business.

In many cases, the price changes that affect a business may not correspond to the general price changes occurring within the economy (although, for the sake of convenience, we assumed in earlier examples that the specific price of goods changed in line with the general rate of inflation). Referring to Example 9.4, let us assume that, although the general rate of inflation was 5 per cent during the period, the rise in the cost of the particular stocks traded was 10 per cent. Using the specific purchasing power approach to accounting for inflation, the profit for the period would be:

	£
Sales revenue	2,500
Less Cost of sales (2,000 × 110/100)	2,200
Profit	300

Each approach is concerned with maintaining capital intact. However, the two approaches have different views concerning what form of capital should be kept intact. The general purchasing power approach is concerned with ensuring the *owners'* purchasing power over general goods and services within the economy is maintained, whereas the specific purchasing power approach is concerned with ensuring that the *business* is able to maintain its purchasing power over the specific goods and services that it needs to continue trading at the same level. Both views have their advantages and disadvantages and there has been a great deal of debate concerning which view should prevail. At present, the specific purchasing power approach probably has the greater support. However, the fairly low rates of inflation in recent years have meant that many businesses no longer see this form of reporting as being as important as in earlier periods when inflation rates were much higher. In practice, few businesses produce supplementary reports that account for the effects of inflation. Those that do normally use a particular form of specific purchasing power accounting referred to as **current cost accounting (CCA)**. This method is based largely (but not exclusively) on the use of replacement cost (that is, the cost of replacing an item) figures rather than historic cost figures.

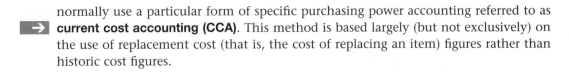

Environmental reporting

In recent times there has been an increasing awareness of how fragile our natural environment is in the face of continuing economic development. There has been a growing concern that the policies pursued by businesses will inflict major environmental damage on our planet from which it may never recover. Environmental issues such as acid rain, destruction of the rainforests, the use of non-renewable resources, the treatment of hazardous waste, damage to the ozone layer and pollution of rivers have received much media coverage. This, in turn, has led to demands for businesses to be more accountable for their activities.

Conventional accounting fails to recognise the impact of the business on its environment. Accounting is based on transactions between parties who have property rights. The exchange of these rights (for example, the purchase of an asset by a business for cash) will give rise to transactions that are quantifiable in monetary terms and which the accounting system can record. However, the impact of the business on aspects of the environment over which there are no property rights is not recorded by the accounting system, so does not appear in the financial statements. The principle that 'the polluter must pay' is, however, gaining greater recognition and this means that the financial statements will, at least, record the cost of negative environmental impacts.

Some businesses have responded to the increase in environmental awareness, and the criticisms levelled at the business community, by producing an **environmental report**. Generally speaking, large businesses have responded more readily to this new challenge than small and medium-sized ones. There is still much work to be done in encouraging small and medium-sized businesses to produce environmental reports. Apart from overcoming the scepticism that such businesses may have towards such reports, there is often the added problem that they do not have the internal environmental management systems to produce them.

Where environmental reports are being produced, it can be either as part of the annual financial report or as a separate report to users. The motive for producing environmental reports will vary. For some businesses, it may be to reassure the public or regulatory authorities that the business is a good 'corporate citizen', whereas for others it may be to change the views of users and regulators about the activities of the business so as to avoid any harmful reactions. Industrial sectors such as oil, chemicals and privatised utilities are well represented among those businesses producing such reports.

Styles of environmental reporting

Environmental reports are produced voluntarily and there is no consensus regarding 'best practice' in this area. As a result, the reports vary considerably in style, content and depth. It has been suggested, however, that they can be classified according to one of three levels (see reference 2 at the end of the chapter). These are:

- *Level 1.* A statement simply setting out the environmental policies of the business and an explanation of its environmental management systems and responsibilities.
- *Level 2.* A qualitative report that builds on the Level 1 statement and sets out the performance of the business on environmental matters in qualitative terms. For example, reports may indicate that the business is meeting, or exceeding, national, or international, standards on particular environmental matters.
- *Level 3.* A quantitative report providing a detailed breakdown of the performance of the business on environmental matters. Performance is set against clear quantitative targets. The report may also quantify the financial impact of managing the environment.

Most businesses that prepare environmental reports confine themselves to either Level 1 or Level 2 reporting, although an increasing number of businesses have introduced reporting using quantitative data.

Content of environmental reports

A key issue facing businesses is what should be included in an environmental report. One suggestion (see reference 3 at the end of the chapter) is that the following should be included by each business in its environmental report:

- The environmental policy of the business.
- The identity of the director with overall responsibility for environmental issues.
- The environmental objectives of the business expressed in such a way that performance can be measured against them. (In so far as possible, environmental targets and performance should be expressed in quantifiable technical or financial terms.).
- Information on actions taken in pursuit of environmental objectives (including details of expenditure incurred).
- The key impact of the business on the environment and, where practical, related measures of environmental performance.
- The extent of compliance with any regulations and/or industry guidelines.
- Significant environmental risks.
- Key features of external audit reports on the environmental activities of the business.

However, there is no real agreement on this issue and other forms of reporting have been proposed.

Developing performance indicators

One of the key points mentioned above concerns the measurement of environmental performance. Many believe that each business must determine its own environmental performance indicators (EPIs). The diversity of business operations means that a 'one size fits all' approach to measurement is impractical. To develop appropriate EPIs, the following five-step approach has been suggested (see reference 4 at the end of the chapter):

- *Identify environmental aspects.* This involves examining the operations of the business and identifying the likely effects of these on the environment.
- *Establish the key performance indicators.* These should reflect the key dimensions of environmental impact. There should not be too many and they should be a mixture of lagging and leading indicators. A lagging indicator reflects past outcomes, such as actual leakages from nuclear sites. A leading indicator monitors activities before an impact, such as the number of maintenance checks undertaken on a particular device designed to eliminate leakages. Leading indicators can help predict the likelihood of particular outcomes. For example, a high frequency of maintenance checks may help to predict a low level of leakages.
- *Establish targets.* These should be challenging but achievable.
- *Develop a stewardship/reporting process.* Reporting the outcomes is vitally important to ensuring that EPIs are taken seriously.
- *Review and adjust.* Changes in the nature of business operations, and the fact that environmental performance measurement is a developing area, mean that regular reviews should be carried out and targets adjusted if necessary.

This five-step process is summarised in Figure 9.3. This approach, however, raises issues of comparability. It is very difficult for users of environmental reports to make comparisons between businesses when each business has developed its own unique set of indicators. There is always a tension between the need for comparability and the need for flexibility when measuring performance. This tension also occurs in conventional financial reporting, but it is a particular problem in emerging areas such as environmental reporting. To help to strike a better balance between comparability and flexibility, there has been increasing guidance from environmental bodies concerning EPIs and, over time, this should help to narrow the range of measures employed. We shall consider this issue in more detail later in the chapter.

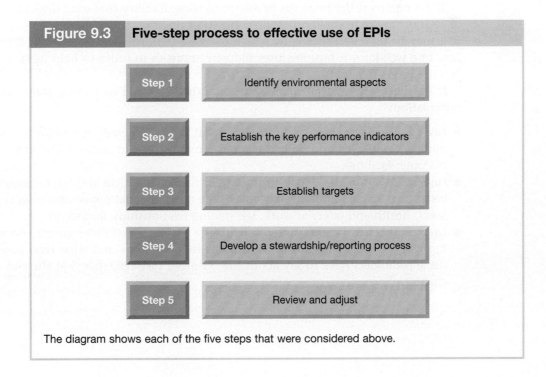

Figure 9.3   Five-step process to effective use of EPIs

Step 1	Identify environmental aspects
Step 2	Establish the key performance indicators
Step 3	Establish targets
Step 4	Develop a stewardship/reporting process
Step 5	Review and adjust

The diagram shows each of the five steps that were considered above.

Social reporting

A business has a number of groups, or stakeholders, that have an interest in, and will be affected by, its operations. The rights of shareholders and lenders concerning the business are well established in law. However, other stakeholders such as suppliers, customers, employees and the communities in which the business operates are increasingly recognised as having rights. Thus, modern businesses have a broad constituency to whom they are accountable and to whom they should report concerning the way in which they conduct their operations.

This wider responsibility has led a number of businesses to report the social aspects of their operations. Although such reports are still in their infancy, their importance is growing and they are being viewed increasingly as an integral part of the annual reporting cycle – at least for larger businesses.

Styles of social reports

Social reports, like environmental reports, are voluntarily produced. They also vary considerably in style, content and depth. Indeed, there is probably greater variation in the styles of social reports than in the styles of environmental reports produced. The social dimensions of business operations are not well defined and so it is inevitable that they are interpreted by different businesses in different ways. It seems that any form of interaction that a business has with society could be included within a social report. However, as our views on social performance crystallise, a growing consensus should emerge about what should be reported and how. In practice, areas such as equal opportunities, employee relations, human rights and community development feature largely in such reports.

Social reports suffer from the problems of comparability that were discussed earlier in relation to environmental reports. However, in some areas there are benchmarks that may be used as a means by which to assess performance. **Real World 9.1** shows how one well-known business uses industry statistics in order to help users to judge performance.

It has been argued that a social report can be viewed as having three layers of information:

● *Layer 1.* This is descriptive information that provides details of employees (such as numbers employed and skills categories), involvement in community projects, and customer facilities.
● *Layer 2.* This provides details of the extent to which ethical and legal standards are being met. These standards may cover such areas as equal opportunities in employment, health and safety at work, fair trading relationships, and so on.
● *Layer 3.* This involves consultation with the various stakeholder groups concerning the way in which the business conducts its operations and then reporting what the stakeholders have to say about the business. (See reference 5 at the end of the chapter.)

REAL WORLD 9.1

Is sugar safe?

Tate and Lyle plc is a leading producer of sweeteners and starches. Its 2003 annual report provided information concerning the recordable injury rate within its key business units as part of its reporting of its social responsibilities. The business also provided safety statistics published by the US Bureau of Labor Safety Statistics as a benchmark with which to compare its performance. The figures provided were set out in the form of a diagram as shown in Figure 9.4.

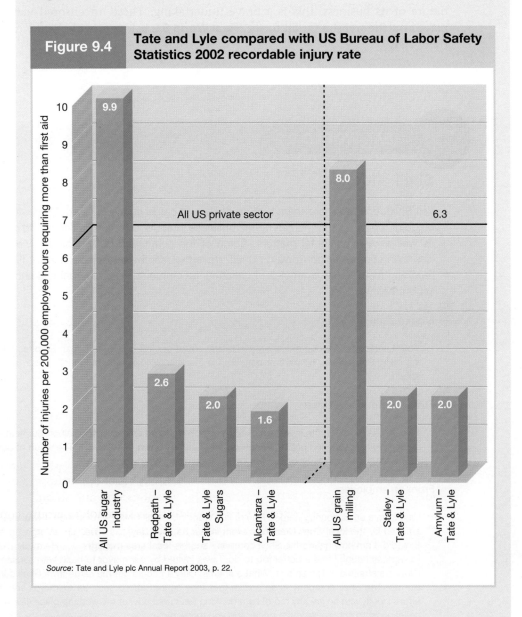

Figure 9.4   Tate and Lyle compared with US Bureau of Labor Safety Statistics 2002 recordable injury rate

Source: Tate and Lyle plc Annual Report 2003, p. 22.

Tate and Lyle also announced that the recordable injury rate had decreased by 29% compared to the previous year.

Dialogue with stakeholders

A recurring theme in the literature is the need for a business to have a dialogue with its stakeholders over social and environmental issues. It is a useful means of demonstrating a concern for their views and can provide valuable information with which to improve performance. One particularly interesting method of doing this has been adopted by Royal Dutch Shell plc (Shell), the oil business. Shell has a web forum 'Tell Shell' (www.shell.com/tellshell). The business is committed to having an open and transparent debate with its stakeholders, who can use the website to express their views on a variety of matters. Given the environmentally sensitive nature of its business, this is a brave undertaking. These uncensored views are displayed on the website for all to see. **Real World 9.2** below provides some examples of these views.

REAL WORLD 9.2

Shell shocked

Tell Shell received more than 1,500 e-mails and cards during 2002, dealing with a wide range of topics such as human rights, business integrity, directors' salaries and dividends as well as environmental matters. Some of the comments posted on the website are less than complimentary towards Shell. Nevertheless, the business does not flinch from reporting them. A few examples of unflattering comments from different stakeholders are set out below:

From a shareholder:

> Your Lubricants IT group in Houston is totally out of control in terms of cost. Empires are growing daily. Once again, no care or concern for the shareholder and how much of our money you spend.

From a (former) customer:

> I would like to inform the investors of Shell petroleum that I am boycotting all products at service stations in New Zealand until the price of petrol comes down to below $1. The value of our dollar to the American dollar is high, so our petrol should be under a dollar.

From an employee:

> I am from a small country named Romania. I work in a small Shell petrol station. I was surprisedly amazed by the local Shell Branch to work in our national day. . . . It was an unforgiving mistake they did. I am now hating the Shell company and his local area manager. . . . He made me come to work, although I had a better job to do. I was invited by our mayor to bean with sausages and I was constrained to refuse him. What a shame! Only if I could get the same from Shell company. But no! The Shell company is so selfish that they cannot afford such an extraordinary financial effort! I work with no joy any more! I am drinking beer right now at my working place (like my other colleagues) to compensate the deception you made me.

Source: Tell Shell (www.shell.com/tellshell).

Criticisms of social and environmental reporting

Some commentators are unimpressed by the quality of social and environmental reporting to date. They point out that there is a lack of an agreed framework for each type of reporting, which leads to partial and unsystematic reports. As these reports are a voluntary exercise, there is little incentive for a business to disclose the adverse effects of its policies on society or the environment. There may well be incentives to emphasise any positive effects, however. It has also been argued that there is a general lack of quantitative measures and targets. There is also the failure of many businesses to have their social and environmental management efforts audited by external bodies. These factors make it difficult to assess how well businesses discharge their responsibilities. This has led some commentators to dismiss these reports as little more than a public relations exercise.

However, these reports are still at an early stage of development and there is evidence to suggest that their quality is improving each year. Systems and procedures are being developed that address many of the concerns that have been raised. We shall review these in the next section. The pressure on businesses to produce social and environmental reports is likely to increase rather than decrease. It may well be that regulations will be imposed in the future. If this occurs, even faster progress will be made.

Auditing social and environmental reports

The credibility of published reports dealing with social and environmental issues is an important issue. The reports can provide an opportunity for unscrupulous directors to manipulate information in an attempt to portray a picture that they would like users of the reports to see rather than one which faithfully reflects reality. One way of giving users greater confidence in the integrity of the reports is through an independent audit. A number of businesses now have their reports audited, but the general quality of the data and unresolved measurement issues make the process much more difficult than for conventional financial statements. Hence, auditors are usually cautious in providing assurances to users. **Real World 9.3** describes the audit process for the Shell Report.

REAL WORLD 9.3

Auditing the Shell Report

The Shell Report 2002 runs to almost 50 pages and contains a wealth of information concerning the economic, social and environmental performance of the business. This report also contains an assurance report from independent auditors. The auditors were a multi-disciplinary team consisting of financial auditors as well as environmental and social specialists. They examined selected data, graphs and statements in the Shell Report and provided an opinion on them.

The wide range of information checked made it impossible to examine the reliability and accuracy of all elements with the same degree of completeness. Hence, the information checked was divided into three groups:

Real World 9.3 continued

- Information that was checked by testing the systems used to generate, analyse and report the data. In this case, the auditors gave an opinion that the information properly reflected performance.
- Information that was checked by reviewing systems and documentation and confirming the accurate use of information from external sources. In this case, the auditors gave the opinion that underlying evidence supported the information.
- Information that was checked by testing the accuracy of the data received from countries in which Shell operates. In this case, the auditors did not give an assurance on the reliability of the data but gave the opinion that the information was properly reported.

Source: Royal Dutch Shell plc, The Shell Report 2002, pp. 44 and 45.

There are mixed views as to whether the audit of social and environmental reports is a good thing. These types of reporting are at an early stage of development and there is a danger that experimentation with new measures and the inclusion of new forms of information will be hindered by the need to satisfy the auditors. There is also a danger that, in the absence of agreed rules about the content of such reports or the measures to be used, the auditors' responsibilities will be set out by the business. As a result, the credibility of the audit process will be undermined.

Social and environmental reporting frameworks

We have already mentioned the wide variations that exist in the content and depth of social and environmental reports. Some businesses refer to particular social and environmental issues almost as an aside in their annual financial reports. Other businesses have a separate section, or sections, of the annual report devoted exclusively to these issues. In some cases, such as Severn Trent plc (the water supply and waste business) and Royal Dutch Shell plc, there are quite separate and lengthy reports relating to social and environmental issues.

In recent years, various bodies have sought to establish standards and guidelines for reporting. An important contribution has been AA1000, a standard developed by the Institute of Social and Ethical Accountability to provide a single accounting, auditing and reporting framework for social and ethical issues. The standard is based on the ideas of responsibility for continuous improvement of performance, transparency towards stakeholders and compliance with agreed standards. Another important contribution has been the Global Reporting Initiative Guidelines, an international development. Businesses that draw up their reports in accordance with the guidelines must adhere to a number of principles and report on a number of key indicators. We shall consider these guidelines in more detail a little later in the chapter.

Business in the Community (BiTC) has developed a framework to help businesses to assess and report their impact in five areas spanning both social and environmental topics. This is a UK-based development. These areas are the marketplace, the environment, the workplace, the community and human rights. The framework offers progression over three levels. Level 1 is for businesses just beginning to measure progress and concerned with providing fairly basic data. Level 2 is for businesses that wish to go further and to include some performance and impact measures. Level 3 is for businesses going further still and providing quantitative as well as qualitative information. The BiTC framework is shown opposite.

	Marketplace	Environment	Workplace	Community	Human rights
Level 1	• Customer complaints about products and services • Advertising complaints upheld • Complaints about late payment of bills • Upheld cases of anti-competitive behaviour	• Overall energy consumption • Water usage • Quantity of waste produced (by weight) • Upheld cases of prosecution for environmental offences	• Workforce profile – gender, race, disability and age • Staff absenteeism • Number of legal non-compliances on health and safety and equal opportunities legislation • Number of staff grievances • Upheld cases of corrupt or unprofessional behaviour • Number of recordable incidents (fatal and non-fatal) including subcontractors	• Cash value of business support as % of pre-tax profit • Estimated combined value of staff business time, gifts in kind and management costs	• Any upheld non-compliances with domestic human rights legislation • Existence of confidential grievance procedures for workers • Wage rates
Level 2	• Customer satisfaction levels • Customer retention • Provision for customers with special needs • Average time to pay bills of suppliers	• CO$_2$/greenhouse gas emissions • Other emissions (such as Ozone, Radiation, and so on) • Use of recycled material	• Staff turnover • Value of training and development provided to staff • Pay and conditions compared with local equivalent averages • Workforce profile compared with the community profile for travel to work area – gender, race, disability and age	• Individual value of staff time, gifts in kind and management costs • Project progress and achievement measures • Leverage of other resources	• Progress measures against adherence to stated business principles on human rights as stated by UK law and international human rights standards • Proportion of suppliers and partners screened for human rights compliance
Level 3	• Customer loyalty measures • Recognising and catering for diversity in advertising and product labelling • Social impact, cost of benefits, of business's core products and services	• Percentage of waste recycled • Net CO$_2$ contribution made • Environmental impact over the supply chain • Environmental impact, benefits or costs, of business's core products and services	• Impact evaluations of the effect of downsizing, restructuring, and so on • Perception measures of the business by its employees	• Impact evaluations carried out on community programmes • Perception measures of the business as a good neighbour	• Proportion of suppliers and partners meeting the business's expected standards on human rights • Proportion of the business's managers meeting the business's standards on human rights within their area of operation • Perception of the business's performance on human rights by employees, the local community and other stakeholders

Source: Adapted from *Winning with Integrity*, BITC, 2002.

BiTC has also developed a Corporate Responsibility Index, which aims to compare the performance of different businesses. The index comprises both core and industry-specific indicators. Businesses are ranked according to these measures. However, such an index is fraught with problems of comparison, as businesses appearing towards the bottom of the rankings will no doubt agree!

Towards an integrated approach

There has been a growing recognition that environmental and social issues are inextricably linked. For example, a debate on issues relating to our natural environment will usually raise issues concerning the welfare of communities, the distribution of wealth, social justice and so on. This implies that a more complete approach to reporting would deal with both the environmental and social dimensions of business operations as well as report the effectiveness of the business in generating economic wealth.

Sustainable development

A framework that can be used to bring together all three dimensions in a systematic way is based on the concept of **sustainable development**. This concept has been defined as 'meeting the needs of the present without compromising the ability of future generations to meet their own needs' (see reference 6 at the end of the chapter).

Supporters of sustainable development believe that economic viability must go hand in hand with a concern for the environment and for social equity. To enable us to survive and prosper over the longer term, businesses must have proper regard for the effect on the natural and human resources that they use. This means that businesses should manage environmental and human resources with the same kind of care as they manage their financial resources. This idea appears to be gaining ground and a number of businesses are now committed to what has been termed 'sustainable value creation'.

Sustainable development and triple bottom line reporting

Some believe that the best way to assess the effectiveness with which a business implements environmental, social and economic policies is through **triple bottom line reporting**. This means that, in addition to reporting economic value added, a business should also report environmental value added and social value added.

Environmental value added would measure the renewable natural resources consumed (such as wood and fish stocks), as well as the non-renewable resources consumed (such as fossil fuels).

Social value added would attempt to measure the 'intellectual resources' (that is knowledge and skills) that the business has developed or lost. It would also take account of the extent to which the business has developed or damaged the level of respect and trust within the communities in which it operates. The economic value added (such as profit) could then be viewed in the context of the environmental and social value added by the business. If all three forms could be quantified in monetary terms, it would be possible to deduce the *total net value added* by a business, which would be the sum of the three dimensions.

It is an extremely ambitious idea that raises huge problems and issues.

Activity 9.9

Can you think of some of the key issues that will have to be addressed in order to produce a triple bottom line for a business?

The issues that we thought of are:

- How are environmental and social dimensions to be defined? In other words, what items should be included and what should be excluded?
- How can environmental value added and social value added be measured in monetary terms?
- How can there be an independent audit of these measures so as to lend credibility to the reporting process?
- How can benchmarks be developed against which we can assess progress?

This is not an exhaustive list, you may have thought of others.

Despite the problems, there has already been some progress towards developing this type of reporting framework. A few progressive businesses, such as BAA plc (the airport operator) and Royal Dutch Shell plc, have already begun to develop sustainable development frameworks.

Key areas for sustainability reporting

Although the development of triple bottom line reporting is a mammoth task, a sensible starting point is to identify a small number of key areas for consideration. Having done this, we can then try to develop appropriate indicators of performance and targets against which performance can be assessed. The Global Reporting Initiative Sustainability Reporting Guidelines has suggested the following key areas for sustainability reporting:

Direct economic impacts	Environmental	Labour practices and decent work conditions	Human rights	Society	Product responsibility
• Customers • Suppliers • Employees • Providers of capital • Public sector	• Materials • Energy • Water • Biodiversity • Emissions, effluents and waste • Suppliers • Products and services • Compliance • Transport • Overall	• Employment • Labour/ management relations • Health and safety • Training and education • Diversity and opportunity	• Strategy and management • Non-discrimination • Freedom of association and collective bargaining • Child labour • Forced and compulsory labour • Disciplinary practices • Security practices • Indigenous rights	• Community • Bribery and corruption • Political contributions • Competition and pricing	• Customer health and safety • Products and services • Advertising • Respect for privacy

Source: Global Reporting Initiative Sustainability Reporting Guidelines (www.globalreporting.org).

One of the topics mentioned under the general heading 'Society' relates to the reporting of bribery and corruption. **Real World 9.4** shows how Royal Dutch Shell plc reports this particular problem.

REAL WORLD 9.4

Bribery and corruption

The Shell Report 2002 deals with bribery and corruption in a quantitative manner. It shows figures for a five-year period as follows:

	1998	1999	2000	2001	2002
Reported cases of bribery					
Number of bribes ($value)					
Bribes offered and/or paid by Shell company employees to third parties	1 ($300)	1 ($300)	0	0	0
Bribes paid by intermediaries or contractor employees to third parties	N/C	0	1 ($4,562)	0	0
Bribes accepted by Shell company employees	4 ($75,000)	3 ($153,000)	4 ($89,000)	4 ($25,668)	4 (unknown)
Bribes accepted by intermediaries, contractor employees or others	N/C	1 (unknown)	0	1 ($18,072)	0

Source: Royal Dutch Shell plc, The Shell Report 2002, p. 48.

Reporting the key areas

At this point, it is probably worth looking at an example of a business that provides information to users relating to all three aspects of performance: economic, social and environmental. **Real World 9.5** reproduces an extract from the Severn Trent plc 2003 sustainable development report. The extract shows the quantitative measures used in all three areas.

REAL WORLD 9.5

Severn Trent plc

Severn Trent plc is a large environmental services business. It provides water, waste and utility services and has operations in the UK, US and Europe. It has annual revenue of £1.8bn and employs more than 14,000 people (2003). The following extract from its 2003 sustainable development report focuses on the quantitative measures used by the business to assess its performance.

Key performance data

			2002/03	2001/02	2000/01
Marketplace and economic					
Stakeholders					
Customers	Sales	£m	1,852.0	1,794.3	1,681.6
Suppliers	Cost of goods and services	£m	(1,016.3)	(970.1)	(889.4)
	Exceptional items	£m	(40.8)	(17.0)	(15.5)
Employees	Total payroll	£m	(452.0)	(432.5)	(409.8)
Providers of capital	Interest	£m	(159.4)	(159.0)	(161.1)
	Dividends	£m	(157.6)	(157.6)	(154.5)
Government	Taxation	£m	(84.3)	(58.4)	(64.8)
Retained loss		£m	(58.4)	(0.3)	(13.5)
Environment					
Climate change (direct and indirect emissions) (Note 1)					
Total emissions		tCO_2e	1,969,355	2,389,603	1,667,668
Renewable energy exports		tCO_2e	(204,569)	(172,722)	(144,568)
Net total CO_2 equivalent emissions		tCO_2e	1,764,786	2,216,881	1,523,100
Energy use					
Total energy use		GJ	6,851,896	6,561,792	5,624,833
Purchased electricity used		MWh	1,180,267	1,141,834	941,824
Total renewable electricity generated		MWh	543,221	462,910	394,058
Transport					
Total business distance travelled		million kms	188.46	188.73	164.36
Waste handled					
Total solid waste handled		tonnes	7,969,238	8,522,450	8,695,542
Solid waste handled for recycling		tonnes	822,500	730,516	560,542
Liquid waste handled for recycling		tonnes	1,022,431,326	1,022,202,523	896,250,113
Waste generated					
Total waste generated		tonnes	369,623	396,949	329,513
Total waste recycled		tonnes	205,876	196,572	161,332
Water consumption					
Water consumption		Megalitres/day	7.0	9.3	8.3
Biodiversity					
Coverage of operations by biodiversity action plans		% by turnover	77	50	50
Compliance					
Proportion of drinking water samples meeting standards (UK operations)		%	99.9	99.9	99.9
Proportion of sewage works meeting sanitary consents (UK operations)		%	99.9	99.6	99.6
Air Quality (direct and indirect emissions) (Note 2)					
Total NOx emissions		tonnes	2,219	2,143	1,753
Total SOx emissions		tonnes	2,080	1,993	1,822
Standards					
ISO 14001 Certification		Number	16	18	10
EMAS		Number	2	2	0
Environmental prosecutions					
Convictions for environmental offences		Number	4	1	2
Amount of fines including costs imposed		£	38,301	1,600	13,159

→

Real World 9.5 continued

Workplace and community		2002/03	2001/02	2000/01
Employees (Notes 3 and 4)				
Total number of employees	Average number of full time equivalents	14,647	14,372	14,057
Ethnic minorities	% of Total Workforce	9.0	–	–
Female employees	% of Total Workforce	26.5	–	–
Employee turnover	% of Total Workforce	11.0	11.0	–
Employee training	Number of days	69,084	67,371	61,008
Health and Safety				
Reportable incidents	Rate per 1,000 employees	27.17	24.37	22.12
Days lost	Number of days	12,608	11,179	14,559
Customers				
Households receiving water and waste services	Millions	7.24	7.17	7.08
Community investment				
Donations	£m	0.98	0.96	0.48
In kind	£m	2.36	2.01	2.27
Leveraged donations	£m	2.17	1.90	1.06

Notes

1   Measured in accordance with the UK Department for Environment, Food and Rural Affairs (DEFRA) guidelines for company reporting on greenhouse gas emissions. US emission factors derived from Emissions Factors, Global Warming Potentials, Unit Conversions, Emissions and Related Facts, compiled by ICF Consulting, November 1999.
2   Excludes businesses based in the US.
3   Certain employee information is only available for 2002/2003.
4   Employee turnover includes voluntary resignations only.

Source: Severn Trent plc Stewardship 2003, Sustainable Development Report, pp. 34–35.

SUMMARY

The main points of this chapter may be summarised as follows:

Value added statement (VAS)

● Aims to foster a team spirit among stakeholders.

● Value added = total outputs less total inputs.

● The VAS consists of two elements, the first derives a measure of value added and the second shows how the value added was applied.

● The VAS has a number of problems, including the team concept and the classification of items.

● Value added is not a substitute for profit within a capitalist economy.

● Nowadays, relatively few businesses incorporate the VAS in their annual reports but they are still used in reports to employees.

Inflation accounting and reporting

● Inflation tends to lead to an overstatement of profit and an understatement of asset values.

- Inflation can also obscure the fact that the capital base of a business is being eroded.
- Holding monetary items during a period of inflation can lead to gains and losses that are not recorded in the conventional financial statements.
- CPP accounting aims to maintain the general purchasing power of owners.
- CCA accounting aims to ensure the business can maintain its scale of operations.
- The debate concerning the merits of each method has subsided in recent years as rates of inflation have been low.

Environmental reporting

- Reflects an increasing concern for the environment.
- Environmental reports are produced voluntarily and vary in style, content and depth.
- They can be classified on a scale of 1 to 3. Level 1 reports are very basic and set out policies and systems in place. Level 3 reports provide a detailed review of performance along with detailed targets.

Social reporting

- Recognises the rights of various stakeholders in a business, such as employees, customers and the community.
- Social reports are also produced voluntarily and vary in style, content and depth.
- They can be classified on a scale of 1 to 3 according to the layers of information provided. Layer 1 provides descriptive information relating to the business and its community involvement; Layer 2 provides details of ethical and legal standards being met; and Layer 3 involves consultation with stakeholders.

Social and environmental reporting

- Has been criticised for not having agreed frameworks concerning what to measure and report and for not requiring that reports be audited.
- Auditing does occur in some cases but auditors are cautious about giving assurances because of the quality of the underlying data.
- Reporting frameworks have been developed in recent years by various bodies.

Towards an integrated approach

- There is growing recognition of the interrelationship between economic, social and environmental dimensions.
- The concept of sustainable development provides a framework for bringing these dimensions together.
- Sustainable development involves meeting current needs without compromising future needs.
- Triple bottom line reporting involves measuring economic valued added, social value added and environmental value added.
- This is an ambitious idea and initial steps towards this objective are being taken by some businesses.

→ **Key terms**

Value added statement (VAS) p. 306	**Current cost accounting (CCA)** p. 319
Inflation accounting p. 313	
Monetary items p. 316	**Environmental report** p. 319
Current purchasing power (CPP) accounting p. 318	**Social reports** p. 322
	Sustainable development p. 328
	Triple bottom line reporting p. 328

Further reading

If you would like to explore the topics covered in this chapter in more depth, we recommend the following books:

Financial Accounting and Reporting, *Elliot B and Elliot J.*, 8th edn, Prentice Hall Financial Times, 2004, chapters 4 and 5.

Inflation Accounting: An introduction to the debate, *Whittington G.*, Cambridge University Press, 1983.

The areas of environmental and social reporting are fast changing. You may find it useful to consult the following websites to discover the current state of progress:

www.sustainability.co.uk
www.accountability.co.uk
www.globalreporting.org

References

1 **The Corporate Report**, Accounting Standards Committee, ASC, 1975.

2 'Corporate environmental reporting in practice', *Bullough M. and Johnson D.*, in **Business Strategy and the Environment**, Vol. 4, 1995, pp. 36–39.

3 **Business, Accountancy and the Environment: A policy and research agenda**, *Macve R. and Carey A.*, ICAEW, 1992.

4 'Sustainable development – what is it?', *Elkington J.*, **www.sustainability.com**

5 'Environment and social reporting', *Gray R., Collison D. and Debbington J.*, in **Financial Reporting Today: Current Trends and Emerging Issues**, Accountancy Books, 1998.

6 **Our Common Future** (The Brutland Report), World Commission on Environment and Development, 1987, p. 8.

REVIEW QUESTIONS

Answers to these questions can be found on the students' side of the Companion Website at www.pearsoned.co.uk/atrillmclaney.

9.1 It has been suggested that if an accountant is asked by the board of directors, 'What is the value added for a period?', he or she could easily reply, 'What figure do you have in mind?' Explain why such a reply could be made.

9.2 Do environmental reporting and social reporting really fall within the scope of accounting? Are accountants really the best people to prepare and audit such reports?

9.3 Are there any arguments for using the historic cost approach to accounting during a period of inflation?

9.4 Should reporting of sustainable value creation be a voluntary exercise or should there be a legal obligation to produce such reports?

EXERCISES

Exercises 9.6 to 9.8 are more advanced than 9.1 to 9.5. Those with a coloured number have answers at the back of the book.

9.1 'The value added statement simply rearranges information contained within the conventional profit and loss account. As a result it is of little value to users.' Discuss the validity of this statement.

9.2 The following information has been taken from the accounts of Buttons Ltd, a retail business, for the year ended 30 September.

	£	£
Revenue		950,000
Cost of sales:		
Materials	(220,000)	
Wages and salaries	(160,000)	
Other expenses	(95,000)	
Interest	(45,000)	
Depreciation	(80,000)	
		(600,000)
		350,000
Taxation		(110,000)
		240,000
Dividends paid		(120,000)
Retained profit		120,000

Required:

(a) Prepare a value added statement for Buttons Ltd for the year ended 30 September.

(b) State and comment upon the reasons why a business may present a value added statement to its shareholders in addition to a profit and loss account.

9.3   Refer to your answer to Exercise 9.2 above. Calculate ratios that you believe could be used to interpret the VAS for Buttons Ltd. Explain the purpose of each ratio.

9.4   Rose Limited operates a small chain of retail shops. Abbreviated and unaudited financial statements are given below.

Profit and loss accounts for the years ended 31 March

	Last year		This year	
	£000	£000	£000	£000
Revenue		7,800		12,080
Cost of sales		(4,370)		(6,282)
Gross profit		3,430		5,798
Labour costs	(2,106)		(2,658)	
Depreciation	(450)		(625)	
Other operating costs	(92)		(1,003)	
		(2,648)		(4,286)
Net profit before interest		782		1,512
Interest payable		–		(66)
Net profit before tax		782		1,446
Tax payable		(158)		(259)
Net profit after tax		624		1,187
Dividend paid		(250)		(300)
Retained profit for year		374		887
Retained profit brought forward		498		872
Retained profit carried forward		872		1,759

Required:
Prepare a value added statement for the year ended 31 March this year.

9.5   Comment on each of the following statements:

(a) 'Inflation-adjusted accounts do not justify the additional cost of their preparation. The historic cost accounts are all that is required by users.'
(b) 'Publishing environmental reports may not be in the interests of a business.'

9.6   Most businesses that produce environmental reports and/or social reports believe that it is a good thing to have these reports independently audited. However, not everyone agrees with this.

What do you think are the arguments for and against having these reports independently audited?

9.7   It is often argued that it is difficult to make comparisons between the environmental reports of different businesses even when they are in the same industry.

Examine the most recent environmental report of Severn Trent plc (available on www.severn-trent.com) and compare it with another water utility business of your choice. What problems do you experience in making comparisons?

9.8   Milton Friedman, a famous economist, once wrote:

> There is one and only one social responsibility of business – to use its resources and engage in activities designed to increase profits.

Preparing social reports and pursuing social objectives can be costly and so it might be argued that a business should not do this as it is not consistent with the need to maximise profits over the long term.

Do you agree with this view? Discuss.

Supplementary information

This section provides information that is supplementary to the main text of the book.

Appendix A takes the format of a normal textual chapter and describes the way in which financial transactions are recorded in books of accounts. Generally, this is by means of the 'double entry' system, described in basic terms in the Appendix.

Appendix B gives definitions of the key terms highlighted throughout the main text and listed at the end of each chapter. The aim of the Appendix is to provide a single location to check on the meanings of the major accounting terms used in this book and in the world of finance.

Appendices C and D give answers to some of the questions set in the main text. Appendix C gives answers to the self-assessment questions, and Appendix D to those of the exercises that are marked as having their answers provided in the book.

Appendix A
Recording financial transactions

OBJECTIVES

When you have completed this Appendix, you should be able to:

- Explain the basic principles of double-entry bookkeeping.

- Write up a series of business transactions and balance the accounts.

- Extract a trial balance and explain its purpose.

- Prepare a set of financial statements from the underlying double-entry accounts.

INTRODUCTION

In Chapters 2 and 3 we saw how the financial transactions of a business may be recorded by making a series of entries on the balance sheet and/or profit and loss account (income statement). Each of these entries had its corresponding 'double', meaning that both sides of the transaction were recorded. However, adjusting the financial statements, by hand, for each transaction can be very messy and confusing. With a reasonably large number of transactions it is pretty certain to result in mistakes.

For businesses whose accounting systems are on a computer, this problem is overcome because suitable software can deal with a series of 'plus' and 'minus' entries very reliably. Where the accounting system is not computerised, however, it would be helpful to have some more practical way of keeping accounting records. Such a system not only exists but, before the advent of the computer, was the routine way of keeping accounts. It is this system that is explained in this Appendix. We should be clear that the system we are going to consider follows exactly the same rules as those that we have already met. Its distinguishing feature, for those keeping accounting records by hand, is its ability to provide a methodical approach that allows each transaction to be clearly identified and errors to be minimised.

The basics of double-entry bookkeeping

When we record accounting transactions by hand, we use a recording system known as **double-entry bookkeeping**. This system does not use plus and minus entries on the face of a balance sheet and profit and loss account to record a particular transaction, in the way described in Chapters 2 and 3. Instead, these are recorded in accounts. An **account** is simply a record of one or more transactions relating to a particular item, such as cash, fixtures and fittings, loans outstanding, sales revenues, rent payable and capital. A business may keep few or many accounts, depending on the size and complexity of its operations. Broadly, businesses tend to keep a separate account for each item that appears in either the profit and loss account or the balance sheet.

An example of an account, in this case the cash account, is as follows:

Cash

£		£

We can see that an account has three main features:

- A title indicating the item to which it relates.
- A left-hand side, known as the **debit** side.
- A right-hand side, known as the **credit** side.

One side of an account will record increases in the particular item and other will record decreases. This, of course, is slightly different from the approach we used when adjusting the financial statements. When adjusting the balance sheet, for example, we put a reduction in an asset or claim in the same column as any increases, but with a minus sign against it. However, when accounts are used, a reduction is shown on the opposite side of the account.

The side on which an increase or decrease is shown will depend on the nature of the item to which the account relates. For example, an account for an asset, such as cash, will show increases on the left-hand (debit) side of the account and decreases on the right-hand (credit) side. However, for claims (that is, capital and liabilities) it is the other way around. An increase in the account for capital or for a liability will be shown on the right-hand (credit) side and a decrease will be shown on the left-hand (debit) side.

To understand why this difference exists, we should recall from Chapter 2 that the balance sheet equation is:

$$\text{Assets} = \text{Capital} + \text{Liabilities}$$

We can see that assets appear on one side of the equation and capital and liabilities appear on the other. Recording transactions in accounts simply expresses this difference in the recording process. Increases in assets are shown on the left-hand side of an account and increases in capital and liabilities are shown on the right-hand side of the account. We should recall the point made in Chapter 2, that each transaction has two aspects. Thus, when we record a particular transaction, two separate accounts will be affected. Recording transactions in this way is known as double-entry bookkeeping.

It is worth going through a simple example to see how transactions affecting balance sheet items would be recorded under the double-entry bookkeeping system. Suppose a new business started on 1 January with the owner putting £5,000 into a newly opened business bank account, as initial capital. This entry would appear in the cash account as follows:

Cash

	£		£
1 January Capital	5,000		

The corresponding entry would be made in the capital account as follows:

Capital

	£			£
		1 January Cash		5,000

It is usual to show, in each account by way of note, where the other side of the entry will be found. Thus, someone looking at the capital account will know that the £5,000 arose from a receipt of cash. This provides potentially useful information, partly because it establishes a 'trail' that can be followed when checking for errors. Including the date of the transaction provides additional information to the reader of the accounts.

Now suppose that, on 2 January, £600 of the cash is used to buy some stock. This would affect the cash account as follows:

Cash

	£		£
1 January Capital	5,000	2 January Stock	600

This cash account, in effect, shows 'positive' cash of £5,000 and 'negative' cash of £600, a net amount of £4,400.

Activity A.1

As you know, we must somehow record the other side of the transaction involving the acquisition of the stock for £600. See if you can work out what to do in respect of the stock.

We must open an account for stock. Since stock is an asset, an increase in it will appear on the left-hand side of the account, as follows:

Stock

	£		£
2 January Cash	600		

What we have seen so far highlights the key rule of double-entry bookkeeping: each left-hand entry must have a right-hand entry of equal size. Using the jargon, we can say that *every debit must have a credit.*

It might be helpful at this point to make clear that the words 'debit' and 'credit' are no more than accounting jargon for left and right, respectively. It general English (that is, when not referring to accounting), people tend to use credit to imply something good and debit something undesirable. Debit and credit have no such implication in accounting. Each transaction requires both a debit and a credit entry. This is equally true whether the transaction is a 'good' one, such as being paid by a debtor, or a 'bad' one such as having to treat a debtor's balance as worthless because the debtor has gone bankrupt.

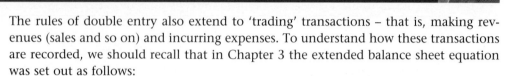

Recording trading transactions

The rules of double entry also extend to 'trading' transactions – that is, making revenues (sales and so on) and incurring expenses. To understand how these transactions are recorded, we should recall that in Chapter 3 the extended balance sheet equation was set out as follows:

$$\text{Assets = Capital + (Revenues – Expenses) + Liabilities}$$

This equation can be rearranged so that:

$$\text{Assets + Expenses = Capital + Revenues + Liabilities}$$

We can see that increases in expenses are shown on the same side as assets and this means that they will be dealt with in the same way for recording purposes. Thus, an increase in an expense, such as wages, will be shown on the left-hand (debit) side of the wages account and a decrease will be shown on the right-hand (credit) side. Increases in revenues are shown on the same side as capital and liabilities and so will be dealt with in the same way. Thus, an increase in revenues, such as sales, will be shown on the right-hand (credit) side and a decrease will be shown on the left-hand (debit) side.

To summarise, therefore, we can say that:

● Debits (left-hand entries) represent increases in assets and expenses and decreases in claims and revenues.
● Credits (right-hand entries) represent increases in claims and revenues and decreases in assets and expenses.

Let us continue with our example by assuming that, on 3 January, the business paid £900 to rent business premises for the three months to 31 March. To record this transaction, we should normally open a 'rent account' and make entries in this account and in the cash account as follows:

Rent

		£			£
3 January	Cash	900			

Cash

		£			£
1 January	Capital	5,000	2 January	Stock	600
			3 January	Rent	900

The fact that assets and expenses are dealt with in the same way should not be surprising since assets and expenses are closely linked. Assets actually transform into expenses as they are 'used up'. Rent, which, as here, is usually paid in advance, is an asset when it is first paid. It represents the value to the business of being entitled to occupy the premises for the forthcoming period (until 31 March in this case). As the three months progress, this asset becomes an expense; it is 'used up'. We need to remember that the debit entry in the rent account does not necessarily represent either an asset or an expense; it could be a mixture of the two. Strictly, by the end of the day on which it was paid (3 January), £30 would have represented an expense for the three days; the remaining £270 would have been an asset. As each day passes, an additional £10 (that is, £900/90 (there are 90 days in January, February and March all together)) will transform from an asset into an expense. As we have already seen, it is not necessary for us to make any adjustment to the rent account as the days pass.

Assume, now, that on 5 January the business sold stock costing £200 for £300 on credit. As usual, when we are able to identify the cost of the goods sold at the time of sale, we need to deal with the sale and the cost of the stock sold as two separate issues, each having its own set of debits and credits.

Firstly, let us deal with the sale. We now need to open accounts for both 'sales revenues' and 'trade debtors' – which do not, as yet, exist. The sale is an increase in revenue and so there is a credit entry in the sales revenues account. The sale also creates an asset of trade debtors and so there is debit entry in trade debtors:

Sales revenues

	£		£
		5 January Trade debtors	300

Trade debtors

	£		£
5 January Sales revenues	300		

Let us now deal with the stock sold. Since the stock sold has become the expense 'cost of sales', we need to reduce the figure on the stock account by making a credit entry and to make the corresponding debit in a 'cost of sales' account, opened for the purpose:

Stock

	£		£
2 January Cash	600	5 January Cost of sales	200

Cost of sales

	£		£
5 January Stock	200		

We shall now look at the other transactions for our hypothetical business for the remainder of January. These can be taken to be as follows:

8 January	Bought some stock on credit costing £800
11 January	Bought some office furniture for £600, paying by cheque
15 January	Sold stock costing £600 for £900, on credit
18 January	Received £800 from trade debtors
21 January	Paid trade creditors £500
24 January	Paid wages for the month £400
27 January	Bought stock on credit for £800
31 January	Borrowed £2,000 from the Commercial Finance Company

Naturally, we shall have to open several additional accounts to enable us to record all of these transactions in any meaningful way. By the end of January, the set of accounts would appear as follows:

Cash

		£			£
1 January	Capital	5,000	2 January	Stock	600
18 January	Trade debtors	800	3 January	Rent	900
31 January	Comm. Fin. Co.	2,000	11 January	Office furniture	600
			21 January	Trade creditors	500
			24 January	Wages	400

Capital

		£			£
			1 January	Cash	5,000

Stock

		£			£
2 January	Cash	600	5 January	Cost of sales	200
8 January	Trade creditors	800	15 January	Cost of sales	600
27 January	Trade creditors	800			

Rent

		£		£
3 January	Cash	900		

Sales revenues

	£			£
		5 January	Trade debtors	300
		15 January	Trade debtors	900

Trade debtors

		£			£
5 January	Sales revenues	300	18 January	Cash	800
15 January	Sales revenues	900			

Cost of sales

		£		£
5 January	Stock	200		
15 January	Stock	600		

Trade creditors

		£			£
21 January	Cash	500	8 January	Stock	800
			27 January	Stock	800

Office furniture

		£			£
11 January	Cash	600			

Wages

		£			£
24 January	Cash	400			

Loan creditor – Commercial Finance Company

		£			£
			31 January	Cash	2,000

All of the transactions from 8 January onwards are quite similar in nature to those up to that date, which we discussed in detail, and so we should be able to follow them using the date references as a guide.

Balancing accounts and the trial balance

Businesses keeping their accounts in the way shown would find it helpful to summarise their individual accounts periodically – perhaps weekly or monthly – for two reasons:

- To be able to see at a glance how much is in each account (for example, to see how much cash the business has left).
- To help to check the accuracy of the bookkeeping so far.

Let us look at the cash account again:

Cash

		£			£
1 January	Capital	5,000	2 January	Stock	600
18 January	Trade debtors	800	3 January	Rent	900
31 January	Comm. Fin. Co.	2,000	11 January	Office furniture	600
			21 January	Trade creditors	500
			24 January	Wages	400

Does this account tell us how much cash the business has at 31 January? The answer is partly yes and partly no.

We do not have a single figure showing the cash balance but we can fairly easily deduce this by adding up the debit (receipts) column and deducting the sum of the credit (payments) column. However, it would be better if a cash balance were provided for us.

 To summarise or **balance** this account, we add up the column with the largest amount (in this case, the debit side) and put this total on *both* sides of the account. We then put in, on the credit side, the figure that will make that side add up to the total that appears in the account. We cannot put in this balancing figure only once as the double-entry rule would be broken. Thus, to preserve the double entry, we also put it in on the other side of the same account below the totals, as follows:

Cash

		£			£
1 January	Capital	5,000	2 January	Stock	600
18 January	Trade debtors	800	3 January	Rent	900
31 January	Comm. Fin Co	2,000	11 January	Office furniture	600
			21 January	Trade creditors	500
			24 January	Wages	400
			31 January		
				Balance carried down	4,800
		7,800			7,800
1 February					
	Balance brought down	4,800			

Note that the balance carried down (usually abbreviated to 'c/d') at the end of one period becomes the balance brought down ('b/d') at the beginning of the next. Now we can see at a glance what the present cash position is, without having to do any mental arithmetic.

Activity A.2

Try balancing the stock account and then say what we know about the stock position at the end of January.

The stock account will be balanced as follows:

Stock

		£			£
2 January	Cash	600	5 January	Cost of sales	200
8 January	Trade creditors	800	15 January	Cost of sales	600
27 January	Trade creditors	800	31 January	Balance c/d	1,400
		2,200			2,200
1 February	Balance b/d	1,400			

We can see at a glance that the business held stock that had cost £1,400 at the end of January. We can also see quite easily how this situation arose.

We can balance all of the other accounts in similar fashion. However, there is no point in formally balancing accounts that have only one entry at the moment (for example, the capital account) because we cannot summarise one figure; it is already in as summarised a form as it can be. After balancing them, the remaining accounts will be as follows:

Capital

	£			£
		1 January	Cash	5,000

Rent

		£		£
3 January	Cash	900		

Sales revenues

		£			£
31 January	Balance c/d	1,200	5 January	Trade debtors	300
			15 January	Trade debtors	900
		1,200			1,200
			1 February	Balance b/d	1,200

Trade debtors

		£			£
5 January	Sales revenues	300	18 January	Cash	800
15 January	Sales revenues	900	31 January	Balance c/d	400
		1,200			1,200
1 February	Balance b/d	400			

Cost of sales

		£			£
5 January	Stock	200	31 January	Balance c/d	800
15 January	Stock	600			
		800			800
1 February	Balance b/d	800			

Trade creditors

		£			£
21 January	Cash	500	8 January	Stock	800
31 January	Balance c/d	1,100	27 January	Stock	800
		1,600			1,600
			1 February	Balance b/d	1,100

Office furniture

		£		£
11 January	Cash	600		

Wages

		£		£
24 January	Cash	400		

Loan creditor – Commercial Finance Company

	£			£
		31 January	Cash	2,000

Activity A.3

If we now separately total the debit balances and the credit balances for each of the above accounts, what should we expect to find?

....

We should expect to find that these two totals are equal. This must, in theory, be true since every debit entry was matched by an equally-sized credit entry.

Let us see if our expectation in Activity A.3 works in our example, by listing the debit and credit balances as follows:

	Debits £	Credits £
Cash	4,800	
Stock	1,400	
Capital		5,000
Rent	900	
Sales revenues		1,200
Trade debtors	400	
Cost of sales	800	
Trade creditors		1,100
Office furniture	600	
Wages	400	
Loan creditor		2,000
	9,300	9,300

→ This statement is known as a **trial balance**. The fact that it agrees gives us *some* indication that we have not made bookkeeping errors.

This situation, does not, however, give us total confidence that no error could have occurred. Consider the transaction that took place on 3 January (paid rent for the month of £900). In each of the following cases, all of which would be wrong, the trial balance would still have agreed:

● The transaction was completely omitted from the accounts; that is, no entries were made at all.
● The amount was misread as £9,000 but then (correctly) debited to the rent account and credited to cash.
● The correct amount was (incorrectly) debited to cash and credited to rent.

Nevertheless, a trial balance that agrees does give some confidence that accounts have been correctly written up.

Activity A.4

Why do you think the words 'debtor' and 'creditor' are used to describe those who owe money or are owed money by a business?

....

The answer simply is that debtors have a debit balance in the books of the business, whereas creditors have a credit balance.

Preparing the financial statements (final accounts)

If the trial balance agrees and we are confident that there are no errors in recording, the next stage is to prepare the profit and loss account (income statement) and balance sheet. Preparing the profit and loss account is simply a matter of going through the individual accounts, identifying those amounts that represent revenues and expenses of the period, and transferring them to a profit and loss account, which is itself part of the double-entry system.

We shall now do this for the example we have been using. The situation is complicated slightly for three reasons:

1 As we know, the £900 rent paid during January relates to the three months January, February and March.
2 The business's owner estimates that the electricity used during January is about £110. There is no bill yet from the electricity supply business because it normally only bills customers at the end of each three-month period.
3 The business's owner believes that the office furniture should be depreciated by 20 per cent each year (straight-line).

These three factors need to be taken into account. As we shall see, however, the end-of-period adjustments of these types are very easily handled in double-entry accounts. Let us deal with these three areas first.

The rent account will appear as follow, after we have completed the transfer to the profit and loss account:

Rent

		£			£
3 January	Cash	900	31 January	Profit and loss	300
				Balance c/d	600
		900			900
1 February	Balance b/d	600			

At 31 January, because two months' rent is still an asset, this is carried down as a debit balance. The remainder (representing January's rent) is credited to the rent account and debited to a newly opened profit and loss account. As we shall shortly see, the £600 debit balance remaining will appear in the 31 January balance sheet.

Now let us deal with the electricity. The electricity account will be as follows after the transfer to the profit and loss account:

Electricity

	£			£
		31 January	Profit and loss	110

Because there has been no cash payment or other transaction recorded so far for electricity, we do not already have an account for it. It is necessary to open one. We need to debit the profit and loss account with the £110 of electricity used during January and credit the electricity account with the same amount. At 31 January, this credit balance reflects the amount owed by this business to the electricity supplier. Once again, we shall shortly see that this balance will appear on the balance sheet as at the end of January.

Next we shall consider what is necessary regarding the office furniture. The depreciation for the month will be $20\% \times £600 \times \frac{1}{12}$, that is, £10. Normal accounting practice is to charge (debit) this to the profit and loss account, with the corresponding credit going to a 'provision for depreciation of office furniture' account. The latter entry will appear as follows:

Provision for depreciation of office furniture account

	£			£
		31 January	Profit and loss	10

This £10 balance will be reflected in the balance sheet at 31 January by being deducted from the office furniture itself, as we shall see.

The balances on the following accounts represent straightforward revenues or expenses for the month of January:

- Sales revenues
- Cost of sales
- Wages.

The balances on these accounts will simply be transferred to the profit and loss account.

To transfer balances to the profit and loss account, we simply debit or credit the account concerned, such that any balance amount is eliminated, and make the corresponding credit or debit in the profit and loss account. Take sales revenues, for example. This has a credit balance (because the balance represents a revenue). We must debit the sales revenues account with £1,200 and credit the profit and loss account with the same amount. So a credit balance on the sales revenues account becomes a credit entry in the profit and loss account. For the three accounts, then, we have the following:

Sales revenues

		£			£
31 January	Balance c/d	1,200	5 January	Trade debtors	300
			15 January	Trade debtors	900
		1,200			1,200
31 January	Profit and loss	1,200	1 February	Balance b/d	1,200

Cost of sales

		£			£
5 January	Stock	200	31 January	Balance c/d	800
15 January	Stock	600			
		800			800
1 February	Balance b/d	800	31 January	Profit and loss	800

Wages

		£			£
24 January	Cash	400	31 January	Profit and loss	400

The profit and loss account will now look as follows:

Profit and loss account

		£			£
31 January	Cost of sales	800	31 January	Sales revenues	1,200
31 January	Rent	300			
31 January	Wages	400			
31 January	Electricity	110			
31 January	Depreciation	10			

We must now transfer the balance on the profit and loss account (a debit balance of £420).

Activity A.5

What does the balance on the profit and loss account represent, and to where should it be transferred?

The balance is either the profit or the loss for the period. In this case it is a loss as the total expenses exceed the total revenues. This loss must be borne by the owner, and it must therefore be transferred to the capital account.

The two accounts would now appear as follows:

Profit and loss account

		£			£
31 January	Cost of sales	800	31 January	Sales revenues	1,200
31 January	Rent	300			
31 January	Wages	400			
31 January	Electricity	110			
31 January	Depreciation	10	31 January	Capital (net loss)	420
		1,620			1,620

Capital

		£			£
31 January	Profit and loss (net loss)	420	1 January	Cash	5,000
31 January	Balance c/d	4,580			
		5,000			5,000
			1 February	Balance b/d	4,580

The last thing done was to balance the capital account.

Now all of the balances remaining on accounts represent either assets or claims as at 31 January. These balances can now be used to produce a balance sheet, as follows:

Balance sheet as at 31 January

	£	£
Non-current assets		
Property, plant and equipment		
Office furniture: cost		600
depreciation		(10)
		590
Current assets		
Stock	1,400	
Prepaid expense	600	
Trade debtors	400	
Cash	4,800	
	7,200	
Current liabilities		
Accrued expense	(110)	
Trade creditors	(1,100)	
	(1,210)	5,990
		6,580
Less **Non-current liability**		
Loan creditor		2,000
		4,580
Capital		4,580

The profit and loss account could be written in a more stylish manner, for reporting to users, as follows:

Profit and loss account for the month ended 31 January

	£	£
Sales revenues		1,200
Cost of sales		800
Gross profit		400
Less Rent	300	
Wages	400	
Electricity	110	
Depreciation	10	
		820
Net loss for the month		(420)

The ledger and its division

The book in which the accounts are traditionally kept is known as the ledger, and 'accounts' are sometimes referred to as 'ledger accounts', even where they are computerised.

In a handwritten accounting system, the ledger is often divided into various sections. This tends to be for two main reasons:

1 Having all of the accounts in one book means that it is only possible for one person at a time to use the accounts, either to make entries or to extract useful information.

2 Dividing the ledger along logical grounds can allow specialisation, so that various individual members of the accounts staff can look after their own part of the system. This can lead to more efficient record-keeping. It can also lead to greater security, that is, less risk of error and fraud, by limiting an individual's access to only part of the entire set of accounts.

There are no clear, universal rules on the division of the ledger, but the following division is fairly common:

- *The cash book.* This tends to be all of the accounts relating to cash either loose or in the bank.
- *The sales (or trade debtors) ledger.* This contains the accounts of all of the business's individual trade debtors.
- *The purchases (or trade creditors) ledger.* This consists of the accounts of all of the business's individual trade creditors.
- *The nominal ledger.* These accounts tend to be those of expenses and revenues, for example sales revenues, wages, rent, and so on.
- *The general ledger.* This contains the remainder of the business's accounts, mainly those to do with fixed assets and long-term finance.

SUMMARY

The main points of this Appendix may be summarised as follows:

Double-entry bookkeeping = a system for keeping accounting records by hand, such that a relatively large volume of transactions can be handled effectively and accurately

- A separate account for each asset, claim, expense and liability that needs to be separately identified.
- Each account looks like a letter T.
- Left-hand (debit) side of the account records increases in assets and expenses and decreases in revenues and claims.
- Right-hand (credit) side records increases in revenues and claims and decreases in assets and expenses.
- There is an equal credit entry in one account for a debit entry in another.
- Double-entry bookkeeping can be used to record day-to-day transactions.
- Can also follow through to generate the profit and loss account.
- The balance sheet is a list of the net figure (the 'balance') on each of the accounts after appropriate transfers have been made to the profit and loss account.
- The accounts are traditionally kept in a 'ledger,' a term that persists even with computerised accounting.
- The ledger is traditionally broken down into several sections, each containing particular types of account.

→ **Key terms**

Double-entry bookkeeping p. 340   **Credit** p. 340
Account p. 340   **Balance** p. 345
Debit p. 340   **Trial balance** p. 348

Further reading

If you would like to explore the topics covered in this appendix in more depth, we recommend the following books:

Foundations of Business Accounting, *Dodge R.*, 2nd edn, Thomson Business Press, 1997, chapter 3.

An Introduction to Financial Accounting, *Thomas A.*, 4th edn, McGraw-Hill, 2001, chapters 3–6.

Practical Accounting, *Benedict A. and Elliott B.*, Financial Times Prentice Hall, 2001, chapters 2–5.

Financial Accounting, *Bebbington J., Gray R. and Laughlin R.*, 3rd edn, Thomson Learning, 2001, chapters 2–7.

EXERCISES

All three exercises have answers at the back of the book.

A.1 In respect of each of the following transactions, state in which two accounts must an entry be made and whether the entry is a debit or a credit. (For example, if the transaction were purchase of stock for cash, the answer would be debit the stock account and credit the cash account.)

(a) Purchased stock on credit.
(b) Owner made cash drawings.
(c) Paid interest on a business loan.
(d) Purchased stock for cash.
(e) Received cash from a credit customer.
(f) Paid wages to employees.
(g) The owner received some cash from a credit customer, which was taken as drawings rather than being paid into the business's bank account.
(h) Paid a credit supplier.
(i) Paid electricity bill.
(j) Made cash sales.

A.2 (a) Record the following transactions in a set of double-entry accounts:

1 February	Lee (the owner) put £6,000 into a newly opened business bank account to start a new business
3 February	Purchased stock for £2,600 for cash
5 February	Purchased some equipment (non-current asset) for cash for £800
6 February	Purchased stock costing £3,000 on credit
9 February	Paid rent for the month of £250
10 February	Paid fuel and electricity for the month of £240
11 February	Paid general expenses of £200
15 February	Sold stock for £4,000 in cash; the stock had cost £2,400
19 February	Sold stock for £3,800 on credit; the stock had cost £2,300
21 February	Lee withdrew £1,000 in cash for personal use
25 February	Paid £2,000 to trade creditors
28 February	Received £2,500 from trade debtors

(b) Balance the relevant accounts and prepare a trial balance (making sure that it agrees).
(c) Prepare a profit and loss account for the month and a balance sheet at the month end. Assume that there are no prepaid or accrued expenses at the end of the month and ignore any possible depreciation.

A.3   The following is the balance sheet of David's business at 1 January of last year.

	£	£		£
Non-current assets			Capital	25,050
Property, plant and equipment				
Buildings		25,000	Non-current liability	
Fittings: cost	10,000		Loan	12,000
dep'n	(2,000)			
		8,000		
			Current liabilities	
Current assets			Trade creditors	1,690
Stock of stationery		140	Accrued electricity	270
Stock-in-trade		1,350		
Prepaid in rent		500		
Trade debtors		1,840		
Cash		2,180		
		39,010		39,010

The following is a summary of the transactions that took place during the year:

1   Stock was purchased on credit for £17,220.
2   Stock was purchased for £3,760 cash.
3   Credit sales revenues amounted to £33,100 (cost £15,220).
4   Cash sales revenues amounted to £10,360 (cost £4,900).
5   Wages of £3,770 were paid.
6   Rent of £3,000 was paid. The annual rental amounts to £3,000.
7   Electricity of £1,070 was paid.
8   General expenses of £580 were paid.
9   Additional fittings were purchased on 1 January for £2,000. The cash for this was raised from an additional loan of this amount. The interest rate is 10% a year, the same as for the existing loan.
10   £1,000 of the loan was repaid on 30 June.
11   Cash received from debtors amounted to £32,810.
12   Cash paid to creditors amounted to £18,150.
13   The owner withdrew £10,400 cash and £560 stock.

At the end of the year it was found that:

(a)   The electricity bill for the last quarter of the year for £290 had not been paid.
(b)   It was also found that trade debts amounting to £260 were unlikely to be received.
(c)   The value of stationery remaining was estimated at £150. Stationery is included in general expenses.
(d)   Depreciation to be taken at 20% on the cost of the fittings owned at the year end. Buildings are not depreciated.

Required:
(1)   Open ledger accounts and bring down all of the balances in the opening balance sheet.
(2)   Make entries to record the transactions 1 to 13 (above), opening any additional accounts as necessary.
(3)   Open a profit and loss account (part of the double entry, remember). Make the necessary entries for the items a to d (above) and the appropriate transfers to the profit and loss account.
(4)   List the remaining balances in the same form as the opening balance sheet (above).

Appendix B
Glossary of key terms

Account A section of a double-entry bookkeeping system that deals with one particular asset, claim, expense or revenue. *p. 340*

Accounting The process of identifying, measuring and communicating information to permit informed judgements and decisions by users of the information. *p. 2*

Accounting conventions Accounting rules that have evolved over time in order to deal with practical problems rather than to reflect some theoretical ideal. *pp. 13, 43*

Accounting information system The system used within a business to identify, record, analyse and report accounting information. *p. 11*

Accounting (financial reporting) standards Rules established by the UK accounting profession, which should be followed by preparers of the annual accounts of companies. *p. 139*

Accruals accounting The system of accounting that follows the accruals convention. This is the system followed in drawing up the balance sheet and profit and loss account. *p. 72*

Accruals convention The convention of accounting that asserts that profit is the excess of revenue over expenses, not the excess of cash receipts over cash payments. *p. 72*

Accrued expense An expense that is outstanding at the end of an accounting period. *p. 69*

Acid test ratio A liquidity ratio that relates the current assets (less stocks) to the current liabilities. *p. 217*

Allotted share capital *See* Issued share capital. *p. 118*

Asset A resource held by a business, that has certain characteristics. *pp. 29*

Associate company A company over which considerable influence, but not full control, may be exercised by another company. *p. 293*

Auditor A professional whose main duty is to make a report as to whether, in his or her opinion, the accounting statements of a company do that which they are supposed to do, namely show a true and fair view and comply with statutory, and accounting standard, requirements. *p. 149*

Authorised share capital The maximum amount of share capital that directors are authorised by the shareholders to issue. *p. 118*

Average settlement period for creditors The average time taken by a business to pay its creditors. *p. 211*

Average settlement period for debtors The average time taken for debtors to pay the amounts owing. *p. 210*

Average stock turnover period An efficiency ratio that measures the average period for which stocks are held by a business. *p. 209*

Bad debt An amount owed to the business that is considered to be irrecoverable. *p. 87*

Balance The net of the debit and credit totals in an account in a double-entry book-keeping system. *p. 345*

Balance sheet A statement of financial position that shows the assets of a business and the claim on those assets. *p. 25*

Bonus issue Reserves that are converted into shares and given 'free' to shareholders. *p. 116*

Bonus shares *See* Bonus issue. *p. 116*

Business entity convention The convention that holds that, for accounting purposes, the business and its owner(s) are treated as quite separate and distinct. *p. 43*

Called-up share capital That part of a company's share capital for which the share-holders have been asked to pay the agreed amount. Part of the claim of the owners against the business. *p. 118*

Capital The owner's claim on the assets of the business. *p. 31*

Capital expenditure The outlay of funds on non-current assets.

Capital reserve A reserve that arises from an unrealised 'capital' profit or gain rather than from normal trading activities. *p. 113*

Capital reserve arising on consolidation The excess of the fair value of the assets over the amount paid for them in a takeover. It is the equivalent of 'negative' goodwill arising on consolidation in the consolidated balance sheet. *p. 273*

Cash flow statement A statement that shows the sources and uses of cash for a period. *p. 25*

Cash flows from financing activities That part of the cash flow statement that deals with raising and redeeming long-term finance. *p. 175*

Cash flows from investing activities That part of the cash flow statement that deals with cash flows to acquire and dispose of non-current assets. *p. 176*

Cash flows from operating activities That part of the cash flow statement that deals with cash flows arising from day-to-day trading operations. *p. 176*

Cash generated from operations per ordinary share An investment ratio that relates the cash generated from operations available to ordinary shareholders to the number of ordinary shares. *p. 227*

Cash generated from operations to maturing obligations ratio A liquidity ratio that compares the cash generated from operations with the current liabilities of the business. *p. 217*

Claim An obligation on the part of a business to provide cash or some other benefit to an outside party. *p. 29*

Combined Code A code of practice for companies listed on the London Stock Exchange that deals with corporate governance matters. *p. 107*

Common-size financial statements   Normal financial statements (such as the profit and loss account, balance sheet and cash flow statement) that are expressed in terms of some base figure. *p. 235*

Comparability   The requirement that items that are basically the same should be treated in the same manner for measurement and reporting purposes. Lack of comparability will limit the usefulness of accounting information. *p. 7*

Consistency convention   The accounting convention that holds that, when a particular method of accounting is selected to deal with a transaction, this method should be applied consistently over time. *p. 87*

Consolidated financial statement   A group financial statement (balance sheet and so on) where the results of subsidiary companies are 'consolidated' into the results of the parent company. *p. 266*

Consolidating   Reducing the number of shares by increasing their nominal value. *p. 115*

Corporate governance   Systems for directing and controlling a company. *p. 106*

Corporation tax   Taxation that a limited company is liable to pay on its profits. *p. 105*

Cost of sales   The cost of the goods sold during a period. Cost of sales can be derived by adding the opening stock held to the stock purchases for the period and then deducting the closing stocks held. *p. 62*

Creative accounting   Adopting accounting polices to achieve a particular view of performance and position that preparers would like users to see rather than what is a true and fair view. *p. 160*

Credit   An entry made in the right-hand side of an account in double-entry bookkeeping. *p. 340*

Current asset   An asset that is not held on a continuing basis. Current assets include cash itself and other assets that are expected to be converted to cash at some point in the future. *p. 37*

Current cost accounting (CCA)   A method of accounting for inflation, based on maintaining the existing scale of business operations. It seeks to maintain the purchasing power of the business over specific goods and services utilised. *p. 319*

Current liabilities   A claim against the business which is expect to be settled within the normal course of the business's operating cycle or within 12 months of the balance sheet date *or* they are held primarily for trading purposes; and the business does not have the right to defer settlement beyond 12 months after the balance sheet date. *p. 39*

Current purchasing power (CPP) accounting   A method of accounting for inflation based on maintaining the owners' purchasing power over general goods and services within the economy. *p. 318*

Current ratio   A liquidity ratio that relates the current assets of the business to the current liabilities. *p. 216*

Debenture   A long-term loan, usually made to a company, evidenced by a trust deed. *p. 119*

Debit   An entry made in the left-hand side of an account in double-entry bookkeeping. *p. 340*

Depreciation   A measure of that portion of the cost of a non-current asset that has been consumed during an accounting period. *p. 73*

Direct method   An approach to deducing the cash flows from operating activities, in a cash flow statement, by analysing the business's cash records. *p. 178*

Director   An individual who is elected to act as the most senior level of management of a company. *p. 106*

Directors' report   A report containing information of a financial and non-financial nature that the directors must produce as part of the annual financial report to shareholders. *p. 149*

Discriminate function   An equation (model) that is capable of deriving a value that can indicate that likelihood of some future outcome, such as failure or being a takeover target. *p. 242*

Dividend   The transfer of assets (usually cash) made by a company to its shareholders. *p. 111*

Dividend cover ratio   An investment ratio that relates the earnings available for dividends to the dividend announced, to indicate how many times the former covers the latter. *p. 225*

Dividend payout ratio   An investment ratio that relates the dividends announced for the period to the earnings available for dividends that were generated in that period. *p. 224*

Dividend per share   An investment ratio that relates the dividends announced for a period to the number of shares in issue. *p. 226*

Dividend yield ratio   An investment ratio that relates the cash return from a share to its current market value. *p. 225*

Double-entry bookkeeping   A system for recording financial transactions where each transaction is recorded twice, once as a debit and once as a credit. *p. 340*

Dual aspect convention   The accounting convention that holds that each transaction has two aspects and that each aspect must be recorded in the financial statements. *p. 46*

Earnings per share (EPS)   An investment ratio that relates the earnings generated by the business during a period, and available to shareholders, to the number of shares in issue. *p. 226*

Environmental report   A report that accounts for the impact of the business on the environment. *p. 319*

Equity   Ordinary shares and reserves of a company. *p. 111*

Expense   A measure of the outflow of assets (or increase in liabilities) incurred as a result of generating revenue. *p. 59*

Fair value   The value ascribed to an asset as an alternative to historic cost. It is usually the current market value (that is, the exchange values in an arm's-length transaction). *pp. 49, 285*

Final accounts   The profit and loss account, cash flow statement and balance sheet taken together. *p. 28*

Financial accounting   The measuring and reporting of accounting information for external users (those users other than the managers of the business). *p. 11*

Financial gearing   The existence of fixed payment-bearing securities (for example, loans) in the capital structure of a business. *p. 219*

First in, first out (FIFO)   A method of stock valuation that assumes that the earlier stocks are to be sold first. *p. 83*

Fixed asset *See* Non-current asset. *p. 38*

Framework of principles The main principles that underpin accounting, which can help in identifying best practice and in developing accounting rules. *p. 150*

Fully paid shares Shares on which the shareholders have paid the full issue price. *p. 118*

Gearing ratio A ratio that relates the contribution of long-term lenders to the total long-term capital of the business. *p. 221*

Going concern convention The accounting convention that holds that it is assumed that the business will continue operations for the foreseeable future, unless there is a reason to believe otherwise. In other words, there is no intention, or need, to liquidate the business. *p. 45*

Goodwill arising on consolidation Anything paid in excess of the underlying net asset value of the subsidiary's shares. *p. 273*

Gross profit The amount remaining (if positive) after trading expenses (for example, cost of sales) have been deducted from trading revenue (for example, sales revenue). *p. 61*

Gross profit margin ratio A profitability ratio relating the gross profit for the period to the sales revenue for the period. *p. 207*

Group balance sheet A balance sheet for a group of companies, prepared from the perspective of the parent company's shareholders. *p. 266*

Group cash flow statement A cash flow statement for a group of companies, prepared from the perspective of the parent company's shareholders. *p. 291*

Group financial statements Sets of financial accounting statements that combine the performance and position of a group of companies that are under common control. *p. 258*

Group of companies A situation that arises where one company is able to exercise control over one or more other companies. *p. 258*

Group profit and loss account A profit and loss account (income statement) for a group of companies, prepared from the perspective of the parent company's shareholders. *p. 288*

Historic cost What an asset cost when it was originally acquired. *p. 44*

Historic cost convention The accounting convention that holds that assets should be recorded at their historic (acquisition) cost. *p. 44*

Holding company *See* Parent company. *p. 258*

Horizontal analysis An approach to common-size financial statements where all of the figures in equivalent statements over time are expressed in relation to the equivalent figure for the base period (year, month and so on). So, for example, the sales revenue figure for each year will be expressed in terms of the sales revenue figure of the base year. *p. 238*

Income statement *See* Profit and loss account. *p. 25*

Indirect method An approach to deducing the cash flows from operating activities, in a cash flow statement, by analysing the business's final accounts. *p. 178*

Inflation accounting A means of accounting for a fall in the purchasing power of money. *p. 313*

Intangible assets Assets that do not have a physical substance (for example, patents, goodwill and debtors). *p. 31*

Interest cover ratio A gearing ratio that divides the net profit before interest and taxation by the interest payable for a period. *p. 222*

International accounting (financial reporting) standards Transnational accounting rules that have been adopted, or developed, by the International Accounting Standards Board and which should be followed in preparing the published financial statements of limited companies. *p. 140*

Issued share capital That part of the authorised share capital which has been issued to shareholders. Also known as allotted share capital. *p. 118*

Last in, first out (LIFO) A method of stock valuation that assumes that the latest stocks are the first to be sold. *p. 83*

Liabilities Claims of individuals and organisations, apart from the owner, that have arisen from past transactions or events such as supplying goods or lending money to the business. *p. 32*

Limited company An artificial legal person that has an identity separate from that of those who own and manage it. *pp. 17, 101*

Limited liability The restriction of the legal obligation of shareholders to meet all of the company's debts. *p. 103*

Loan stock *See* debenture. *p. 119*

Management accounting The measuring and reporting of accounting information for the managers of a business. *p. 11*

Margin of safety The extent to which the planned level of output or sales revenue lies above the break-even point. *p. 123*

Matching convention The accounting convention that holds that, in measuring income, expenses should be matched to revenue which they helped generate in the same accounting period as that revenue was realised. *p. 68*

Materiality The requirement that material information should be disclosed to users of financial reports. *p. 8*

Materiality convention The accounting convention that states that, where the amounts involved are immaterial, only what is expedient should be considered. *p. 71*

Minority interests That part of the net assets of a subsidiary company that is financed by shareholders other than the parent company and that part of group's profit attributable to those shareholders. Also known as outsiders' interests. *p. 271*

Monetary items Items appearing on the balance sheet that have a fixed number of £s attached to them and which cannot be changed as a result of inflation. *p. 316*

Money measurement convention The accounting convention that holds that accounting should deal only with those items which are capable of being expressed in monetary terms. *p. 43*

Multiple discriminate analysis A statistical technique used to predict financial distress, which involves using an index based on a combination of financial ratios. *p. 242*

Net profit The amount remaining (if positive) after the total expenses for a period have been deducted from total revenue. *p. 61*

Net profit margin ratio A profitability ratio relating the net profit for the period to the sales revenue for the period. *p. 206*

Nominal value   The face value of a share in a company. (Also called *par value*.) *p. 111*

Non-current asset   An asset held with the intention of being used to generate wealth rather than being held for resale. Non-current assets can be seen as the tools of the business and are held on a continuing basis. (Also known as *fixed assets*.) *p. 38*

Non-current liability   A claim against the business that is not within the definition of a current liability. *p. 39*

Objectivity convention   The convention that holds that, in so far as is possible, the financial statements prepared should be based on objective verifiable evidence rather than matters of opinion. *p. 47*

Operating and financial review   A narrative report that helps users to understand the operating and financial results of a business for a period. *p. 155*

Operating profit   The profit achieved from business operations before any financing expenses are taken into account. *p. 127*

Ordinary shares   Shares of a company owned by those who are due the benefits of the company's activities after all other stakeholders have been satisfied. *p. 112*

Overtrading   The situation arising when a business is operating at a level of activity which cannot be supported by the amount of finance which has been committed. *p. 233*

Paid-up share capital   That part of the share capital of a company that has been called and paid. *p. 118*

Par value   *See* Nominal value. *p. 111*

Parent company   A company that is able to exercise control over another (subsidiary) company, usually, but not necessarily, because it owns a majority of the shares of the subsidiary. Sometimes known as a holding company. *p. 258*

Partnership   A form of business unit where there are at least two individuals, but usually no more than twenty, carrying on a business with the intention of making a profit. *p. 16*

Preference shares   Shares of a company owned by those who are entitled to the first part of any dividend which the company may pay. *p. 112*

Prepaid expenses   Expenses that have been paid in advance at the end of the accounting period. *p. 71*

Price/earnings ratio   An investment ratio that relates the market value of a share to the earnings per share. *p. 227*

Private company   A limited company for which the directors can restrict the ownership of its shares. *p. 104*

Profit   The increase in wealth attributable to the owners of a business that arises through business operations. *p. 59*

Profit and loss account   A financial statement (also known as *income statement*) that measures and reports the profit (or loss) the business has generated during a period. It is derived by deducting from total revenue for a period, the total expenses associated with that revenue. *pp. 25, 61*

Provision for doubtful debts   An amount set aside out of profits to provide for anticipated losses arising from debts that may prove irrecoverable. *p. 88*

Prudence convention   The accounting convention that holds that financial statements should err on the side of caution. *p. 46*

Public company   A limited company for which the directors cannot restrict the ownership of its shares. *p. 104*

Realisation convention   The accounting convention that holds that revenue should be recognised only when it has been realised. *p. 65*

Reducing-balance method   A method of calculating depreciation that applies a fixed percentage rate of depreciation to the written-down value of an asset in each period. *p. 76*

Relevance   The ability of accounting information to influence decisions; regarded as a key characteristic of useful accounting information. *p. 6*

Reliability   The requirement that accounting should be free from material error or bias. Reliability is regarded as a key characteristic of useful accounting information. *p. 6*

Reserves   Part of the owners' claim on a limited company that has arisen from profits and gains, to the extent that these have not been distributed to the shareholders. *p. 111*

Residual value   The amount for which a non-current asset is sold when the business has no further use for it. *p. 75*

Return on capital employed (ROCE)   A profitability ratio expressing the relationship between the net profit (before interest and taxation) and the long-term capital invested in the business. *p. 206*

Return on ordinary shareholders' funds (ROSF)   A profitability ratio that compares the amount of profit for the period available to the ordinary shareholders with their stake in the business. *p. 205*

Revenue   A measure of the inflow of assets (for example, cash or amounts owed to a business by debtors), or a reduction in liabilities, that arises as a result of trading operations. *p. 59*

Revenue reserve   Part of the owners' claim on a company that arises from realised profits and gains, including after-tax trading profits and gains from disposals of non-current assets. These profits and gains have been reinvested in the company rather than distributed to the owners. *p. 111*

Sales revenue per employee ratio   An efficiency ratio that relates the sales revenue generated during a period to the average number of employees of the business. *p. 213*

Sales revenue to capital employed ratio   An efficiency ratio that relates the sales revenue generated during a period to the capital employed. *p. 212*

Segmental financial reports   Reports that break down the operating results of a business according to its business or geographical segments. *p. 153*

Share   A portion of the ownership, or equity, of a company. *pp. 6, 101*

Share premium account   A capital reserve reflecting any amount, above the nominal value of shares, that is paid for those shares when issued by a company. *p. 114*

Social reports   Reports that are produced to reveal the way in which a business interacts with society. *p. 322*

Sole proprietorship   An individual in business on his or her own account. *p. 16*

Stable monetary unit convention   The accounting convention that assumes that money, which is the unit of measurement in accounting, will not change in value over time. *p. 47*

Statement of changes to equity   A financial statement, required by IAS 1, which shows the effect of gains/losses and capital injections/withdrawals on the equity base of a company. *p. 146*

Straight-line method   A method of accounting for depreciation that allocates the amount to be depreciated evenly over the useful life of the asset. *p. 75*

Subsidiary company   A company over which another (parent) company is able to exercise control, usually, but not necessarily, because a majority of its shares are owned by the parent company. *p. 258*

Summary financial statement   A summarised version of the complete annual financial statements, which shareholders may receive as an alternative to the complete statements. *p. 160*

Sustainable development   Meeting the needs of the present without compromising the ability of future generations to meet their own needs. *p. 328*

Takeover   The acquisition of control of one company by another, usually as a result of acquiring a majority of the ordinary shares of the former. *p. 258*

Tangible assets   Those assets that have a physical substance (for example, plant and machinery, motor vehicles.) *p. 31*

Target company   A company that is the subject of a takeover bid. *p. 261*

Transfer price   The price at which goods or services are sold, or transferred, between divisions or segments of the same business. *p. 154*

Trial balance   A totalled list of the of the balances on each of the accounts in a double-entry bookkeeping system. *p. 348*

Triple bottom line reporting   The combined reporting of economic value added, environmental value added and social value added by a business. *p. 328*

Understandability   The requirement that accounting information should be understood by those for whom the information is primarily compiled. Lack of understandability will limit the usefulness of accounting information. *p. 7*

Univariate analysis   Drawing conclusions based on consideration of just one variable. Applied when considering just one accounting ratio. *p. 242*

Value added statement   A performance statement, based on a rearrangement of the information contained in the profit and loss account, that reveals the income (value added) attributable to employees, government and suppliers of capital. *p. 306*

Vertical analysis   An approach to common-size financial statements where all of the figures in the particular statement are expressed in relation to one of the figures in that same statement, for example sales revenue or total long-term funds. *p. 238*

Weighted average cost (AVCO)   A method of valuing stocks that assumes that stocks entering the business lose their separate identity and any issues of stock reflect the weighted average cost of the stocks held. *p. 83*

Written-down value (WDV)   The difference between the cost (or revalued amount) of a non-current asset and the accumulated depreciation relating to the assets. The written-down value is also referred to as the net book value (NBV). *p. 76*

Appendix C
Solutions to self-assessment questions

Chapter 2

2.1 The balance sheet you prepare should be set out as follows:

Simonson Engineering
Balance sheet as at 30 September 2005

	£	£	£
Non-current assets			
Freehold premises			72,000
Plant and machinery			25,000
Motor vehicles			15,000
Fixtures and fittings			9,000
			121,000
Current assets			
Stock-in-trade		45,000	
Trade debtors		48,000	
Cash in hand		1,500	
		94,500	
Current liabilities			
Trade creditors	(18,000)		
Bank overdraft	(26,000)		
		(44,000)	
			50,500
Total assets less current liabilities			171,500
Non-current liabilities			
Loan			(51,000)
Net assets			120,500
Capital			
Opening balance			117,500
Add Profit			18,000
			135,500
Less Drawings			15,000
			120,500

Chapter 3

3.1   TT and Co.

Balance sheet as at 31 December 2004

Assets	£	Claims	£
Delivery van		Capital	
(12,000 – 2,500)	9,500	(50,000 + 26,900)	76,900
Stock-in-trade (143,000 +			
12,000 – 74,000 – 16,000)	65,000	Trade creditors	
		(143,000 – 121,000)	22,000
Trade debtors			
(152,000 – 132,000 – 400)	19,600	Accrued expenses	
		(630 + 620)	1,250
Assets	**£**	**Claims**	**£**
Cash at bank (50,000 – 25,000			
– 500 – 1,200 – 12,000 – 33,500			
– 1,650 – 12,000 + 35,000 –			
9,400 + 132,000 – 121,000)	750		
Prepaid expenses			
(5,000 + 300)	5,300		
	100,150		100,150

Profit and loss account for the year ended 31 December 2004

	£	£
Sales revenue (152,000 + 35,000)		187,000
Less Cost of stock sold		
(74,000 + 16,000)		90,000
Gross profit		97,000
Less		
Rent	20,000	
Rates (500 + 900)	1,400	
Wages (33,500 + 630)	34,130	
Electricity (1,650 + 620)	2,270	
Bad debts	400	
Van depreciation [(12,000 – 2,000)/4]	2,500	
Van expenses	9,400	
		70,100
Net profit for the year		£26,900

The balance sheet could now be rewritten in a more stylish form as follows:

Balance sheet as at 31 December 2004

Non-current assets	£	£	£
Motor van			9,500
Current assets			
Stock-in-trade	65,000		
Trade debtors	19,600		
Prepaid expenses	5,300		
Cash	750		
		90,650	
Less **Current liabilities**			
Trade creditors	22,000		
Accrued expenses	1,250		
		23,250	
			67,400
			76,900

Capital

Original	50,000
Retained profit	26,900
	76,900

Chapter 4

4.1 Dev Ltd

(a) The summarised balance sheet of Dev Ltd, immediately following the rights and bonus issue, is as follows:

Balance sheet as at 31 December 2005

	£
Net assets [235 + 40 (cash from the rights issue)]	275,000
Equity	
Share capital: 100,000 shares @ £1 [(100 + 20) + 60]	180,000
Share premium account (30 + 20 − 50)	–
Revaluation reserve (37 − 10)	27,000
Profit and loss account balance	68,000
	275,000

Note that the bonus issue of £60,000 is taken from capital reserves (reserves unavailable for dividends) as follows:

	£
Share premium account	50,000
Revaluation reserve	10,000
	60,000

More could have been taken from the revaluation reserve and less from the share premium account without making any difference to dividend payment possibilities.

(b) There may be pressure from a potential creditor for the business to limit its ability to pay dividends. This would place creditors in a more secure position because the maximum buffer or safety margin between the value of the assets and the amount owed by the business is maintained. It is not unusual for potential creditors to insist on some measure to lock up shareholders' funds in this way as a condition of granting the loan.

(c) The summarised balance sheet of Dev Ltd, immediately following the rights and bonus issue, assuming a minimum dividend potential objective, is as follows:

Balance sheet as at 31 December 2005

	£
Net assets [235 + 40 (cash from the rights issue)]	275,000
Equity	
Share capital: 100,000 shares @ £1 ((100 + 20) + 60)	180,000
Share premium account (30 + 20)	50,000
Revaluation reserve	37,000
Profit and loss account balance (68 − 60)	8,000
	275,000

(d) Before the bonus issue, the maximum dividend was £68,000. Now it is £8,000. Thus the bonus issue has had the effect of locking up an additional £60,000 of the business's assets in terms of the business's ability to pay dividends.

(e) Before the issues, Lee had 100 shares worth £2.35 (£235,000/100,000) each or £235 in total. Lee would be offered 20 shares in the rights issue at £2 each or £40 in total. After the rights issue, Lee would have 120 shares worth £2.2917 (£275,000/120,000) each or £275 in total.

  The bonus issue would give Lee 60 additional shares. After the bonus issue, Lee would have 180 shares worth £1.5278 (£275,000/180,000) each or £275 in total.

  None of this affects Lee's wealth. Before the issues, Lee had £235 worth of shares and £40 more in cash. After the issues, Lee has the same total wealth but all £275 is in the value of the shares.

(f) The things that we know about the company are as follows:

  (i)   It is a private (as opposed to a public) limited company, for it has 'Ltd' (limited) as part of its name, rather than plc (public limited company).

  (ii) It has made an issue of shares at a premium, almost certainly after it had traded successfully for a period. (There is a share premium account. It would be very unlikely that the original shares, issued when the company was first formed, would have been issued at a premium.)

  (iii) Certain of the assets in the balance sheet have been upwardly revalued by at least £37,000. (There is a revaluation reserve of £37,000. This may just be what is left after a previous bonus issue had taken part of the balance.)

  (iv) The company has traded at an aggregate profit (though there could have been losses in some years), net of tax and any dividends paid. (There is a positive balance on the profit and loss account.)

Chapter 5

5.1 J Baxter plc

We can see from the table below that the Italian segment generates the highest revenue, but also generates the lowest profit. We shall be considering financial ratios in detail in Chapter 7, however, it is helpful to compare the profit generated with the sales for each geographical segment. We can see from the table below that the French segment generates the most profit in relation to sales revenue. Fifteen per cent or £0.15 in every £1, of profit is derived from the sales revenue generated. However, for the Italian segment, only 2.1%, or £0.02 in every £1, of profit is derived from the sales revenue generated.

  We can also compare the profit generated with the net assets employed (that is, total assets – total liabilities) for each segment. We can see from the table below that the UK segment produces the best return on net assets employed: £0.36 for every £1 invested. Once again, the Italian segment produces the worst results.

  The reasons for the relatively poor results from the Italian segment need further investigation. There may be valid reasons; for example, this segment may have deliberately engaged in low pricing during the period in an attempt to increase market share. However, it may suggest that the business needs to re-evaluate its presence in this geographical region.

  It is interesting to note that the Italian segment benefited most from capital expenditure during the period. The reasons for such a large investment in such a poorly-performing segment needs to be justified. It is possible that the business will reap rewards for the investment in the future; however, we do not have enough information to understand the reasons for the investment decision.

  The reasons why the depreciation charges in the Italian segment are significantly lower than in the other geographical segments should also be investigated. The depreciation charge as a percentage of total assets is much lower. It is possible that the mix of assets is different in the Italian segment from that in the other two segments. If, however, this is not the case and a higher depreciation charge is really warranted, the profitability of this segment would be even worse.

Table of key results

	UK	France	Italy
Total revenue	270	200	390
Segment result	34	30	8
Net assets	94	122	94
Segment result as a percentage of sales revenue	12.6%	15.0%	2.1%
Segment result as a percentage of net assets employed	36.2%	24.6%	8.5%
Capital expenditure	£20m	£15m	£35m
Depreciation as a percentage of total assets	21.7%	23.3%	9.5%

Chapter 6

6.1   Touchstone plc

Cash flow statement for the year ended 31 December 2005

	£m	£m
Cash flows from operating activities		
Net profit, after interest, before taxation		
(see Note 1 below)	60	
Adjustments for:		
Depreciation	16	
Interest expense (Note 2)	4	
	80	
Increase in trade debtors (26 – 16)	(10)	
Decrease in trade creditors (38 – 37)	(1)	
Decrease in stocks (25 – 24)	1	
Cash generated from operations	70	
Interest paid	(4)	
Corporation tax paid (Note 3)	(12)	
Dividend paid	(18)	
Net cash from operating activities		36
Cash flows from investing activities		
Payments to acquire tangible non-current assets (Note 4)	(41)	
Net cash used in investing activities		(41)
Cash flows from financing activities		
Issue of debenture stock (40 – 20)	20	
Net cash used in financing activities		20
Net increase in cash and cash equivalents		15
Cash and cash equivalents at 1 January 2005		
Cash		4
Cash and cash equivalents at 31 December 2005		
Cash		4
Treasury bills		15
		19

To see how this relates to the cash of the business at the beginning and end of the year it can be useful to provide a reconciliation as follows:

Analysis of cash and cash equivalents during the year ended 31 December 2005

	£m
Cash and cash equivalents at 1 January 2005	4
Net cash inflow	15
Cash and cash equivalents at 31 December 2005	19

Notes

1 This is simply taken from the profit and loss account for the year.
2 Interest payable expense must be taken out, by adding it back to the profit figure. We subsequently deduct the cash paid for interest payable during the year. In this case the two figures are identical.
3 Tax is paid by companies 50% during their accounting year and the other 50% in the following year. Thus the 2005 payment would have been half the tax on the 2004 profit (that is, the figure that would have appeared in the current liabilities at the end of 2004), plus half of the 2005 tax charge (that is, $4 + (1/2 \times 16) = 12$).
4 Since there were no disposals, the depreciation charges must be the difference between the start and end of the year's non-current asset values, adjusted by the cost of any additions.

	£m
Book value, at 1 January 2005	147
Add Additions (balancing figure)	41
	188
Less Depreciation (6 + 10)	16
Book value, at 31 December 2005	172

Chapter 7

7.1 Financial ratios

In order to answer this question you may have used the following ratios:

	Ali plc	Bhaskar plc
Current ratio	$\dfrac{853.0}{422.4} = 2.0$	$\dfrac{816.5}{293.1} = 2.8$
Acid test ratio	$\dfrac{(853.0 - 592.0)}{422.4} = 0.6$	$\dfrac{(816.5 - 403.0)}{293.1} = 1.4$
Gearing ratio	$\dfrac{190}{(687.6 + 190)} \times 100 = 21.6\%$	$\dfrac{250}{(874.6 + 250)} \times 100 = 22.2\%$
Interest cover ratio	$\dfrac{(131.9 + 19.4)}{19.4} = 7.8$ times	$\dfrac{(139.4 + 27.5)}{27.5} = 6.1$ times
Dividend payout ratio	$\dfrac{135.0}{99.9} \times 100 = 135\%$	$\dfrac{95.0}{104.6} \times 100 = 91\%$
Price/earnings ratio	$\dfrac{£6.50}{31.2\text{p}} = 20.8$ times	$\dfrac{£8.20}{41.8\text{p}} = 19.6$ times

Ali plc has a much lower current ratio and acid test ratio than does Bhaskar plc. The reasons for this may be partly due to the fact that Ali plc has a lower average settlement period for debtors. The acid test ratio of Ali plc is substantially below 1.0: this may suggest a liquidity problem.

The gearing ratio of each business is quite similar. Neither business has excessive borrowing. The interest cover ratio for each business is also similar. The respective ratios indicate that both businesses have good profit coverage for their interest charges.

The dividend payout ratio for each business seems very high. In the case of Ali plc, the dividends announced for the year are considerably higher than the earnings generated during the year that are available for dividend. As a result, part of the dividend was paid out of retained profits from previous years. This is an unusual occurrence; although it is quite legitimate, such action may nevertheless suggest a lack of prudence on the part of the directors.

The P/E ratio for both businesses is high, which indicates market confidence in their future prospects.

Chapter 8

8.1 Great plc

Group balance sheet as at 31 December last year

	£m	£m
Non-current assets		
Property, plant and equipment (at cost less depreciation)		
Land (80 + 14 + 5)		99
Plant		53
Vehicles		31
		183
Intangible asset		
Goodwill arising on consolidation*		5
		188
Current assets		
Stocks	29	
Debtors	27	
Cash	22	
	78	
Less **Current liabilities**		
Creditors	(22)	
Net current assets		56
Total assets less current liabilities		244
Less **Non-current liabilities**		
Debentures		(50)
		194
Equity		
Called-up share capital: ordinary shares of £1 each, fully paid		100
Profit and loss account		81[†]
Minority interests (60 + 5) × 20%		13
		194

* Goodwill arising on consolidation: 53 – (80% × (20 + 35 + 5)) = 5.

[†] Apart from the fact that this is the closing profit and loss account balance (see below), it can be shown to be correct as:

	£m
Great plc's balance	77
Great plc's share of Small plc's post-acquisition profits (40 – 35) × 80%	4
	81

Group profit and loss account for last year

	£m	£m
Turnover		144
Cost of sales		(70)
Gross profit		74
Administration expenses	(17)	
Distribution expenses	(11)	(28)
Profit before tax		46
Taxation		(17)
Profit after tax		29
Attributable to minorities (20% × 10)		(2)
Profit after tax attributable to Great plc shareholders		27
Profit and loss account balance brought forward from the previous year (there was no post-acquisition balance brought forward for Small plc)		65
		92
Dividend on ordinary shares		(11)
Profit and loss account balance carried forward to the following year		81

Chapter 9

9.1 Samodiva Limited

(a)

Value added statement for the year ended 30 September

	£000	£000	%
Revenue (less bad debts)		5,998	
Less Bought-in goods and services		2,488	
Value added		3,510	
Distributed to			
Employees			
Wages	628		
Benefits	82	710	20.2
Government – taxation (62 + 128 + 244)		434	12.4
Providers of capital			
Shareholders	500		14.3
Debenture holders	320	820	9.1
Retained within company			
Depreciation	854		24.3
Retained earnings	692	1,546	19.7
		3,510	100.0

(b) The ratios reveal that a large percentage of total value added (44.0%) is retained within the business. Providers of capital take 23.4% of value added and employees take only 20.2%. This last figure seems quite low. It is not unusual for 70% or more of value added by a business to be paid to employees.

Appendix D
Solutions to selected exercises

Chapter 2

2.1

Cash flow statement for day 4

	£
Opening balance (from day 3)	59
Cash from sale of wrapping paper	47
	106
Cash paid to purchase wrapping paper	(53)
Closing balance	53

Profit and loss account for day 4

	£
Sales revenue	47
Cost of goods sold	(33)
Profit	14

Balance sheet at the end of day 4

	£
Cash	53
Stock of goods for resale (23 + 53 − 33)	43
Total business wealth	96

2.2

	£
Cash introduced by Paul on day 1	40
Profit of day 1	15
Profit of day 2	18
Profit of day 3	9
Profit of day 4	14
	96

Thus the wealth of the business, all of which belongs to Paul as sole owner, consists of the cash he put in to start the business plus the profit earned each day.

2.3

Profit and loss account for day 1

	£
Sales revenue (70 × £0.80)	56
Cost of sales (70 × £0.50)	(35)
Profit	21

Cash flow statement for day 1

	£
Opening balance	40
Add Cash from sales	56
	96
Less Cash for purchases (80 × £0.50)	40
Closing balance	56

Balance sheet as at end of day 1

	£
Cash balance	56
Stock of unsold goods (10 × £0.50)	5
Helen's business wealth	61

Profit and loss account for day 2

	£
Sales revenue (65 × £0.80)	52.0
Cost of sales (65 × £0.50)	(32.5)
Profit	19.5

Cash flow statement for day 2

	£
Opening balance	56.0
Add Cash from sales	52.0
	108.0
Less Cash for purchases (60 × £0.50)	30.0
Closing balance	78.0

Balance sheet as at end of day 2

	£
Cash balance	78.0
Stock of unsold goods (5 × £0.50)	2.5
Helen's business wealth	80.5

Profit and loss account for day 3

	£
Sales revenue (20 × £0.80) + (45 × £0.40)	34.0
Cost of sales (65 × £0.50)	(32.5)
Profit	1.5

Cash flow statement for day 3

	£
Opening balance	78.0
Add Cash from sales	34.0
	112.0
Less Cash for purchases (60 × £0.50)	30.0
Closing balance	82.0

Balance sheet as at end of day 3

	£
Cash balance	82.0
Stock of unsold goods	–
Helen's business wealth	82.0

2.5   (a)

Crafty Engineering Ltd
Balance sheet as at 30 June last year

	£000	£000	£000
Non-current assets			
Freehold premises			320
Machinery and tools			207
Motor vehicles			38
			565
Current assets			
Stock-in-trade		153	
Debtors		185	
		338	
Less **Current liabilities**			
Creditors	86		
Bank overdraft	116	202	
			136
			701
Less **Non-current liabilities**			
Loan from Industrial Finance Co.			260
			441
Capital (missing figure)			441

(b) The balance sheet reveals a high level of investment in non-current assets. In percentage terms, we can say that more than 60% of the total investment in assets (565/903) has been in non-current assets. The nature of the business may require a heavy investment in non-current assets. The investment in current assets exceeds the current liabilities by a large amount (approximately 1.7 times). As a result, there is no obvious sign of a liquidity problem. However, the balance sheet reveals that the business has no cash balance and is therefore dependent on the continuing support of the bank (in the form of a bank overdraft) in order to meet obligations when they fall due. When considering the long-term financing of the business, we can see that about 37% [260/(260 + 441)] of the total long-term finance for the business has been supplied by loan capital and about 63% [441/(260 + 441)] by the owners. This level of borrowing seems quite high but not excessive. However, we would need to know more about the ability of the business to service the loan capital (that is, make interest payments and loan repayments) before a full assessment could be made.

2.8   (a) The profit and loss account shows the increase in wealth, as a result of trading, generated during the period (revenue), the decrease in wealth caused by the generation of that revenue (expenses) and the resulting net increase (profit) or decrease (loss) in wealth for the period. Though most businesses hold some of their wealth in cash, wealth is held in many other forms: non-current assets, debtors and so on.

(b) Assets, to be included in a balance sheet, must be judged as likely to produce future economic benefits. The economic benefit may come from selling the asset in the short term, in which case the statement is broadly true for those assets that it is the intention of the business to liquidate (turn into cash) in the short term. Many assets have an economic benefit that is related not to liquidation value but to use – for example, in production. For these types of asset, the statement is certainly *not* true.

There are other conditions that must be met in order for an item to be included in the balance sheet. These are:

● the business must have an exclusive right to control the asset
● the benefit must arise from some past transaction or event
● the asset must be measurable in monetary terms.

(c) The balance sheet equation is:

Assets = Capital + Liabilities

(d) Non-current assets are assets that do not meet the criteria for current assets. They are held for the long-term operations of the business. Some non-current assets may be immovable (for example, freehold land), but others are not (for example, motor vans).

(e) Working capital is the name given to the sum of the current assets *less the sum of the current liabilities*.

Chapter 3

3.1 (a) Capital does increase as a result of the owners introducing more cash into the business, but it will also increase as a result of introducing other assets (for example, a motor car) and by the business generating revenue by trading. Similarly, capital decreases not only as a result of withdrawals of cash by owners but also by withdrawals of other assets (for example, stock for the owners' personal use) and through trading expenses being incurred. For the typical business in a typical accounting period, capital will alter much more as a result of trading activities than for any other reason.

(b) An accrued expense is not one that relates to next year. It is one that needs to be matched with the revenue of the accounting period under review, but that has yet to be met in terms of cash payment. As such, it will appear on the balance sheet as a current liability.

(c) The purpose of depreciation is not to provide for asset replacement. Rather, it is an attempt to allocate the cost, or fair value, of the asset (less any residual value) over its useful life. Depreciation is an attempt to provide a measure of the amount of the non-current asset that has been consumed during the period. This amount will then be charged as an expense for the period in deriving the profit figure. Depreciation is a book entry (the outlay of cash occurs when the asset is purchased) and does not normally entail setting aside a separate amount of cash for asset replacement. Even if this were done, there would be no guarantee that sufficient funds would be available at the end of the asset's life for its replacement. Factors such as inflation and technological change may mean that the replacement cost is higher than the original cost of the asset.

(d) In the short term, it is possible for the current value of a non-current asset to exceed its original cost. However, nearly all non-current assets will wear out over time as a result of being used to generate wealth for the business. This will be the case for freehold buildings. As a result, some measure of depreciation should be calculated to take account of the fact that the asset is being consumed. Some businesses revalue their freehold buildings where the current value is significantly different from the original cost. Where this occurs, the depreciation charged should be based on the revalued amount. This will normally result in higher depreciation charges than if the asset remained at its historic cost.

3.3 The existence of profit and downward movement in cash may be for various reasons, which include the following:

- The purchase of assets for cash during the period (for example, motor cars and stock), which were not all consumed during the period and are therefore not having as great an effect on expenses as they are on cash.
- The payment of an outstanding liability (for example, a loan), which will have an effect on cash but not on expenses in the profit and loss account.
- The withdrawal of cash by the owners from the capital invested, which will not have an effect on the expenses in the profit and loss account.
- The generation of revenue on credit where the cash has yet to be received. This will increase the sales revenue for the period but will not have a beneficial effect on the cash balance until a later period.

3.5 (a) Rent payable – expense for period   £9,000
      (b) Rates and insurance – expense for period   £6,000
      (c) General expenses – paid in period   £7,000
      (d) Loan interest payable – prepaid   £500
      (e) Salaries – paid in period   £6,000
      (f) Rent receivable – received during period   £3,000

3.7

WW Limited
Balance sheet as at 31 December 2005

Assets	£	Claims	£
Machinery		Capital	
(+25,300 + 6,000 + 9,000 – 13,000 + 3,900 – 9,360)	21,840*	(+48,900 – 23,000 + 26,480)	52,380
Stock-in-trade			
(+12,200 + 143,000 + 12,000 – 127,000 – 25,000)	15,200		
		Trade creditors	
		(+16,900 + 143,000 – 156,000)	3,900
Trade debtors	34,300	Accrued expenses	860
(+21,300 + 211,000 – 198,000)		(+1,700 – 1,700 + 860)	
Cash at bank (overdraft)	–19,700		
(+8,300 – 23,000 – 25,000 – 2,000 – 6,000 – 23,800 – 2,700 – 12,000 + 42,000 + 198,000 – 156,000 – 17,500)			
Prepaid expenses	5,500		
(+400 – 400 + 500 + 5,000)			
	57,140		57,140

	£
Cost less accumulated depreciation at 31 December 2004	25,300
Less Book value of machine disposed of (£13,000 – £3,900)	9,100
	16,200
Add Cost of new machine	15,000
	31,200
Depreciation for 2005 (£31,200 × 30%)	9,360
Net book value of machine at 31 December 2005	21,840

Profit and loss account for the year ended 31 December 2005

	£	£
Sales revenue (+211,000 + 42,000)		253,000
Less Cost of stock sold (+127,000 + 25,000)		152,000
Gross profit		101,000
Less		
Rent (+20,000)	20,000	
Rates (+400 + 1,500)	1,900	
Wages (–1,700 + 23,800 + 860)	22,960	
Electricity (+2,700)	2,700	
Machinery depreciation (+9,360)	9,360	
Loss on disposal of the old machinery (+13,000 – 3,900 – 9,000)	100	
Van expenses (+17,500)	17,500	
		74,520
Net profit for the year		26,480

The loss on disposal of the old machinery is the book value (cost less depreciation) less the disposal proceeds. Since the machinery had only been owned for one year, with a depreciation rate of 30%, the depreciation on it so far is £3,900 (that is, £13,000 × 30%). The effective disposal proceeds were £9,000 because, as a result of trading it in, the business saved £9,000 on the new asset.

The depreciation expense for 2005 is based on the cost less accumulated depreciation of the assets owned at the end of 2005. Accumulated depreciation must be taken into account because the business uses the reducing-balance method.

The balance sheet could now be rewritten in a more stylish form as follows:

WW Limited
Balance sheet as at 31 December 2005

	£	£	£
Non-current assets			
Machinery			21,840
Current assets			
Stock-in-trade	15,200		
Trade debtors	34,300		
Prepaid expenses	5,500		
		55,000	
Less **Current liabilities**			
Trade creditors	3,900		
Accrued expenses	860		
Bank overdraft	19,700		
		24,460	30,540
			52,380
Capital			
Original			48,900
Profit			26,480
			75,380
Less Drawings			23,000
			52,380

3.8 An examination of the trading and profit and loss accounts for the two years reveals a number of interesting points, which include:

● An increase in sales value and gross profit of 9.9% in 2005.
● The gross profit expressed as a percentage of sales revenue remaining at 70%.
● An increase in salaries of 7.2%.
● An increase in selling and distribution costs of 31.2%.
● An increase in bad debts of 392.5%.
● A decline in net profit of 39.3%.
● A decline in the net profit as a percentage of sales revenue from 13.3% to 7.4%.

Thus, the business has enjoyed an increase in sales revenue and gross profits, but this has failed to translate to an increase in net profit because of the significant rise in overheads. The increase in selling costs during 2005 suggests that the increase in sales revenue was achieved by greater marketing effort, and the huge increase in bad debts suggests that the increase in sales revenue may be attributable to selling to less creditworthy customers or to a weak debt-collection policy. There appears to have been a change of policy in 2005 towards sales, and this has not been successful overall as the net profit has shown a dramatic decline.

Chapter 4

4.1 Limited companies can no more set a limit on the amount of debts they will meet than can human beings. They must meet their debts up to the limit of their assets, just as we as individuals must. In the context of owners' claim, 'reserves' mean part of the owners' claim against the assets of the company. These assets may or may not include cash. The legal ability of the company to pay dividends is not related to the amount of cash that it has.

Preference shares do not carry a guaranteed dividend. They simply guarantee that the preference shareholders have a right to the first slice of any dividend that is paid. Shares of many companies can, in effect, be bought by one investor from another through the Stock Exchange. Such a transaction has no direct effect on the company, however. These are not new shares being offered by the company, but existing shares that are being sold 'second-hand'.

4.2 (a) The first part of the quote is incorrect. Bonus shares should not, of themselves, increase the value of the shareholders' wealth. This is because reserves, belonging to the share-holders, are used to create bonus shares. Thus, each shareholder's stake in the company has not increased.

Share splits should not increase the wealth of the shareholder, and so that part of the quote is correct.

(b) This statement is incorrect. Shares can be issued at any price, provided that it is not below the nominal value of the shares. Once the company has been trading profitably for a period, the shares will not be worth the same as they were (the nominal value) when the company was first formed. In such circumstances, issuing shares at above their nominal value would not only be legal, but essential to preserve the wealth of the existing shareholders relative to any new ones.

(c) This statement is incorrect. From a legal perspective, the company is limited to a max-imum dividend of the current extent of its revenue reserves. This amounts to any after-tax profits or gains realised that have not been eroded through, for example, payments of previous dividends. Legally, cash is not an issue; it would be perfectly legal for a com-pany to borrow the funds to pay a dividend – although whether such an action would be commercially prudent is another question.

(d) This statement is partly incorrect. Companies do indeed have to pay tax on their profits. Depending on their circumstances, shareholders might also have to pay tax on their dividends.

4.4 **Iqbal Ltd**

Year	Maximum dividend £	
2002	0	No profit exists out of which to pay a dividend
2003	0	There remains a cumulative loss of £7,000. Since the revaluation represents a gain that has not been realised, it cannot be used to justify a dividend
2004	13,000	The cumulative net realised gains are derived as (–£15,000 + £8,000 + £15,000 + £5,000)
2005	14,000	The net realised profits and gains for the year
2006	22,000	The net realised profits and gains for the year

4.6   **Pear Limited**

Balance sheet as at 30 September 2005

	£000	£000
Non-current assets		
Property, plant and equipment		
Cost (1,570 + 30)	1,600	
Depreciation (690 + 12)	<u>702</u>	
		898
Current assets		
Stock	207	
Debtors (182 + 18 − 4)	196	
Cash at bank	<u>21</u>	
	424	
Less **Current liabilities**		
Trade creditors	88	
Other creditors (20 + 30 + 15 + 2)	67	
Taxation	17	
Dividend approved	25	
Bank overdraft	<u>105</u>	
	302	
Net current assets		122
Less **Non-current liabilities**		
10% debenture – repayable 2008		<u>(300)</u>
		720
Equity		
Shares capital		300
Share premium account		300
Retained profit at beginning of year	104	
Retained profit for year	<u>16</u>	<u>120</u>
		720

Profit and loss account for the year ended 30 September 2005

	£000	£000
Revenue (1,456 + 18)		1,474
Cost of sales		<u>(768)</u>
Gross profit		706
Less Salaries	220	
Depreciation (249 + 12)	261	
Other operating costs [131 + (2% × 200) + 2]	<u>137</u>	
		<u>(618)</u>
Operating profit		88
Interest payable (15 + 15)		<u>(30)</u>
Profit before taxation		58
Taxation (58 × 30%)		<u>(17)</u>
Profit after taxation		41
Dividend approved		<u>(25)</u>
Retained profit for the year		<u>16</u>

4.7 **Chips Limited**

Balance sheet as at 30 June 2005

	Cost £000	Depreciation £000	£000
Non-current assets			
Property, plant and equipment			
Buildings	800	(112)	688
Plant and equipment	650	(367)	283
Motor vehicles (102 − 8); (53 − 5 + 19)	94	(67)	27
	1,544	(546)	998
Current assets			
Stock		950	
Trade debtors (420 − 16)		404	
Cash at bank (16 + 2)		18	
		1,372	
Less **Current liabilities**			
Trade creditors (361 + 23)		(384)	
Other creditors (117 + 35)		(152)	
Taxation		(26)	
		(562)	
Net current assets			810
Less **Non-current liabilities**			
Secured 10% loan			(700)
			1,108
Equity			
Ordinary shares of £1, fully paid			800
Reserves at 1 July 2000		248	
Retained profit for year		60	308
			1,108

Profit and loss account for the year ended 30 June 2005

	£000	£000
Revenue (1,850 − 16)		1,834
Cost of sales (1,040 + 23)		1,063
Gross profit		771
Less Depreciation [220 − 2 − 5 + 8 + (94 × 20%)]	(240)	
Other operating costs	(375)	
		(615)
Operating profit		156
Interest payable (35 + 35)		(70)
Profit before taxation		86
Taxation (86 × 30%)		(26)
Profit after taxation		60

Chapter 5

5.1 Many believe that the annual reports of companies are becoming too long and contain too much information. To illustrate this point, a few examples of the length of the 2003 financial statements of large companies are as follows:

Rolls-Royce plc	76 pages
The Boots Company plc	68 pages
Cadbury Schweppes plc	148 pages
Vodafone Group plc	152 pages

There is a danger that users will suffer from 'information overload' if they are confronted with an excessive amount of information and that they will be unable to cope with it. This may, in turn, lead them to:

- fail to distinguish between important and less important information;
- fail to approach the analysis of information in a logical and systematic manner;
- feel a sense of confusion and avoid the task of analysing the information.

Lengthy annual reports are likely to be a particular problem for the less sophisticated user. This problem, however, has been recognised and many companies publish abridged financial statements for private investors, which include only the key points. However, for sophisticated users the problem may be that the annual reports are still not long enough. They often wish to glean as much information as possible from the company in order to make investment decisions.

5.3

I. Ching (Booksellers) plc
Profit and loss account for the year ended 31 December 2005

	£000
Revenue	943
Cost of sales	(460)
	483
Other income	42
	525
Distribution costs	(110)
Administrative expenses	(314)
Other expenses	(25)
Finance costs	(40)
Total expenses	(489)
Profit before tax	36
Corporation tax	(9)
Profit for the period	27

5.4

Manet plc
Statement of changes in equity for the year ended 30 June 2005

	Share capital £m	Share premium £m	Reval. reserve £m	Translat. reserve £m	Retained earnings £m	Total £m
Balance as at 30 June 2004	250	50	120	15	380	815
Changes in equity for the year ended 30 June 2005						
Gain on revaluation of properties			30			30
Exchange differences on translation of foreign operations	—	—	—	(5)	—	(5)
Net income recognised directly to equity			30	(5)		25
Profit for the period	—	—	—	—	160	160
Total recognised income and expense for the period			30	(5)	160	185
Dividends					(80)	(80)
Balance at 30 June 2005	250	50	150	10	460	920

5.5 Here are some points that might be made concerning accounting regulation and accounting measurement:

For

- It seems reasonable that companies, particularly given their limited liability, should be required to account to their members and to the general public and that the law should prescribe how this should be done – including how particular items should be measured. It also seems sensible that accounting standards should amplify these rules, to try to establish some uniformity of practice. Investors could be misled if the same item appeared in the financial statements of two separate companies but had been measured in different ways.

- Companies would find it difficult to attract finance, credit and possibly employees without publishing credible information about themselves. An important measure of performance is profit, and investors often need to make judgements concerning relative performance within an industry sector. Without clear benchmarks by which to judge performance, investors may not invest in a company.

Against

- Some would argue that it is up to the companies to decide whether or not they can survive and prosper without publishing information about themselves. If they can, then so much the better for them as they will have saved large amounts of money by not doing so. If it is necessary for a company to provide financial information in order to be able to attract investment finance and other necessary factors, then the company can make the necessary judgement of how much information is necessary and what forms of measurement are required.

- Not all company managements view matters in the same way. Allowing companies to select their own approaches to financial reporting enables them to reflect their personalities. Thus, a conservative management will adopt conservative accounting policies such as writing off research and development expenditure quickly, whereas more adventurous management may adopt less conservative accounting policies such as writing off research and development expenditure over several years. The impact of these different views will have an effect on profit and will give the reader an insight to the approach adopted by the management team.

5.8 **Unilever plc**

(a) We can see from the first table that the Personal Care segment has the both the highest sales revenue (turnover) and the highest profit. Revenue is approximately three times higher and profit is approximately four times higher that of the smallest segment: the Health and Wellness and Beverages segment.

The Personal Care segment also generates the highest profit when expressed as a percentage of sales revenue. It is almost twice that of the Home Care and Professional Cleaning segment, which produces the lowest return in relation to sales revenue (excluding other operations). This wide difference in returns between the segments may reflect factors such as differences in the competitive environment, differences in pricing policies and so on. The Personal Care segment also produces the highest profit when expressed as a percentage of the assets employed. It is more than twice the return of the next best segment, the Spreads and Cooking Products segment. Personal Care seems to be the 'star' segment.

The Savoury and Dressings segment has substantially more assets employed than other segments and the return on assets employed is very low in relation to other segments (excluding other operations). The reasons for this should be established, as it seems that assets are not being used as productively in this segment as in the others. The capital expenditure as a percentage of sales revenue is fairly low for all of the business segments.

The geographical analysis shown in the second table is not very helpful as around two-thirds of both assets and revenue have been lumped together under the heading of 'other'. We can see, however, that the US segment is significantly larger than the UK segment in terms of both revenue and assets employed.

Tables of key results

	Business segments						
	Savoury and dressings	Spreads and cooking products	Health & wellness and beverages	Ice cream and frozen foods	Home care & professional cleaning	Personal care	Other operations
Group revenue (turnover)	9,272	6,145	4,064	7,456	8,565	12,236	532
Trading result	1,362	834	504	704	725	1,976	27
Capital expenditure	202	166	167	270	215	251	27
Total assets by operation	19,717	3,610	4,095	3,851	3,581	4,066	2,662
Segment result as a percentage of revenue (turnover)	14.7%	13.6%	12.4%	9.4%	8.5%	16.1%	5.1%
Segment result as percentage of total assets	6.9%	23.1%	12.3%	18.3%	20.2%	48.6%	1.0%
Capital expenditure as a percentage of revenue (turnover)	2.2%	2.7%	4.1%	3.6%	2.5%	2.1%	5.1%

Geographical segments

	UK	US	Other	Total
Revenue (turnover) as a percentage of total revenue	11.2%	23.7%	65.1%	100.0%
Property, plant and equipment as a percentage of total property, plant and equipment	13.2%	21.0%	65.8%	100.0%

(b) Information on the liabilities relating to each business segment would be helpful. This information is a requirement under IAS 14 *Segment Reporting*. In addition, a more detailed breakdown of geographical segments would be helpful, along with information relating to the profits generated by each segment.

Chapter 6

6.1 (a) An increase in the level of stock-in-trade (inventory) would, ultimately, have an adverse effect on cash.

(b) A rights issue of ordinary shares will give rise to a positive cash flow, which will be included in the 'financing' section of the cash flow statement.

(c) A bonus issue of ordinary shares has no cash flow effect.

(d) Writing off some of the value of the stock (inventory) has no cash flow effect.

(e) A disposal for cash of a large number of shares by a major shareholder has no cash flow effect as far as the business is concerned.

(f) Depreciation does not involve cash at all. Using the indirect method of deducing cash flows from operating activities involves the depreciation expense in the calculation, but this is simply because we are trying to find out from the profit (after depreciation) figure what the profit before depreciation must have been.

6.3

Torrent plc
Cash flow statement for the year ended 31 December 2005

	£m	£m
Cash flows from operating activities		
Net profit, after interest, before taxation (see Note 1 below)	170	
Adjustments for:		
Depreciation (Note 2)	78	
Interest expense (Note 3)	26	
	274	
Decrease in stock (41 − 35)	6	
Increase in trade debtors (145 − 139)	(6)	
Decrease in trade creditors (54 − 41)	(13)	
Cash generated from operations	261	
Interest paid	(26)	
Corporation tax paid (Note 4)	(41)	
Dividend paid	(60)	
Net cash from operating activities		134
Cash flows from investing activities		
Payments to acquire plant and machinery	(67)	
Net cash used in investing activities		(67)
Cash flows from financing activities		
Redemption of debenture stock (250 − 150) (Note 5)	(100)	
Net cash used in financing activities		(100)
Net decrease in cash and cash equivalents		(33)
Cash and cash equivalents at 1 January 2005		
Bank overdraft		(56)
Cash and cash equivalents at 31 December 2005		
Bank overdraft		(89)

To see how this relates to the cash of the business at the beginning and end of the year it can be useful to provide a reconciliation as follows:

Analysis of cash and cash equivalents during the year ended 31 December 2005

	£m
Cash and cash equivalents at 1 January 2005	(56)
Net cash outflow	(33)
Cash and cash equivalents at 31 December 2005	(89)

Notes
1 This is simply taken from the profit and loss account for the year.
2 Since there were no disposals, the depreciation charges must be the difference between the start and end of the year's plant and machinery values, adjusted by the cost of any additions.

	£m
Book value, at 1 January 2005	325
Add Additions	67
	392
Less Depreciation (balancing figure)	78
Book value, at 31 December 2005	314

3 Interest payable expense must be taken out, by adding it back to the profit figure. We subsequently deduct the cash paid for interest payable during the year. In this case the two figures are identical.

4 Companies pay 50% of tax during their accounting year and 50% in the following year. Thus the 2005 payment would have been half the tax on the 2004 profit (that is, the figure that would have appeared in the current liabilities at the end of 2004), plus half of the 2005 tax charge (that is, $23 + (^1/_2 \times 36) = 41$).

5 It is assumed that the cash payment to redeem the debentures was simply the difference between the two balance sheet figures.

It seems that there was a bonus issue of ordinary shares during the year. These increased by £100m. At the same time, the share premium account balance reduced by £40m (to zero) and the revaluation reserve balance fell by £60m.

6.6

Blackstone plc

Cash flow statement for the year ended 31 March 2005

	£m	£m
Cash flows from operating activities		
Net profit, after interest, before taxation (see Note 1 below)	1,853	
Adjustments for:		
Depreciation (Note 2)	1,289	
Interest expense (Note 3)	456	
	3,598	
Increase in stocks (2,410 – 1,209)	(1,201)	
Increase in trade debtors (1,173 – 641)	(532)	
Increase in trade creditors (1,507 – 931)	576	
Cash generated from operations	2,441	
Interest paid	(456)	
Corporation tax paid (Note 4)	(300)	
Dividend paid	(400)	
Net cash from operating activities		1,285
Cash flows from investing activities		
Proceeds of disposals	54	
Payment to acquire intangible non-current asset	(700)	
Payments to acquire property, plant and equipment	(4,578)	
Net cash used in investing activities		(5,224)
Cash flows from financing activities		
Bank loan	2,000	
Net cash from financing activities		2,000
Net decrease in cash and cash equivalents		(1,939)
Cash and cash equivalents at 1 April 2004		
Cash at bank		123
Cash and cash equivalents at 31 March 2005		
Bank overdraft		(1,816)

To see how this relates to the cash of the business at the beginning and end of the year it can be useful to provide a reconciliation as follows:

Analysis of cash and cash equivalents during the year ended 31 March 2005

	£m
Cash and cash equivalents at 1 April 2004	123
Net cash outflow	(1,939)
Cash and cash equivalents at 31 March 2005	1,816

Notes

1 This is simply taken from the profit and loss account for the year.

2 The full depreciation charge was that stated in Note 1 to the question (£1,251m), plus the deficit on disposal of the non-current assets. According to the table in Note 4 to the question, these non-current assets had originally cost £581m and had been depreciated by £489m, that is a net book value of £92m. They were sold for £54m, leading to a deficit on disposal of £38m. Thus the full depreciation expense for the year was £1,289m (that is, £1,251m + £38m).

3 Interest payable expense must be taken out, by adding it back to the profit figure. We subsequently deduct the cash paid for interest payable during the year. In this case the two figures are identical.

4 Tax is paid by companies 50% during their accounting year and the other 50% in the following year. Thus the 2005 payment would have been half the tax on the 2004 profit (that is, the figure that would have appeared in the current liabilities at 31 March 2004), plus half of the 2005 tax charge (that is, $105 + (1/2 \times 390) = 300$).

6.7

York plc
Cash flow statement for the year ended 30 September 2005

	£m	£m
Cash flows from operating activities		
Net profit, after interest, before taxation		
(see Note 1 below)	10.0	
Adjustments for:		
Depreciation (Note 2)	9.8	
Interest expense (Note 3)	3.0	
	22.8	
Increase in stock and debtors (122.1 – 119.8)	(2.3)	
Increase in creditors (82.5 – 80.0)	2.5	
Cash generated from operations	23.0	
Interest paid	(3.0)	
Corporation tax paid (Note 4)	(2.3)	
Dividend paid	(3.5)	
Net cash from operating activities		14.2
Cash flows from investing activities		
Proceeds of disposals (Note 2)	5.2	
Payments to acquire non-current assets	(20.0)	
Net cash used in investing activities		(14.8)
Cash flows from financing activities		
Increase in long-term loan	3.0	
Share issue (Note 5)	5.0	
Net cash from financing activities		8.0
Net increase in cash and cash equivalents		7.4
Cash and cash equivalents at 1 October 2004		
Cash at bank		9.2
Cash and cash equivalents at 30 September 2005		
Cash at bank		16.6

To see how this relates to the cash of the business at the beginning and end of the year it can be useful to provide a reconciliation as follows:

Analysis of cash and cash equivalents during the year ended 30 September 2005

	£m
Cash and cash equivalents at 1 October 2004	9.2
Net cash inflow	7.4
Cash and cash equivalents at 30 September 2005	16.6

Notes

1 This is simply taken from the profit and loss account for the year.

2 The full depreciation charge was the £13.0m, less the surplus on disposal (£3.2m), both stated in Note 1 to the question.

   According to the table in Note 3 to the question, the non-current assets disposed of had a net book value of £2.0m. To produce a surplus of £3.2m, they must have been sold for £5.2m.

3 Interest payable expense must be taken out, by adding it back to the profit figure. We subsequently deduct the cash paid for interest payable during the year. In this case the two figures are identical.

4 Companies pay 50% of tax during their accounting year and the other 50% the following year. Thus the 2005 payment would have been half the tax on the 2004 profit (that is, the figure that would have appeared in the current liabilities at 30 September 2004), plus half of the 2005 tax charge (that is, $1.0 + (^1/_2 \times 2.6) = 2.3$).

5 This issue must have been for cash since it could not have been a bonus issue – the share premium is untouched and the 'Reserves' had only altered over the year by the amount of the 2005 retained profit. The shares seem to have been issued at par (that is, at their nominal value). This is a little surprising since the business has assets that seem to be above that value. On the other hand, were this a rights issue, the low issue price would not have disadvantaged the existing shareholders since they were also the beneficiaries of the advantage of the low issue price.

6.8

Axis plc
Cash flow statement for the year ended 31 December 2005

	£m	£m
Cash flows from operating activities		
Net profit, after interest, before taxation		
(see Note 1 below)	34	
Adjustments for:		
Depreciation (Note 2)	19	
Interest expense (Note 3)	2	
	55	
Decrease in stock (25 – 24)	1	
Increase in debtors (26 – 16)	(10)	
Increase in creditors (36 – 31)	5	
Cash generated from operations	51	
Interest paid	(2)	
Corporation tax paid (Note 4)	(15)	
Dividend paid	(14)	
Net cash from operating activities		20
Cash flows from investing activities		
Proceeds of disposals (Note 2)	4	
Payments to acquire non-current assets	(25)	
Net cash used in investing activities		(21)
Cash flows from financing activities		
Issue of debentures	20	
Net cash from financing activities		20
Net increase in cash and cash equivalents		19
Cash and cash equivalents at 1 January 2005		
Cash at bank		nil
Short-term investments		nil
		nil
Cash and cash equivalents at 31 December 2005		
Cash at bank		7
Short-term investments		12
		19

To see how this relates to the cash of the business at the beginning and end of the year it can be useful to provide a reconciliation as follows:

Analysis of cash and cash equivalents during the year ended 31 December 2005

	£m
Cash and cash equivalents at 1 January 2005	nil
Net cash inflow	19
Cash and cash equivalents at 31 December 2005	19

Notes

1   This is simply taken from the profit and loss account for the year.

2   The full depreciation charge for the year is the sum of two figures labelled 'depreciation' and the deficit on disposal of non-current assets (that is, £2m + £16m + £1m = £19m). These were detailed in the profit and loss account (income statement).

  According to the note in the question, the non-current assets disposed of had a net book value of £5.0m (that is, £15m – £10m). To produce a deficit of £1m, they must have been sold for £4m.

3   Interest payable expense must be taken out, by adding it back to the profit figure. We subsequently deduct the cash paid for interest payable during the year. In this case the two figures are identical.

4   Companies pay 50% tax during their accounting year and the other 50% in the following year. Thus the 2005 payment would have been half the tax on the 2004 profit (that is, the figure that would have appeared in the current liabilities at 31 December 2004), plus half of the 2005 tax charge (that is, $7 + (\frac{1}{2} \times 16) = 15$).

Chapter 7

7.1   Jiang Ltd

The effect of each of the changes on ROCE is not always easy to predict.

(i)   On the face of it, an increase in the gross profit margin would tend to lead to an increase in ROCE. An increase in the gross profit margin *may*, however, lead to a decrease in ROCE in particular circumstances. If the increase in the margin resulted from an increase in price, which in turn led to a decrease in sales revenue, a fall in ROCE can occur. A fall in sales revenue can reduce the net profit (the numerator (top part of the fraction) in ROCE) if the overheads of the business did not decrease correspondingly.

(ii)   A reduction in sales revenue can reduce ROCE for the reasons mentioned above.

(iii)   An increase in overhead expenses will reduce the net profit and this in turn will result in a reduction in ROCE.

(iv)   An increase in stocks held would increase the amount of capital employed by the business (the denominator (bottom part of the fraction) in ROCE) where long-term funds are employed to finance the stocks. This will, in turn, reduce ROCE.

(v)   Repayment of the loan at the year end will reduce the capital employed and this will increase the ROCE, assuming that the year-end capital employed figure has been used in the calculation. Since the net profit was earned during a period in which the loan existed, there is a strong argument for basing the capital employed figure on what was the position during the year, rather than at the end of it.

(vi)   An increase in the time taken for debtors to pay will result in an increase in capital employed if long-term funds are employed to finance the debtors. This increase in long-term funds will, in turn, reduce ROCE.

7.2

The ratios for Amsterdam Ltd and Berlin Ltd reveal that the debtors turnover ratio for Amsterdam Ltd is three times that for Berlin Ltd. Berlin Ltd is therefore much quicker in collecting amounts outstanding from customers. On the other hand, there is not much difference between the two businesses in the time taken to pay trade creditors.

It is interesting to compare the difference in the debtor and creditor collection periods for each business. As Amsterdam Ltd allows an average of 63 days' credit to its customers, yet pays creditors within 50 days, it will require greater investment in working capital than Berlin Ltd, which allows an average of only 21 days to its debtors but takes 45 days to pay its creditors.

Amsterdam Ltd has a much higher gross profit percentage than Berlin Ltd. However, the net profit percentage for the two businesses is identical. This suggests that Amsterdam Ltd has much higher overheads (as a percentage of sales revenue) than Berlin Ltd. The stock turnover period for Amsterdam Ltd is more than twice that of Berlin Ltd. This may be due to the fact that Amsterdam Ltd maintains a wider range of goods in stock in an attempt to meet customer requirements. The evidence therefore suggests that Amsterdam Ltd is the one that prides itself on personal service. The higher average settlement period for debtors is consistent with a more relaxed attitude to credit collection (thereby maintaining customer goodwill) and the high overheads are consistent with incurring the additional costs of satisfying customers' requirements. Amsterdam Ltd's high stock levels are consistent with maintaining a wide range of stock, with the aim of satisfying a range of customer needs.

Berlin Ltd has the characteristics of a more price-competitive business. Its gross profit percentage is much lower than that of Amsterdam Ltd, that is, a much lower gross profit for each £1 of sales revenue. However, overheads have been kept low, the effect being that the net profit percentage is the same as Amsterdam Ltd's. The low stock turnover period and average collection period for debtors are consistent with a business that wishes to minimise investment in current assets, thereby reducing costs.

7.6 Bradbury Ltd

(a)

	2004	2005
(i) Net profit margin		
914/9,482 × 100%	9.6%	
1,042/11,365 × 100%		9.2%
(ii) ROCE		
914/11,033 × 100%	8.3%	
1,042/13,943 × 100%		7.5%
(iii) Current ratio		
4,926/1,508	3.3:1	
7,700/5,174		1.5:1
(iv) Gearing ratio		
1,220/11,033 × 100%	11.1%	
3,674/13,943 × 100%		26.4%
(v) Days debtors		
(2,540/9,482) × 365	98 days	
(4,280/11,365) × 365		137 days
(vi) Sales revenue to capital employed		
9,482/(9,813+1,220)	0.9 times	
11,365/(10,269 + 3,674)		0.8 times

(b) The net profit margin was slightly lower in 2005 than in 2004. Though there was an increase in sales revenue in 2005, this could not prevent a slight fall in ROCE in 2005. The lower net profit margin and increases in sales revenue may well be due to the new contract. The capital employed of the company increased in 2005 by a larger percentage than the increase in revenue. Hence, the sales revenue to capital employed ratio decreased over the period. The increase in capital during 2005 is largely due to an increase in borrowing. However, the gearing ratio is probably still low in comparison with that of other businesses. Comparison of the freehold premises and loans figures indicates possible unused debt capacity.

The major cause for concern has been the dramatic decline in liquidity during 2005. The current ratio has more than halved during the period. There has also been a similar decrease in the acid test ratio, from 1.7:1 in 2004 to 0.8:1 in 2005. The balance sheet shows that the business now has a large overdraft and the trade creditors outstanding have nearly doubled in 2005.

The trade debtors outstanding and stocks have increased much more than appears to be warranted by the increase in sales revenue. This may be due to the terms of the contract that has been negotiated and may be difficult to influence. If this is the case, the business should consider whether it is overtrading. If the conclusion is that it is, increasing its long-term funding may be a sensible policy.

7.7   Harridges Ltd

(a)

	2004	*2005*
ROCE	$\dfrac{310}{1,600} = 19.4\%$	$\dfrac{350}{1,700} = 20.6\%$
ROSF	$\dfrac{155}{1,100} = 14.1\%$	$\dfrac{175}{1,200} = 14.6\%$
Gross profit margin	$\dfrac{1,040}{2,600} = 40\%$	$\dfrac{1,150}{3,500} = 32.9\%$
Net profit margin	$\dfrac{310}{2,600} = 11.9\%$	$\dfrac{350}{3,500} = 10\%$
Current ratio	$\dfrac{735}{400} = 1.8$	$\dfrac{660}{485} = 1.4$
Acid test ratio	$\dfrac{485}{400} = 1.2$	$\dfrac{260}{485} = 0.5$
Days debtors	$\dfrac{105}{2,600} \times 365 = 15 \text{ days}$	$\dfrac{145}{3,500} \times 365 = 15 \text{ days}$
Days creditors	$\dfrac{235}{1,560} \times 365 = 55 \text{ days}$	$\dfrac{300}{2,350^*} \times 365 = 47 \text{ days}$
Stock turnover period	$\dfrac{250}{1,560} \times 365 = 58 \text{ days}$	$\dfrac{400}{2,350} \times 365 = 62 \text{ days}$
Gearing ratio	$\dfrac{500}{1,600} = 31.3\%$	$\dfrac{500}{1,700} = 29.4\%$
EPS	$\dfrac{155}{490} = 31.6\text{p}$	$\dfrac{175}{490} = 35.7\text{p}$

* Used because the credit purchases figure is not available.

(b) There has been a considerable decline in the gross profit margin during 2005. This fact, combined with the increase in sales revenue by more than one-third, suggests that a price-cutting policy has been adopted in an attempt to stimulate sales. The resulting increase in sales revenue, however, has led to only a small improvement in ROCE and ROSF. Similarly, there has only been a small improvement in EPS.

Despite a large cut in the gross profit margin, the net profit margin has fallen by less than 2%. This suggests that overheads have been tightly controlled during 2005. Certainly, overheads have not risen in proportion to sales revenue.

The current ratio has fallen and the acid test ratio has fallen by more than half. Even though liquidity ratios are lower in retailing than in manufacturing, the liquidity of the business should now be a cause for concern. However, this may be a passing problem. The business is investing heavily in non-current assets and is relying on internal funds to finance this growth. When this investment ends, the liquidity position may improve quickly.

The debtors period has remained unchanged over the two years, and there has been no significant change in the stock turnover period in 2005. The gearing ratio is quite low and provides no cause for concern given the profitability of the business.

Overall, the business appears to be financially sound. Though there has been rapid growth during 2005, there is no real cause for alarm provided that the liquidity of the business can be improved in the near future. In the absence of information concerning share price, it is not possible to say whether or not an investment should be made.

7.8 Genesis Ltd

(a) and (b)

These parts have been answered in the text of the chapter and you are referred to it for a discussion on overtrading and its consequences.

(c)

$$\text{Current ratio} = \frac{232}{550} = 0.42$$

$$\text{Acid test ratio} = \frac{104}{550} = 0.19$$

$$\text{Stock turnover period} = \frac{128}{1,248} \times 365 = 37 \text{ days}$$

$$\text{Average settlement period for debtors} = \frac{104}{1,640} \times 365 = 23 \text{ days}$$

$$\text{Average settlement period for creditors} = \frac{184}{1,260} \times 365 = 53 \text{ days}$$

(d) Overtrading must be dealt with either by increasing the level of funding to match the level of activity, or by reducing the level of activity to match the funds available. The latter option may result in a reduction in profits in the short term but may be necessary to ensure long-term survival.

Chapter 8

8.1

Group balance sheet of Giant and its subsidiary as at 31 March

	£m	£m
Non-current assets (at cost less depreciation)		
Land		39
Plant		63
Vehicles		25
		127

	£m	£m
Current assets		
Stocks	46	
Debtors	59	
Cash	27	
	132	
Less **Current liabilities**		
Creditors	60	
Net current assets		72
Total assets less current liabilities		199
Less **Non-current liabilities**		
Debentures		63
		136
Equity		
Called-up share capital:		
ordinary shares of £1 each, fully paid		50
Share premium account		40
Profit and loss account		46
		136

Note that the group balance sheet is prepared by adding all like items together. The investment in 10 million shares of Jack Ltd (£30m), in the balance sheet of Giant plc, is then compared with the equity (in total) in Jack Ltd's balance sheet. Since Giant paid exactly the balance sheet values of Jack's assets *and* bought all of Jack's shares, these two figures are equal and can be cancelled.

8.2 The balance sheet of Jumbo plc and its subsidiary will be as follows:

Balance sheet as at 31 March

	£m	£m
Non-current assets (at cost less depreciation)		
Land		102
Plant		67
Vehicles		57
		226
Current assets		
Stocks	87	
Debtors	70	
Cash	24	
	181	
Less **Current liabilities**		
Creditors	80	
Net current assets		101
Total assets less current liabilities		327
Less **Non-current liabilities**		
Debentures		170
		157
Equity		
Called-up share capital:		
ordinary shares of £1 each, fully paid		100
Profit and loss account		41
		141
Minority interests		16
		157

Note that the normal approach is taken with various assets and external claims. The 'minority interests' figure represents the minorities' share (8 million of 20 million ordinary shares) in the equity of Nipper plc.

8.3   Toggles plc

(a) (i) 'Minority interests' represents the portion, either of net assets (balance sheet) or after-tax profit (profit and loss account), which is attributable to minority shareholders. Minority shareholders are those shareholders in the subsidiaries other than the parent company. Since, by definition, the parent company is the major shareholder in each of its subsidiaries, any other shareholders in any other subsidiary must be a minority, in terms of number of shares owned.

(ii) 'Goodwill arising on consolidation' is the difference, at the time that the parent acquires the subsidiary, between what is paid for the subsidiary company shares and what they are 'worth'. 'Worth' normally is based on the fair values of the underlying assets that appear in the balance sheet of the subsidiary. This is not necessarily, nor usually, the balance sheet values. Goodwill, therefore, represents the excess of what was paid over the fair values of the assets that appear in the balance sheet of the subsidiary. As such, the excess is an intangible asset that represents the amount that the parent was prepared to pay for the reputation, staff loyalty, and so on, of the subsidiary; it is what we normally refer to as goodwill.

(iii) The retained profit of the parent company will be its own cumulative profits net of tax and dividends paid. This will include dividends received from its subsidiaries, which represent part of the company's income.

When the results of the subsidiaries are consolidated with those of the parent, the parent's share of the post-acquisition retained profits of its subsidiaries is added to its own retained profit figure. In this way the parent is, in effect, credited with its share of all the subsidiaries' after-tax profit, not just with the dividends that the subsidiaries have paid.

(b) The objective of preparing consolidated financial statements is to reflect the underlying economic reality that the assets of the subsidiary companies are as much under the control of the shareholders of the parent, acting through their board of directors, as are the assets owned directly by the parent. This will be true despite the fact that the subsidiary is strictly a separate company from the parent. It is also despite the fact that the parent may not own all of the shares of the subsidiaries.

Consolidated financial statements provide an example where accounting tends to put 'content' before 'form' in the UK. That is to say that it tries to reflect economic reality rather than the strict legal position. This is to try to provide more useful information.

8.4   Arnold plc and Baker plc

Group profit and loss account for the year ended 31 December

	£m	£m	Notes
Revenue (83 + 47)		130	
Cost of sales (36 + 19)		(55)	
Gross profit		75	
Administration expenses (14 + 7)	(21)		
Distribution expenses (21 + 10)	(31)	(52)	
Profit before tax		23	
Taxation (4 + 3)		(7)	
Profit after tax		16	
Attributable to minorities (25% × 8)		(2)	1
Profit after tax attributable to Arnold plc shareholders		14	
Profit and loss account balance brought forward			
from previous year [34 + ((21 − 17) × 75%)]		37	2
		51	
Dividend on ordinary shares		(12)	3
Profit and loss account balance carried forward			
to the following year		39	

Notes

1 This is the minorities share of the after-tax profit of Baker plc (taken from that company's profit and loss account).
2 This is Arnold plc's balance brought forward (£34m), plus Arnold plc's share of Baker plc's retained profit earned since the takeover. £17m was the value of Baker plc's profit and loss account balance at the date of the takeover (see preamble to the question) and £21m the balance at the start of the current year (see Baker plc's profit and loss account).
3 This is just the dividend paid by Arnold plc.

8.5 The balance sheet of Apple Ltd and its subsidiary will be as follows:

Balance sheet as at 30 September

	£000	£000
Non-current assets (at cost less depreciation)		
Goodwill arising on consolidation (see Note 2)		24
Property, plant and equipment (950 + 320)		1,270
		1,294
Current assets		
Stocks (320 + 160)	480	
Debtors (180 + 95)	275	
Cash at bank (41 + 15)	56	
	811	
Less **Current liabilities**		
Trade creditors (170 + 87)	257	
Taxation (54 + 55)	109	
	366	
Net current assets		445
Total assets less current liabilities		1,739
Less **Non-current liabilities**		
Long-term loans (500 + 160)		660
		1,079
Equity		
£1 fully paid ordinary shares		700
Reserves		307
		1,007
Minority interests (see Note 3)		72
		1,079

Notes

1 The normal approach is taken with various assets and external claims.
2 The goodwill arising on consolidation is the difference between what Apple Ltd paid for the shares in Pear Ltd (150,000 × £1.60 = £240,000), less the fair value of the net assets acquired (150,000/200,000 × £288,000 = £216,000). That is £24,000.
3 The minority interest figure is simply the minority shareholders' stake in the net assets of Pear Ltd. This is 50,000/200,000 × £288,000 = £72,000.

Chapter 9

9.1 The VAS is, in effect, a rearrangement of the information already contained within the profit and loss account. However, it does not automatically follow that the VAS will be of little value to users. Its purpose is different from that of the profit and loss account, which is geared towards providing a measure of income for the shareholders of the business. However, there are other groups with a stake in the business and which benefit from its activities. The VAS attempts to measure the value added by the collective effort of the various groups and the benefits that each group has received from the business. It is, therefore, a much broader measure of income than the profit and loss account. The benefits of the VAS have been dealt with in the chapter. However, it is worth mentioning again the use of the VAS in promoting a team spirit among the various stakeholders.

Some, however, believe the VAS was a child of its time. It was first proposed at a time when industrial relations in the UK were at a low ebb and employee/management disputes were widespread. Promoting team spirit and showing the proportion of value added that employees receive from the business were therefore seen as a good idea. However, the combined effects of recession, high levels of unemployment, industrial relations legislation and increased global competitiveness over the past few decades have resulted in far fewer disputes and managers are less concerned with this aspect of their duties. This may help to explain, in part, the decline in popularity of the VAS.

9.2   Buttons Ltd

(a) The value added statement for the year ended 30 September is:

	£000	£000
Sales revenue		950
Less Bought-in materials and services (220 + 95)		315
Value added		635
Applied as follows:		
To employees		160
To pay government		110
To suppliers of capital:		
Interest	45	
Dividends	120	165
For maintenance and expansion of assets:		
Depreciation	80	
Retained profit	120	200
		635

(b) The VAS is seen as promoting a measure of income which is generated through the collective effort of the key 'stakeholders' of the business. The VAS tries to encourage a team spirit among managers, shareholders, employees and so on, and to reduce conflict. The VAS also permits the calculation of various ratios (as seen in the chapter) which may help in assessing financial performance.

As the amount of value added received by employees is often high in relation to that received by other groups, the VAS is useful in reinforcing the fact that employees are significant beneficiaries of the business. However, some are suspicious of the motives of management in presenting financial information in this way.

9.3

$$\text{Value added to sales revenue} = \frac{635}{950} \times 100\% = 66.8\%$$

The lower this ratio, the greater the reliance of the business on outside sources of materials and services and the more vulnerable the business will be to difficulties encountered by external suppliers.

$$\text{Value added per £1 of wages} = \frac{635}{160} = 4.0$$

This ratio is a measure of labour productivity. In this case, the employees are generating £4.0 of value added for every £1 of wages expended. The higher the ratio, the higher the level of productivity. This ratio may be useful when making comparisons between businesses.

$$\text{Dividends to value added} = \frac{120}{635} \times 100\% = 18.9\%$$

This ratio calculates that portion of value added that will be received in cash more or less immediately by shareholders. The trend of this ratio may provide an insight to the distribution policy of the business over time. It is important to remember, however, that shareholders also benefit, in the form of capital growth, from amounts reinvested in the business. Thus, the ratio is only a partial measure of the benefits received by shareholders.

$$\text{Depreciation and retentions to value added} = \frac{200}{635} \times 100\% = 31.5\%$$

This ratio may provide an insight to the ability or willingness of the business to raise finance for new investment from internal operations rather than external sources. A high ratio may suggest a greater ability or willingness to raise finance internally than a low ratio.

9.4   Rose Ltd

Value added statement for the year ended 30 September

	£000	£000
Revenue		12,080
Less Bought-in materials and services (6,282 + 1,003)		7,285
Value added		4,795
Applied as follows:		
To employees		2,658
To pay government		259
To suppliers of capital:		
Interest	66	
Dividends	300	366
For maintenance and expansion of assets:		
Depreciation	625	
Retained profit	887	1,512
		4,795

9.5

(a) Although the historic cost financial statements have certain redeeming features, such as objectivity, it is difficult to argue that they are all that users require. During a period of inflation, historic cost accounting tends to result in an overstatement of profit and an understatement of financial position for the business. In the absence of additional information, users of the historic cost financial statements will be required to make their own adjustments in order to take into account the effects of inflation on the financial statements.

The value of inflation-adjusted financial statements will depend on the levels of inflation within the economy. The higher the rates of inflation, the greater the distortion of the historic cost financial statements and, therefore, the greater the need for some sort of inflation-adjusted statement. However, the problems that exist during periods of inflation still persist during periods of low inflation and their cumulative effect can be significant over a number of years.

We should always bear in mind the fact that the preparation of inflation-adjusted information has a cost to the business, and the benefits of preparation should exceed the costs. This means, amongst other things, that the form of inflation-adjusted financial statements should be given careful consideration. We saw in the chapter, however, that there is more than one approach to dealing with the problem of inflation adjustment. The debate as to which is the best method to use has not been resolved. Until this is done, the case for inflation-adjusted financial statements is certainly weakened.

(b) Publishing environmental reports can have its drawbacks. There is a danger that publication could open up opportunities for litigation against the business if any shortcomings are exposed. There is also the danger that the expectations of stakeholders will be raised as a result of publishing such information and the business will be required to adopt increasingly stringent environmental standards that will prove very costly. For many businesses, the publication of environmental reports would, first of all, require the development of an internal environmental management system, which could be both time-consuming and costly.

However, there are likely to be costs associated with not providing such information. Businesses are under increasing pressure from a variety of sources, including customers, other businesses within the same industry and green campaigners, to produce such reports. Failure to respond to such pressures may not be in the longer-term interests of the business. Unless these groups can be reassured by environmental policies adopted by the business, there is the risk of strict legislation being imposed (leading to higher costs) and lost sales.

Appendix A

A.1

Account to be debited	Account to be credited
(a) Stock	Trade creditors
(b) Capital (or a separate drawings account)	Cash
(c) Loan interest	Cash
(d) Stock	Cash
(e) Cash	Trade debtors
(f) Wages	Cash
(g) Capital (or a separate drawings account)	Trade debtors
(h) Trade creditors	Cash
(i) Electricity (or heat and light)	Cash
(j) Cash	Sales revenue

Note that the precise name given to an account is not crucial so long as those who are using the information are clear as to what each account deals with.

A.2 (a) and (b)

Cash

		£			£
1 Feb	Capital	6,000	3 Feb	Stock	2,600
15 Feb	Sales revenue	4,000	5 Feb	Equipment	800
28 Feb	Trade debtors	2,500	9 Feb	Rent	250
			10 Feb	Fuel and electricity	240
			11 Feb	General expenses	200
			21 Feb	Capital	1,000
			25 Feb	Trade creditors	2,000
			28 Feb	Balance c/d	5,410
		12,500			12,500
1 Mar	Balance b/d	5,410			

Capital

		£			£
21 Feb	Cash	1,000	1 Feb	Cash	6,000
28 Feb	Balance c/d	5,000			
		6,000			6,000
			1 Mar	Balance b/d	5,000
28 Feb	Balance c/d	7,410	28 Feb	Profit and loss	2,410
		7,410			7,410
			1 Mar	Balance b/d	7,410

Stock

		£			£
3 Feb	Cash	2,600	15 Feb	Cost of sales	2,400
6 Feb	Trade creditors	3,000	19 Feb	Cost of sales	2,300
			28 Feb	Balance c/d	900
		5,600			5,600
1 Mar	Balance b/d	900			

Equipment

		£			£
5 Feb	Cash	800			

Trade creditors

		£			£
25 Feb	Cash	2,000	6 Feb	Stock	3,000
28 Feb	Balance c/d	1,000			
		3,000			3,000
			1 Mar	Balance b/d	1,000

Rent

		£			£
9 Feb	Cash	250	28 Feb	Profit and loss	250

Fuel and electricity

		£			£
10 Feb	Cash	240	28 Feb	Profit and loss	240

General expenses

		£			£
11 Feb	Cash	200	28 Feb	Profit and loss	200

Sales revenue

		£			£
28 Feb	Balance c/d	7,800	15 Feb	Cash	4,000
			19 Feb	Trade debtors	3,800
		7,800			7,800
28 Feb	Profit and loss	7,800	28 Feb	Balance b/d	7,800

Cost of sales

		£			£
15 Feb	Stock	2,400	28 Feb	Balance c/d	4,700
19 Feb	Stock	2,300			
		4,700			4,700
28 Feb	Balance b/d	4,700	28 Feb	Profit and loss	4,700

Trade debtors

		£			£
19 Feb	Sales revenue	3,800	28 Feb	Cash	2,500
			28 Feb	Balance c/d	1,300
		3,800			3,800
1 Mar	Balance b/d	1,300			

(b) Trial balance as at 28 February

	Debits	Credits
	£	£
Cash	5,410	
Capital		5,000
Stock	900	
Equipment	800	
Trade creditors		1,000
Rent	250	
Fuel and electricity	240	
General expenses	200	
Sales revenue		7,800
Cost of sales	4,700	
Trade debtors	1,300	
	13,800	13,800

(c)   **Profit and loss account**

		£			£
28 Feb	Cost of sales	4,700	28 February	Sales revenue	7,800
28 Feb	Rent	250			
28 Feb	Fuel and electricity	240			
28 Feb	General expenses	200			
28 Feb	Capital (net profit)	2,410			
		7,800			7,800

Balance sheet as at 28 February

	£	£
Non-current assets:		
Equipment		800
Current assets:		
Stock	900	
Trade debtors	1,300	
Cash	5,410	
	7,610	
Current liabilities		
Trade creditors	1,000	
		6,610
		7,410
Capital		7,410

Profit and loss account for the month ended 28 February

	£	£
Sales revenue		7,800
Cost of sales		4,700
Gross profit		3,100
Less Rent	250	
Fuel and electricity	240	
General expenses	200	
		690
Net profit for the month		2,410

A.3

Buildings

		£			£
1 Jan	Balance brought down	25,000			

Fittings – cost

		£			£
1 Jan	Balance brought down	10,000	31 Dec	Balance carried down	12,000
	Cash	2,000			
		12,000			12,000
1 Jan	Balance brought down	12,000			

Fittings – depreciation

		£			£
31 Dec	Balance carried down	4,400	1 Jan	Balance brought down	2,000
			31 Dec	Profit and loss	
				(£12,000 × 20%)	2,400
		4,400			4,400
			1 Jan	Balance brought down	4,400

General expenses

		£			£
1 Jan	Balance brought down	140	31 Dec	Profit and loss	570
	Cash	580		Balance carried down	150
		720			720
1 Jan	Balance brought down	150			

Stock-in-trade

		£			£
1 Jan	Balance brought down	1,350	31 Dec	Cost of sales	15,220
31 Dec	Trade creditors	17,220		Cost of sales	4,900
	Cash	3,760		Capital	560
				Balance carried down	1,650
		22,330			22,330
1 Jan	Balance brought down	1,650			

Cost of sales

		£			£
31 Dec	Stock-in-trade	15,220	31 Dec	Profit and loss	20,120
	Stock-in-trade	4,900			
		20,120			20,120

Rent

		£			£
1 Jan	Balance brought down	500	31 Dec	Profit and loss	3,000
31 Dec	Cash	3,000		Balance carried down	500
		3,500			3,500
1 Jan	Balance brought down	500			

Trade debtors

		£			£
1 Jan	Balance brought down	1,840	31 Dec	Cash	32,810
31 Dec	Sales revenue	33,100		Profit and loss (bad debt)	260
				Balance carried down	1,870
		34,940			34,940
1 Jan	Balance brought down	1,870			

Cash

		£			£
1 Jan	Balance brought down	2,180	31 Dec	Stock-in-trade	3,760
31 Dec	Sales revenue	10,360		Wages	3,770
	Loan	2,000		Rent	3,000
	Trade debtors	32,810		Electricity	1,070
				General expenses	580
				Fittings	2,000
				Loan	1,000
				Trade creditors	18,150
				Capital	10,400
				Balance carried down	3,620
		47,350			47,350
1 Jan	Balance brought down	3,620			

Capital

		£			£
31 Dec	Stock-in-trade	560	1 Jan	Balance brought down	25,050
	Cash	10,400		Profit and loss (profit)	10,900
	Balance carried down	24,990			
		35,950			35,950
			1 Jan	Balance brought down	24,990

Loan

		£			£
30 June	Cash	1,000	1 Jan	Balance brought down	12,000
31 Dec	Balance carried down	13,000		Cash	2,000
		14,000			14,000
			1 Jan	Balance brought down	13,000

Trade creditors

		£			£
30 June	Cash	18,150	1 Jan	Balance brought down	1,690
31 Dec	Balance carried down	760	31 Dec	Stock-in-trade	17,220
		18,910			18,910
			1 Jan	Balance brought down	760

Electricity

		£			£
31 Dec	Cash	1,070	1 Jan	Balance brought down	270
31 Dec	Balance carried down	290	31 Dec	Profit and loss	1,090
		1,360			1,360
			1 Jan	Balance brought down	290

Sales revenue

		£			£
31 Dec	Profit and loss	43,460	31 Dec	Trade debtors	33,100
				Cash	10,360
		43,460			43,460

Wages

		£			£
31 Dec	Cash	3,770	31 Dec	Profit and loss	3,770

Loan interest

	£			£
		31 Dec	Profit and loss	1,350
			[(6/12 × 14,000) +	
			(6/12 × 13,000)] × 10%	

(3)

Profit and loss

		£			£
31 Dec	Cost of sales	20,120	31 Dec	Sales revenue	43,460
	Depreciation	2,400			
	General expenses	570			
	Rent	3,000			
	Bad debts (Trade debtors)	260			
	Electricity	1,090			
	Wages	3,770			
	Loan interest	1,350			
	Profit (Capital)	10,900			
		43,460			43,460

(4) **Balance sheet as at 31 December last year**

Non-current assets	£	£	Capital	£ 24,990
Buildings		25,000		
Fittings: cost	12,000		Non-current liability	
depreciation	4,400	7,600	Loan	13,000
			Current liabilities	
			Trade creditors	760
Current assets			Accrued electricity	290
Stock of stationery		150	Accrued loan interest	1,350
Stock-in-trade		1,650		
Prepaid rent		500		
Trade debtors		1,870		
Cash		3,620		
		40,390		40,390

Index